Problem Solving Using
Pascal
Algorithm Development
and Programming Concepts

Romualdas Skvarcius
Boston University

PWS PUBLISHERS
Boston

PWS PUBLISHERS

Prindle, Weber & Schmidt • ♟ • Willard Grant Press • **WG** • Duxbury Press • ♠ • B/C Engineering • ⚘
Statler Office Building • 20 Park Plaza • Boston, Massachusetts 02116

PWS Publishers is a division of Wadsworth, Inc.

Library of Congress Cataloging in Publication Data

Skvarcius, Romualdas.
   Problem solving using Pascal.

   Includes index.
   1. PASCAL (Computer program language)   2. Electronic digital computers—Programming.   3. Problem solving.   4. Algorithms.   I. Title.
QA76.73.P2S58 1984   001.64'2   83-19474
ISBN 0-87150-440-5

ISBN 0-87150-440-5

Cover photos courtesy of Dave Kamins, Computer Graphics Laboratory, Boston University.

Cover and text design by Trisha Hanlon. Composition by Carlisle Graphics. Artwork by Arvak. Text printed and bound by Halliday Lithograph. Cover printed by Lehigh Press Lithographers

Printed in the United States of America

85   86   87   88 — 10   9   8   7   6   5   4   3

To my family,
Dianne, Erika, Kenneth, and Andrew

Preface

This book is intended for a one- or two-term introductory course in computer programming. It is also appropriate for students whose first course was in a programming language other than Pascal. No background other than high school algebra is assumed. Students, however, should be able to follow a carefully structured argument.

It is well recognized that problem solving should be taught in the first programming course. Both the new Advanced Placement course in Computer Science for advanced high school students and the undergraduate college course, CS1 as described in ACM Curriculum '78 [Communications of the ACM, **22**, 3 (March 1979), 147–166], emphasize this point. The ACM recommendations also provide a list of topics to be covered in the introductory course. This text is compatible with these recommendations.

The primary goal of the text is to teach problem solving and algorithm development through the technique of stepwise refinement. This approach is illustrated repeatedly in the solution of the problems presented in the text. Students are encouraged to outline their algorithms in English-like pseudocode and then to refine carefully each of the steps on an individual basis. Algorithm development issues are discussed formally at two points in the text: Chapter 3 and Chapter 8. The principles of program design, however, are best learned by practice. Therefore, techniques such as stepwise refinement and the use of modules are presented mainly by example. Students see these techniques being used and are encouraged to use them throughout the text.

The text is designed so that students can begin programming as soon as possible. As each new feature of the language is introduced, it is immediately used to illustrate the solution to some problem. The examples embedded in the text are deliberately small and easy to understand. They generally focus on a single idea. Great care is taken not to use, at this point, an example that is too complex for students to comprehend easily. However, students should also see examples complex enough to illustrate major applications, as well as techniques of algorithm development. For this reason a section is provided at the end of each chapter illustrating one or more major applications of the ideas covered in that chapter. These application sections serve a double purpose. They provide examples of relevant and interesting applications, as well as illustrate problem solving and algorithm development in a meaningful context.

An extensive set of homework problems appears at the end of each chapter. The problems are graded from very easy ones, testing direct understanding of the reading material, to progressively more complex programming exercises. Solutions to selected problems are provided at the end of the text. Great care is taken to make the programming exercises both relevant and interesting. Each chapter also includes self-test quizzes, which allow students to quickly check their understanding of the material just covered.

Topics are sequenced in such a way as to make it possible to write progressively more complex programs as early as possible. Thus some topics are delayed until they can be used in meaningful programs. For example, characters are covered only after loops are discussed, since not much can be done with single characters until then.

—Chapter 1 presents the concepts of computer systems, programming languages, and computer programming. Except for some common vocabulary, this material may be postponed until students have gained some experience, or it may be assigned as independent reading.

—Chapter 2 presents enough Pascal to make it possible to write simple yet complete programs.

—Chapter 3 introduces problem definition and algorithm design. Although the subset of Pascal available at this point makes it impossible to write programs of any complexity, the early discussion of these topics sets the tone for a systematic approach to problem solving and starts students thinking about the process.

—Chapter 4 discusses branching and introduces boolean variables. The **if . . . then . . . else, if . . . then,** and **case** control structures are presented in this chapter.

—Chapter 5 covers loops by presenting the **while, repeat,** and **for** control structures. Character data types, as well as user-defined data types, are introduced in this chapter. The end of the chapter provides a summary of all control structures and discusses structured programming.

—Chapter 6 presents arrays, as well as various algorithms involving arrays, such as sorting and searching. Character strings are also presented in this chapter.

—Chapter 7 covers procedures and functions. It starts with user-defined functions, continues with procedures, parameter passing, and block structure, and ends with a detailed discussion of recursion.

—Chapter 8 presents a detailed and extensive discussion of modular design and testing. This is done via two large examples: a game and a set of routines for string processing.

—Chapter 9 covers sets. Sets are easier to understand than records and for this reason are presented before records.

—Chapter 10 covers the concept of records, including variant records. It concludes with some detailed examples of applications programs involving record structures.

—Chapter 11 discusses the Pascal implementation of sequential files. Classic file update and file sorting algorithms conclude this chapter.

—Chapter 12 is an introduction to pointers and dynamic data structures. Algorithms for traversal, deletion, and insertion of elements into linked lists are presented in detail, as are simple algorithms to manipulate trees.

Each chapter, except for the first one, contains a chapter review and a discussion of common programming problems. Discussions of these problems are, of course, also omitted from chapters 3 and 8.

The text adheres to the proposed ISO standard. Students are given the customary warnings when particular implementations of Pascal may differ in some respects on a particular Pascal feature being discussed.

Pascal syntax is presented through explanations and illustrations, as well as syntax diagrams. This makes the text suitable for beginners and more accomplished programmers. A summary of all syntax diagrams is available in the Appendix.

As with any project of this size, many people contributed to its success. The following colleagues used the manuscript in its early versions, and in the process, they helped find errors and provided many suggestions for improving the book: Harpal S. Dhama, Karen Levin, Paul Shiman, and Caroline Wardle.

I would also like to thank the people who reviewed the manuscript: Ann E. Fleury, SUNY, College at Plattsburgh; Gary A. Ford, University of Colorado, Colorado Springs; Paul Gormley, Villanova University; Wayne T. Graybeal; John E. Herman, Western Michigan University; Robert Holloway, University of Wisconsin, Madison; William B. Jones, California State University, Dominguez Hills; Alan L. Tharp, North Carolina State University, Raleigh; Carol E. Wolf, Iowa State University.

Finally many thanks are due to Augusta Devine, who attended to the fine points in the manuscript; to Theron Shreve, who helped launch the entire project and provided support through its early stages; and to Karin Ellison, my editor at PWS, who not only showed enthusiasm for the project but also managed to exert the right pressure to keep the project on time.

R.S.
Boston

Contents

1. Computer Systems

**1.1
COMPUTER
SYSTEMS**

Modern electronic digital computers are powerful devices that are used to collect, analyze, and process enormous amounts of information at extremely high speeds and with a high degree of accuracy.

A common misconception about computers is that a computer consists only of complex circuitry and other impressive looking devices, such as those shown in Figure 1.1. In fact, what you see is only one of the major components of a computer system: its **hardware**.

More specifically, the hardware of a computer system consists of the physical equipment that forms the computer and its peripheral devices. The hardware includes all equipment for input, processing, and output functions of the system.

Another, just as important, component of a computer system is its **software**. Software is the set of programs and associated documentation that is needed to operate the system. Computers without software are merely a collection of electronic devices incapable of

Figure 1.1 A typical computer installation (Courtesy of International Business Machines Corporation)

doing anything useful. In the remainder of this chapter we will examine computer hardware and software in more detail.

1.2 HARDWARE

The major hardware elements of a computer system are shown in Figure 1.2.

Input Unit The input unit links the computer system to the outside world. This portion of the computer is designed to input information into the rest of the system. It obtains information (data and programs) from various input devices and places this information into main storage.

Main Storage The main storage unit of a computer system is sometimes called *primary storage* or *primary memory*. It is used to store information that is received from the input unit so that this information is available to the units involved in processing it. Main storage also stores already processed information so that it can be output on various output devices.

Auxiliary Storage Auxiliary storage, also known as *secondary storage*, is used for storing large volumes of information. In contrast to main storage, which is used primarily to store only information currently being processed, auxiliary storage provides more permanent information storage. Before information in auxiliary storage can be used by the computer system, however, it must be transferred to main storage.

Central Processing Unit The central processing unit, often called the CPU, consists of components that perform calculations

Figure 1.2 Functional components of a computer system

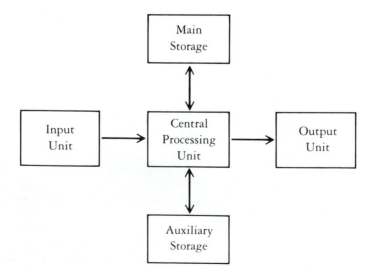

and logical operations. Additionally, the central processing unit controls the operation of all of the other components of the computer system.

Output Unit The output unit, just as the input unit, allows the computer to communicate with the outside world. It is used to transfer information from main storage to various output devices.

Input of Information

Information enters the computer via the input unit, which in turn obtains the information from some input device. Among the input devices found on computer systems, two common ones are card readers and terminals.

A **card reader** is a device designed to read punched cards. Information is stored on a card by punching holes into it with a device called a **keypunch**. Figure 1.3 illustrates how various patterns of holes can be used to represent information on a card. The particular scheme shown is called Hollerith coding, after the inventor Herman Hollerith. This is the most common scheme for punching information into cards, but it is not the only one.

To enter information into a computer system, a person types the information onto cards using a keypunch. The cards are then taken to a card reader and read into main storage by the input unit. The card reader, using a series of lights (one for each column of the card), is capable of sensing the holes in a card. As the card passes over these lights, one column at a time, the light shines through the hole and triggers an electronic impulse, which is sent to the central processing unit. The contents of that column, as represented by the holes in it and the resulting electronic impulses, are then stored in main storage.

Figure 1.3 A punched card

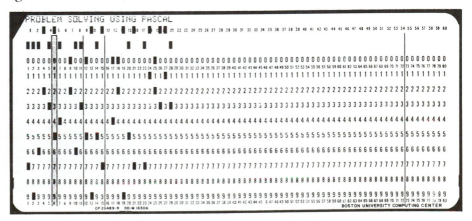

For many years cards were the most common way to communicate with computers. Today, although cards are still being used,
terminals are a more popular means of entering information into
the computer system. A *terminal* differs from a card reader in one
major way. It allows information to be entered by hand directly into
main storage. As information is entered at the keyboard, it goes directly to main storage via the input unit. A great variety of terminals
are available. Some resemble typewriters (Figure 1.4); others use
cathode-ray-tubes (CRT) (Figure 1.5). Although every computer uses
at least one input device, it is not uncommon for the input unit to
have several input devices attached to it.

Main Storage

Once information enters a computer system through an input device, it is, at least temporarily, stored in main storage where it is used
by other parts of the computer system. Information is moved into
and out of main storage and from place to place within main storage.
So that the computer system can keep track of the location of information, main storage is organized as a large array of individual stor-

Figure 1.4 A type-
writerlike terminal
(Courtesy of Digital
Equipment Corpo-
ration)

Figure 1.5 A CRT terminal (Courtesy of Digital Equipment Corporation)

age locations, each with its own **address** much like an array of mail boxes for a large apartment building. The information stored in a given location may be data, an instruction for the computer, or the address of a location for another item of data or instruction.

How is information represented in main storage? If we were able somehow to examine a location in main storage that is capable of holding a piece of information, we would see that it is composed of single storage units. Each unit is capable of representing a single **binary digit**, or **bit**. Physically, the storage location containing a bit is capable of only two states: on and off. The "on" state represents the binary digit 1 and the "off" state represents the binary digit 0. All information in main storage is composed solely of 1s and 0s. This is known as **binary coding**. The group of bits that forms a location in main storage that is capable of holding the information of, say, one column of a card is known as a **byte**. The number of bits that make up a byte differs from computer to computer. However, on most systems a byte consists of eight bits.

The size of a main storage location identified by a given address is not the same in all computer systems. On some computers, the byte is the fundamental unit of the computer's main storage and, therefore, each byte has an address associated with it. Most computers also use larger storage units consisting of a fixed number of bytes. These storage units are called **words**. The most common word sizes are 1, 2, or 4 bytes. Thus, just as the size of a byte can vary from computer system to computer system, so the size of a word can vary.

We can think of computer main storage as being made up of either byte-size or word-size locations, each with its own address. Thus the CPU can retrieve or change the contents of a byte-size or word-size location. Figure 1.6 shows the layout of bytes in main storage. The address of each byte is shown to the left. Note that we start addresses at 0.

Computer manufacturers express the size of main storage in terms of the number of bytes or words. A commonly used unit is the *kilobyte*. Kilo often is abbreviated to K and, in everyday usage, stands for 1000. However, when used to describe the size of a computer's main storage, K stands for 1024 because in the computer field we count by powers of 2, $2^{10} = 1024$.

Small computers usually have between 4K bytes and 64K bytes of main storage. Large systems may have upwards of 16 million bytes of main storage.

Before we discuss auxiliary storage and the CPU, let us examine how information is stored in main storage. Data in main storage usually consist of characters or numbers.

Character Codes Characters (alphabetic letters and symbols) can be represented in binary coding. A character generally requires one byte of storage. To represent a character in a byte, such as the letter *A*, a pattern of 1s and 0s or "ons" and "offs" is used. The actual

Figure 1.6 Layout of bytes in main storage

Address

0000	Byte
0001	Byte
0002	Byte
0003	Byte
	⋮

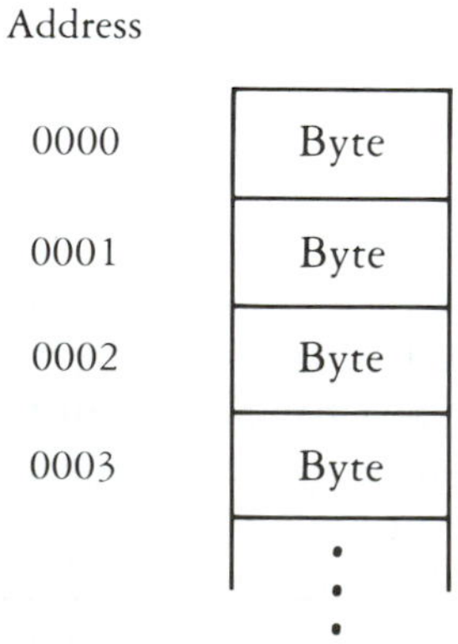

pattern used for a particular character is arbitrary. However, there are a few standardized patterns used by most computer manufacturers. One of the most commonly used schemes for encoding characters is the American Standard Code for Information Interchange, or ASCII. In this scheme, the character *A* is encoded as:

1000001

In ASCII code, an *A* is represented by a pattern of seven bits, where all the bits except the first and the last are "off." The leftmost eighth bit is not used.

Another commonly used encoding scheme is the Extended Binary Coded Decimal Interchange Code, or EBCDIC. In EBCDIC, the *A* is encoded as:

11000001

In this scheme the *A* is represented by a pattern of eight bits in which all but three bits are "off." The ASCII and EBCDIC conventions for encoding characters are described in more detail in the Appendix.

Numeric Codes A character can easily be stored in a byte, because most encoding schemes require at most eight bits. To store numbers we usually need a word or more of storage. For illustration purposes, let us consider the storage of numbers in a word consisting of two bytes. The bits of a word (or byte) are numbered from right to left as illustrated in Figure 1.7. Because the computer uses only the symbols 0 and 1, we use the *base-2* or *binary* number system to represent numbers in main storage. The digits of a binary number, taken from right to left, represent increasing powers of 2. Thus, the rightmost bit (bit 0) represents 1s. The next bit (bit 1) represents 2s. The next bit (bit 2) represents 4s, and so on. Thus, the digits of the binary number

1011

represent

eights   fours   twos   ones
  1   0   1   1

Figure 1.7 Numbering of bits in a word

0	1	1	0	0	0	0	1	1	0	1	0	0	1	0	1
15	14	13	12	11	10	9	8	7	6	5	4	3	2	1	0

and the decimal equivalent of the number is

$(1 \times 8) + (0 \times 4) + (1 \times 2) + (1 \times 1) = 11$

The decimal equivalent of the binary number 0110000110100101, which is stored in the word of Figure 1.7, is:

$16384 + 8192 + 256 + 128 + 32 + 4 + 1 = 24897$

Note that because we are using a fixed number of bits (16 in our example) to represent a whole number, a limit on the largest integer that can be represented in this fashion clearly exists.

Other schemes to represent whole numbers in main storage exist. Another approach, for example, stores a decimal digit in each half of a byte. Numbers that are stored by this scheme are called **binary coded decimals**. (By the way, a half a byte is often called a nibble!) Consider the following byte:

```
  tens   ones
 ⏜⏜⏜ ⏜⏜⏜
 0 1 0 0 0 0 0 1
```

If we interpret this byte to contain a binary coded decimal, then it is storing the number 41. A four is stored in the left half of the byte and a one is stored in the right half. On the other hand, if the byte is considered as a single unit that holds a binary number, then the number stored is 65.

As this example illustrates, we cannot tell what is stored in a main storage location by simply examining its contents. Not only can the above byte be considered to contain the integer 41 or the integer 65, depending on the coding scheme used, but also, if we consider the pattern of bits as representing an ASCII character, then the byte is storing an *A*. Thus, it is how a given storage location is used that determines how the contents are to be interpreted.

The above examples illustrate the representation of positive whole numbers. Negative numbers and numbers with fractional parts also can be represented in binary notation.

Instruction Codes In addition to storing information in the form of encoded characters and numbers, main storage locations can also hold instructions for manipulating this information; these instructions also are encoded in binary codes. As was stated earlier, the contents of a main storage location can be interpreted and used in a variety of different ways: characters, numbers, or instructions, among other things. The ability to store not only the data being processed but also the instructions for what to do with the data makes the computer the general purpose information processing device that it is. By changing the set of instructions, we can readily change how the computer handles a given set of data values.

A computer has a set of instructions that allow it to manipulate the contents of bytes and words. The ability to understand and execute these instructions is built into its hardware. The set of all these instructions is called the computer's **instruction set**. With most computers, the operations that the CPU can carry out on bytes and words include the usual operations of arithmetic, as well as the instructions to move information from one location to another and to compare the contents of bytes or words. A computer instruction must specify two things: (1) the operation to be performed, and (2) the address or addresses of the value or values on which the operation is to be carried out. These addresses are known as the **operands** of the instruction. A typical instruction format with a single operand appears in Figure 1.8.

In this instruction format, bits 6 through 15 specify the operation to be performed. That is, these bits contain the operation code. Bits 0 through 5 specify the operand. That is, they contain the address of the value on which the operation is to be performed. An actual instruction in this format would appear as shown in Figure 1.9. In the example of Figure 1.9, the operation code in bits 6–15 is represented by the binary code 0000101010. This code, when interpreted by the appropriate components of the CPU, may indicate that the operation of adding a one (incrementing) to the contents of location 110111 is to be performed. The value 110111 in bits 0–5 provides us with the address of the number to be incremented by one. When the instruction is executed, a one will be added to the contents of location 110111.

In practice, instructions may be much longer, and, for example, may require a full word for each of the addresses. Also not all instruc-

Figure 1.8 Single operand instruction format

Operation Code										Operand					
15	14	13	12	11	10	9	8	7	6	5	4	3	2	1	0

Figure 1.9 Example of a machine instruction

0	0	0	0	1	0	1	0	1	0	1	1	0	1	1	1
15	14	13	12	11	10	9	8	7	6	5	4	3	2	1	0

tions require one operand. Some need two operands and some do not need any at all. For example, the instruction to halt execution needs only an operation code. A **machine language program** consists of a sequence of such binary coded instructions.

Auxiliary Storage

Auxiliary storage, you will recall, is necessary because main storage can be used only temporarily. Once information has been processed in main storage by a given program, that program must yield main storage to another program. Auxiliary storage is used to store data and programs more permanently. The two primary media used for long-term storage of data and programs are *tape* and *magnetic disk*.

Figure 1.10 Magnetic tape drive (Courtesy of International Business Machines Corporation)

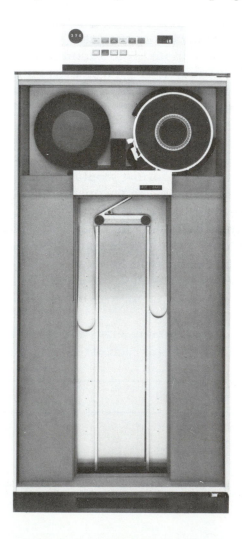

Magnetic tape looks like the tape used in home tape recorders. The tape has an iron oxide coating that can be magnetized. Information is stored as extremely small magnetized spots, which can be read or written by a device called a *tape drive* (see Figure 1.10). The schemes used to encode information on tape are similar to the ones used to store information in main storage.

Magnetic disk is another common form of auxiliary storage. A magnetic disk is a metal platter with an iron oxide coating that looks like a long-playing stereo record. Generally, several disks are assembled together into a disk pack. Disk storage belongs to a class of devices called direct access storage devices. With such devices one can go directly to the information one wants without going through all the preceding information. Information on a tape, on the other hand, must be accessed sequentially. That is, to get at the information you need, you must first go through all the preceding information. The ability to access information on a disk directly is its main advantage over tape. One of its main disadvantages is its cost. Disk storage units are considerably more expensive than tape. Figure 1.11 shows disk storage. It has a capacity of 317.5 million bytes.

Figure 1.11 The IBM 3350 Disk Storage (Courtesy of International Business Machines Corporation)

Central Processing Unit

When the computer is running, the instructions that tell it what to do must be in main storage. They are fetched from main storage and executed by the CPU. The CPU consists of two distinct functional parts: the Arithmetic and Logic Unit (ALU) and the Control Unit. They are shown in Figure 1.12.

Arithmetic and Logic Unit, (ALU) The ALU is responsible for performing such calculations as addition, subtraction, multiplication, and division. It can also perform certain logical operations, such as the comparison of the contents of two memory locations to see if they are equal.

Control Unit The control unit coordinates the activities of the CPU as it executes the programs in main storage. It can access instructions from programs stored in main storage, interpret these instructions, and then activate appropriate units of the computer system to execute them. It generates control and timing signals for the input and output units and routes data between the ALU and main storage.

The control unit and the arithmetic and logic unit use special storage locations called **registers** to perform their functions. These locations are not part of the main storage. They are instead components of the CPU. Figure 1.13 illustrates an even more detailed view of the CPU for a simple, hypothetical computer.

The CPU executes the instructions in its main storage one at a time. In order to do this, the CPU performs a sequence of operations known as the **instruction execution cycle** for each instruction. The *program counter register* and *instruction decoder register* are used by the control unit of the CPU as it goes through the instruction execution cycle. The *accumulator* is a register in the arithmetic and logic unit of the CPU, which is used as a "scratch pad" to perform calculations and to temporarily store results of such calculations. Many computer systems actually have more than one register that can be used to do calculations. For simplicity, we will assume only one such

Figure 1.12 Components of the central processing unit

Central Processing Unit

Arithmetic and Logic Unit
Control Unit

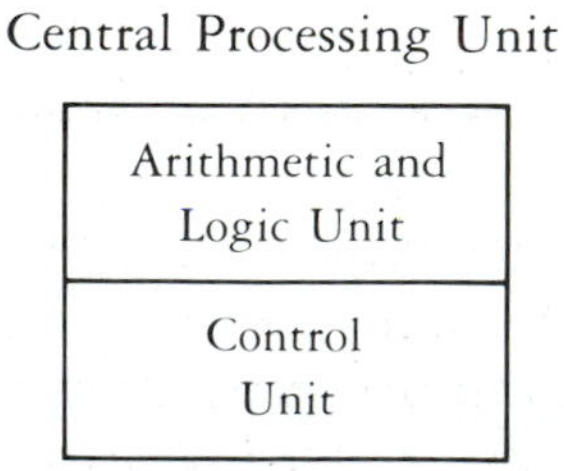

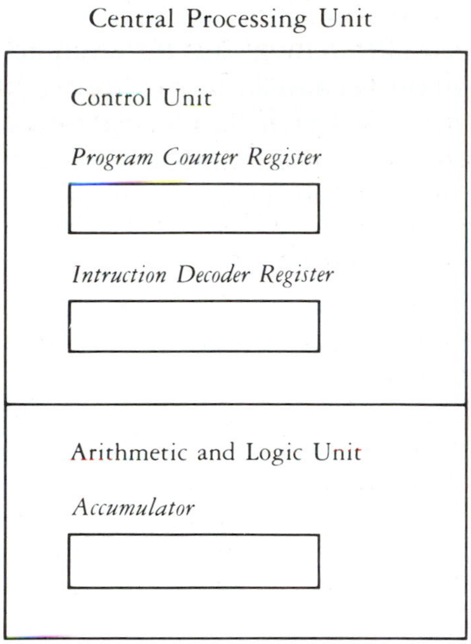

Figure 1.13 Details of hypothetical central processing unit

Central Processing Unit

Control Unit

Program Counter Register

Intruction Decoder Register

Arithmetic and Logic Unit

Accumulator

register. To illustrate how all of the components of the CPU work, let us now follow the course of execution of the short sequence of instructions given in Example 1.1.

EXAMPLE 1.1 Machine Language Instructions

Main Storage Location	Instruction Stored	Meaning
000100	0010000000 111000	Load contents of main storage location 111000 into the accumulator.
000101	0011000000 111001	Add the contents of main storage location 111001 to contents of accumulator.
000110	0101000000 111010	Store the contents of the accumulator in location 111010

Our example uses three instructions. We add two numbers—one at location 111000 (56 in decimal notation), the other at location 111001 (57 in decimal notation)—and store the result at location 111010 (58 in decimal notation). This is accomplished by first loading (copying) the contents of location 111000 into the accumulator. The second instruction then adds the contents of location 111001 to the contents of the accumulator. The result of the addition remains in the accumulator. Finally, the last instruction stores (copies) the contents of the accumulator into location 111010. The program itself is in main storage with the first instruction at location 000100 (4 in decimal notation).

When execution of the program is initiated, the program counter must contain the address of the first instruction. Suppose that when the program starts the state of our computer is as shown in Figure 1.14. The symbol ?????? indicates that we do not know the

Figure 1.14 Beginning of instruction execution cycle

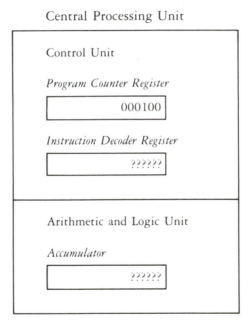

contents of either the register or the main storage location. When the CPU goes through an instruction execution cycle, the control unit performs the following operations:

1. Fetch the instruction whose memory address is in the program counter register and copy it into the instruction decoder register.
2. Increment the contents of the program counter register by 1 so that the address of the next instruction will be available at the beginning of the next cycle.
3. Decode the contents of the instruction decoder register and fetch the data needed to execute the instruction.
4. Execute the instruction.

At the end of the first instruction execution cycle the state of the machine is shown in Figure 1.15. Note the changes in the CPU. The program counter now contains the address of the next instruction to be executed. The instruction decoder contains the instruction that was just executed. And the accumulator contains the same value as memory location 111001. Nothing was changed in main storage.

The CPU will now perform the next instruction execution cycle. This process continues until an instruction to halt or an invalid instruction is encountered. You should now execute the remaining two instructions by hand and note the corresponding changes in both the CPU and main storage.

As can be seen from our example, the hardware organization of even a simple computer can be quite complex. Current technology is now capable of building much more complex CPUs on a tiny chip. Figure 1.16 shows a microprocessor built by INTEL Corporation. This chip is a tiny CPU, much more powerful than the one described in the text. When augmented by main storage and input/output devices, the chip becomes a microcomputer more powerful than some of the early computers that cost 1000 times more than current microcomputers.

Output of Information

Various types of printing devices are used to output information, and the most common form of output from computer systems is on paper. Of the devices used, *line printers* commonly are used with large computer systems. A line printer assembles all the characters to be output on a line and prints them on paper almost instantaneously.

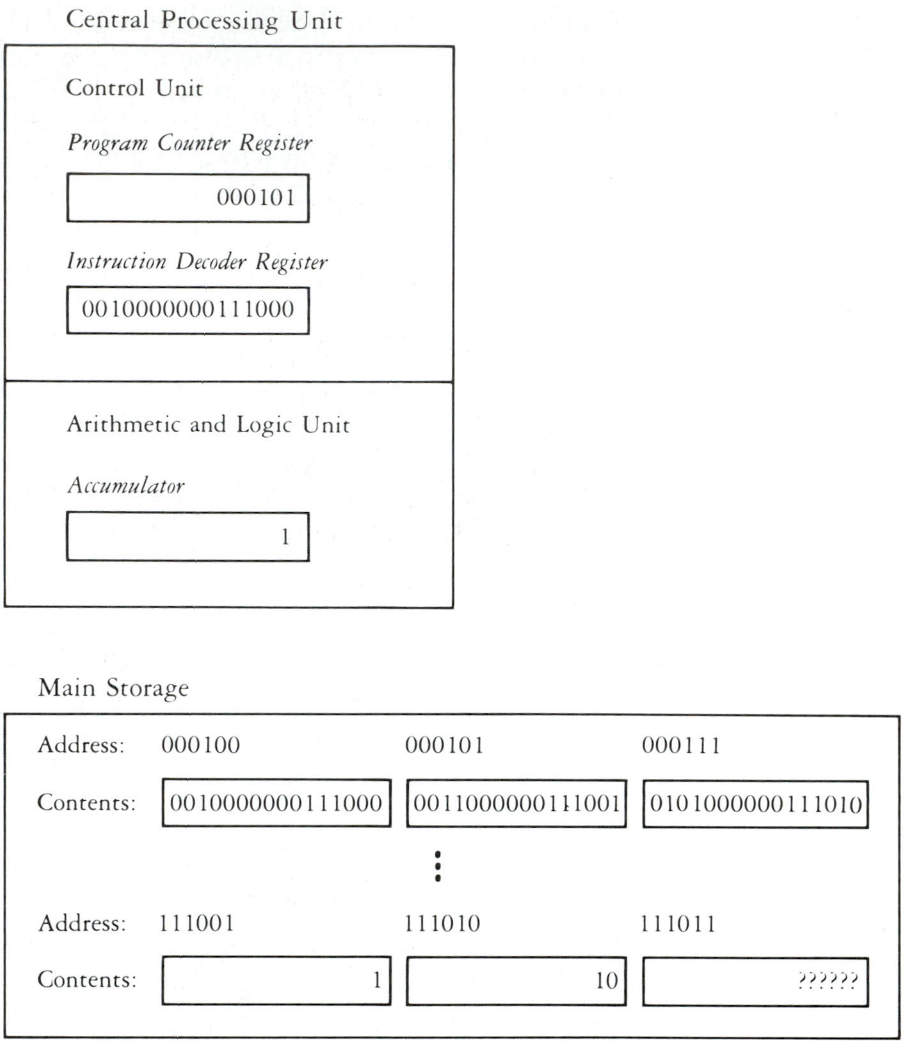

Figure 1.15 End of
first instruction
execution cycle

Central Processing Unit

Control Unit

Program Counter Register

| 000101 |

Instruction Decoder Register

| 0010000000111000 |

Arithmetic and Logic Unit

Accumulator

| 1 |

Main Storage

Address:	000100	000101	000111
Contents:	0010000000111000	0011000000111001	0101000000111010

⋮

Address:	111001	111010	111011
Contents:	1	10	??????

Line printer speeds average about 1200 lines per minute, but some
printers are as fast as 21,000 lines per minute. Another device, the *laser printer* (Figure 1.17) uses a laser beam to form characters on paper. This printer is capable not only of extremely fast speeds but also
of extremely high-quality printing.

    With smaller systems, slower, but also less expensive, character
printers are popular. A *character printer* is like a typewriter, and
prints character by character across the page, from one side to the
other. Figure 1.18 illustrates one type of character printer that uses a
print thimble with raised characters. As the thimble rotates to a de-

Figure 1.16 A microprocessor chip (Courtesy of Intel Corporation)

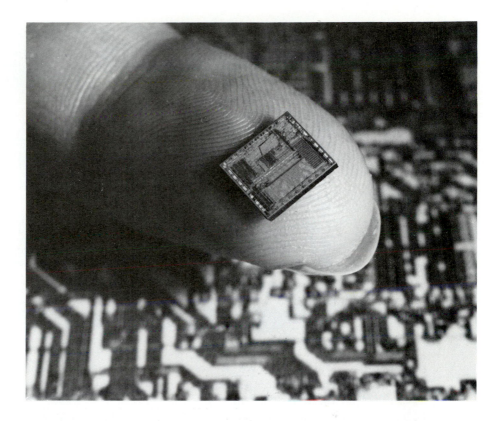

Figure 1.17 A laser-electrophotographic printer (Courtesy of International Business Machines Corporation)

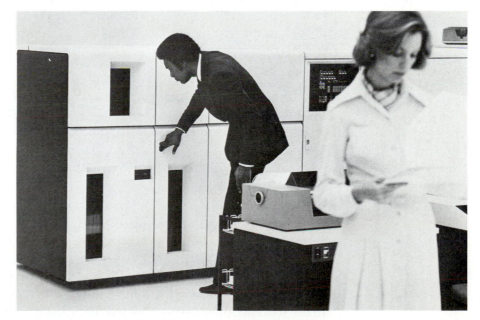

Figure 1.18 A
character printer
(Courtesy of Digital
Equipment
Corporation)

sired character, the character is struck by a small hammer to produce
the imprint on paper. These printers are noted also for their high-
quality printing.

Output also can be produced on CRT terminals and plotters, to
name some other devices. Output can also take the form of color
graphics, electronic signals, sound, and many other forms in addition to printed paper.

SELF-TEST 1

1. Differentiate between the hardware and software of a computer
system.
2. What are the major hardware components of a computer system?
Explain the function of each component.
3. What is the relationship between bit, byte, and word?
4. Consider the byte

01010011

(a) What binary number is stored in that byte?
(b) What binary coded decimal is stored in that byte?

5. The maximum number of bytes in the main storage of a computer
is determined by the size of the operands in a machine instruction.
Since operands are main storage addresses, the maximum number of
main storage locations corresponds to the largest possible operand.

What is the maximum possible size (in bytes) for each of the following operand sizes?

(a) 10 bits (b) 16 bits (c) 18 bits

Answers

1. Hardware is the physical equipment or devices making up the computer and its peripheral equipment. Software is a set of programs and associated documentation concerned with the operation of the computer system.

2. The major hardware components of a computer system are: (a) Input Unit—used to enter information into the computer system. It obtains information (data and programs) from various input devices and places this information into main storage. (b) Main Storage—used to store information that is received from the input unit so that this information is available to the units involved in processing it. It also stores already processed information so that it can be output on various output devices. (c) Auxiliary Storage—used for storing large volumes of information. It provides more permanent information storage. Before this information can be used by the computer system, however, it must be transferred to main storage. (d) Central Processing Unit—consists of components that perform such things as calculations and logical operations. Additionally, the central processing unit controls the operation of all of the other components of the computer hardware. (e) Output Unit—used to output results of processing by the computer. It is used to transfer information from main storage to various output devices.

3. A bit is a single binary digit. It is either a 1 or a 0. A byte is a group of consecutive bits. All the bits of a byte are manipulated usually as a unit. A word is a group of bytes that can be processed as a single unit.

4. (a) 83 (b) 53

5. (a) 1024 bytes or 1 kilobyte
   (b) 65536 bytes or 64 kilobytes
   (c) 262244 bytes or 256 kilobytes.

1.3 SOFTWARE

Our attention up to this point has been focused on computer hardware. We will now examine some of the procedures used to make this hardware perform its tasks. These procedures are referred to collectively as computer *software*. Software is a general term for the programs that control computer systems as they are used to solve various problems. Designing programs to perform various tasks is, of course, the subject of the rest of this book. At this point, we simply want to discuss the software that is generally available on computer systems that makes it possible for users to interact with the system in order to use it.

Programs used with computers can be divided into three major groups. One such group is *operating systems*. These programs provide overall control and management of computer resources. *Language translators* are programs that do what their name implies—they translate instructions written in a programming language, such as Pascal, into the binary code that the computer hardware "understands" directly. *Application programs* are programs used to perform specific tasks, such as weekly payroll processing.

Operating Systems

Simply put, an operating system is a set of programs that manage the resources of a computer system as it performs its operations. Such programs sometimes are called *supervisory programs* or *monitors*. The operating system consists of programs to supervise the execution of other programs; control the location, storage, and retrieval of information; and schedule jobs for continuous processing. Because operating systems perform many routine system operations, users of the system can focus their attention on solving problems of interest to them instead of worrying about machine-oriented details. One of the primary benefits of having an operating system is that you, as a programmer, can share the resources of the computer system with other users without concern about how it is done or what the other users are doing. It is the function of the operating system to make the sharing of resources among users possible.

Among the resources of an operating system is a *system program library*. This library is a set of programs and routines that can be used by programmers. The major types of routines provided by an operating system are various utility programs, such as input/output utilities and mathematical and statistical routines.

You are likely to encounter an important system program called a *text editor*. A text editor is a program that eases the job of modifying files that are stored on the system. Operating under the control of a text editor, simple codes are used for inserting, deleting, and otherwise modifying characters, words, or lines within a file that usually contains text. This system program is very useful to programmers because it allows them to enter and modify their own programs.

Language Translators

Language translators are programs in the system program library that translate programs written by programmers to machine language (the combination of 1s and 0s recognized by the hardware). As we will see shortly, most programmers do not write their programs in machine language directly. Because of this, a language translator program is used to translate the programs prepared by programmers into machine language programs that then can be executed by the computer. Language translator programs are also called *assemblers* or *compilers*. These will be discussed in the next section.

Application Programs

Application programs are generally the programs that are used to perform the tasks for which the computer system was bought. Typical examples of application programs are programs used to process mailing lists, to maintain inventory control and accounting records, to maintain personnel records, to compute and print payroll information, and so on.

1.4 PROGRAM-MING LANGUAGES

When we discussed the operation of the CPU, we saw how instructions are represented within main storage and how the CPU fetches and executes the instructions. Instructions written in a format that can be understood directly by the CPU are said to be in *machine language*. Instructions in machine language are all binary. It should be apparent from the machine language example presented in Example 1.1 that it would be a horrifying prospect to write a large program in such a language.

Consider some of the difficulties involved in writing machine language programs. First of all, we have to remember, or look up, long binary strings for operation codes. Because these codes are arbitrary patterns of 1s and 0s, there is nothing in the code that helps us to remember what code represents "add," "store," or any other instruction. Second, each operation performed by the computer hardware is usually a very small step in the overall program we are trying to write. For example, in order to add two numbers we may be required to write as many as three machine language instructions. That is, we may be required to load (copy) one of the numbers into the accumulator, add the second number, and store the result. Finally, we are required to keep track of the locations of values in main storage because instructions must specify operands as addresses.

Another problem with machine languages is the fact that machine languages differ from one computer to another. A machine language program written for one computer will not run on another computer. Of course, these characteristics of machine language became apparent to many other people, and thus, other programming languages were invented.

Assembly Language

The first step in making programming languages easier to use was to introduce *assembly languages*. In an assembly language, the operation codes and operands of machine language are stated in alphabetic mnemonics, which are easier to remember. For example, the machine instructions of Example 1.1 can be stated in assembly language as:

Mnemonic Code	Meaning
LD X	load *X*
ADD Y	add *Y*
ST Z	store *Z*

Note how much more easily the assembly language instructions can be read. Note also that addresses have been replaced by letters.

Figure 1.19 Sample assembly language program

Machine Language			Assembly Language			Comments
1				.LIST	TTM	
2				.TITLE	ASSEMBLER DEMO	
3	000000	016700	START:	MOV	NUM1,R0	;LOAD FIRST NUMBER
		000012				
4	000004	066700		ADD	NUM2,R0	;ADD SECOND NUMBER
		000010				
5	000010	010067		MOV	R0,RESULT	;PLACE SUM IN RESULT
		000006				
6	000014	000000		HALT		;HALT THE COMPUTER
7			;			
8	000016	000123	NUM1:	.WORD	123	;FIRST NUMBER
9	000020	000456	NUM2:	.WORD	456	;SECOND NUMBER
10	000022		RESULT:	.BLKW	1	;THE RESULT
11		000000'		.END	START	

However, before an assembly language program can be executed, it must be translated to machine language. The assembly language program must be passed as input data to another program called an *assembler*, which performs that translation. Early assemblers required a one-to-one correspondence between instructions written in assembly language and machine language. Assemblers in use today allow for assembly language instructions that translate to more than one machine language instruction. But because most assembly language instructions correspond directly to single-machine language instructions, assembly languages are as machine dependent as are machine languages. Each computer system has its own assembly language. Figure 1.19 shows an actual assembly language program and the corresponding machine language program.

High-Level Languages

The next refinement in languages made them procedure oriented. A *procedure-oriented language* differs from an assembly language in that each program statement is related to a procedural task and may translate to many machine language instructions. As an example of a program written in a procedural language, consider the following Pascal program.

```
program AddNumbers (input,output);

var
   Num1, Num2, Result : integer;

begin
   read (Num1,Num2);
   Result := Num1 + Num2;
   writeln (Result)
end.
```

Even without any knowledge of the Pascal programming language, it is obvious what the program does. One of the features of procedural languages, such as Pascal, is that program statements appear in English-like sentences or mathematical formulas. They are clearly easier to understand than machine and assembly languages. Translations of these languages to machine languages, however, are more complex than for assembly languages.

The line

```
Result := Num1 + Num2;
```

is equivalent to the whole assembly language program of Figure 1.19. We know that the computer cannot execute a statement such as the above in one instruction; many, much smaller steps are involved in the execution of that statement. In other words, the translator that translates a Pascal program to machine language has to generate many machine language instructions for each Pascal statement. Such a translator is called a *compiler.* A compiler's task is much more complex than that of an assembler, because procedure-oriented languages are much further removed from machine language than are assembly languages. Thus, procedure-oriented languages are often called *high-level* languages and assembly languages are called *low-level* languages. While machine and assembly languages are tied to particular computers, high-level languages are not. A compiler for Pascal, for example, can be written for a wide range of computers. Thus, a program written in a high-level language can be translated and executed by many different computers. This makes high-level language programs "portable."

Compilers do not necessarily translate a high-level language directly to machine language. The result of the compiler's translation may be an assembly language program or sometimes even another high-level language program, which in turn requires further translation. We say that a compiler translates a *source program* written in some high-level language into an *object program* written in some other language.

Another type of translator that is sometimes used to translate high-level language programs is called an *interpreter*. An interpreter translates and executes a high-level language program one instruction at a time. By contrast, a compiler translates the whole high-level language program and then executes the translated version. When an interpreter is used, it appears as if the computer can execute a high-level language program directly.

Common High-Level Languages

The following are some of the more commonly available high-level languages:

1. Ada (named in honor of Lady Ada Lovelace, reputed to be the world's first computer programmer)   A new language designed to write systems programs, which was designed and implemented for the Department of Defense.
2. ALGOL (ALGOrithmic Language) A numerically oriented procedural language widely used in Europe.

3. APL (A Programming Language) A highly mathematical language. It is used in scientific computing.

4. BASIC (Beginners' All Purpose Symbolic Instruction Code) A teaching language designed to be used by students working at online terminals. It is commonly used to teach programming at an introductory level.

5. COBOL (COmmon Business-Oriented Language) The first complete language developed and designed for business applications.

6. FORTRAN (FORmula TRANslator) The first complete compiler language. It was designed for use in scientific problem solving and remains one of the most popular languages for scientific programming.

7. LISP A special-purpose language developed primarily for list processing and symbolic manipulation.

8. Pascal (named in honor of Blaise Pascal, a seventeenth-century French mathematician) A general-purpose language specifically designed as a teaching language.

9. PL/I (Programming Language 1) A general purpose language developed by IBM. It has many of the commercial capabilities of COBOL and many of the scientific capabilities of FORTRAN, as well as some of the better features of ALGOL. It is an extremely complex language.

The Pascal Language

The development of a new language is usually motivated by some perceived need and a conviction that existing languages do not satisfy the need. Pascal began in the late 1960s as a teaching experiment by Professor Niklaus Wirth. The experiment was to teach programming in a systematic fashion using a highly structured way of representing programs. The following quote of Professor Wirth states the purpose of Pascal:

> The development of the language Pascal is based on two principal aims. The first is to make available a language suitable to teach programming as a systematic discipline based on certain fundamental concepts clearly and naturally reflected by the language. The second is to develop implementations of this language which are both reliable and efficient on presently available computers.
>
> The desire for a new language for the purpose of teaching programming is due to my dissatisfaction with the presently used major

languages whose features and constructs too often cannot be explained logically and convincingly and which too often defy systematic reasoning. Along with this dissatisfaction goes my conviction that the language in which a student is taught to express his ideas profoundly influences his habits of thought and invention, and that the disorder governing these languages directly imposes itself on the programming style of the students. [Quoted from the second edition of the *Pascal User's Manual and Report* by Kathleen Jensen and Niklaus Wirth (Springer Verlag, New York, 1974), p. 133.]

Since the time of Pascal's creation by Professor Wirth, the language has become widespread, primarily because the features that make it such a good teaching language are also the features that make it useful for developing systems and applications software. The acceptance of Pascal has been so widespread that Pascal compilers for most of the common microprocessors in the personal computing field, as well as many large computers, now exist.

SELF-TEST 2

1. What are the major functions of an operating system?
2. Differentiate between a machine language and a high-level language.
3. What is a compiler? What is its main function?

Answers

1. The major functions of an operating system are: (a) supervision of the execution of other programs; (b) control of the location, storage, and retrieval of information; (c) scheduling of jobs for continuous processing.

2. A machine language program is directly interpreted by the computer without further modification. A high-level language program must be translated into a machine language before the program can be executed.

3. A compiler is a program that translates the source program (usually written in a high-level language) into an object program (often a machine language) for a particular computer.

1.5 GLOSSARY

Accumulator A special storage location in the ALU that stores the results of a computation. It is also called a register.

Address A particular location in main storage, usually a byte, that has its own unique address or number, just as a post office box.

Application program A computer program that performs a specific function for a user of the computer system. An order-entry program or a sales-report program are examples of applications programs.

Arithmetic and Logic Unit (ALU) The component in the CPU that performs the arithmetic and logical operations.

ASCII (*American Standard Code for Information Interchange*) A standard binary code that is used to represent information inside the computer's main storage.

Assembler A program that translates a program written in assembly language to machine language.

Assembly language A programming language that lets programmers write programs at the machine-language level but uses mnemonic representations of operators and symbolic representations of operand addresses.

Auxiliary storage A permanent storage of data and instructions that is distinguished from main storage by the fact that the contents of auxiliary storage must first be moved to main storage before they can be used.

Bit A single binary digit that is either 0 or 1.

Byte A storage unit that usually consists of eight bits, which is capable of storing a character of information.

Card reader An input device that reads punched cards and converts the pattern of holes in the card into electronic impulses, and transmits the impulses to main storage.

Central Processing Unit (CPU) The component of a computer system that controls and executes a program.

Compiler A program that translates a high-level language into machine language.

Control unit The part of the CPU that performs the primary functions of the computer. It obtains, decodes, and executes each instruction of a machine-language program.

Cathode-Ray Tube (CRT) A video terminal that may be both an input and output device.

EBCDIC (*Extended Binary Coded Decimal Interchange Code*) A standard code used to store and retrieve information. Primarily used by IBM.

Hardware The physical components such as the CPU and all peripheral devices, that make up the computer.

High-level language A problem-oriented language that is designed to allow programmers to concentrate on the problem they are solving and eliminates the requirement that programmers have an intimate knowledge of the computer's machine language.

Hollerith code A punched-card code. Hollerith cards contain 80 columns of information, coded as the presence or absence of holes.

Input unit The component of a computer system that is used to input information.

Instruction A command to a computer that consists of an operation code and one or more operands.

Instruction execution cycle The steps that are performed by the CPU to execute an instruction in machine language. The steps are: fetch the instruction, decode it, and execute it.

Instruction set The set of instructions that was designed and built into the computer.

Interpreter A translator program that translates and executes each line of a source program as it is encountered.

Kilobyte A commonly used designator of main storage size that equals one thousand bytes.

Machine language The language that can be understood by the computer without requiring translation

Main storage The part of the computer system where programs currently being executed are stored.

Object program A program that is the output of a compiler.

Operating system A set of programs that are used to manage the resources of a computer system.

Operation code The part of a computer instruction that specifies what the instruction does.

Program A step-by-step set of instructions that directs the computer to perform certain operations to solve a problem.

Register A temporary storage location in the CPU that is used for arithmetic and logic operations.

Software The programs and associated documentation that make the hardware perform various tasks.

Source program A program that is written in a procedure-oriented language. Source programs are the input to a compiler.

Terminal A device that enters information into, or outputs information from, a computer.

Text editor A program that modifies stored files. It provides a set of simple commands for inserting, deleting, or changing entries within the file.

Word A collection of bytes (usually one, two, or four bytes) that is commonly used to store numbers.

1.6 EXERCISES

1.1. Fill in the blank for each of the following:

(a) The _____ is a complex set of electrical circuitry that executes machine instructions.
(b) Another name for a binary digit is _____ .
(c) The physical equipment of a computer system is called the _____ .
(d) The programs available to run a computer system are called _____ .
(e) The arithmetic and logic unit is part of the _____ .
(f) The instruction execution cycle is carried out by the _____ .
(g) The two most common forms of output devices are _____ and _____ .
(h) A _____ translates a high-level language program into a machine language program.

1.2. Answer each of the following *true* or *false*. If your answer is *false*, state why.

(a) A program is a sequence of instructions that directs the computer to perform specific tasks.
(b) The CPU controls the computer and carries out the operations called for by the program.
(c) An assembler translates a machine language program to assembly language.
(d) Input units and output units are part of a computer's software.
(e) The central processing unit accepts data directly from the output unit.
(f) Add, subtract, multiply, and divide are examples of operands.
(g) The operation code portion of an instruction indicates the operation to be performed.
(h) Pascal is an example of an assembly language.

1.3. What are the major hardware elements of a computer? Explain the functions of each of these elements.

1.4. Why are binary digits used as the basis for the codes used to represent information in computers?

1.5. Convert the following binary numbers to base 10.

(a) 010101
(b) 111111
(c) 100000

1.6. Consider the following hypothetical machine language:

Instruction	Meaning
0010000000xxxxxx	Load contents of main storage location xxxxxx into accumulator.
0101000000xxxxxx	Store contents of accumulator in location xxxxxx.
0011000000xxxxxx	Add contents of main storage location xxxxxx to contents of accumulator. Leave result in accumulator.
0110000000xxxxxx	Subtract contents of main storage location xxxxxx from contents of accumulator. Leave result in accumulator.
0000000000	Halt.

(a) Write a machine language program to add the contents of location 001111 to the contents of location 010000, store the result in location 010000, and halt.

(b) Write a machine language program to subtract the contents of location 000100 from the contents of location 000101, store the result in location 000110, and halt.

(c) Write a machine language program to add the contents of location 000100 to the contents of location 000101, subtract from the result the contents of location 000110, store the final result in location 000111, and halt.

(d) Write a machine language program to move the contents of location 000111 to location 001001.

1.7. Execute the machine language programs of Exercise 1.6 by hand. Show the contents of the appropriate registers and main storage locations for each machine execution cycle.

1.8. What is an operating system?

1.9. What is software?

1.10. Distinguish between main storage and auxiliary storage.

1.11. Explain the following terms: (a) source program (b) object program.

1.12. What do FORTRAN, COBOL, and Pascal stand for? Give an example of a suitable problem for programming in each of the languages and state the reason for your choice.

1.13. Now that we have high-level languages, can we do without assembly and machine languages? Explain your answer.

1.14. What are the advantages of programming in a high-level language? What are the disadvantages?

2. Introduction to Pascal

2.1 THE PASCAL PROGRAM

A Pascal program is divided into two parts: a **heading** and a body, called a **block**. The heading provides the program name and lists the program's interfaces with its environment. In Example 2.1 the program will input data and output a result.

The block, in our example, consists of three sections. The first two sections describe the data used by the program and are usually called the **declaration part** of the program. The first section of the block defines the **const**ant pi to be 3.14159. The second section of the block declares the **var**iables Radius, Circumference, and Area to be real variables. The third section of the block describes the actions to be performed by the program and is called the **statement part** of the program. This consists of the description of four actions enclosed by the symbols **begin** and **end**. First we read the value of the Radius. Next we compute the Circumference, and then we compute the Area. Finally, we write the values of the Radius, Circumference, and Area. The program is terminated by a period following the symbol **end**.

EXAMPLE 2.1 Program to Compute the Circumference and Area of a Circle

Heading

```
program Circle (input, output);

{ Program to compute the circumference
  and area of a circle given the radius }
```

Block

```
const
    pi = 3.14159;
var
    Radius, Circumference, Area : real;

begin
    read (Radius);
    Circumference := 2 * pi * Radius;
    Area := pi * sqr(Radius);
    writeln (Radius, Circumference, Area)
end.
```

Figure 2.1 The shell of a Pascal program

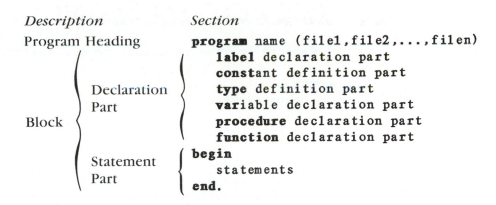

Description | *Section*

Program Heading — **program** name (file1,file2,...,filen)

Block
  Declaration Part
    label declaration part
    constant definition part
    type definition part
    variable declaration part
    procedure declaration part
    function declaration part
  Statement Part
    begin
        statements
    end.

The part of the program enclosed in braces, { }, is called a **comment**. It conveys no information to the computer. It is intended to provide information to the human reader. The comment in our example simply describes the function of the program. Comments are often used to indicate the author's name, the date the program was written, and so forth.

The Shell of a Pascal Program

All Pascal programs will have one or more of the sections listed, in order, in Figure 2.1. These sections, with the exception of the program heading and the statement part, may or may not be present in a given program. In Example 2.1 only the program heading, constant definition part, variable declaration part, and statement part are present. We will discuss these parts in the remainder of this chapter. Label declarations and type definitions will be discussed in Chapter 5. Procedure and function declarations will be discussed in Chapter 7. Here are some additional examples of simple Pascal programs.

EXAMPLE 2.2 A Simple Addition Program

```
program Addition (input, output);

{ Program to compute and print the sum of two numbers. }

var
    FirstNumber, SecondNumber, Sum : integer;

begin
    read (FirstNumber);
    read (SecondNumber);
    Sum := FirstNumber + SecondNumber;
    writeln (Sum)
end.
```

**EXAMPLE 2.3
Program to
Convert
Inches to
Centimeters**

```
program Convert (input, output);

{ Program to convert inches to centimeters. }

const
    ConversionFactor = 2.54;
var
    Inches, Centimeters : real;
begin
    read (Inches);
    Centimeters := ConversionFactor * Inches;
    writeln (Centimeters)
end.
```

**EXAMPLE 2.4
Program to
Print a Mes-
sage**

```
program Message (output);

begin
    writeln ('Hello this is your friendly computer')
end.
```

Identifiers

In Pascal, as in other programming languages, we are often required to name objects in the program. In the program heading we name the program; in the constant definition section we name constants; in the variable declaration section we name variables. In subsequent chapters we will see that types, procedures, and functions also must be named.

The sequence of characters that forms the name of a program, constant, type, variable, procedure, or function is called an **identifier**. In Pascal *an identifier consists of a letter followed by a sequence of letters and/or digits*.

As a visual aid to mastering rules of Pascal, we use Pascal **syntax diagrams**. The syntax diagram for an identifier in Pascal is given in Figure 2.2. To use the diagram, simply follow the arrows through the chart. This diagram offers many options but requires that the first character of every identifier be a letter. Note that the diagram does not specify whether the letters should be lowercase (*a*, *b*, *c*, etc.) or uppercase letters (*A*, *B*, *C*, etc.). Many compilers recognize both but often do not distinguish between matching uppercase and lowercase letters. That is, they would regard "Amount" and "amount" as the same identifier.

Figure 2.2 Syntax diagram for identifier

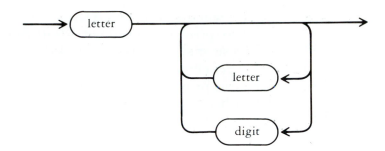

The following are examples of *valid* Pascal identifiers:

A	count	number8
I	total	hoursworked
y2	partnumber	LunchTime
minimum	Value	ThisIsaVeryLongIdentifier

The syntax diagram does not specify the length of identifiers. Thus we can have identifiers of any length. Most compilers, however, only recognize the first eight characters of an identifier; so the identifier "hoursworked" would appear as "hourswor" and would not be differentiated from the identifier "hoursworried." Therefore, when you select identifiers for distinct objects, be sure that they differ in their first eight characters.

Here are some *invalid* identifiers.

Identifier	Reason Identifier Is Invalid
2ndnumber	Identifier must begin with a letter.
First Name	Embedded blanks are not permitted.
$value	Only letters and numbers should be used.
array	Array is a reserved word in Pascal.

Pascal has some keywords, or **reserved words**, which cannot be used as identifiers. These words have a fixed meaning and cannot be used for any other purpose. Reserved words in Pascal are

and	do	function	nil	program	type
array	downto	goto	not	record	until
begin	else	if	of	repeat	var
case	end	in	or	set	while
const	file	label	packed	then	with
div	for	mod	procedure	to	

In this book we will use **bold-faced** letters for all reserved words.

Pascal also provides **standard identifiers** with predefined meanings. These may, if needed, be redefined to have different meanings, but redefining a standard identifier can lead to confusion for a reader of the program. Thus it is not recommended. A redefined standard identifier cannot be used for its original purpose. The standard identifiers in Pascal are

Constants:	false, true, maxint
Types:	integer, boolean, real, char, text
Functions:	abs, arctan, chr, cos, eof, eoln, exp, ln, odd, ord, pred, round, sin, sqr, sqrt, succ, trunc
Procedures:	get, new, pack, page, put, read, readln, reset, rewrite, unpack, write, writeln
Files:	input, output

Identifiers should be chosen to give a clear indication of their purpose in the program. In Example 2.1, we chose the identifier Radius to represent the radius of a circle. We could have chosen the identifier x for this purpose, but clearly Radius is much more meaningful. Meaningful identifiers make programs more understandable. Identifiers that are obscure or meaningless should be avoided, as they are often the major stumbling block to understanding a program.

Comments

Even when a programmer is careful to use meaningful identifiers, it is still often difficult to read a program and understand what various parts do without some explanatory comments. Comments easily can be inserted in Pascal programs. A **comment** in Pascal has the following form:

```
{ string of characters }
```

or

```
(* string of characters *)
```

The string of characters may contain any characters except the brace symbol, }. The compound symbols (∗ and ∗) can be used where { and } are not available. Comments are ignored by the compiler when the program is translated. To the compiler, a comment is equivalent to a blank, and so a comment may be inserted anywhere a blank is allowed in the program. The braces allow the compiler to distinguish a comment from the rest of the program easily. (That is, of course, unless we forget the closing brace, }, at the end of the comment, in which case the compiler would consider everything until the next } a comment!)

However, it is good practice to make comments stand out from program statements. Although the compiler has no difficulty distinguishing a comment from the rest of the program, a person reading a program often needs some visual cues other than { and } to separate comments from program text. A simple way to do this is to insert blank lines before and after comments. A better way is to use easily seen characters, such as *, to frame a comment. We could have made the comment in the program at the beginning of the chapter stand out by framing it with asterisks as follows:

```
{*****************************************
* Program to compute the circumference  *
* and area of a circle given the radius *
*****************************************}
```

Comments can be overdone. For example, the comments in the following statements are superfluous:

```
read (Radius) {** read the value of radius **}
writeln (Area)  {** write the value of area **}
```

Program Heading

The program heading is the first line of every Pascal program. The word **program** is the first symbol in the program heading and is always followed by the **program name**. The name is of your choosing and serves to identify the program. It is required by the compiler, but is not otherwise significant inside, or outside of the program. The remaining part of the heading is a list of file names enclosed in parentheses. It is through this list of files that the program communicates with its environment. We will discuss these files in greater detail when we examine how to get data to a program and how to output results.

The syntax diagram for a program heading is given in Figure 2.3. The first identifier is the name of the program. The other identifiers are names of files. In the next chapters we will need only input

Figure 2.3 Syntax
diagram for
program heading

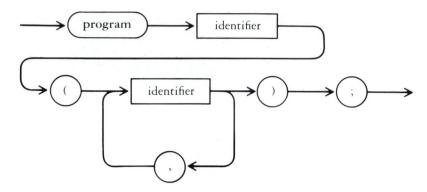

and output files. In the chapter on files we will introduce other file
concepts.

A typical program heading takes the form:

program identifier (input, output);

The files "input" and "output" indicate that the program will
read data from an input file and write results to an output file. In
computer programming, any source from which information can be
obtained, or to which information can be sent, is often called a file.
Thus, the term not only refers to actual data files, but also to such devices as printers and terminals.

Note that the last symbol on the line is a semicolon (;). The semicolon is not part of the heading. It is used to *separate* the heading
from whatever follows it; for example, a definition, a declaration, or
a statement. In Pascal the semicolon is used as a **statement separator** and appears wherever one statement must be separated from another statement.

Constant Definition

When writing a program, we frequently need to use values that are
known before the program is executed, and that remain constant
during program execution. Such values are therefore called **constants**. An example of such a value is the value of pi in the program at
the beginning of the chapter.

Whenever we are using constants in a Pascal program, we can
use the actual value of the constant, such as 3.14159, or we can give
the constant an identifier and then use the identifier throughout the
program. To name a constant in Pascal, the **const** definition section
of the program is used. The general form of the **const** definition is

Figure 2.4 Syntax diagram for **const** definition

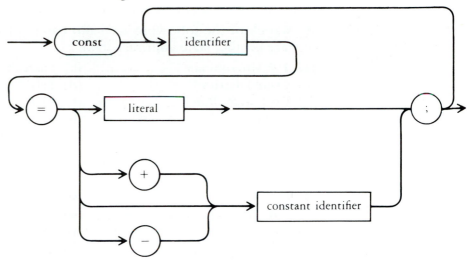

```
const
    identifier1 = constant1;
    identifier2 = constant2;
                  .
                  .
                  .
```

The syntax diagram for a constant definition is given in **Figure 2.4**. Thus,

```
const
    pi = 3.14159;
    e  = 2.7182818;
    accuracy = 2;
```

defines the constants pi, e, and accuracy for use throughout the program. It is no longer necessary to type either 3.14159 or 2.7182818 in the several places where these constants may be required by the program. Instead, we can simply type pi or e. More importantly, by using names such as "accuracy," we make the program more understandable. Finally, if future versions of the program require modifications of constant values, it is easier to alter the single definition of a constant than to change its value everywhere it appears in the program.

SELF-TEST 1

1. A Pascal program is divided into two parts. What are they?

2. Which of the following are valid Pascal identifiers? If you think any are invalid, state your reason(s).

(a) 1981Incometax   (b) District8
(c) CourtDistrict8   (d) Feb7Payroll
(e) Exchange Rate   (f) case4
(g) CASE4   (h) Record
(i) Sales$ (j) A*BMarkets

3. Classify each of the following as Pascal reserved words, standard identifiers, or neither.

(a) and   (b) begin
(c) number   (d) ending
(e) abs   (f) integer
(g) program   (h) if
(i) false   (j) set

4. Which of the following constant definitions are invalid? If they are invalid, correct them.

(a) **const**   (b) **const**
    Difference : 4;   NoOfPages = 23;
(c) **const**   (d) **const**
    LineWidth = 60;   Weight = 23.44.

Answers

1. The heading and the block
2. (a) Invalid, must start with a letter (b) Valid (c) Valid   (d) Valid   (e) Invalid, a blank is not a valid character (f) Valid   (g) Valid (h) Invalid, "record" is a reserved word   (i) Invalid, "$" is not a valid character   (j) Invalid, "*" is not a valid character

3. (a) Reserved word (b) Reserved word (c) Neither (d) Neither   (e) Standard identifier (f) Standard identifier (g) Reserved word (h) Reserved word (i) Standard Identifier (j) Reserved word

4. (a) **const**   (b) Valid
    Difference = 4;   (d) **const**
(c) Valid   Weight = 23.44;

2.2 VARIABLES

A **variable** can be thought of as a location in the computer's main storage that retains a value and has a name associated with it. It is important to distinguish between the *name* or identifier associated with a variable and its *current value*. Figure 2.5 shows the relation between names, locations, and values.

Figure 2.5 Varia-
bles as named
locations in main
storage

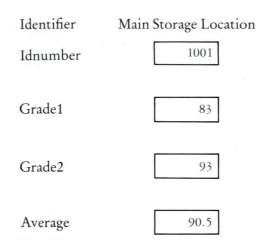

Identifier   Main Storage Location

Idnumber   1001

Grade1   83

Grade2   93

Average   90.5

In Figure 2.5, the identifier "Idnumber" names a certain main storage location. The value associated with Idnumber, in this case 1001, is stored in the designated location. In English, we might say something like "the value stored in the main storage location named Idnumber is 1001." Since this is a somewhat clumsy statement, we usually say "Idnumber equals 1001" with the understanding that we are talking about the current value of the location named "Idnumber."

When a variable is created, a physical location in main storage is reserved to hold its value. The creation of a variable occurs in the variable declaration section of the block. The name of the variable cannot be changed within the block where it is declared. As the computer executes the program, it will usually modify data stored in main storage. The value stored in a particular location, and therefore the value of a variable, will usually change as the program executes. That is why we refer to the value of a variable at a given point as its *current value*.

To declare the variables contained in a block, we use the **var** declaration, which has the following general format:

var

        identifier-list-1 : data-type;
        identifier-list-2 : data-type;
                    .
                    .
                    .
        identifier-list-n : data-type;

Figure 2.6 Syntax diagram for **var** declaration

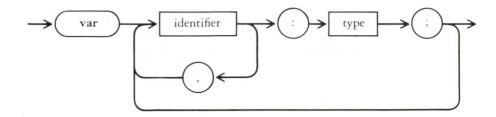

The syntax diagram for a variable declaration is shown in Figure 2.6. Figure 2.6 is incomplete because *type* is not yet defined. A complete syntax diagram for type is provided in Appendix C. Initially, we will not need the full definition of type, so the syntax diagram in Figure 2.7 will suffice for now.

The following is an example of a variable declaration section:

```
var
    Count, IdNumber, HoursWorked : integer;
    Total, Radius, Area : real;
```

As the syntax diagram illustrates, the **var** declaration not only assigns identifiers to variables, thereby reserving main storage locations to hold their values, but it also specifies the **type** of values these locations may contain. The **type** of a variable, like the variable name, is permanent and cannot be changed once it is declared. In the above declaration, the variable IdNumber is declared to be an integer. Thus, it can hold values such as 1001, − 1, or 0, but it cannot hold values such as 13.3 or − 21.67. The meaning of various variable types, such as integer and real, will be discussed later in this chapter.

Note that when variables are declared, the symbol **var** occurs only once. It is followed by a list of all the variable identifiers used in

Figure 2.7 Syntax diagram for simple **type**

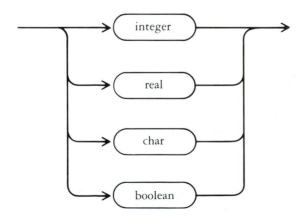

the block. We can declare each variable individually by specifying the type of each separately, or we can declare variables of the same type together, separating the variable names with commas and specifying their type once. Thus, the following declaration:

```
var
    Count, IdNumber, HoursWorked : integer;
```

is equivalent to

```
var
    Count : integer;
    IdNumber : integer;
    HoursWorked : integer;
```

In all cases the colon (:) is used to separate variable names from their types.

SELF-TEST 2

1. Define a variable.
2. Choose meaningful identifiers and write **var** declarations to represent the following variables:

(a) Selling price
(b) Number of pages in a book
(c) Grade point average
(d) Age in years

3. Consider the following variable declaration:

```
var
    Total : integer;
    Counter : integer;
    Average : real;
```

(a) Write an equivalent declaration without repeating the type integer.
(b) Write an equivalent declaration, including descriptive comments, to describe the function of each variable.

4. Given the following variables:

Identifier	Location
IdNumber	37
TestGrade	75.5

(a) What is the current value of IdNumber?

(b) What is the current value of TestGrade?

(c) Write a Pascal declaration for the above variables.

5. There are several errors in the following program. Make all the necessary corrections.

```
program Change Money (input,output)

(Program to convert US dollars to Japanese yen)

const
   ExchangeRate = 3.75;
var
   US$, Yen : real;
begin
   read (US$)
   Yen := ExchangeRate * US$;
   writeln (Yen)
end.
```

Answers

1. A variable is a named location in the computer's main storage in which a value may be stored.

2. (a) **var**
        SellingPrice : real;

(b) **var**
        NoOfPages : integer;

(c) **var**
        GradePointAverage : real;

(d) **var**
        Age : integer;

3. (a) **var**
        Total, Counter : integer;
        Average : real;

(b) **var**
        Total : integer; {Total of all Scores}
        Counter : integer; {Counter for number
                             of scores}
        Average : real; {Average of all scores}

4. (a) 37   (b) 75.5

(c) **var**
        IdNumber : integer;
        TestGrade : real;

5. The corrected program is:

```
program ChangeMoney (input,output);

{Program to convert US dollars to Japanese yen}

const
    ExchangeRate = 3.75;
var
    US, Yen : real;
begin
    read (US);
    Yen := ExchangeRate * US;
    writeln (Yen)
end.
```

2.3 SCALAR TYPES

In Pascal, all variables must be declared and their data types must be specified. This is not true of all programming languages. BASIC and FORTRAN, for example, do not require variable declarations. These languages have data type *defaults*. Either they have no restrictions on what values are assigned to a variable, or they use certain spelling conventions to determine the data type of a variable. For example, in FORTRAN a variable whose identifier starts with the letter i, j, k, l, m, or n is of type integer, unless otherwise specified. This is a potential source of error and confusion. Furthermore, in such a language, if a variable is misspelled, the compiler simply assumes it to be a new variable and gives it the default data type. Such languages are called **weakly typed**.

Pascal takes the opposite approach. Data type defaults do not exist in Pascal. Therefore Pascal is considered a **strongly typed** language. Although having to declare the data type of every variable may at first appear a time-consuming inconvenience, Pascal's strong typing actually works to your advantage. It makes it easier for you to detect typographical and logical errors in your program.

Pascal offers a rich variety of data types, ranging from simple types to very complex data structures. The simplest data types in Pascal are called **scalar types**. These are the primitive types from which everything else is built. The scalar data types are themselves divided into two groups: the *standard* scalar types and the *user-defined* scalar types.

Four standard scalar data types are provided automatically by the Pascal language. They are **integer**, **real**, **character**, and **bool-**

ean. User-defined data types are defined by the programmer to aid in the solution of a particular problem.

Scalar data types are *unstructured* types. That is, they consist of single distinct values. Pascal also has *structured* data types that are composed of scalar data types that can take on an ensemble or group of values.

The formalization of the concept of data type is one of Pascal's most fundamental contributions to programming languages. Table 2.1 summarizes the different data types of Pascal. Although we will not discuss most of these until much later in the text, the table shows the full scope and richness of the data-typing capabilities of Pascal.

The Type Integer

The term *integer* in Pascal is used in its everyday mathematical sense. Integers are whole numbers and may be positive, zero, or negative. Thus −13, 0, and 2341 are examples of integers and are called *integer literals* in Pascal. When writing integer literals, Pascal does not allow the use of commas or spaces to set off groups of digits. That is, 2,341 and 2 341 are not allowed.

Any computer can represent only a finite subset of the integers. The set represented will vary, depending on the particular computer system being used. Pascal provides a predefined constant, *maxint*, which refers to the largest integer available on any particular computer system. Care must be taken to ensure that the results of calculations with integers always lie between −maxint and maxint. If the result of an integer calculation is outside this range, *overflow* is said to have occurred, either giving unpredictable results, or abruptly terminating the execution of your program. On a system such as an IBM/370, which uses 32 bits to represent integers, maxint is $2^{31} - 1$, or 2147483647. On a system such as a DEC PDP-11, which uses 16

Table 2.1 Data types of Pascal

Scalar		Structured		Pointer
Standard	**User Defined**	**Standard**	**User Defined**	
integer	enumerated	text	array	
real	subrange		set	
boolean			record	
char			file	

bits to represent integers, it is $2^{15} - 1$, or 32767. Although the differences from system to system can be dramatic, in most cases, even the limited range is adequate. However, if you are doing calculations that could lead to very large integers, you should exercise care not to cause an overflow.

To declare a variable of type *integer*, the following format is used:

```
var
    Count, IdNumber : integer;
```

The Type Real

Real numbers, or **reals**, are used for data that can take on a continuum of possible values, such as length or area, and are thus represented as numbers with fractional portions. As we saw earlier, because a main storage location consists of a finite number of bits, integers are restricted to a maximum, maxint. Real numbers have both a maximum value and a finite precision. Therefore, in contrast to integers, real numbers are not exact. In main storage, real numbers are stored in **floating-point** representation, which is similar to scientific notation. That is, they are represented as a fractional part called the *mantissa* and a power of ten. For example, we often write:

2.5×10^9 instead of 2500000000

and

2.5×10^{-7} instead of 0.00000025

In both of these examples the mantissa is 2.5. In the first number, 10 is raised to the 9th power, and in the second number, 10 is raised to the -7 power. The number of digits in the mantissa is the **precision** of the floating point number.

To see how scientific and exponential notation works, consider the several alternative ways of writing 98.765. The following all represent the value 98.765:

$98765 \quad \times 10^{-3}$
$9876.5 \quad \times 10^{-2}$
$987.65 \quad \times 10^{-1}$
$98.765 \quad \times 10^{0}$
$9.8765 \quad \times 10^{1}$
0.98765×10^{2}

When the exponent is positive, it indicates how many places the decimal point should be moved to the right in order to obtain a decimal representation without a power of ten. For example,

0.98765×10^2

can be written as

098.765   or   98.765

If the exponent is negative, it indicates how many places the decimal point is to be moved to the left. The range of real numbers that can be represented for a specific large computer is shown in Figure 2.8. Similar implementation-dependent ranges exist on other computer systems.

Because most computer terminals do not have the capability to write an exponent to the upper right of a 10, a comparable, but slightly different, notation is used in Pascal. The way of writing 9.8765×10^1 in Pascal is:

9.8765E1

The 1 following the letter *E* is the exponent. Similarly, 98765×10^{-3} would be written as:

98765.0E − 3

Pascal requires that real number **literals**, such as 0.98765E2, 0.51, or 3.0, be written with at least one digit to the left and to the right of the decimal point. If the literal is written in exponential form, the exponent must be an integer. The following real literals are *invalid* for the indicated reasons:

.35   no digit to left of decimal point
4.   no digit to right of decimal point
3.1E2.5   exponent not an integer

Figure 2.8 Range
for real numbers

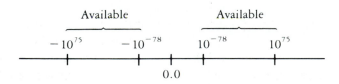

To create variables in Pascal to store values that are real numbers, we use a declaration such as:

```
var
    Area, Radius, Perimeter : real;
```

Variables of type *real* should be used whenever calculations involve a wide range of possible values, and whenever you need to represent values involving fractional parts.

SELF-TEST 3

1. Which of the following are valid Pascal literals and what is the type of each? If a constant is not valid, state why.

(a) 34 (b) maxint
(c) 34. (d) .34
(e) 2,345 (f) 2.0E3
(g) −2.0E−5 (h) 34.56

2. Write the following numbers as valid Pascal literals.

(a) 23,987 (b) One-tenth
(c) 2.3×10^{-3} (d) 1.2 million (integer)

3. Rewrite each of the following in exponential notation.

(a) 23978.5 (b) −98.765
(c) 0.0000005 (d) −0.123

4. Rewrite each of the following without exponents.

(a) 1.23E5 (b) −12.4E3
(c) 1.23E−5 (d) −3.67E−4

Answers

1. (a) Valid integer (b) Valid integer (c) Not valid, should be 34.0 (d) Not valid, should be 0.34 (e) Not valid, should be 2345 (f) Valid real (g) Valid real (h) Valid real

2. (a) 23987 (b) 0.1 (c) 2.3E−3 (d) 1200000

3. (a) 2.39785E4 (b) −9.8765E1 (c) 5E−7 (d) −1.23E−1

4. (a) 123000 (b) −12400 (c) 0.0000123 (d) −0.000367

**2.4
ARITHMETIC
EXPRESSIONS**

One of the important concepts in programming is that of an *expression*. The simplest expressions are literals such as 2, 98.765, and 9.8765E1, or variables such as radius, count, and total. In general an expression can include a number of terms, or **operands**, and **opera-**

tors by which operands are combined to yield a single value. We used expressions on the right-hand side of many statements in the sample programs of this chapter. Some examples of expressions are:

```
2 * pi * radius
FirstNumber + SecondNumber
Conversionfactor * Inches
```

Arithmetic Operators

Pascal provides a number of arithmetic operators, which take integer operands and produce integer results. The operators are:

+	addition
−	subtraction
*	multiplication
div	integer division
mod	remainder after integer division

These operators are **binary infix** operators, which means that they are written *between* their *two* operands.

Some examples of integer expressions using integer operators are:

Operation	Result
9 + 5	14
9 − 5	4
9 * 5	45
9 **div** 5	1
9 **mod** 5	4

The operators + and − may also be used with single values such as +a and −a to indicate the sign of an expression. The operator + used with a single operand is called the **unary +** operator and a − used with a single operand is called the **unary −** operator. Of course, integer operators also can be used with variables. Thus, if we have the following declarations:

```
const
     Maximum = 20;
var
     Count, Middle, Smallest : integer;
```

then the following are valid integer expressions:

```
Count + Middle
Count - Middle * Smallest
Smallest + Maximum
Middle div 10 + Smallest
```

The binary infix operators $+$, $-$, and $*$ represent the familiar operations of addition, subtraction, and multiplication. The integer division operator **div**, however, may not be as familiar. Integer division always results in a value where the remainder is ignored; thus,

5	**div**	2 is	2
2	**div**	2 is	1
7	**div**	2 is	3
-7	**div**	-2 is	3
-7	**div**	2 is	-3
7	**div**	-2 is	-3

The operator **mod** is used when the remainder is required. Thus,

21	**mod**	5 is	1
13	**mod**	10 is	3
5	**mod**	6 is	5

Pascal also defines a number of arithmetic operators that take real operands and return real results. These operators are:

$+$	addition
$-$	subtraction
$*$	multiplication
$/$	division

As with the integer operators, these are binary infix operators. The operators $+$ and $-$ can also be used as unary $+$ and $-$ operators respectively, if they are used with a single operand.

Some examples of real expressions are given below.

Operation	Result
3.5 + 4.3	7.8
3.5 - 4.3	-0.8
3.5 * 4.3	15.05
3.5 / 4.3	0.81395

The binary operators $+$, $-$, and $*$ are the same as the corresponding integer operators. The binary operator $/$ is used for real division. As was pointed out in the section dealing with type *real* (p. 47), the representation of real numbers in a computer is not exact. As a consequence, it is possible that, for real values a and b, the relation $(a/b)*b = a$ may not always hold true on the computer.

Unlike most programming languages, Pascal has no special operator for exponentiation.

Precedence of Operators

When an expression involves several operators, the order in which the operators should be evaluated may be ambiguous. For example, is the value of $2 + 3 * 4$ equal to 20 or 14? That is, should $2 + 3 * 4$ be interpreted as $(2 + 3) * 4$ or $2 + (3 * 4)$? Because of such possible ambiguities, programming languages, including Pascal, have adopted rules specifying the order in which operations should be performed. These are called *operator precedence rules*, and, in Pascal, they correspond to the rules used in algebra. The precedence for the operators we have seen thus far, from the highest to the lowest are:

1. $*$ $/$ **div**   **mod**
2. $+$ $-$

Pascal rules for evaluating expressions reflect the different precedence classes of operators and the ability to override these precedences by using parentheses.

1. First, evaluate expressions enclosed in parentheses, beginning with the innermost set of parentheses.
2. Perform all multiplications and/or divisions ($*$,$/$, **div, mod**) from left to right.
3. Perform all additions and/or subtractions from left to right.

For example, consider the expression

(Cost - Salvage)/Life

Suppose Cost = 500.00, Salvage = 100.00, and Life = 10.0. Then, using the rules for evaluating expressions, we have

	Expression Evaluated	Result	Remains to Be Evaluated
Rule 1	Cost − Salvage	400.00	400.00/Life
Rule 2	400/Life	40.00	

Let us look at a more complex example.

$$(c * d \textbf{ div } (a \textbf{ mod } b)) + b - c * d \textbf{ mod } a$$

Suppose $a = 3, b = 4, c = 5, d = 6$. Then we have

	Expression Evaluated	Result	Remains to Be Evaluated
Rule 1	$a \textbf{ mod } b$	3	$(c * d \textbf{ div } 3) + b - c * d \textbf{ mod } a$
Rule 2	$c * d$	30	$(30 \textbf{ div } 3) + b - c * d \textbf{ mod } a$
Rule 1	$30 \textbf{ div } 3$	10	$10 + b - c * d \textbf{ mod } a$
Rule 2	$c * d$	30	$10 + b - 30 \textbf{ mod } a$
Rule 2	$30 \textbf{ mod } a$	0	$10 + b - 0$
Rule 3	$10 + b$	14	$14 - 0$
Rule 3	$14 - 0$	14	

If you are unsure of the precedence rules in a particular calculation, you can always force the order of evaluation to be performed in the sequence you want by using parentheses.

Compatibility of Types

In mathematics, integers can be considered as a subset of the real numbers. In a computer, they are actually represented differently. Pascal, however, allows us to partially ignore this difference by automatically converting each integer, which occurs where a real number is required, to an equivalent real. The converse, however, is not true. When Pascal expects an integer value it will *not* accept a real value. Finally, Pascal allows mixing of integers and reals, but the result of such mixed expressions is always real. For example, suppose we have declared the following variables:

```
var
    value1, value2 : real;
    count : integer;
```

then the expressions

```
value1 + value2
count * value1
value - 5
(value1 + value2)/2
```

produce results that are real.
    The expressions

```
count + 5
count div 5
```

produce results that are integer. Only an expression with all integer operands produces an integer result.
    The expressions

```
value1 div value2
value1 mod   count
```

are *not* valid because only integers are expected for the **div** and **mod** operators and real values will not be accepted.

SELF-TEST 4

1. Which of the following are valid expressions? If you think the expression is invalid, give your reason.
(a) 10 **mod** 4 + 1   (b) maxint − 3.5
(c) 34.0/2   (d) (0.34 − 23.4)/2E2
(e) 7 * 2 **mod** 1.8   (f) 4.6 **div** 2.3 − 3
(g) − 2E − 5 * 5   (h) 34.56 + 4 **div** 2

2. If $x = 4, y, = 2.1, z = 1$, factor $= 0.75$, evaluate each of the following, if possible. If it is not possible, state the reason.
(a) $(x + y)*$factor   (b) $(z \bmod x) \mathbf{div}\, x *$ factor
(c) $(x + y) \mathbf{div}$ factor   (d) $(((x * y) * 3) + z)$

3. Given the expression $ax^3 + bx^2 - cx + d$, which of the following are correct Pascal statements for this expression?

(a) $a * x * x * x + b * x * x - c * x + d$
(b). $a (x * x * x) + b (x * x) - c(x) + d$
(c) $a * (x * x * x) + b * (x * x) - c * (x) + d$
(d) $a * xxx + b * xx - c * x + d$

Answers

1. (a) Valid   (b) Valid   (c) Valid   (d) Valid   (e) Not valid. Real operand cannot be used with **mod**.   (f) Not valid. Real operand cannot be used with **div**.   (g) Valid   (h) Valid

2. (a) 4.575   (b) 0   (c) Not possible. "Factor" is a real number and cannot be used with **div**.   (d) 26.2

3. (a) Valid   (b) Not valid. The operator * is missing in three locations.   (c) Valid   (d) Not valid. The operator * is missing between the xs.

2.5 ASSIGNMENT STATEMENT

The general form of an assignment statement in Pascal is

identifier : = expression

The assignment statement is by far the most widely used statement in Pascal, and in most programming languages for that matter. It is the primary means of performing calculations, moving data, and changing the values of variables. The two-character symbol, : = , is called the **assignment operator** and is read "is replaced by." Examples of assignment statements we have already seen are:

```
Circumference := 2 * pi * Radius
Radius := 5.0
Sum := FirstNumber + SecondNumber
Centimeters := Conversionfactor * Inches
```

An assignment statement causes the following to occur:

1. The expression on the right side of the assignment operator : = is evaluated.

2. The value of the expression is stored in (assigned to) the location named by the identifier on the left side of the assignment operator.

The arithmetic assignment statement, then, specifies that the variable on the left side of the assignment operator be given, or assigned, the value equivalent to the expression on the right of the assignment operator. This destroys whatever value the variable may have contained previously.

In order to be able to assign a value to the variable on the left of the := , all variables appearing in the expression on the right must have values associated with them. That is, they must be defined. Thus, when using assignment statements, it is important to sequence them properly. Consider Examples 2.5 and 2.6.

The value of z output by the program in Example 2.5 will be 2, since x := 5 assigns x the value 5, the y := x + 3 assigns y the value 8, and finally z := y − 6 assigns z the value 2.

If we were to rearrange the statements as in Example 2.6 we not only would fail to produce the same result as in Example 2.5, but, in fact, would not produce any result at all. The assignment statement

EXAMPLE 2.5
A Program to Illustrate Sequence of Execution

```
program Sequence1 (output);

var
    x, y, z : integer;

begin
    x  := 5;
    y  := x + 3;
    z  := y - 6;
    writeln ( z )
end.
```

EXAMPLE 2.6
A Program to Illustrate Incorrect Sequence

```
program Sequence2 ( output );

var
    x, y, z : integer;

begin
    y  := x + 3;
    x  := 5;
    z  := y - 6;
    writeln ( z )
end.
```

$y := x + 3$ would result in an error because x has no value associated with it. The variable x is *undefined* at this point in the program.

The data types of both sides of the $:=$ should be the same. Recall, however, that an integer will be accepted where a real is expected, but not the converse. Thus, given the variable declaration:

```
var
   a, b : integer;
   x, y : real;
```

the following assignment statements are valid:

```
x := y
```

```
x := a
```

```
x := a + b
```

```
x := y + b
```

However, the following assignment statements are *not* valid:

```
a := x
```

```
a := x + y
```

```
a := x + b
```

```
a := 5.0
```

2.6 BUILT-IN FUNCTIONS

Many calculations that occur quite frequently, such as computing the square root of a number, cannot be easily performed using the operators $+$, $-$, $*$, $/$, **div**, or **mod**. To make such computations easy to perform, most languages, including Pascal, provide a number of standard mathematical *functions*. For example, to compute the square root of 10.5 and assign the result to the variable y in Pascal, we need only write:

```
y := sqrt(10.5)
```

The value computed by the function instance sqrt (10.5) is 3.4037. This value is assigned to y. The value 10.5 is called the **argument** or **actual parameter** of the function. Given an argument, a

Table 2.2
Mathematical
functions

Name	Description	Argument	Value of Function
abs (x)	Absolute value of *x*	Integer or Real	Same as argument
arctan (x)	Inverse tangent of *x*	Integer or Real	Real
cos (x)	Cosine of *x*	Integer or Real	Real
exp (x)	Exponential function	Integer or Real	Real
1n (x)	Natural logarithm	Integer or Real	Real
round (x)	*x* rounded	Real	Integer
sin(x)	Sine of *x*	Integer or Real	Real
sqr (x)	Square of *x*	Integer or Real	Same as argument
sqrt (x)	Square root of *x*	Integer or Real	Real
trunc (x)	*x* truncated	Real	Integer

function always computes a *single* value called the *value of the function*. In our example, the value of the function is 3.4037.

The function sqrt is supplied with the Pascal language and, therefore, is called a **predefined** or **built-in function**. Table 2.2 gives the names and descriptions of the predefined mathematical functions of Pascal.

To use a function, we write its name followed by its argument, or actual parameter, enclosed in parentheses. Such an expression is called a *function designator*. Any legal expression can be used as an actual parameter as long as the *type* of the expression is of the type the function expects. The following are all valid statements that use functions:

```
hyp := sqrt(sqr(a) + sqr(b))

w := abs(-3.5)

number := trunc(3.5 * length - 1.0)
```

Note that the argument can be a literal, variable, arithmetic expression, or even the value of a function.

All of the above functions will take a real argument; all except round and trunc also will take an integer argument.

The function abs returns the absolute value of a number. That is, if $x < 0$ abs returns *-x* and if $x \geq = 0$, it returns *x*. The following examples illustrate the abs function:

Expression	Value
abs (2)	2
abs (− 7)	7
abs (− 6.3)	6.3
abs (8.2 − 7.1)	1.1

The functions arctan, cos, and sin compute the corresponding trigonometric or inverse trigonometric functions. The trigonometric functions cos and sin take as arguments angles measured in radians. The inverse trigonometric function arctan returns the radian measure of an angle.

The function exp is the exponential function with base e and the function ln is the inverse of exp. That is, ln computes the natural logarithm (the logarithm to the base e) of its argument.

The functions sqr and sqrt, respectively, return the square and the square root of a number. Below are some examples of both functions.

Expression	Value
sqr (2)	4
sqr (− 1.2)	1.44
sqrt (900)	30.0
sqrt (2)	1.414

The functions round and trunc take real arguments and return integer values. Both are used to convert real values to integer values. The function round rounds a real number to the closest integer. The function trunc, on the other hand, changes a real number to an integer by truncating it—discarding the fractional part of the real number. The following examples illustrate the use of both the round and trunc functions:

Expression	Value
round (3.1)	3
round (3.9)	4
trunc (3.1)	3
trunc (3.9)	3

SELF-TEST 5

1. After the declarations

var
    a,b,c,d,e : integer;
    r,s,t,u,v : real;

which of the following are valid assignment statements? If a statement is not valid, state why.

(a) a := b*c+a−e   (b) b := r + 5
(c) c := d / 3   (d) a := a*r+a−e
(e) s := a * 13   (f) t := e / a

2. If a and b are integers and x and y are reals, what value, if any, is assigned to the last left-side identifier in the following sequences?

(a) a := 8;
    b := a+1;
    x := sqrt(b)+2

(b) b := −17;
    a := abs(b) −10;
    y := a mod b

(c) x := 5.0;
    y := sqr(x) − 20.0;
    x := y * 2

(d) x := 11.44;
    a := trunc(x) − 15;
    b := abs(a−5)

3. In the assignment statement

a := ((b + 5) **div** c) * 13

list the order in which the operations are performed.

4. In each of the following assignment statements, delete the unnecessary parentheses.

(a) c := sqrt((a*a)−(b*b))
(b) a := (b+c)/d
(c) x := −(b) + sqrt((b*b−(4*(a*c))))/(2*a*c)
(d) s := (1/2)*g*(sqr(t))

Answers

1. (a) Valid   (b) Not valid, right side is a real expression. Left side is an integer variable.   (c) Not valid, right side is a real expression since / is used. Left side is an integer variable.   (d) Not valid, right side is a real expression since the variable r is real. Left side is an integer variable.   (e) Valid   (f) Valid

2. (a) 5.0   (b) 7   (c) 10.0   (d) 9

3. +, **div**, *

4. (a) c := sqrt (a * a − b * b)   (b) a := (b + c)/d   (c) x := −b + sqrt (b * b − 4 * a * c)/(2 * a * c)   (d) s := (1/2)* g * sqr (t)

2.7 OUTPUT OF DATA

The basic output statement in Pascal takes one of two forms:

write (output-list)
writeln (output-list)

where "output-list" is a list of values to be output. The items of the output list can be expressions, certain variables, or characters enclosed by apostrophes.

Note the following in Example 2.7:

1. The computer printed the numerical values in fixed **field widths**: ten columns for integer values and twenty-two columns for real values. The field width is the exact number of print positions allowed for the value, and varies from one computer system to another. The field widths used in our example are typical but do not apply to every computer system. Therefore, you should either obtain and read your system's manuals

**EXAMPLE 2.7
A Program to Illustrate Output Formatting**

```
program PrintValues (output);

var
    value1 : integer;
    value2 : real;

begin
    value1 := 5;
    value2 := 3.5;
    write (value1, -15);
    writeln (-15 + value1);
    write (value2, -0.55);
    writeln (value2 * -0.55);
    writeln (sqrt(4))
end.
```

The output of this program is

```
|  |  |  |  |  |  |  | 5 |  |  |  |  | - 1 5 |  |  |  |  | - 1 0 |
```

```
⌐ 3.500000000000000E+00-5.500000000000000E-01-1.925000000000000E+00
```

```
⌐ 2.000000000000000E+00
```

on Pascal or write and run a simple program, such as our example, to determine this information for your system.

2. The integer values are printed flush right or *right justified* in their fields. Blanks are filled in on the left. Thus, there are nine blanks preceding the 5 and seven blanks preceding the − 15.

3. Real values are printed in scientific notation with trailing zeros used to fill the field.

4. The writeln instruction outputs the values of the expressions in its output list on the current line, and then issues a carriage return, which causes any following output to start at the beginning of the next line.

5. An expression in the output list can be as simple as a single variable or literal, or it can be arbitrarily complex.

Printing Integers

We may find at times that the field widths on a particular system are not what we would like to have. Pascal gives us the option of specifying the exact spacing we want. We do this for integers by using *field width parameters* with the write and writeln statements.

For example, consider the following statement:

```
write (value1 :3, -15 :4)
```

where value1 is the same as in our previous example. The output will appear as

⌷⌷⌷5⌷⌷−15

The field width parameter for item1 is 3. Thus there are only two blanks preceding the 5. Similarly, there is only one blank preceding the − 15. For both of the above values, the field width parameters are large enough to accommodate the values printed. If the value being printed requires more spaces than specified in the field width parameter, then the parameter is ignored and the printed value takes up as many columns as needed. For example, the result of executing

```
write (value1 :1, -15 :1)
```

will be

5−15

Printing Real Numbers

When we use a single field width parameter with real numbers, we still get floating-point notation, as we did when no field width parameter was specified. Thus,

```
write (-0.55 :8)
```

will output

```
-5.5E-01
```

Note that eight columns are used. To get conventional decimal notation we have to use two field width parameters. The first parameter is the true field width. The second field width parameter specifies how many digits to the right of the decimal will be printed.

```
write (value2 :4 :1, -0.55 :7 :3)
```

will output:

```
 3.5 -0.550
```

The following is another example of field width parameters for real numbers, where *a*, *b*, *c* are real variables with values 9.8765, 12.345, and −555.66, respectively:

```
write (a, b :10, c :10 :1)
```

The output is

```
 9.876500000000000E+00 1.2345E+01     -555.6
```

Constructing Output Lines

In order to provide greater output flexibility, Pascal allows us to construct output lines one item at a time. To do this, the *write* statement is used. The *write* and *writeln* statements produce printed output by copying the values of the variables or constants in their output lists into an *output buffer*—a location in main storage set aside just for the construction of lines to be printed. The difference between the write and writeln statements is the way they cause the contents of the output buffer to be printed. The writeln statement, after placing the value of the last variable in its output list into the output buffer,

forces the contents of the buffer to be printed. With the write statement, values are added to the output buffer but the buffer is not
printed (unless it becomes full). To print the contents of the buffer, a
writeln statement is used. For example, if we have the sequence of
statements,

```
write (x);
write (y, z);
writeln (a);
writeln (b, c)
```

the values of x, y, z, and a will be output on one line and the values of
b and c on the next line. On the other hand,

```
write (x);
write (y, z);
write (a);
write (b, c);
writeln
```

will output the values of all the variables on a single line. The writeln
statement forces the buffer to be emptied (i.e., printed). We could
have achieved the same result with other combinations of write and
writeln statements. For example,

```
write (x, y, z, a, b);
writeln (c)
```

would produce the same output. Here again, the write statement
only places values into the output buffer while the writeln statement
not only places values into the buffer, but also forces the contents of
the buffer to be printed.

Labeling Output

Consider the program in Example 2.8. Although we probably can
guess the meaning of such output, its meaning could be improved
easily by adding appropriate labels. Labels can be created by placing
character strings, as well as variables, in the output list of the writeln
statement. A **character string** is a group of characters enclosed in
single quotes. For example,

```
'a'
'Hello'
'+'
'sum='
' '
```

**EXAMPLE 2.8
Program with
Unlabeled
Output**

```
program Sum (output);

var
   a, b : integer;

begin
   a := 5;
   b := 3;
   writeln (a :3, b :2, a + b :2)
end.
```

Its output will be:

5 3 8

---

are all character strings. A character string is printed exactly as it appears but without the surrounding quotes. Consider now our previous program rewritten to include character strings in the output list of the writeln statement.

Character strings are often used to identify values by printing the identifiers. Character strings consisting of blanks are often used to control spacing. Character strings may be of any length, but if they are longer than the number of columns available on a line, they may spill over into the next line.

Character strings are written in exactly the number of columns equal to the length of the string unless a field width parameter is

**EXAMPLE 2.9
Program to
Illustrate
Labeled
Output**

```
program Sum (output);

var
   a, b : integer;

begin
   a := 5;
   b := 3;
   writeln (a:3,' +',b:2,' =',a+b:2)
end.
```

The output of this program looks like this:

5 + 3 = 8

---

specified. Then the string is written right justified in the number of columns specified by the parameter. For example,

```
writeln ('Hello':15, ' How are you ?')
```

will produce the output:

|||||||||||Hello How are you ?

with ten blanks in front of "Hello." If the field width parameter is not large enough to accommodate the string, then the string is truncated as in the following example:

```
writeln('Hello':2)
```

which will produce the output:

```
He
```

Since the single quote is used to delimit a character string, we must provide two consecutive single quotes if we want a single quote to appear in our output. Thus,

```
writeln ('John''s program')
```

will print:

```
John's program
```

To print a single quote by itself, four quotes are required: two quotes to delimit the string and two to produce the quote for output.

```
writeln ('''')
```

will output a single quote as below:

```
'
```

SELF-TEST 6   1. What will be the output of each of the following writeln statements?

(a) `writeln(123)`   (b) `writeln(123 :5)`
(c) `writeln(123 :1)`   (d) `writeln(1:4,1:3,1:2,1:1)`

2. What will be the output of each of the following writeln statements?

(a) `writeln(123.5)`   (b) `writeln(123.5 :10)`
(c) `writeln(123.5 :9:1)`   (d) `writeln(123.5 :8:2)`

3. What is the output of the following program?

```
program Question3 (output);

var
   a,b : integer;
   x,y : real;
begin
   a := 1;
   b := 2;
   x := 10.0;
   y := 20.5;
   writeln (a,b,a+b);
   writeln (a+5,x);
   writeln (trunc(y-x))
end.
```

4. What will be the output of each of the following program segments?

(a) `write(1:3);`   (b) `writeln(1:3);`
    `write(2:3);`   `writeln(2:3);`
    `write(3:3);`   `writeln(3:3);`
    `writeln(4:3)`   `writeln(4:3)`

(c) `writeln(1:3);`   (d) `write(1:3);`
    `write(2:3);`   `writeln(2:3);`
    `writeln(3:3);`   `write(3:3);`
    `writeln(4:3)`   `writeln(4:3)`

5. What will be the output of the following program segments?

(a) `write (' The sum of ');`
    `write (5:2,' and',4:2);`
    `writeln(' is',5+4:2)`

(b) `writeln (' The sum of ':12);`
    `writeln (' 5 and 4  is ');`
    `writeln (' 5+4')`

Answers

1. (a) |║║║║║║║║ 123   (b)|║║║123
   (c) 123   (d)|║║║║1║║║1║║11

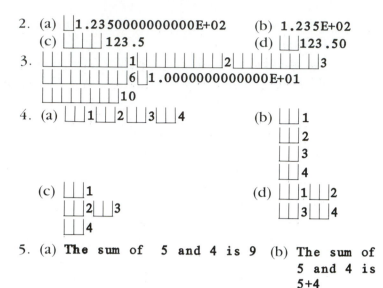

2. (a) ⌴⌴1.2350000000000E+02   (b) **1.235E+02**
    (c) ⌴⌴⌴⌴⌴123.5   (d) ⌴⌴123.50
3. ⌴⌴⌴⌴⌴⌴⌴⌴⌴⌴1⌴⌴⌴⌴⌴⌴⌴⌴⌴⌴2⌴⌴⌴⌴⌴⌴⌴⌴3
    ⌴⌴⌴⌴⌴⌴⌴⌴6⌴1.0000000000000E+01
    ⌴⌴⌴⌴⌴⌴⌴⌴10
4. (a) ⌴⌴1⌴⌴2⌴⌴3⌴⌴4   (b) ⌴⌴1
                                   ⌴⌴2
                                   ⌴⌴3
                                   ⌴⌴4
    (c) ⌴⌴1   (d) ⌴⌴1⌴⌴2
        ⌴⌴2⌴⌴3   ⌴⌴3⌴⌴4
        ⌴⌴4
5. (a) **The sum of 5 and 4 is 9** (b) **The sum of**
                                        5 and 4 is
                                        5+4

2.8 INPUT OF DATA

Both input and output statements are essential in all computer languages. We saw earlier how to output the results of computations by using the write and writeln statements. However, unless we also have means of inputting data, our programs will only be able to operate on fixed values. If we need to use new data, the program would have to be rewritten. This is certainly inconvenient.

An input statement allows a program to obtain data values from outside the program. As the program executes, data values are input and assigned to variables. This allows actions to be carried out on different data values without changing the program. Only the values we provide for input need to be changed.

Pascal provides two input statements:

read (input-list)
readln (input-list)

where "input-list" is a series of variable identifiers separated by commas. When a read or readln statement is executed, as many values as there are identifiers in the input list are obtained from the standard input file and assigned to the variables in the list. For example, the statement

read (firstnumber)

will obtain the next value from the standard input file and assign this value to the variable firstnumber. Similarly,

```
read (a, b, c, d)
```

will obtain the next four values from the standard input file and assign them to the variables *a*, *b*, *c*, and *d*, in that order.

Standard Input and Output Files

When we are talking about an *input file*, we are referring to any source of input data. This source could be any of the input or peripheral storage devices discussed in Chapter 1. Thus, an input file can refer to a magnetic disk, a terminal keyboard, a card reader, or any other such device. Similarly, an *output file* is simply a name for any destination of output data and thus could be a magnetic disk, a terminal printing element, a video screen, a card-punch, and so forth.

Every computer installation has a given input and output device designated as the *standard* input and output devices. These designated devices are usually the typical devices that most programmers use to communicate with the system and are referred to as the **standard input file** and the **standard output file** respectively. The devices differ from system to system. For example, on one system the standard input file could be a terminal keyboard and the standard output file a terminal printing element or video screen. On another system the standard input file might be a magnetic disk and the standard output file a high-speed printer.

In Pascal, the standard input file is designated by the predefined identifier **input**. The standard output file is designated by the predefined identifier **output.** When either of these files is used in a program, it has to be declared in the program heading. The heading

```
program example ( input, output );
```

indicates that the program will use both the standard input and output files. When a read or readln statement is executed in this program, the data will be read from these files. Similarly, when a write or writeln statement is executed, data will be output to the standard output file. It is, of course, possible to read data from a file other than the standard input file and write them to a file other than the standard output file. In fact, it is often necessary to use more than one input and output file in a given program. We will, however, defer any discussion of nonstandard files until Chapter 11.

Input of Numeric Data

A read or a readln statement can be considered an assignment state-ment that obtains its values from the standard input file instead of an expression. Just as with an assignment statement, the value obtained must be compatible in type to the variable to which it is to be as-signed.

The instruction

```
read(Number)
```

where Number is of data type real or integer, will cause the computer to scan the standard input file until it encounters a nonblank charac-ter. If the first nonblank character is a digit, the number of which this digit is a part is read and assigned to the variable Number. If the first nonblank character the computer finds is not a digit (or + or −), then an error results, and the message "type error in read" is dis-played. An error will also result if Number is of type integer and the value read from the input file is of type real.

Suppose we have the following declarations:

```
var
   Id, HoursWorked : integer;
   HourlyRate      : real;
```

and we would like to read the values of Id, HoursWorked, and Hour-lyRate from the standard input file.

The read statements

```
read (Id, HoursWorked);
read (HourlyRate)
```

coupled with the following arrangement of data in the input file

123   38   5.85

would result in the desired assignment of 123 to Id, 38 to Hours-Worked, and 5.85 to HourlyRate. Pascal relies on *positional corre-spondence* for correct assignment of input values. The position of the variables in the read statement must correspond to the position of data values in the input file.

To input a series of values, one or more read statements can be used. The sequence

```
read (Id);
read (HoursWorked);
read (HourlyRate)
```

is equivalent to the pair of read statements we used earlier and is also equivalent to the single statement:

```
read (Id, HoursWorked, HourlyRate)
```

Just as many arrangements of read statements, all yielding the same result, are possible, many arrangements of data in the input file are possible. For example,

```
123
  38   5.85
```

and

```
123
  38
5.85
```

are all arrangements that are equivalent to our initial example.

The readln statement operates in the same manner with respect to inputting data as the read statement. The only difference occurs at the end of the input operation. After the computer inputs the number for the last variable in the input list of the readln statement, it skips over the rest of the current line. The next read or readln statement will begin reading in the first column of the next line in the input file. Consider the following statements:

```
read (a);
readln (b, c);
read (d);
read (e, f)
```

with the following arrangement of input data:

```
10   11   12   13   14
15   16   17   18
19   20   21
```

Execution of the above statements results in the following assignments:

a ←——10
b ←——11
c ←——12
d ←——15
e ←——16
f ←——17

A readln statement can also be used without an input list to skip the rest of the current line of the input file.

SELF-TEST 7

1. Suppose the data given on the input file are

1   2   3   4   5

What would be the values of variables *a*, *b*, and *c* after execution of the following statement?

```
read (a,b,c)
```

2. Suppose that the data given on the input file are

1   2   3   4   5
6
7   8

What would be the values of *a*, *b*, and *c* after execution of the following statements?

```
read(a);
readln(b);
read(c)
```

3. Write a read statement and a data list to assign the value 3.54 to *a*, the value 17.4 to *b*, and the value 3 to *c*.

Answers

1. *a* is assigned 1, *b* is assigned 2, *c* is assigned 3
2. *a* is assigned 1, *b* is assigned 2, *c* is assigned 6
3. read (a,b,c) data arrangement 3.54   17.4   3

We have now covered enough Pascal to be able to write some simple but useful programs. Let us examine one such program. It computes the sales tax for a given purchase amount.

APPLICATION

Sales Tax Calculation

Given the amount of a purchase, we need to compute the tax and print the amount of the purchase, the tax, and the total bill. Our first attempt at the solution may look like this:

begin
      Obtain the amount of purchase
      Compute the tax and bill
      Output results
end.

Note that we did not write this in Pascal. Instead, we wrote it in ordinary English, making it look somewhat like a Pascal program. This is easier than writing a solution directly in Pascal; and therefore, it is a good way to begin the development of a program. We will have a lot more to say about the development process in the next chapter.

The first action described above, Obtain the amount of purchase, consists of inputting the purchase amount:

Input amount of purchase

The second action, Compute the tax and bill, consists of two assignment statements, each one involving a computation:

Compute the tax
Compute the total bill

The third action, output results, consists of three output statements:

Output amount of purchase
Output tax
Output total bill

Now we can translate each of our actions into Pascal, add the required definitions of constants and declarations of variables, and put together the final version of the program.

Note the use of semicolons in our program listing. Remember that *semicolons are used as statement separators*. A semicolon is used at the end of each assignment, writeln, or readln statement, ex-

APPLICATION

Sales Tax Calculation (*continued*)

cept the last one, to separate it from the next statement. No semicolon is used after the last statement because it is followed by the reserved word **end.**, which is not a statement.

```pascal
program Salestax (input, output);

{**********************************************
* This program computes the sales tax and     *
* total amount of the bill for a given amount *
* of purchase. It then prints out the         *
* amount of purchase, tax, and total bill.    *
**********************************************}

const
    Taxrate = 0.06; { tax rate is 6% }

var
    Purchase, Tax, AmountOfBill : real;

begin
    {** obtain amount of purchase **}

    read (Purchase);

    {** compute tax and total bill **}

    Tax := Taxrate * Purchase;
    AmountOfBill := Purchase + Tax;

    {** output results **}

    writeln (' Purchase Amount :', Purchase :6:2);
    writeln (' Tax             :', Tax:6:2);
    writeln (' Total Bill      :', AmountOfBill :6:2)
end.
```

If the input to our program is

3.75

the output will be:

```
Purchase Amount :    3.75
Tax             :    0.22
Total Bill      :    3.97
```

**2.9
CHAPTER
REVIEW**

A Pascal program is divided into two parts: a heading and a body, called a block. The block is further divided into a declaration part and a statement part. The declaration part of the block describes the data to be used by the program. The actions to be performed by the program are indicated in the statement part. The statement part of the block is bracketed by the words **begin** and **end**.

Comments are enclosed in curly braces, { and }, or the compound symbols (∗ and ∗). Comments convey no information to the computer; they are strictly for the benefit of the human reader. Comments may be inserted anywhere a blank is allowed in a program.

The general form of a Pascal program is:

program name (file1,...,file2,...,filen)
    label declaration part
    constant definition part
    type definition part
    variable declaration part
    procedure declaration part
    function declaration part
begin
    statements
end.

The sequence of characters that forms the name of a program, constant, type, variable, procedure, or function is called an identifier. An identifier consists of a letter followed by a sequence of letters and/or digits.

The program heading is the first line of every Pascal program. The heading is usually followed by comments that indicate what the program is to accomplish.

The semicolon (;) is used as a statement separator.

Constants are values that remain fixed while a program executes. Constants are defined in the **const** definition section.

Variables are values that may change while a program executes. The identifier that names the variable corresponds to the name of a location in the computer's memory. The current value of the variable corresponds to the value contained in that memory location. Variables are declared in the **var** declaration section. The data type of a variable, like the variable name, cannot be changed once it is declared. The colon (:) is used to separate variable names from their types. Every variable used in a Pascal program must be declared, and its data type must be specified.

The predefined constant *maxint* represents the largest integer constant for a particular computer system. The type integer is used to represent whole numbers. The type real is used to represent data that can take on a continuum of values. The computer stores real numbers in floating-point notation, consisting of a mantissa and a power of ten.

Arithmetic operations are performed according to the rules of operator precedence. First, parenthesized expressions are evaluated starting with the innermost set of parentheses. Then, multiplications and divisions (∗, /, **div**, **mod**) are performed left to right. Finally, additions and subtractions are performed left to right.

The assignment statement is the most common statement used in most programming languages. The assignment operator is written as a colon followed by an equals sign (:=) and is read "is replaced by." The expression on the right of the assignment operator is evaluated, and then the result is stored in the variable specified by the identifier on the left of the assignment operator. Movement across the := operator is from right to left, and only a single variable name may be mentioned on the left of an assignment operator.

Pascal also provides built-in or predefined functions. The predefined mathematical functions, such as abs, sin, exp, etc., are useful in mathematical applications.

Output of data is accomplished by either of the statements:

write (output-list)

or

writeln (output-list)

Output list is a list of expressions and/or character strings separated by commas. Integers are printed right justified. Reals are printed in scientific notation. Output after a write statement continues on the same line. Output after a writeln statement continues on the next line. Write (a : b) writes whole number a in b positions (right justified). If b is too small, then b is ignored and the full number is printed. Write (a : b : c) writes real number a in b positions, of which c positions to the right of the decimal point are printed.

Input of data is accomplished with the statements:

read (input-list)

or

readln (input-list)

Input-list is a list of variable names separated by commas. Values are obtained from the standard input file. The next read operation after a read continues on the same line. The next read operation after a readln continues on the next line.

2.10 EXERCISES

2.1. Fill in the blanks in each of the following:

(a) The _____ part of a Pascal program describes data used by the program.

(b) The _____ part of a Pascal program describes the actions to be performed by the program.

(c) A portion of a Pascal program enclosed in { and } or (* and *) is called a(n) _____ .

(d) The sequence of characters that forms the name of a program, constant, type, variable, procedure, or function is called a(n) _____ .

(e) The _____ is the first line of every Pascal program.

(f) The _____ character is used as a statement separator in Pascal.

(g) Values that do not change while a program runs are called _____ . Values that do change when a program runs are called _____ .

(h) In the computer's main storage, the value of a variable corresponds to the _____ of the location assigned to that variable.

(i) The predefined constant _____ refers to the largest integer available on a particular computer system.

(j) Variables of type _____ should be used whenever calculations involve a wide range of values, and whenever you need to represent values involving fractional parts.

(k) The Pascal operator _____ determines the quotient, and the operator _____ determines the remainder after integer division.

(l) Functions _____ and _____ are used to change real numbers to integers.

2.2. Answer each of the following true or false. If your answer is false, state why.

(a) A comment in curly braces helps the computer to understand the function to be performed by the program.

(b) The Pascal statement

```
{sum := first + second }
```

causes the computer to add the values of variables *first* and *second* and store the result in the variable *sum*.

(c) Standard identifiers in Pascal have a predefined meaning, and thus they may not be redefined in a program.

(d) Identifier names should always be as short as possible (i.e., one, two, or three characters, preferably) to save time in typing Pascal programs and to minimize the chance of typing errors.

(e) In Pascal, all variables must be declared and their data types must be specified.

(f) Pascal requires that real number constants be written with at least one digit to the left and at least one digit to the right of the decimal point.

(g) The function *sqrt* will take either a real or integer argument but will always return a real result.

(h) If an expression contains many operators, Pascal performs the indicated operations from left to right.

(i) Only an expression with all real operands produces a real result.

2.3. Describe the function(s) performed by each of the following Pascal statements:

(a) **program** Area (output);

(b) **const**
         Factor = 2.54;

(c) **var**
         Length, Width, Area : real;

(d) **begin**

(e) **end**

(f) Length := 3.65

(g) Area := Length * Width

(h) write (Length, Width, Area)

(i) writeln (Length, Width, Area)

(j) Count := Count + 1

(k) { Calculate area of a rectangle }

(l) writeln ('area of the rectangle is ...')

(m) **var**
         Employee : integer;

(n) Number := 9 **mod** 4 (* number is an integer *)

(o) Depreciation := (Cost−Salvage)/Life { all reals }

(p) writeln (Cost−Salvage)/Life) (* all reals *)

(q) write (1 : 3, 27 : 3, −142 : 4, −142 : 5)

(r) write (0.98 : 9)

(s) write (−0.98 : 9 : 3)

(t) writeln (7, 8, 9 : 10, 1.2, 3.1416, 10 : 5)

(u) writeln ('''')

(v) writeln ('right−justification' : 25)

(w) read (Length, Width)

(x) readln (Length, Width)

(y) readln

2.4. Given the equation

$$y = ax^2 + bx + c$$

which of the following Pascal statements are correct representations of the above equation? For those that are not, state why.

(a) `y := a * x ** 2 + b * x + c`
(b) `y := a * x * x + b * x + c`
(c) `y := a * sqr(x) + b * x +c`
(d) `y := axx+bx+c`
(e) `y := (((a * ((x) * (x))) + ((b) * (x)) + (c))`
(f) `y := (((a) * ((x) * (x))) + ((b) * (x)) + (c))`

2.5. What does each of the following Pascal statements print?

(a) `write (3 + 2 - 1 * (3))`
(b) `write (2 + 2 * 2 * 2 div 2 mod 2 - 2)`
(c) `writeln`
(d) `write (9 mod 4 + 11 mod 9 + 13 div 4)`
(e) `writeln ('''') (* all single quotes *)`

2.6. Write Pascal statements to accomplish each of the following tasks:

(a) Write the program heading for a program that calculates income taxes due. The program reads a person's gross income from the standard input file and writes the income tax due on the standard output file.

(b) A program for converting litres to quarts uses the relationship:

1 litre = 1.0567 quarts

Write a constant declaration defining the conversion factor needed to convert litres to quarts.

(c) Write a variable declaration section for a program that calculates total pay for an employee, given that employee's 9-digit Social Security number, hours worked, hourly salary. The program calculates overtime hours (i.e., hours worked over 40) and pays the employee time-and-a-half for overtime hours worked.

(d) Write an assignment statement that calculates the volume of a sphere according to the relationship:

$$\frac{4}{3} \times \pi \times r^3$$

where π is 3.14159 and r is the radius of the sphere.

2.7. Neatly organized and carefully labeled output is essential to quality computer programming. Write output statements to accomplish each of the following tasks:

(a) Print the following report heading.

* * * WEEKLY PRODUCTIVITY SUMMARY * * *

(b) Print a single blank line. (Note: Printing blank or empty lines is a useful way of spacing the information on reports to improve readability and presentation.)

(c) Print the line

––EMPLOYEE NUMBER–– ––UNITS PRODUCED––

(d) Assume that the employee numbers are stored in variables e1, e2, e3, e4, and e5. Assume that the units produced by these employees last week are stored in u1, u2, u3, u4, and u5. Print one line of the report for each of the five employees. Use the following format:

116345687 114

where the first number is the employee's 9-digit Social Security number and the second number is the units produced by that employee last week.
(e) Print a line to summarize the work of all five employees for the week. Use the following format:

∗∗∗ TOTAL UNITS ∗∗∗   3421

2.8. Write a complete Pascal program that reads two numbers and produces the sum, difference, product, quotient, and average of the two numbers. Assume both numbers are reals. Use literals to label your outputs.
2.9. Write a complete Pascal program for each of the following:

(a) Print the numbers from 1 to 10 on a single line, separated by one space each.
(b) Print the numbers from 1 to 10, each with a field width of precisely 10 characters adjacent to one another. This printout will occupy exactly 100 print positions, and depending upon the line width of your computer system, may cause printing to continue on a subsequent line.
(c) Print the following pattern:

(d) Print the following pattern. (Note: Later in the text we will ask you to do this with a program that contains only a single asterisk!)

(e) Print the following pattern. (Note: You guessed it! Here, too, we will eventually ask you to do this with a program that contains only a single write statement and only a single asterisk!)

2.10. Write a program that will print the numbers from 1 to 15 using the smallest number of statements you can.

2.11. People have become concerned with the mileage obtained by their automobiles because of the high price of gasoline. One young woman recently bought a car that was advertised to get 27 miles-per-gallon in city driving. She wants to know if the car actually does as well as advertised. She has kept track of her last six fillups and has recorded the following information.

Date	Gallons Taken	Miles Driven
Jan 13	18.9	532
Jan 28	19.2	529
Feb 13	17.0	498
Feb 26	21.2	568
Mar 11	16.1	481
Mar 29	20.2	555

Assume that during this period, the woman did city driving exclusively. Assume that on each date, the tank was completely filled with gasoline. Given that the car was full of gas on January 13, write a Pascal program that reads the gallons taken and the miles driven for each of the next five tankfuls. Print the miles-per-gallon obtained on each tankful and the overall miles-per-gallon for the five fillups from January 28th through March 29th. This information will help the woman determine if her car is performing properly.

2.12. In this text, we will present many applications in the field of computer graphics. We will use the computer to draw bar charts, pie charts, diagrams, and pictures. As an introduction to computer graphics, you have drawn certain patterns in earlier problems in this chapter. In this problem you will explore computer graphics in more depth.

Computers often print letters in "dot-matrix" form in which letters, numbers, and special symbols are formed from an array of dots. We can simulate the dot-matrix form; for example, the letter E can be made from asterisks in the following manner:

```
*****
*
*
*****
*
*
*****
```

This letter E is made in a 7 by 5 array of asterisks and spaces. Use graph paper to design the letters of your name using 7 by 5 format. Then write a Pascal program to print your name composed of 7 by 5 asterisk characters. You could also design a complete set of letters and digits for fun.

2.13. In this chapter, we devoted a great deal of time to introducing elementary concepts of computer programming. Yet, we were unable to include a discussion of one of the most important functions performed by computers, namely the repetition of a given task at enormous speed. In subsequent chapters, we will discover that one criterion for determining whether or not it is useful to solve a problem on a computer is repetition. Most computer languages include features to facilitate the solution of problems containing repetition. Even though we haven't introduced Pascal's features for handling repetition, it is still possible for you to write programs to solve repetitive problems, albeit awkward.

Write a complete Pascal program to print powers of 2 from 2^0 to 2^{15}.

3. Algorithm Design

3.1
THE CONCEPT OF AN ALGORITHM

In the previous chapter we learned enough about the programming language Pascal to be able to write simple, yet meaningful programs. We will now examine the process of writing a computer program in greater detail. The reason, of course, we write programs is to solve problems of interest to us. The problems may be simple, such as:

Given the weight of an object in pounds and ounces, find the equivalent weight in kilograms.

Or, they may be complex:

Devise a procedure to maintain student grade records for your college or university.

We all solve many problems every day. For example, we successfully dress, go to work or school, use telephones, and so on. The way we solve such problems is generally very informal, and solutions are developed at a subconscious level. The informal solution process of our everyday problems is perfectly satisfactory. However, when we use a computer to solve a problem, we must be much more precise.

When computers are involved, problem solving generally leads to the development of an **algorithm**. Simply stated, an algorithm is a set of instructions that is organized and detailed enough to lead to the solution of a problem. The meaning of the term is quite similar to recipe, process, or method. In computer programming, however, the term algorithm has acquired a more precise meaning. The instructions that tell a computer how to perform a task are, of necessity, much more precise than the instructions that tell a cook how to bake a cake, or that tell the buyer of a bicycle how to assemble it.

Thus, the process of solving problems with a computer is often much more formal than the process we follow in solving everyday problems. The problem-solving process consists of two distinct components:

1. Analysis, or definition, of the problem
2. Design and implementation of an algorithm to solve the problem

3.2 PROBLEM DEFINITION

An important aspect of developing a solution to any problem is the preliminary analysis of the problem. Knowing exactly what the problem is, is vital to the design of good algorithms and the construction of good programs. An incomplete or poorly defined problem implies that the problem is not clearly understood. The importance of properly defining a problem cannot be overstated. A solution to the wrong problem is no solution at all. The best available set of instructions on how to assemble a bicycle will not help us bake an apple pie.

Beginning programmers often assume that defining the problem to be solved is trivial. Nothing could be further from the truth. In fact, a careful and precise definition of the problem often may be as much as half of the entire solution to the problem. Failure to develop careful, albeit laborious, definitions can lead not only to solution of the wrong problem, but more often can lead to a solution only of a portion of the desired problem or a solution much more complex than is required to solve the problem.

When we solve the wrong problem, we waste a lot of our effort, and obviously, the results are useless. A partial solution of a problem, because of an incomplete problem definition, may be equally useless, especially if we are attempting to solve precisely for that part of the problem whose description was omitted. Finally, if our solution is more complex than is needed to solve our problem, unnecessary effort was used to develop it.

Some problems are much easier to define precisely than others. Certainly, the translation of weights from ounces and pounds to grams is much easier than maintaining the academic records for all the students in a college or university. There is no well-organized universal approach to problem definition. However, our chances of success should improve if we follow some important steps. Above all, good problem definition involves plain hard work. You have to resist the temptation to skip over the definition and "to get on with the job."

Problem definition can be divided into two phases: (1) input specifications, and (2) output specifications.

Input-Output Specifications

An important step in the analysis of a problem is to describe the data that constitute the input to the problem. In order to do this we need to be aware of such things as:

1. What is the input?
2. What is the format of the input?
3. What are the legal and illegal input values?
4. Are there any restrictions on the use of input values?
5. How many input values are there, or, how will we know that all values have been exhausted?

Similarly we need to describe the required output data. Output specifications generally consist of answers to questions such as:

1. What values will be output?
2. What should be the format of the output?
3. Are headers, annotations, or other explanatory notes to be output?
4. What is the amount of output data?

Let us analyze a problem and describe the input and output specifications.

Initial Description

We wish to write a program to compute the commission of a salesperson using the formula: Commission = $50 + 0.10 * Sales. The value of "Sales" will be provided to the program.

Although this is a simple problem, it is not well described. We can easily improve the description.

First Refinement

We wish to compute the commission of a salesperson using the formula: Commission = $50 + 0.10 * Sales. "Sales" represents the total sales figure in dollars for the salesperson in question. The value of Sales will be provided as input. If a negative value for Sales is provided, an error message will be printed. If a value greater than $50,000 is provided, a message to check the amount for correctness will be printed along with the commission. Otherwise, the commission will be calculated and printed.

We now have a much clearer idea of what the program is to do. We can refine our description even further; that is, state more precisely the problem, the input and output data requirements, and conditions that will affect the solution to our problem.

Second Refinement

1. *Problem Outline:* We wish to compute the commission of a single salesperson using the formula: Commission = $50 + 0.10 * Sales, where "Sales" represents the total sales figure in dollars for the salesperson in question.

2. *Input:* The input to the program will consist of a line of data with a single real number.

3. *Output:* The output of the program is to consist of the original value of "Sales," as well as the value of "Commission," and is to be printed in the following format:

   SALES   = $ddddd.dd
   COMMISSION = $ddddd.dd

   where the *d*s represent decimal digits.

4. *Exceptional Conditions:* If an input value is negative, the following message should be printed.

   ERROR: Negative sales figure provided.

   If an input value exceeds $50,000, the following output should be generated.

   SALES   = $ddddd.dd
   COMMISSION = $ddddd.dd
   Warning: Sales above $50,000. Check for accuracy.

Given the last problem specification with its detailed description of input, output, and handling of invalid data values, we now should have no difficulty in understanding what is desired.

Let us consider one more example.

Initial Description

We wish to write a program that will allow someone to estimate the heat loss through a window in a home in a cold climate. There are two causes of heat loss:

1. Heat is lost through the glass. This loss (in BTUs/hour) is given by the formula:

(Glass Area) ∗ (Temperature Difference) /R-rating

The Glass Area is given in square feet; the Temperature Difference is given in degrees Fahrenheit. The R-rating is a measure of insulating effectiveness—0.9 for single-thickness glass, 1.6 for double-thickness glass, and 1.8 for storm windows.

2. Heat is lost through air leakage. This loss (in BTUs/hr) is

((Air Leakage) ∗ 0.075∗0.24∗ (Temperature Difference)∗Length)

where Air Leakage per hour per foot of crack is approximately 39 for a wooden window frame, 24 for a weather-stripped wooden window frame, 72 for an aluminum frame, and 13 for a storm window; Length is the length of the crack between the upper and lower sashes of a double-hung window and is given in feet; Temperature Difference is, again, given in degrees Fahrenheit. The constant, 0.075, is the approximate density of air, and the constant, 0.24, is the specific heat of air.

From the above description, it certainly is not clear what the input data will be nor what its format will be. Nor do we know exactly what output our program should produce. The description can be improved.

Refinement

1. *Problem Outline*: We wish to write a program that will allow someone to estimate the heat loss through a window in a home in a cold climate. There are two causes of heat loss.

   a. Heat is lost through the glass. The quantities to be considered are:

HeatLossGlass	The heat loss through the glass (BTUs/hr).
GlassArea	Glass area of window (square feet).

TempDiff	Temperature difference between inside house and outside house (degrees F).
R-rating	Measure of insulating effectiveness:
	0.9 for single-thickness glass
	1.6 for double-thickness glass
	1.8 for storm windows

The above quantities are related by the formula:

HeatLossGlass = ((GlassArea)*(TempDiff))/R-rating

b. Heat is lost through air leakage. The quantities involved are:

HeatLossLeak	The heat loss through air leakage (BTUs/hr).
AirLeakage	Amount of air leaking out per hour per foot of crack (Cubic feet/hour/foot):
	39 for a wooden window frame
	24 for a weather-stripped wooden window frame
	72 for an aluminum frame
	13 for a storm window.
TempDiff	Temperature difference between inside and outside of house (degrees F).
Length	Length of crack between the sashes of a double-hung window (feet).

These quantities are related by the formula:

HeatLossLeak = ((AirLeakage *0.075*0.24*(TempDiff)*Length)

The total heat loss through the window is given by:

Total Loss = HeatLossGlass + HeatLossLeak

2. *Input*: The input of the program is a line of data appearing as follows:

   dd.dd   dd   d   d   dd.dd
GlassArea TempDiff WindowType FrameType Length

where the *d*s represent decimal digits such that

GlassArea	=	Window glass area in square feet.
TempDiff	=	Temperature difference in degrees F.
WindowType	=	1 if single-thickness glass
		2 if double-thickness glass
		3 if storm window.

FrameType   =   1 if wooden
                      2 if wooden with weather stripping
                      3 if aluminum
                      4 if storm window.

3. *Output*: The output of the program is to consist of the value of the total heat loss printed in the following format:

Heat Loss: dddddd BTUs/hr

4. *Exceptional Conditions*: If the window type is not a value between 1 and 3, inclusive, the program should print:

ERROR: Incorrect window type.

If the frame type is not a value between 1 and 4, inclusive, the program should print:

ERROR: Incorrect frame type.

This refinement of the original problem description makes it much easier to develop the algorithm and to write the program.

3.3 ALGORITHM DEVELOP-MENT

After the problem has been properly defined and analyzed, an algorithm must be developed for the problem's solution. Now we can be more precise in our definition of algorithm. An algorithm consists of

1. A procedure that is made up of a set of unambiguous instructions

2. Operations specified by the instructions that are executed in a certain sequence

3. A procedure that must give a solution to a general class of problems

4. A solution that must be obtained in a finite number of steps; that is, the solution must have a terminating point

All algorithms share the above features. Each instruction must describe exactly what action is to be performed. Every instruction must be stated explicitly, because there are no assumed or understood steps. The instructions must be specified in a precise sequence.

Further, in order to be useful, an algorithm must solve a general problem. An algorithm to average the numbers 2, 3, 6, and 7 has no generality at all. An algorithm to find the average of any four numbers is somewhat more general, and one which will find the average of n numbers is more general yet.

Finally, all algorithms must terminate. When an algorithm is being executed, the execution must eventually reach the point where there are no more instructions to be executed. Because we specified a finite set of instructions, you may wonder how any algorithm could fail to terminate. After all, when all the instructions are executed, what else is there left to do? The problem is that an algorithm may demand that some instructions be repeated until some condition occurs. If the condition fails to occur, the repetition may go on indefinitely.

The process of developing an algorithm to solve a particular problem is usually no easy matter. It usually requires many attempts with insertions, deletions, or modifications of the original algorithm. Sometimes, one is even required to scrap a particular attempt and to begin anew.

The task of designing and implementing an algorithm consists of many steps. The process is outlined below.

1. *An informal description of the algorithm is developed*. This initial outline of a solution describes the approach to the problem in terms of tasks that will need elaboration in subsequent steps.

2. *The initial outline is refined*. Each task and subtask used to describe the algorithm in the previous step is now refined until it leads to a sufficiently detailed description of the algorithm to allow it to be coded into a computer language, such as Pascal. In order to achieve this goal, this step may need to be repeated many times.

3. *The algorithm is coded into a computer language*. Only after the algorithm is completely described and all the step-by-step details have been developed, do we consider writing it in a computer language. The process of translating an algorithm into a computer language (called coding) is usually one of the easiest parts of the process, but it must be done with care. The result of this step is a computer program.

4. *The computer program developed in the previous step is converted to machine-readable form*. This may mean typing it on a typewriterlike keyboard or punching it into cards. The machine-readable program together with a set of text data are submitted to the computer for execution.

5. *The machine-readable program now is tested and debugged*. A beginning programmer soon learns that a program is far from complete when it is run for the first time. There will be inevita-

ble errors, which must be located and corrected. Debugging is a time-consuming and often difficult task. Also, results obtained from a program are not enough; the results must be correct. Furthermore, we would like to make sure that the program will produce correct results everytime it is used, even when it is used with data that it explicitly was not tested with.

6. *The documentation on the completed program is prepared.* Documentation describes what the program does, how to use it, who wrote it, what its limitations are, etc. This step is really part of all the preceding steps. The problem specifications, the algorithm, and the program are all part of the documentation. At this stage we ensure that everything is complete and in a usable form.

7. *The program is used, maintained, and often, modified.* The final step, of course, is using the program, but programs are rarely static entities. They often need to be changed when previously undiscovered errors are found, or when the problem specifications change. A well-written and well-documented program makes this task much easier.

Stepwise Refinements

Once we have a solid definition of a problem, we design the algorithm, usually in levels. That is, initially we concentrate on critical, broad issues that are relevant to the problem solution and postpone the details until lower levels. Each level is refined until we obtain a complete algorithm that easily can be transformed into code. This process of designing the algorithm in levels is called *stepwise refinement*.

Consider the following example that uses a simplified version of a problem we defined earlier—the computation of a salesperson's commission. In designing this solution, we will ignore, for simplicity's sake, all the error handling described in the original problem definition.

Initial Description of Algorithm

begin
    Input the sales amount
    Compute the commission
    Print the sales amount and the commission
end.

The initial description of the algorithm does no more than recognize the major components of the solution. The description of these components is only general at this stage. The next step is to refine each of the components in turn.

Refinement of Algorithm

begin
    Input sales amount
    Commission is 50 + 0.10 * sales
    Print sales amount
    Print commission
end.

The first statement of the original algorithm required no refinements. The next statement, compute commission, simply needed clarification. We replaced it by:

Commission is 50 + 0.10 * sales

The statement "Print sales amount and commission" was refined into the two statements:

Print sales amount
Print commission

The algorithm is now detailed enough to code into Pascal or any other language of our choice.

Pascal Code for Algorithm

```
program SalesCommission (input, output);

{*****************************************************
* This program computes the commission of a single *
* salesperson using the formula:                    *
*        Commission = $50 + 0.10 * Sales            *
* where "Sales" represents the total sales figure   *
* in dollars for the salesperson in question.       *
*                                                   *
* Input: The input to the program consists of a     *
* single real number representing the sales.        *
*                                                   *
* Output: The output of the program consists of     *
* the original value of sales as well as of the     *
* value of the corresponding commission.            *
*****************************************************}
```

```
var
  Sales, Commission : real;

begin
  {Input the sales amount}

  read (Sales);

  {Compute commission}

  Commission := 50 + 0.10 * Sales;

  {Print sales amount and commission}

  writeln ('SALES      = $',Sales :9:2);
  writeln ('COMMISSION = $',Commission :9:2)
end.
```

The comments in the program reflect the problem description and the initial structure of the algorithm. Thus, we can think of the algorithm development process as a stepwise refinement of the comments. We switch to code only at the last step.

Consider another example. This one involves changing a weight from kilograms to pounds and ounces. This is the inverse of the problem we discussed earlier in the chapter.

Problem Description

1. *Problem Outline*: We wish to compute the number of pounds and ounces equivalent to a given number of kilograms. The result should be computed to the nearest ounce.

2. *Input*: The input to the program will consist of a line of data with a single integer corresponding to the number of kilograms.

3. *Output*: The output of the program is to consist of the given number of kilograms and the corresponding number of pounds and ounces printed in the following format:

   ddddd Kilograms equal ddddd Pounds and ddd Ounces
   where the *d*s represent decimal digits.

With the problem description completed, we can now proceed to develop the algorithm using the stepwise refinement approach.

Initial Description of Algorithm

begin
    Input the number of kilograms
    Convert the kilograms to pounds and ounces
    Print the result
end.

We now refine the broad statements in this initial plan of attack. The first statement, Input the number of kilograms, needs no refinements. Neither does the last statement, although it could be clarified somewhat. Instead of "Print the results," we could say "Print the number of kilograms, pounds, and ounces."

On the other hand, the statement "Convert the kilograms to pounds and ounces" needs considerable expansion. We could perform the required conversion many ways. For example, we could convert the kilograms to pounds, then convert the fractional part to ounces; or we could convert everything to ounces and then convert the ounces to pounds and ounces. The choice is ours. We will use the second approach. First, we will convert everything to ounces, then round off the result to the nearest ounce, and then convert the ounces to pounds and ounces. This yields the following refinement of the algorithm:

First Refinement of Algorithm

begin
    Input the number of kilograms
    Convert the kilograms to ounces
    Round off ounces to the nearest ounce
    Convert ounces to pounds and ounces
    Print the number of kilograms, pounds, and ounces
end.

All we need to do now is to specify how each individual conversion is to be performed.

Second Refinement of Algorithm

begin
    Input the number of kilograms
    Compute ounces = kilograms $*$ 35.2
    Round off ounces to the nearest ounce

Number of pounds equals ounces **div** 16
Number of remaining ounces equals ounces **mod** 16
Print the number of kilograms, pounds, and ounces
end.

Here we made use of the Pascal integer operators **div** and **mod**. Now we can code the algorithm into Pascal.

Pascal Code for Algorithm

```
program KilosToPounds (input, output);

{*****************************************************************
* The program computes the number of pounds and ounces  *
* equivalent to a given number of kilograms. The result *
* is computed to the nearest ounce.                     *
*                                                       *
* Input: The input to the program consists of a single  *
* integer corresponding to the number of kilograms.     *
*                                                       *
* Output: The output of the program consists of the     *
* number of kilograms and the corresponding number of   *
* pounds and ounces.                                    *
*****************************************************************}

const
  ConversionFactor = 35.2; {Ounces per kilogram}

var
  Kilograms, RoundedOunces, Pounds : integer;
  Ounces : real;

begin
  {Input the number of kilograms}

  read (Kilograms);

  {Convert kilograms to ounces and round off}

  Ounces := Kilograms * ConversionFactor;
  RoundedOunces := round(Ounces);

  {Convert ounces to pounds and ounces}
```

```
Pounds := RoundedOunces div 16;
RoundedOunces := RoundedOunces mod 16;

{Print the number of kilograms, pounds, and ounces}

writeln (Kilograms :1,' Kilograms equal ',Pounds :1,
         ' Pounds and ',RoundedOunces :1,' Ounces')
end.
```

Algorithm Representation

Our descriptions of algorithms, at least at the upper levels, were machine and language independent. We wrote the algorithms using a notation that meaningfully reflected the problem instead of the rules of any particular language. Why don't we write the algorithm directly in Pascal? The major reason for not doing so is that, when we are solving the problem, we do not want to be concerned about the details of a particular language. We want to feel free to write down in any unambiguous manner what each step is to do without concern for such issues as validity of identifiers, proper use of semicolons, and other details of the language. However, since we will code the algorithm in Pascal, we feel free to use certain Pascal symbols such as

Figure 3.1 Flow-chart symbols

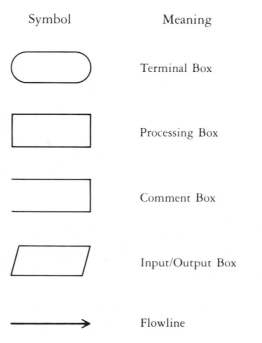

Symbol	Meaning
	Terminal Box
	Processing Box
	Comment Box
	Input/Output Box
	Flowline

Figure 3.2 Flowchart of weight conversion algorithm

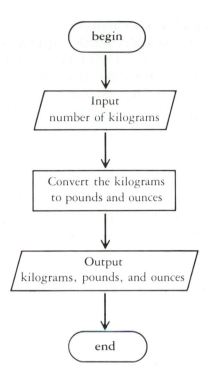

*, **mod**, **div**, **begin**, and **end** in our description. The result of a combination of utilizing English and a particular programming language's symbols and structures is known as **pseudocode**. Pseudocode has the advantage of making the outline of the algorithm resemble the program that will eventually be coded from it. In order to properly use pseudocode, however, we must be familiar with the programming language that will be used to implement the algorithm. In this chapter we only attempt to design algorithms that can be coded with the subset of Pascal we have studied so far. When we study additional features of Pascal, we will introduce the pseudocode together with the corresponding language feature.

The **flowchart** language is another way that algorithms can be described. In flowchart language we use a set of standard geometric symbols to represent various actions of the algorithm. A flowchart pictorially describes the sequence of steps required for the solution of the problem.

Some of the flowchart symbols corresponding to the features of Pascal we have studied, and their meaning, are shown in Figure 3.1.

As an example of a flowchart description of an algorithm, consider Figure 3.2, which depicts the algorithm to convert kilograms to pounds and ounces. This is, of course, the first version of the algorithm (p. 94). Like the initial pseudocode outline, the initial flowchart is quite general. Refinements are made by replacing existing symbols with other flowchart segments that provide more explicit details. The flowchart in Figure 3.3 is equivalent to the last refinement of the algorithm on p. 94.

Figure 3.3 Refinement of weight-conversion flowchart

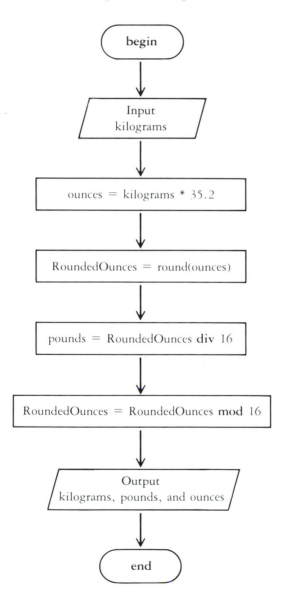

Pseudocode and flowcharts are used for the same purpose. There is no "best" way to represent an algorithm. It is unimportant which technique you use, as long as you are comfortable with it and are able to develop correct algorithms. In this book we use pseudocode for all our algorithms. Periodically we will also use flowcharts to illustrate a particular Pascal instruction.

SELF-TEST 1

1. What are the steps involved in problem description?
2. What are the features of an algorithm?
3. What is pseudocode?
4. Write out a complete problem description for the following problem:

Write a program that computes the interest on a given amount of money.

5. Write an algorithm for the problem specified in the previous question.

Answers

1. The main parts of a problem description are: input specifications and output specifications.

2. An algorithm is a procedure that is made up of a set of unambiguous instructions. The operations specified by the instructions are executed in a certain sequence. The procedure must give a solution to a general class of problems. The solution must be obtained in a finite number of steps.

3. Pseudocode is a language used to describe algorithms that is a combination of English and a particular programming language's symbols and structures.

4. A possible refinement of the problem description is:

(a) *Problem Outline*: We wish to compute the interest on a given amount of money. The program will be provided the principal (amount of money on which the interest is to be computed) and the annual interest rate. The interest will be computed for a one-year period using the formula

Interest = Principal * Rate.

(b) *Input*: The input to the program will consist of a line of data with the principal as a single real number and the interest rate in decimal format.

(c) *Output*: The output of the program is to consist of the principal, interest rate, and interest printed in the following format:

The annual interest on dddddd.dd dollars at dd.dd percent
is ddddd.dd dollars.

where the *d*s represent decimal digits.

5.   An algorithm to solve the above problem is:

begin
   Input the principal and the rate
   Compute interest = principal * rate
   Print the principal, rate, and interest
end.

3.4 PROGRAM RUNNING AND DEBUGGING

Once the algorithm is developed and coded, the next step is to convert it into a *machine-readable form* that can be input into the computer. The way this is done depends on the method used to access the computer. Commonly, computer resources are made available to users in two ways—batch processing and interactive processing.

Batch processing is one of the oldest techniques for running programs and is still widely used for running student jobs. In this technique, the system receives jobs in batches and processes them either in the order in which they are received or according to some priority scheme. Usually the program is first converted to machine-readabale form off-line—that is, without using the computer. This preparation is done by punching each line of the program into an 80-column punch card using a machine called a keypunch. The keypunch was described in Chapter 1. In addition to the program, the control cards required to run a job on the system and the data used by the program must be punched into cards. Figure 3.4 shows an example of a program prepared for batch processing.

Control cards provide the system with information about who you are and what you want to do. In Figure 3.4 the cards begin with the symbol /. The actual format of the cards will differ from system to system, but the information contained in them will generally be similar. Your instructor, or the computing center, will let you know what control cards are needed to run a Pascal program at your installation. A group of cards such as the above is known as a *job deck*.

A program prepared on cards does not enter the computer system until the job deck is read by a card reader. Some computer installations allow individual users to operate the card reader themselves. Others collect all the job decks and put them through the card reader in batches. When the job is run, a compilation listing and the output

Figure 3.4 Sample batch processing for Pascal program

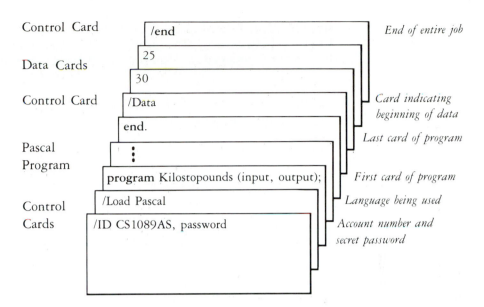

Control Card — /end — *End of entire job*

Data Cards — 25, 30

Control Card — /Data — *Card indicating beginning of data*

end. — *Last card of program*

Pascal Program — **program** Kilostopounds (input, output); — *First card of program*

Control Cards — /Load Pascal — *Language being used*

/ID CS1089AS, password — *Account number and secret password*

generated by the program will be produced on the line printer. The printout generated on the printer is then returned to the person who submitted the job. In many computer installations, users submit job decks at a *batch window* and return later to obtain the resulting printouts.

One of the main disadvantages of batch processing is that the time lag between submission of a job deck and return of the resulting printout (the turnaround time) may vary from a few minutes to several hours. It is not unusual during periods of high activity to have long turnaround times. Therefore, time spent checking a deck before it is submitted is time well spent.

A very important characteristic of batch processing is that it does not allow a user to interact with a program while the program is being executed. All data must be available to the machine at the time the job is run. To be able to run programs that interact with the user during execution requires a technique other than batch processing, which is called *interactive processing*.

In interactive processing, a user usually sits at a terminal with a keyboard and a printing mechanism or a cathode-ray tube (CRT) and enters the program into the system **on-line**. That is, the user communicates directly with the computer through the keyboard. When working with an interactive system, a user carries on a dialogue with the system, entering commands and using various system programs, such as editors, to facilitate program entry and changes. Figure 3.5 il-

Figure 3.5 Sample
interactive session

<u>Hello</u>
User : <u>100,2</u>
Password: <u>passwd</u>   *What you type on this line is not dis-*
                                                        played.
7–FEB–83
Ready

<u>edit/create</u> <u>myprog.pas</u>   *This line tells the system that you*
                                                        are going to create a new Pascal
                                                        program called "myprog.pas."

<u>PROGRAM</u> <u>KilosToPounds</u> <u>(input,output)</u>;
                          .
                          .   *Program lines typed in at terminal.*
                          .

<u>END.</u>
Command: <u>exit</u>   *Leaving the editor.*
saved myprog.pas 23 line(s).   *Program is saved.*
<u>pascal</u>   *Request to compile and run*
program name: <u>myprog</u>   *program "myprog."*

MYPROG   7–FEB–83 15:06   Page 1
                          .
                          .   *Program listing generated by com-*
                          .   *piler.*

Errors detected: 0
Free memory: 6010 words

Ready
*(object)

Ready
*MYPROG   7–FEB–83 15:07   *Output generated by program.*
                          .
                          .
                          .

Ready

        {Here additional requests can be made}

<u>bye</u>   *Request to sign-off.*
Confirm: <u>yes</u>
Saved all disk files; 1964 blocks in use
Job 17 User 100,2 logged off KB11 at 7–FEB–83 11:22 AM
Run time was 56.3 seconds
Elapsed time was 1 hour, 11 minutes
Good morning

lustrates a typical session with an interactive system. The lines typed by the user are underlined in Figure 3.5 to distinguish them from those typed by the computer. This illustration, of course, is an example of a particular system and probably is not the way your system works.

In *interactive processing* the program is typed at a terminal using an editor. A request to execute it is also entered at the terminal, and the program is immediately run. Data may be entered while the program executes or may be retrieved from a previously stored file. Output produced by the program, including the program listing, is produced on the printer or the CRT.

On some systems programs are prepared interactively but executed in batch mode if printed results are desired. With all of these systems, the three basic components of the batch system described earlier are still present: control cards (or statements), the program, and the data.

Program Processing

As we saw in Chapter 1, Pascal or any other high-level language cannot be understood directly by the computer. Before a program can be executed, it must be translated into machine language. We, therefore, need to submit our Pascal program to a Pascal **compiler**. A Pascal compiler translates source programs written in Pascal to object programs written in the machine language of a given computer.

After the program is translated, or compiled, it is executed. Dureing execution, the computer executes the machine language instructions of the resulting object program. Any data that the object program requests will be read, and any output the program generates will be printed. Figure 3.6 illustrates the compilation and execution processes.

The **source listing** is a listing (printed or displayed) of your program generated by the compiler. This is not the output produced by your program at execution time. It is simply a listing of the source code produced by the compiler and, in fact, can be suppressed.

Program Debugging

In most programming environments, the computer proceeds directly from compilation to execution without any intermediate commands, so that we are unaware of the existence of these two distinct steps of running a program. But, we need to be aware of the distinc-

Figure 3.6 Compilation and execution phases

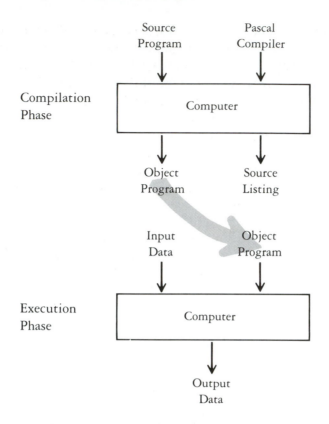

tion, because of the possibility of errors. Three important kinds of errors can occur:

1. *Compile-time errors*. These are errors that can be detected during translation. Typically they will be violations of the grammatical rules of the language; for example, a misspelled reserved word.

2. *Run-time errors*. These are errors that can be recognized during execution of the object program. For example, if a division by zero is attempted when the program executes, the program will fail, since division by zero is not a legal mathematical operation.

3. *Logical Errors*. These errors are not detected either at compilation or execution of the program. The program runs successfully but yields incorrect results.

Figure 3.7 shows how errors are detected at various points of running a Pascal program. Errors detected during compilation appear first. If these errors are serious, the object program will never be executed. Even if the program compiles successfully, it may fail during execution, which will result in run-time errors. Finally, if the program compiles successfully and runs successfully, we will get the output we expected unless there are logical errors, in which case the output will be incorrect.

Debugging is the process of discovering, locating, and correcting all errors that cause a program to produce either incorrect results or no results at all. A beginning programmer usually learns quickly that debugging can be the single most time-consuming part of program development. We will now examine various errors and how to debug them.

For beginning programmers, syntax errors are among the most common; however, they are also the easiest to detect and correct. A **syntax error** is simply a violation of the grammatical rules of the

Figure 3.7 Compilation and execution phases with error detection

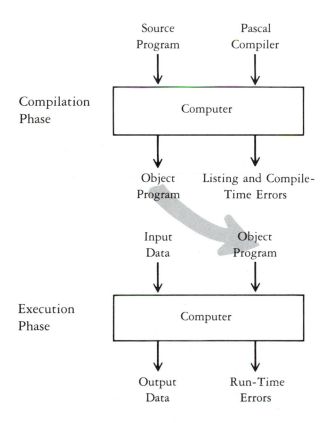

language. For example, the following variable declaration contains a syntax error:

```
var
  Cost : real:
  Count : integer;
```

The colon following real should have been a semicolon.

Syntax errors are easier to correct than most other types of errors because they generally will show up as compile-time errors. When the compiler detects such errors, it will produce a message indicating where and what the mistake is.

Example 3.1 is a program listing with some compile-time errors located and identified by the compiler. The error is the word "read" misspelled as "red."

The compiler uses the symbol ↑ to mark the place where it detected the syntax error. Below the error, it prints a message indicating what it determined the error to be. Finally, it ignores the statement with the error and continues the compilation in order to determine if there are any additional errors. This example, of course, shows how error messages are handled by a particular Pascal compiler. You may be using a system that prints error messages in a different way. The information provided, however, will be similar.

The error message in Example 3.1 is quite clear and explicit about the nature of the mistake, and it is printed at the location of the mistake. Mistakes are not, however, always detected where they are made. This is especially true of omission errors. Example 3.2 illustrates how the compiler detects the omission of a variable declaration. The variable "Ounces" is not declared.

The error is detected when we attempt to reference the undeclared variable Ounces. The error message the compiler prints is the same as in the previous example because it has no way of knowing that "red" is "read" misspelled. The word "red" is just another undeclared identifier. Note that, in this case, the error in the variable declaration resulted in three error messages.

There are cases where error messages are even less clear and helpful than in the above examples. Some error messages tell us nothing more than that an error occurred. It is up to us to determine where and what the error is. As we study new features of the language, we will attempt to point out some of the common errors associated with these features. As you become a more experienced pro-

EXAMPLE 3.1   Program Listing with Syntax Error

KILOSTOPOUNDS   11-Nov-83 15:52   Page 1

```
Line  Stmt Level  Nest    Source Statement

   1                           program KilosToPounds (input, output);
   2
   3                           const
   4                              ConversionFactor = 35.2; {Ounces per kilogram}
   5
   6                           var
   7                              Kilograms, RoundedOunces, Pounds : integer;
   8                              Ounces : real;
   9                           begin
  10                              {Input the number of kilograms}
  11
  12    1    1      1            red (Kilograms);
                                     ↑
******         Undefined symbol

  13
  14                              {Convert kilograms to ounces and round off}
  15
  16    2    1      1            Ounces := Kilograms * ConversionFactor;
  17    3    1      1            RoundedOunces := round(Ounces);
  18
  19                              {Convert ounces to pounds and ounces}
  20
  21    4    1      1            Pounds := RoundedOunces div 16;
  22    5    1      1            RoundedOunces := RoundedOunces mod 16;
  23
  24                              {Print kilograms, pounds, and ounces}
  25
  26    6    1      1            writeln (Kilograms :1,' Kilograms equal ',
  27                                       Pounds :1,' Pounds and ',
  28                                       RoundedOunces :1,' Ounces')
  29                           end.

Errors detected:  1
Free memory:  6002  words
```

EXAMPLE 3.2   Program Listing with Omission Error

KILOSTOPOUNDS   11-Nov-83 15:06   Page 1

```
Line  Stmt Level  Nest    Source Statement

  1                         program KilosToPounds (input, output);
  2
  3                         const
  4                             ConversionFactor = 35.2; {Ounces per kilogram}
  5
  6                         var
  7                             Kilograms, RoundedOunces, Pounds : integer;
  8
  9                         begin
 10                             {Input the number of kilograms}
 11
 12     1    1     1          read (Kilograms);
 13
 14                             {Convert kilograms to ounces and round off}
 15
 16     2    1     1          Ounces := Kilograms * ConversionFactor;
                                                 ↑
****** 	     Undefined symbol

 17     3    1     1          RoundedOunces := round(Ounces);
                                                        ↑
****** 	     Undefined operand
****** 	     Argument must be real
 18
 19                             {Convert ounces to pounds and ounces}
 20
 21     4    1     1          Pounds := RoundedOunces div 16;
 22     5    1     1          RoundedOunces := RoundedOunces mod 16;
 23
 24                             {Print kilograms, pounds, and ounces}
 25
 26     6    1     1          writeln (Kilograms :1,' Kilograms equal ',
 27                                            Pounds :1,' Pounds and ',
 28                                            RoundedOunces :1,' Ounces')
 29                         end.
```

Errors detected: 3
Free memory: 6010 words

grammer, you will be able to correct syntax errors fairly easily. Usually syntax errors can be eliminated by an experienced programmer in two or fewer compilations.

Let us now consider an example with a run-time error. The program in Example 3.3 compiles without errors, but when it is executed it terminates because of a run-time error. The error is due to the attempted division by zero in line 21 of the program.

The statement "Pounds : = RoundedOunces **div** 0;" is syntactically correct and will not produce any error messages at compilation time. However, when the program is executed, this statement will cause the termination of the program. The fact that there is a division by zero is not detected until the object program is actually run. This is why it is termed a run-time error. Note that not only do we have a message indicating what caused the termination, but we are also told where within the program the error occurred. This information, however, is given in terms of the object program so it is not very helpful. In some versions of Pascal, a run-time error will also cause the identifiers and current values of all variables to be printed. This provides us with information about the status of the program when the error occurred and is often called a *post-mortem dump*.

As we stated earlier, there are three types of errors, the last type being a *logical error*. It is the most difficult and time-consuming error to correct. A logical error occurs when your program compiles and executes but yields incorrect results. This is usually due to either an incorrect translation of the algorithm into Pascal, or to an incorrect algorithm. Information about what the logical error is, or where in the program it is located, rarely will be given. An important trouble-shooting step is to carefully compare your program with the algorithm. Another helpful method is to simulate the program with pencil and paper. This allows you to examine the values of the variables as the program executes. Still another very powerful way to locate the error is to insert write and writeln statements at various points in the program. When placing write and writeln statements in a program for debugging purposes, a few general guidelines can be observed. For example, use write or writeln statements after input of data. It is always useful to *echo-print* all input data. Your program may be producing incorrect results not because it is incorrect, but because you are feeding it garbage. Use write or writeln statements to print values of intermediate results of calculations. By comparing actual results with what is expected, we can often determine if the program is proceeding correctly.

EXAMPLE 3.3   Execution of Program with Run-Time Error

KILOSTOPOUNDS   11-Nov-83 15:50   Page 1

Line Stmt Level Nest   Source Statement

```
   1                          program KilosToPounds (input, output);
   2
   3                          const
   4                              ConversionFactor = 35.2; {Ounces per kilogram}
   5
   6                          var
   7                              Kilograms, RoundedOunces, Pounds : integer;
   8                              Ounces : real;
   9                          begin
  10                              {Input the number of kilograms}
  11
  12     1    1     1            read (Kilograms);
  13
  14                              {Convert kilograms to ounces and round off}
  15
  16     2    1     1            Ounces := Kilograms * ConversionFactor;
  17     3    1     1            RoundedOunces := round(Ounces);
  18
  19                              {Convert ounces to pounds and ounces}
  20
  21     4    1     1            Pounds := RoundedOunces div 0;
  22     5    1     1            RoundedOunces := RoundedOunces mod 16;
  23
  24                              {Print kilograms, pounds, and ounces}
  25
  26     6    1     1            writeln (Kilograms :1,' Kilograms equal ',
  27                                       Pounds :1,' Pounds and ',
  28                                       RoundedOunces :1,' Ounces')
  29                          end.
```

Errors detected: 0
Free memory: 6010 words

?Division by zero
I/O status: 34 (?Reserved instruction trap)
Program counter: 1214

Finally, the possibility that the algorithm needs to be reexamined and redesigned always exists. There are many correct ways to debug a program. However, one approach is always wrong—blindly trying something, *anything*, just because you do not know what is wrong is a mistake. Errors are caused by incorrect operations. Until you have an idea which operations are causing the problem, or how to find them, it makes no sense to alter and rerun your program.

SELF-TEST 2

1. What are the three types of errors common to programs?
2. Find and correct all errors in the following program. Characterize each error as either a compile-time, run-time, or logical error. The lines are numbered for ease of reference.

```
1 program Question2 (input,output);
2
3 {This program computes the quotient of two real numbers
4 Number1 and Number2. Both Number1 and Number 2 are read
5 from the input file.}
6
7 var
8     Number1, Number2, Quotient : real;
9
10    negin
11        reed(Number1,Number2);
12        Quotient := (Number2 / Number1);
13        write (Number1 :8:2,' divided by ',Number2 :8:2)
14        writeln (' is ',Quotient :8:2)
15    end.
```

3. Assume that all the errors in the program of the preceding problem have been corrected. If you run the program with the following data, what will be the result?

15.67 0

Answers

1. There are three types of errors: compile-time errors, run-time errors, and logical errors.

2. Errors occur on the following lines:

10 **negin** Compile-time error—should say **begin**

11 reed (Number1,Number2); Compile-time error—reed should say read

12 Quotient := (Number2 **/** Number1); Logical error—the numbers are reversed
13 write (Number1 :8:2, ' divided by ',Number2 :8:2) Compile-time error—missing semicolon.
3. A run-time error indicating division by zero would result.

**3.5
PROGRAM
TESTING**

Program testing is demonstrating that a program will produce correct results for all possible data. Except for the smallest programs, this goal is generally unattainable. Some computer scientists claim that we should be able to prove that programs are correct much in the same way we prove mathematical theorems. Although much work on proof techniques is being done, we are not yet at a stage where we can apply such techniques to anything but very simple, practical problems, such as the problems we have studied so far. These, however, are too simple to be of any real utility. With large and complex problems, we must resort to testing instead of proofs.

Since we generally cannot prove that a complex program is correct, we must convince ourselves that the chances it is incorrect are slim. We do this by testing the program with a sufficient number of well-chosen data sets. If the program produces correct results with all test data, we may say that it is correct and proceed to use it. Obviously, it is possible that errors will go undetected because we failed to test for them.

The most important aspect of program testing is choosing the appropriate sample data. Test cases can be divided into three different types, and a program should be tested with all three.

The first type is **valid** data; that is, data for which our program was designed to produce answers. Our initial tests should be designed to demonstrate that our program works with the data values for which it was designed to work. We should attempt to test all possible alternatives.

The second type involves **special** or unusual cases; that is, data that are not necessarily invalid, but that might require special processing. At this point in our development of algorithms, we are able to design and code only the simplest algorithms, and hence our algorithms do not yet make provisions for processing exceptional cases.

This is also true with the last type of data—the **invalid** cases. Although these cases should not occur when the program operates normally, one can rest assured that every program that is in general use will sooner or later be provided some invalid data to process. Right now, such data would result in a run-time error, or worse, a logical error. We will see in the next chapter how we can protect ourselves from such bad values. Even now, however, you should take care to determine which data will and will not work with your program.

**3.6
PROGRAM
DOCUMENTA-
TION**

We have two major reasons for program documentation: program use and program maintenance. Therefore, the first type of documentation is called **user documentation**, and it is important if the program is to be useful again after it is written. Most programs written by professionals are written to be used by someone else. User documentation provides the information that is needed in order to be able to use the program. It usually includes the following:

1. A description of what the program does so that potential users could decide if the program being considered addresses their problem
2. A description of the data the program needs for input, and its format
3. A description of the output the program produces
4. An explanation of all messages the program produces
5. A description of the limitations and capabilities of the program
6. A description of how the program is to be run

User documentation is much more than a set of instructions on how to run the program. It also must provide enough information to a potential user to determine if the program is suitable for his or her needs.

In addition to the information that may be required by a non-technical user, we also need to document the technical details. Thus, the second type is **technical documentation**, which is written for programmers, including the original author or authors who might have to maintain and modify the program. For example, a bug might turn up after the program has been in use for some time, or additional program features might be needed. Either way, good technical documentation will be necessary. With small programs, well-placed comments, which are written during the algorithm development and coding phases, will suffice. With large programs, it is often necessary to provide separate technical documentation to describe general design strategies and approaches to the problem, as well as relationships between program units. We will postpone detailed discussion of such documentation issues until we are able to write programs of enough complexity to warrant these concerns.

One final point should be made at this time: documentation is an ongoing process. It starts when we first begin to define the problem and continues throughout all phases of algorithm design. It is not something that is done when the program is finished. If we leave documentation until the end, it usually results in a poorly documented program. Although most of the programs you will write as a student will not be large enough to require extensive documentation, and the programs generally will not be written for someone else to use, it is a good idea to get into the habit of well-documented programs from the start. Your programs will certainly be better because of the habit.

Let us now examine in some detail the solution of a complete problem using a computer. We will describe the problem, design and code the algorithm, and run and test the resulting program.

APPLICATION

Making Change

We want to write a program that simulates part of the operation of a cash register. Given the amount of a purchase and the amount of money to pay for the items purchased, the program will tell us what change to return using the appropriate number of correct bills and coins.

Description of Problem

1. *Problem Outline*: We wish to compute change in terms of the specific numbers of coins and bills to be returned to a customer, given the amount of a purchase and the amount tendered to pay for the purchase.

2. *Input*: The input to the program will be a line of data with two real numbers: the amount of the purchase and the amount tendered, both represented in dollars and cents. Each will be less than or equal to $50.00. The program assumes that the amount tendered is always greater than or equal to the purchase amount. It does not check to see whether or not this is the case.

3. *Output*: The output of the program will consist of the purchase amount, the amount tendered, and the change, printed in the following format:

Amount of Purchase = $ddddd.dd
Amount tendered = $ddddd.dd

APPLICATION

**Making
Change
(*continued*)**

Change . . .

d ten-dollar bills.
d five-dollar bills.
d one-dollar bills.
d halves.
d quarters.
d dimes.
d nickels.
d cents.

where the *d*s represent decimal digits.

4. *Exceptional Conditions*: This program is unable to handle any special cases. It assumes the data are valid and the data are entered in the form described in the input specifications.

The inability of our program to handle special cases and to validate the data for correctness is a major drawback. We are forced into this situation because we do not yet know enough Pascal to be able to check our data for validity, but that problem will be addressed in the next chapter, at which time it would be useful to come back to this program and modify it.

Note that the algorithm for this problem is very similar to our previous example that involved the conversion of kilograms to pounds and ounces.

Initial Description of Algorithm

begin
    Input the purchase amount
    Input the amount tendered
    Compute the change
    Print the result
end.

We now proceed to a stepwise refinement of this initial description. The first two statements, "Input the purchase amount" and "Input the amount tendered," need no refinements; but the statement "Compute the change" needs considerable expansion. We will first compute the balance due, then change the amount due to cents, and finally compute the required number of bills and coins of each denomination. Lastly, we will print the amount of the purchase, the amount tendered, and the change. This process yields the first refinement to the algorithm.

First Refinement of Algorithm

begin
    Input the purchase amount
    Input the amount tendered
    Compute the total change
    Change the total change to cents
    Compute the number of ten-dollar bills
    Compute the number of five-dollar bills
    Compute the number of one-dollar bills
    Compute the number of fifty-cent pieces
    Compute the number of quarters
    Compute the number of dimes
    Compute the number of nickels
    Compute the number of pennies
    Print the purchase amount
    Print the amount tendered
    Print the number of ten-dollar bills
    Print the number of five-dollar bills
    Print the number of one-dollar bills
    Print the number of fifty-cent pieces
    Print the number of quarters
    Print the number of dimes
    Print the number of nickels
    Print the number of pennies
end.

    All we need to do now is specify how each individual computation will be performed.

Final Version of Algorithm

begin
    Input PurchaseAmount
    Input AmountTendered
    Compute Change = AmountTendered − PurchaseAmount
    Compute Cents = Round (100*Change)
    Compute Tens = Cents **div** 1000
    Compute Cents = Cents **mod** 1000
    Compute Fives = Cents **div** 500
    Compute Cents = Cents **mod** 500
    Compute Ones = Cents **div** 100
    Compute Cents = Cents **mod** 100
    Compute FiftyCents = Cents **div** 50
    Compute Cents = Cents **mod** 50

APPLICATION

**Making
Change
(*continued*)**

Compute Quarters = Cents **div** 25
Compute Cents = Cents **mod** 25
Compute Dimes = Cents **div** 10
Compute Cents = Cents **mod** 10
Compute Nickels = Cents **div** 5
Compute Pennies = Cents **mod** 5
Print the purchase amount
Print the amount tendered
Print the number of ten-dollar bills
Print the number of five-dollar bills
Print the number of one-dollar bills
Print the number of fifty-cent pieces
Print the number of quarters
Print the number of dimes
Print the number of nickels
Print the number of pennies
end.

Here, as in our previous example, we made use of the Pascal integer operators **div** and **mod**. The **div** was used to obtain the number of coins or bills. The **mod** was used to obtain the corresponding remainders. Now we can code the algorithm into Pascal.

Pascal Code for Algorithm

```
program MakeChange (input, output);

{****************************************************
* This program computes the change to be returned *
* to a customer given the amount of a purchase     *
* and the amount tendered to pay for the purchase.*
*                                                  *
* Input: The input to the program consists of a    *
* line of data with two real numbers. The first    *
* number represents the amount of the purchase in *
* dollars and cents. The second number represents *
* the amount tendered in dollars and cents. The    *
* program assumes that the amount tendered is      *
* greater than or equal to the purchase amount.    *
* It does not check to see if this is the case.     *
*                                                  *
* Output: The output of the program consists of    *
* the purchase amount, the amount tendered and     *
* the change.                                      *
****************************************************}
```

APPLICATION
———————————
**Making
Change**
(*continued*)

```
var
    PurchaseAmount, AmountTendered, Change : real;
    Tens, Fives, Ones, FiftyCents, Quarters, Dimes,
    Nickels, Pennies, Cents : integer;

begin
    {Input purchase amount and amount tendered}

    read (PurchaseAmount);
    read (AmountTendered);

    {Compute total change in cents}

    Change := AmountTendered-PurchaseAmount;
    Cents := round(100*Change);

    {Compute for each denomination}

    Tens := Cents div 1000;
    Cents := Cents mod 1000;
    Fives := Cents div 500;
    Cents := Cents mod 500;
    Ones := Cents div 100;
    Cents := Cents mod 100;
    FiftyCents := Cents div 50;
    Cents := Cents mod 50;
    Quarters := Cents div 25;
    Cents := Cents mod 25;
    Dimes := Cents div 10;
    Cents := Cents mod 10;
    Nickels := Cents div 5;
    Pennies := Cents mod 5;

    {Print the results}

    writeln ('Amount of purchase : $',PurchaseAmount :6:2);
    writeln ('Amount tendered    : $',AmountTendered :6:2);
    writeln;
    writeln ('Change ...');
    writeln;
    writeln (Tens :2,' ten dollar bills');
    writeln (Fives :2,' five dollar bills');
    writeln (Ones :2,' one dollar bills');
    writeln (FiftyCents :2,' fifty cent pieces');
```

APPLICATION

**Making
Change**
(*continued*)

```
writeln (Quarters :2,' quarters');
writeln (Dimes :2,' dimes');
writeln (Nickels :2,' nickels');
writeln (Pennies :2,' cents')
```
end.

    To test the program, we ran it with the input data 34.14 and 40.00. The following was the output:

```
Amount of purchase :  $ 34.14
Amount tendered    :  $ 40.00

Change ...

0 ten dollar bills
1 five dollar bills
0 one dollar bills
1 fifty cent pieces
1 quarters
1 dimes
0 nickels
1 cents
```

    We then ran it again with the input 50.00 and 50.00. The following output resulted.

```
Amount of purchase :  $ 50.00
Amount tendered    :  $ 50.00

Change ...

 0 ten dollar bills
 0 five dollar bills
 0 one dollar bills
 0 fifty cent pieces
 0 quarters
 0 dimes
 0 nickels
 0 cents
```

    Other extreme cases, such as 0.00 0.00, also could have been run. We did not run the program with invalid data because this version of the program cannot check for such data.

3.7 CHAPTER REVIEW

The process of solving problems using a computer consists of two distinct components:

1. Analysis, or definition, of the problem
2. Design and implementation of an algorithm to solve the problem

Problem analysis and definition can be divided into two phases: (1) input specifications and (2) output specifications.

Input specifications should consider such things as:

1. What is the input?
2. What is the format of the input?
3. What are the legal and illegal input values?
4. Are there any restrictions on the use of input values?
5. How many input values are there, or, how will we know that all values have been exhausted?

Similarly, we need to describe the required output data. Output specifications generally consist of answers to questions such as:

1. What values will be output?
2. What should be the format of the output?
3. Are headers, annotations, or other explanatory notes to be output?
4. What is the amount of output data?

After the problem has been properly defined and analyzed, an algorithm must be developed for its solution. An algorithm consists of

1. A procedure that is made up of a set of unambiguous instructions,
2. Operations specified by the instructions that are executed in a certain sequence,
3. A procedure that must give a solution to a general class of problems,
4. A solution that must be obtained in a finite number of steps.

The task of algorithm development consists of many steps, some of which are the following:

1. An informal description of the algorithm is outlined.

2. The initial outline is refined. Each task and subtask used to describe the algorithm is refined until it leads to a sufficiently detailed description of the algorithm to allow it to be coded in a computer language, such as Pascal. This step may be repeated many times.

3. The algorithm is coded into a computer language. The result of this step is a computer program.

4. The program developed in the previous step is converted to machine-readable form. It is either typed in on a terminal or punched into cards. The machine-readable program, together with a set of test data, are submitted to the computer for execution.

5. The machine-readable program is run and debugged. To obtain results from a program is not enough. The results must be correct, so the program is rid of its errors.

6. The completed program is documented; that is, what the program does, how to use it, what its limitations are, etc., are described.

7. The program is used, maintained, and often, modified. Good documentation eases this final step in the process.

We design an algorithm in levels. Initially, we concentrate on broad issues that are critical to the problem solution, postponing details until lower levels. Each level is refined until we obtain a complete algorithm that can be transformed easily into code.

To represent an algorithm we often use a combination of English and the programming language into which the algorithm will be eventually coded. This is known as *pseudocode*.

The *flowchart* language is another common way to represent algorithms. In flowchart language a set of standard geometric symbols is used to represent various actions of the algorithm.

Once the algorithm is fully developed, it is coded into a computer language such as Pascal. The code is converted to machine-readable form and entered into the computer.

Before the Pascal program can be executed, a Pascal *compiler* translates it into the machine language of the particular computer being used.

After the program is translated, or compiled, it is executed. During this step, the computer executes the instructions of the resulting machine language program. Any data that the program requests will be read and any output the program generates will be printed.

Three kinds of errors can occur when a program is being compiled or executed:

1. *Compile-time errors*: These are errors that can be detected during translation. Typically they will be violations of the grammatical rules of the language.

2. *Run-time errors*: These are errors that are discovered by the computer system during execution of the machine language version of the program. They generally are caused by illegal instructions, such as division by zero.

3. *Logical Errors*: These errors are not detected either during compilation or execution of the program. The program runs, but yields incorrect results.

Debugging is the process of locating and correcting all errors that cause either incorrect results or no results at all. It is usually a very time-consuming process.

Once a program is running it should be tested. The most important aspect of program testing is choosing the appropriate data values with which to do the testing. The first tests of a program should be designed to demonstrate that the program works with valid data. A second type of test data should use *special* or unusual cases: not necessarily invalid, but data requiring special processing. Finally, the program should be tested with *invalid* data.

All programs should be documented for two major reasons: program use and program maintenance. User documentation is important if the program is to be used by others once it is written. Technical documentation is important for programmers, including the original author or authors, who might have to maintain and modify the program.

3.8
EXERCISES

3.1. Fill in the blanks in each of the following:

(a) The process of solving problems with a computer involves two distinct steps: _____ and _____ .

(b) List the four properties of an algorithm: (1) _____, (2) _____, (3) _____, and (4) _____.

(c) When defining a problem for computer solution, care must be taken to specify _____ and _____.

(d) The failure to develop a complete problem description can result in an algorithm that _____ or that _____.

(e) The translation of an algorithm into a computer language is called _____.

(f) An English-like language that is used to describe an algorithm is called _____.

(g) A pictorial language used to represent algorithms is _____.

(h) The process that translates a Pascal program into language the computer can understand is _____.

(i) Program documentation is necessary because: _____ and _____.

3.2. Answer each of the following true or false. If your answer is false, state why.

(a) The first step in the development of an algorithm is to define the problem.

(b) When developing an algorithm it is a good idea to write it directly in a programming language, such as Pascal.

(c) Comments in a program should be added after the program is written.

(d) The output of a compiler is a program in object code and a listing with error messages, if any.

(e) A compiler detects run-time, as well as compile-time, errors.

(f) The most difficult errors to correct are compile-time errors.

(g) When a program is being tested, we only need to test it with the data values for which it was designed to work.

(h) User documentation of a program is a set of instructions on how to run the program.

3.3. Develop a thorough and complete problem definition for each of the following problems:

(a) Write a program that reads three numbers and computes and prints their average.

(b) Write a program that converts degrees Fahrenheit (F) to degrees Kelvin (K) using $K = (5/9)(F - 32) + 273$.

(c) Write a program to compute the hypotenuse of a right triangle given the lengths of the perpendicular sides.

(d) Write a program to compute the weekly pay for a worker from the hours worked that week.

(e) Write a program that prints a mailing label given the name and address.

(f) A company has four divisions that sell a variety of products. The company's management wants to know what percentage of total sales is generated by each division. Write a program that reads the gross sales generated by each division and prints the total sales with the corresponding percentages.

3.4. Design algorithms for each part of problem 3.3.

3.5. Write and run Pascal programs for each of the parts of problem 3.3.

3.6. To debug a program we often need to trace it through by hand. Execute the following programs by hand to determine the output produced when the input is:

```
10000.00    3000.00
10
```

Be precise.

(a)
```pascal
program Question6A (input, output);
var
   a,b : real;
   i,j : integer;
begin
   a := 10.0;
   b := 3.0;
   i := 3;
   j := 2;
   write ( i/j, 1.0/b, 2.0/b);
   writeln (a,a-b)
end.
```

(b)
```pascal
program Question6B (input, output):
var
   Cost, SalvageValue, Depreciation : real;
   ServiceLife : integer;
begin
   readln (Cost, SalvageValue);
   readln (ServiceLife);
   Depreciation := (Cost-SalvageValue)/ServiceLife;
   writeln ('Cost: ',Cost : 8:2);
   writeln ('Salvage value: ', SalvageValue : 8:2);
   writeln ('Depreciation: ', Depreciation : 8:2)
end.
```

3.7. What will be the output of problem 3.6 (b), if the input is

1000.00   3000.00
0

3.8. The system of linear equations

$$Ax + By = C$$
$$Dx + Ey = F$$

has the following solution:

$$x = \frac{C * E - B * F}{A * E - B * D}$$

$$y = \frac{A * F - C * D}{A * E - B * D}$$

The problem is to write a program to solve the system given the values of A, B, C, D, E, and F.

(a) Write a complete definition of the problem including special processing.

(b) Design an algorithm to solve the problem. Since you cannot yet test for bad data, assume the data will be valid.

(c) What input values will cause a run-time error?

3.9. When the following Pascal program is executed,

```
program Question9 (input,output);
var
  Number, Digit1, Digit2, Digit3 : integer;
begin
  red (Number);
  Digit1 := Number div 100;
  Number := Number mod 100;
  Digit2 := Number div 10;
  Digit3 := Number mod 0;
  writeln (Digit1, Doigit, Digit3)
end.
```

the compiler used produces the following listing:

```
1    1      program Question9 (input,output);
2    1      var
3    1          Number, Digit1, Digit2, Digit3 : integer;
```

```
   4    1       begin
   5    1           red (Number);
>>>>>> Error    51
   6    1           Digit1 := Number div 100;
   7    1           Number := Number mod 100;
   8    1           Digit2 := Number div 10;
   9    1           Digit3 := Number mod 0;
  10    1           writeln (Digit1, Doigit, Digit3)
>>>>>> Error   104
  11    1       end.
```

Errors:
 51 : **':=' expected**
104 : **Undeclared identifier**

(a) Locate and correct all syntax errors in the program.

(b) Assume that all the syntax errors have been corrected. Will the program execute? Run the program. If run-time errors occur, correct the program to eliminate them.

(c) Describe the function of the program. Modify the program by inserting documentation, changing identifiers if necessary, and improving the output to make its function more apparent.

4. Selection

4.1
CONDITIONAL
EXECUTION

In Chapter 2 we discussed some basic tools of Pascal that allowed us to write simple programs involving input of numeric values, computations, and output of results. In the programs we wrote, statements were executed in sequence until the **end** was reached. Often, however, we need additional capabilities. For example, it is useful to make execution of a statement dependent upon some condition, or to choose to execute one of several statements depending on some condition. This involves the ability to alter the order in which statements are executed or the ability to select the statements to be executed. Consider the following example: We would like to write a program that reads in two real numbers, divides the first number by the second, and then prints the quotient. The algorithm appears simple enough.

```
begin
    Input dividend and divisor
    Divide dividend by divisor
    Output result
end.
```

When the algorithm is translated into Pascal, we obtain the program shown in Example 4.1.

EXAMPLE 4.1
Program to
Perform Divi-
sion with Real
Numbers

```pascal
program Division1 (input, output);

{*************************************
 * Program to input two real numbers, *
 * divide the first by the second,    *
 * and output the result.             *
 *************************************}

var
    Dividend, Divisor : real;

begin
    read (Dividend, Divisor);
    writeln (Dividend :8:2,' / ', Divisor :8:2,
        ' = ', Dividend / Divisor :8:2 )
end.
```

The program in Example 4.1 will work adequately as long as we are careful not to provide as input data a pair of real numbers, such as 12.0 and 0.0. Because division by zero is not permitted, the execution of the program with those values would lead to an error condition. We can improve the above program by first checking to see if the divisor is equal to zero and then performing the division only if it is not zero. The algorithm would now look something like this:

begin
    Input dividend and divisor
    if divisor = 0 **then**
        Output message indicating bad input
    else
        Divide dividend by divisor and output result
end.

The if . . . then . . . else Statement

In order to write the algorithm, we needed a way to represent a condition being tested, with the result of the test affecting what we do next. We did this by using the **if . . . then . . . else** statement. In pseudocode, this statement takes the following general form:

if condition **then**
    operations
else
    operations

The condition between the *if* and the *then* is an expression that is either true or false. If it is true, then the operations following the *then* are performed. If it is false then the operations following the *else* are performed.

In our example, the condition is the expression:

divisor = 0

The operation to be performed if the condition is true is:

output message indicating bad input

The operation to be performed if the condition is false is:

divide dividend by divisor and output result

To code this algorithm into Pascal, we use the **if . . . then . . . else** statement. Its general form is:

if condition **then**
    statement1
else
    statement2

As with pseudocode, the Pascal statement is a *double alternative* statement; that is, there are two alternatives. If the condition is true, then statement1, the "true alternative" (or the **then** clause), is selected. If the condition is false, then statement2, the "false alternative" (or the **else** clause), is selected. Figure 4.1 shows the *flowchart* for the **if . . . then . . . else** statement.

Figure 4.1 Flowchart of **if** . . . **then** . . . **else**

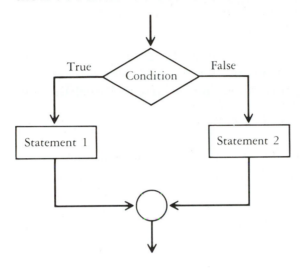

Thus, the program can be written as in Example 4.2.

EXAMPLE 4.2 Program to Divide Two Real Numbers and to Check for Zero Divisors

```
program Division2 (input, output);

{*****************************************
*   Program to input two real numbers,  *
*   divide the first by the second, and *
*   output the result, being careful    *
*   to check division by zero.          *
*****************************************}

var
    Dividend, Divisor : real;

begin
    read (Dividend, Divisor);
    if Divisor = 0 then
        writeln (' The divisor is zero ')
    else
        writeln (Dividend :6:2,' / ', Divisor :6:2,
            ' = ', Dividend/Divisor :6:2)
end.
```

If this program is executed with input values 6.0 and 2.0, the output will be:

`6.00 / 2.00 = 3.00`

On the other hand, if it is executed with input values 6.0 and 0.0, the output will be:

`The divisor is zero`

Note that the **if . . . then . . . else** statement is a single statement. Thus, there is no semicolon after the statement that makes up the **then** clause. Recall that in Pascal the semicolon is a statement separator.

4.2 THE TYPE BOOLEAN

As we just saw, the **if . . . then . . . else** statement allows us to select which of two statements we are to perform depending on the truth value of a condition when the program is being executed. To facilitate our work with expressions that are either true or false, Pascal provides us with a standard data type that has exactly two possible values. These values are:

false   true

Variables that can take only these values are often called *logical variables* or **boolean variables**, in honor of the nineteenth-century British mathematician, George Boole, who developed the algebra of logic.

To declare a variable to be of type boolean, we use a variable declaration of the following form:

```
var
    Flag, p, Found : boolean;
```

The variables "Flag," "p," and "Found" have been declared boolean and now can be assigned the values *true* or *false*. The assignments

`Flag := true`

`p := false`

`Found := true`

are all valid. To print the value of a boolean variable, we include it in the output list of a write or writeln statement. If the variable Found has the value true, then the statement:

`writeln (Found)`

outputs:

`true`

Boolean variables, however, cannot be used in the input list of a read or readln statement. The following read statement is *not* valid if Found is declared to be of type boolean, as above.

`read (Found)`

We will see later how we can write a program segment to input character data and interpret them as boolean values so that external assignments can be made to boolean variables.

Relational Operators

Boolean values usually arise from the evaluation of expressions that involve comparisons. For example, the expression "Divisor = 0," which we used in Example 4.2, produces a boolean result because it is either true or false that the value of Divisor is equal to zero. An expression that yields a boolean value of either true or false is called a *boolean expression*. Thus, Divisor = 0 is a boolean expression. The equal symbol (=) in the expression is called a **relational operator**. In Pascal there are seven relational operators, of which we shall consider six here. (The seventh is used with a data type that we will not study until later.) The relational operators are:

Operator	Meaning
=	is equal to
< >	is not equal to
<	is less than
>	is greater than
< =	is less than or equal to
> =	is greater than or equal to

The symbols $<>$, $<=$, and $>=$ are *compound symbols* and must be written as shown, with no blanks between the individual symbols. The order of the individual symbols may not be reversed. When these operators are used with integer or real expressions they yield boolean values. (They can also be used with expressions involving data types other than integer or real, as we will see later.) Thus, we have:

Expression	Value
$5=6$	false
$2<4$	true
$3.6<>4.1$	true
$7.1<=7.0$	false
$3+5=6$	false

Relational operators are given a lower priority than arithmetic operators; so when expressions involve both types of operators all arithmetic computations are performed before any of the relational operators are used. The precedence rules of arithmetic and relational operators, taken together, are:

1. $*$,$/$,**div**, **mod**
2. $+$, $-$
3. $=$, $<>$, $<$, $>$, $<=$, $>=$

The following examples illustrate the evaluation of expressions involving both arithmetic and relational operators:

$5 + 6 < 3 * 5$ **div** 2

Expression Evaluated	Result	Remains to be Evaluated
$3*5$	15	$5 + 6 < 15$ **div** 2
15 **div** 2	7	$5 + 6 < 7$
$5+6$	11	$11 < 7$
$11<7$	false	

Now let us look at an example involving parentheses:

5 mod 2 < = (7 + 5) **div** 10

Expression Evaluated	Result	Remains to be Evaluated
7 + 5	12	5 **mod** 2 < = 12 **div** 10
5 **mod** 2	1	1 < = **div** 10
12 **div** 10	1	1 < = 1
1 < = 1	true	

Since the result of evaluating a boolean expression is a boolean value, it can be assigned to a boolean variable. Consider the following program fragment:

```
var
    p, q : boolean;
    x, y : integer;

begin
    x := 5;
    y := 0;
    p := x = y;
    q := x+y <= x;
        .
        .
        .
```

After execution of these statements p is false and q is true. The assignment statement:

```
p := x=y
```

states that the expression on the right-hand side of the assignment operator is to be evaluated and the result assigned to p. Since $x = y$ is false, the value false is assigned to p.

Examples 4.3 and 4.4 illustrate some simple uses of boolean variables and expressions. They are self-explanatory and are therefore presented without showing all the steps involved in developing the algorithms.

EXAMPLE 4.3
Program to
Compute
Gross Salary

```
program Pay (input, output);

{*****************************************
* Program to compute the gross pay for *
* an employee.  The employee gets      *
* "straight-time" for the first 40     *
* hours worked and "time-and-a-half"   *
* for all hours worked in excess of    *
* 40 hours.                            *
*****************************************}

var
    HoursWorked :real; {hours worked last week}
    Rate : real;       {hourly salary rate}
    Overtime : real;   {overtime for week}
    Regular : real;    {regular hours for week}
    Salary :real;      {last week's gross pay}

begin
    {input hours worked and hourly rate}

    read (HoursWorked, Rate);

    {compute gross pay}

    if HoursWorked > 40.00 then
        Overtime := HoursWorked - 40.00
    else
        Overtime := 0;
    Regular := HoursWorked - Overtime;
    Salary := Regular * Rate + Overtime * Rate * 1.5;

    {output gross salary}

    writeln (' Gross pay: ',Salary :6:2)
end.
```

The if . . . then Statement

As we have said, the **if . . . then . . . else** construction is used to se-lect which of two statements we want to execute, based on the value of a boolean expression. The **if** statement, however, may also occur without an **else**. This is called the **if . . . then** construction and a flowchart for it is shown in Figure 4.2.

EXAMPLE 4.4
Program to Determine If Three Numbers Could Represent the Lengths of the Sides of a Right Triangle

```
program RightTriangle (input, output);

{***********************************
 * Program to determine if three    *
 * numbers could be the lengths of  *
 * the sides of a right triangle.   *
 * The largest number is input last.*
 ***********************************}

var
    a, b, c : integer; {Sides of triangle}
    Right : boolean;    {Boolean value set to true
                         if the triangle is a right
                         triangle, false otherwise}

begin
    {input the numbers}

    read (a, b, c);

    {test for sides of right triangle}

    Right := a*a + b*b = c*c;
    if Right then
        writeln (' The numbers form a right triangle')
    else
        writeln (' The numbers do not form a right triangle')
end.
```

The **if . . . then** statement is useful when you want to perform an action if a certain condition is true and simply bypass that action if the condition is false. In this case, the **else** is superfluous and may be omitted. For example, consider another version of the gross pay program, Example 4.5.

First we initialize Overtime to zero, then we check to see if the employee worked more than 40 hours. If the employee worked more than 40 hours, we compute the overtime—otherwise we do nothing. Either way, we next compute the regular hours worked, and finally we compute the gross pay. Compare this program to that in Example 4.3, where we used an **if . . . then . . . else** construct to control the order of execution. Note the use of the semicolon to separate the **if . . . then** statement from the statement that follows it.

Figure 4.2 Flow-chart of **if** . . . **then**

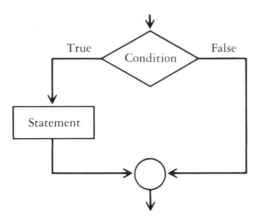

**EXAMPLE 4.5
Program to
Compute
Gross Salary
Using
if . . . then
Statement**

```pascal
program Pay (input, output);

{**********************************************
* Program to compute the gross pay for    *
* an employee.   The employee gets        *
* "straight-time" for the first 40 hours  *
* worked and "time-and-a-half" for all    *
* hours worked in excess of 40 hours.     *
**********************************************}

var
    HoursWorked :real;  {hours worked last week}
    Rate : real;        {hourly salary rate}
    Overtime : real;    {overtime for week}
    Regular : real;     {regular hours worked}
    Salary :real;       {last week's gross pay}

begin
    {input hours worked and hourly rate}

    read (HoursWorked, Rate);

    {compute gross pay}

    Overtime := 0.0;
    if HoursWorked > 40.00 then
        Overtime := HoursWorked - 40.00;
    Regular := HoursWorked - Overtime;
    Salary := Regular * Rate + Overtime * Rate * 1.5;

    {output gross salary}

    writeln (' Gross pay: ',Salary :6:2)
end.
```

Figure 4.3 Syntax diagram for **if** . . . **then** . . . **else**

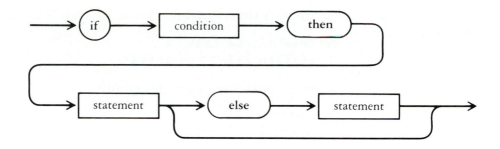

Figure 4.3 shows the syntax diagram for the **if** . . . **then** . . . **else** statement. It shows that the **else** clause is optional, in which case we have the **if** . . . **then** statement.

SELF-TEST 1

1. Determine if the following **if** . . . **then** . . . **else** statements are valid. If they are not valid, state why.

(a) ```
if x=y then
    writeln('They are equal');
else
    writeln('They are unequal')
```

(b) ```
if Weight <= 20.0 then
    Cost := Weight * 0.45
else
    Cost := Weight * 0.35
```

(c) ```
if sqr(b) < 4*a*c then;
    writeln('Complex roots')
else
    writeln('Real roots')
```

(d) ```
if x <> 0 then
    writeln('Not zero');
    x := 0
else
    writeln('Zero')
```

2. Evaluate the following expressions:

(a) $5 + 2 < = 3 - 5$

(b) $18 \bmod 3 < = (5 + 3) \operatorname{div} 2$

(c) $3.4 - 2.5 > 4.7/.2.4$

(d) $\operatorname{abs}(34.6 - 37 - 0) > 0.5$

3. Simplify the following. "Done" is a boolean variable.

```
if Done = true then
    writeln ('Job completed')
```

4. Study the following code carefully:

```
read(x);
if x mod 2 = 0 then
    writeln ('Even');
if x mod 2 <> 0 then
    writeln ('Odd')
```

(a) Rewrite the code using an **if . . . then . . . else** statement instead of two **if . . . then** statements.
(b) Which version is better and why?

Answers

1. (a) Invalid. There cannot be a semicolon before the **else**. (b) Valid. (c) Invalid. There cannot be a semicolon right after the **then** if we have an **else**. (d) Invalid. We cannot have more than one statement as part of the **then** clause.
2. (a) False (b) True (c) False (d) True
3.  ```
if Done then
    writeln ('Job completed')
```

Since Done is a boolean variable its value is either true or false. "Done = true" represents exactly the same value. As originally written, the computer is forced to determine that true = true is true or that false = true is false. This is not necessary.

4.  (a)  ```
read(x);
if x mod 2 = 0 then
    writeln ('Even')
else
    writeln ('Odd')
```

(b) The **if . . . then . . . else** version is better because it requires that the expression x **mod** 2 = 0 be evaluated only once. In the version using only **if . . . then** statements the expression will be evaluated twice, even when this is not necessary.

4.3 COMPOUND STATEMENTS

With the **if . . . then . . . else** and the **if . . . then** statements we have considered so far, we can only execute *one* statement based on the truth or falsity of some boolean expression. If we need to write a program that executes more than one statement based on the truth value of a condition, we would have to resort to the rather clumsy use of more than one **if . . . then** statement. For example, suppose we want to input two integers, *a* and *b*, and if necessary interchange their values so that the larger of the two integers is in *a*. A conditional test can be used to establish if an exchange is needed. If it is, then we will have to save one of the values in a temporary location while we copy the other. The algorithm to make the test and exchange looks like this:

if a < b **then**
    Store *a* in a temporary location
    Copy *b* into *a*
    Copy temporary into *b*

If *a* < *b*, we want to perform all three actions. This is indicated in the algorithm by indenting the statements with respect to the **if**. However, with our current knowledge of Pascal, we have to use two **if . . . then** statements to perform the exchange because the **then** clause in Pascal allows for only one statement.

```
temporary := a;
if temporary < b then
    a := b;
if temporary < b then
    b := temporary
```

Although the code does the job, it is unclear and repetitious. If we had a situation where we wished to execute a large number of statements based on a single condition, this approach would be very cumbersome indeed.

Fortunately, Pascal provides us with an easy way to designate a group of statements so that the whole group is executed as if it were a single statement. When the reserved words **begin** and **end** are used to bracket a group of statements, the whole group is called a **compound statement** and becomes an indivisible unit, as if it were *one* statement. Using a compound statement, we can rewrite our previous example as a single **if . . . then** statement.

```
if a < b then
   begin
      temporary := a;
      a := b;
      b := temporary
   end
```

The body of the compound statement consists of the three individual statements needed to effect the exchange. Here, however, the three statements will be executed in sequence, as if they were a single statement. Figure 4.4 shows the syntax diagram for a compound statement.

Semicolons are used to separate statements within the **begin** and **end** brackets. No semicolon is needed to separate the last statement from the reserved word **end.** Actually, to permit greater freedom in the use of semicolons, Pascal allows a semicolon to be placed at the end of the last statement in the body. The compound statement above can also be written as:

```
begin
   temporary := a;
   a := b;
   b := temporary;
end
```

When this is done, Pascal inserts a statement that does *nothing* between the last semicolon and **end**. This statement is called the *empty statement* or the **null statement**. It exists for the convenience of the programmer, to make the use of semicolons more flexible. In our example, the null statement is inserted where we put our comment.

```
begin
   temporary := a;
   a := b;
   b := temporary;
   {null statement}
end
```

Nested if Statements

The statement following the **then** or **else** in an **if . . . then . . . else** statement can be another **if . . . then . . . else** statement. The pro-

Figure 4.4 Syntax diagram of compound statement

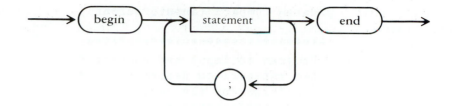

Figure 4.5 Flowchart of a nested **if** . . . **then** . . . **else** statement

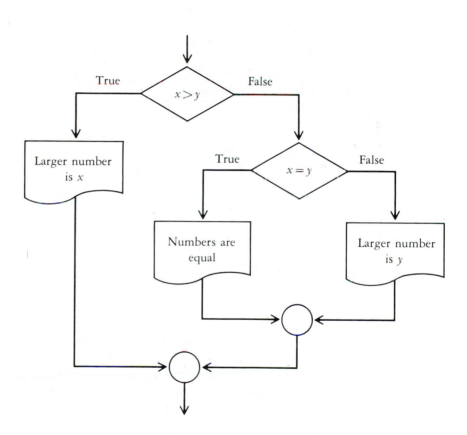

gram of Example 4.6 inputs two integers and prints the larger of the two. If they are equal, it prints the message "The numbers are equal." In order to do this, two **if** . . . **then** . . . **else** statements are needed, with the second **if** . . . **then** . . . **else** statement as the **else** clause of the first. When this occurs, the **if** . . . **then** . . . **else** statements are said to be *nested*. The flow of control of the nested **if** . . . **then** . . . **else** statement is shown in Figure 4.5.

**EXAMPLE 4.6
Program to
Compare Two
Integers**

```pascal
program Compare (input, output);

{*******************************
* Program to input and compare *
* two integers to determine    *
* the larger of the two.       *
*******************************}

var
   x, y : integer;

begin
   {input the numbers}

   read(x, y);

   {compare numbers to determine
    the larger}

   if x>y then
      writeln(' The larger number is ',x)
   else
      if x=y then
         writeln(' The numbers are equal')
      else
         writeln(' The larger number is ',y)
end.
```

When this nested **if . . . then . . . else** statement is executed, the computer first evaluates the boolean expression $x > y$. If the value is true, then the statement

```pascal
writeln(' The larger number is ',x)
```

is executed. If the value of $x > y$ is false, however, the statement to be executed is the second **if . . . then . . . else**. Therefore, the expression $x = y$ is evaluated. If $x = y$ is true then

```pascal
writeln(' The numbers are equal')
```

is executed. If it is false, then

```pascal
writeln(' The larger number is ',y)
```

is executed. Table 4.1 summarizes the flow of control.

Table 4.1 Flow of control for nested **if . . . then . . . else** statement

x > y	x = y	Statement Executed
true		writeln (' The larger number is ',x)
false	true	writeln (' The numbers are equal')
false	false	writeln (' The larger number is ',y)

Because the situation of making decisions based on the outcome of other decisions is very common, nested **if . . . then . . . else** statements occur frequently in computer programs. Great care must be taken when using such statements, since they often can be very difficult to interpret. Consider the following code:

```
if x>2 then
if x=5 then
writeln (x)
else writeln (x+2);
read (x)
```

What statement is executed when the value of x is 2? The difficulty in answering the question lies in determining to which of the two **if** statements the **else** belongs. That is, does the **else** go with **if** $x = 5$ **then** or with **if** $x > 2$ **then**? This well-known ambiguity is called the **dangling else problem**. In Pascal an **else** is always associated with the nearest unpaired **if**. Thus, the **else** of our example is associated with **if** $x = 5$ **then**. Hence, when x is 2 the expression $x > 2$ is false and the statement

```
read (x)
```

is executed.

We can rewrite the above code in a clearer manner by indenting it to make the relationship between an **if** and the corresponding **else** easier to see:

```
if x>2 then
    if x=5 then
        writeln (x)
    else
        writeln (x+2);
read (x)
```

When indentation is used to make the structure of nested **if** statements easier to see, care must be taken to indent properly. For example,

```
if x<5 then
    if x>2 then
        writeln (x)
else
    writeln (x+2);
read (x)
```

is deceptive and does not accurately show the program structure. The Pascal compiler does not see the indentation. It will associate the **else** with **if** x > 2 **then** and *not* with **if** x < 5 **then**, as the indentation implies.

A sometimes useful rule to follow when writing nested **if** statements is to balance every **if** with an **else**. For example,

```
if x<5 then
    if x>2 then
        writeln (x)
    else
        writeln (x+2)
else {do nothing};
read (x)
```

Here we used the null statement, represented by the comment {do nothing} to balance the first **if**. This approach is even more useful if more than two **if** statements are involved. Consider the following code:

```
if x<>9 then
    if x>=3 then
        if x<>5 then
            writeln (x)
        else
            writeln (x*x)
    else {do nothing}
else {do nothing}
```

Compare this to

```
if x<>9 then
if x>=3 then
if X<>5 then
writeln (x)
else writeln (x*x)
```

SELF-TEST 2   1. Determine if the following **if . . . then . . . else** statements are valid. If they are not valid, state why.

(a) ```
if x=y then
    begin
        x := sqr(x) + 3
        y := 0
    end
else
    writeln('They are unequal')
```

(b) ```
if Weight <= 20.0 then
    begin
        writeln(Weight);
        Cost := Weight * 0.45
    else
        Cost := Weight * 0.35
```

(c) ```
if sqr(b) < 4*a*c then
      writeln('Complex roots')
else
    if sqr(b)-4*a*c then
        writeln('One real root')
    else
```

(d) ```
if x = 0 then
    writeln('Zero')
else
    if x < 0 then
        writeln ('Negative')
    else
        writeln ('Positive')
```

2. Given the values 1 4 3 as input, what will be the output of each of the following program segments?

(a) ```
read(a,b,c);
   if a=1 then
     if b=2 then
       if c=3 then
           writeln('Three')
       else
           writeln('Two')
     else
         writeln('One')
   else
     writeln('None')
```

(b) ```
read(a,b,c);
   if a=1 then
      writeln('One');
   if b=2 then
      writeln('Two');
   if c=3 then
      writeln('Three');
   writeln('None')
```

3. Study the following program segment carefully.

```
read(x,y);
if x>=y then
    if y > 0 then
        begin
            x := x + 3;
            y := y - x
        end
    else
        y := y - 5
else
    if x + 5 >= y then
        y := 5 - y
    else
        x := x + y;
writeln(x,y)
```

Determine what the output will be for each of the following possible data values.

(a) 2 3

(b) − 5 20

(c) 5 4

(d) 1 0

Answers

1. (a) Invalid. The individual statements in the compound statement must be separated by semicolons. (b) Invalid. The **begin** of the compound statement is missing an **end**. (c) Invalid. The condition of the second **if** is not a boolean expression. (d) Valid.

2. (a) One   (b) One Three None

3. (a) 2 2   (b) 15 20   (c) 8 − 4   (d) 1 − 5

4.4 PROGRAM READABILILTY

In the previous section we saw how indentation helps to make nested **if . . . then . . . else** statements easier to understand. We have, in fact, been following indentation conventions in all of our programs. These conventions are strictly for the human reader. The Pascal compiler, as we pointed out earlier, ignores all indentations. The following code:

```
if x<5 then if x=2 then writeln(x) else writeln(x+2) else;read(x)
```

is just as understandable to the compiler as

```
if x<5 then
    if x=2 then
        writeln (x)
    else
        writeln (x+2)
else;
read (x)
```

However, the second version clearly is easier for a person to read. The second layout emphasizes the structure of the **if . . . then . . . else** statements, whereas the first layout provides no such information.

Obviously there are different ways to indent various structures of a Pascal program in order to make them more readable. The conventions we use are the most commonly used ones. You should feel free to use your own indentation conventions, but keep in mind that the purpose of indentation is to improve readability. The conventions used in this text are:

1. Line up on the left margin the program heading, **var** and **const**, and the first **begin** and final **end**. For example:

program Name (input, output);
const
  . . .
var
  . . .
begin
  . . .
end.

2. Indent all definitions and declarations with respect to their reserved words. For example:

const
  Largest = 10;
var
  x, y, : integer;
  p   : boolean;

3. Indent statements with respect to **begin . . . end** for the whole program, as well as with **begin . . . end** for compound statements. For example:

```
begin
   read (x);
   writeln (x)
end.
```

4. Do not put more than one statement on a line. For example:

```
read (x);
writeln (x)
```

is better than

```
read (x); writeln (x)
```

5. Indent **if . . . then . . . else** statements as follows:

```
if boolean-expression then
   statement1
else
   statement2
```

or as follows if compound statements are used:

```
if boolean-expression then
   begin
      statement1;
      statement2;
         .
         .
         .
      statementm
   end
else
   begin
      statement1;
      statement2;
         .
         .
         .
      statementn
   end
```

Note that our conventions *always* vertically align **begin** with **end** and **if** with **else**.

As we study new statements in Pascal, we will always use indentation conventions to make them as readable as possible.

SELF-TEST 3

1. The following code does exactly what the programmer intended. Rewrite it so that it is properly indented to reflect its function.

```
program Question1 (input, output);  var x,y,s : real;
begin read(x,y); if x<y then s := x    else if x>y  then
s := y    else  s := 0; writeln (s) end.
```

2. The following code is improperly indented. Indent it so as to reflect the program structure.

```
program Question2 (input, output);
var
   a,b,c : integer;
begin
read(a); read(b); read(c);
   if a > b then
      if c <= 10 then
a := 5
   else
      if c >= 10 then
         a := 10
      else
         a := 15
      else
         a := 20;
      writeln(a)
end.
```

Answers

```
1. program Question1 (input, output);
   var
      x,y,s : real;
   begin
      read(x,y);
      if x<y then
         s := x
      else
         if x>y then
            s := y
         else
            s := 0;
      writeln (s)
   end.
```

```
2. program Question2 (input, output);
   var
       a,b,c : integer;
   begin
       read(a);
       read(b);
       read(c);
       if a > b then
           if c <= 10 then
               a := 5
           else
               if c >= 10 then
                   a := 10
               else
                   a := 15
       else
           a := 20;
       writeln (a)
   end.
```

4.5 LOGICAL OPERATORS

Conditions and boolean variables can be combined by using *logical* or *boolean* operators. These operators are **and**, **or**, and **not**. The binary operators **and** and **or** are used to combine conditions into *compound conditions*. The unary operator **not** is used to reverse the truth value of a condition or boolean variable. Consider the boolean variables *a* and *b*. Table 4.2 illustrates what various operators do.

Table 4.2 Truth values for boolean operators

a	*b*	*a* and *b*
true	true	true
true	false	false
false	true	false
false	false	false

a	*b*	*a* or *b*
true	true	true
true	false	true
false	true	true
false	false	false

a	not *a*
true	false
false	true

Here are some examples of boolean operators used to construct compound conditions:

Expression	Value
(15 < = 20) **or** (55 = 33)	true
(15 < = 20) **and** (55 = 33)	false
not (15 < = 20)	false

The precedence of boolean operators taken together with arithmetic and relational operators is:

1. **not**
2. $*$, /, **div**, **mod**, **and**
3. +, −, **or**
4. =, < >, <, >, < =, > =

Because of the precedence of boolean operators, parentheses always should enclose arithmetic and relational expressions used with boolean operators.

The following example illustrates the evaluation of an expression involving all three types of operators.

(5 + 3 < > 3 − 1) **or** (7 + 5 < = 12 **div** 2)

Expression Evaluated	Result	Remains to be Evaluated
12 **div** 2	6	(5 + 3 < > 3 − 1) **or** (7 + 5 < = 6)
5 + 3	8	(8 < > 3 − 1) **or** (7 + 5 < = 6)
3 − 1	2	(8 < > 2) **or** (7 + 5 < = 6)
7 + 5	12	(8 < > 2) **or** (12 < = 6)
8 < > 2	true	true **or** (12 < = 6)
12 < = 6	false	true **or** false
true **or** false	true	

The expressions in the parentheses are evaluated first. Note that in Pascal:

12 < 14 **and** 2 = 5

is an *invalid* expression. By the precedence rules just described, the **and** operator has the highest precedence. Thus the expression to be evaluated first would have to be 14 **and** 2. This is a meaningless expression since **and** is a boolean operator and 14 and 2 are not boolean values.

Compound Conditions

Compound conditions are often used to make programs with complex nested **if** statements more understandable. For example, the nested conditional

```
if a<4 then
   if b >0 then
      w := a*a - 2*b
   else
      if a=3 then
         w := a*a - 2*b
```

can be written using a compound condition as

```
if ((a<4) and (b>0)) or (a=3) then
   w := a*a - 2*b
```

As an example of a program involving a compound decision, consider the following charge customer screening procedure. Whenever a customer wants to make a charge purchase, the sales clerk determines what to do based on the following information: if the purchase does not exceed $100, the customer's purchase does not include any tobacco, and the customer has brought the credit card, then approve the purchase, otherwise check with the credit department. The program to simulate the sales clerk's behavior is given in Example 4.7.

4.6
THE CASE
STATEMENT

Compound conditions are especially useful in situations where we need to test more than one condition to decide which of two actions to perform. When there are more than two actions to select, we can often use the **case** statement. This statement takes the general form:

```
case expression of
   case-label-list1 : statement1;
   case-label-list2 : statement2;
                .
                .
                .
   case-label-listn : statementn
end
```

**EXAMPLE 4.7
Program
Screen Credit**

```
program Screening (input, output);

{*****************************************
* Program to simulate credit screening  *
* by sales clerk. Clerk checks for       *
* amount of purchase, type of purchase,  *
* and availability of credit card.       *
* Credit is approved if purchase         *
* amount is less than $100, no tobacco   *
* is purchased, and credit card is       *
* available.                             *
*****************************************}

var
    Amount : integer;
    Tobacco: integer; { 1 if tobacco is purchased
                        0 if no tobacco is purchased}
    Card   : integer; { 1 if card is available
                        0 if card is not available}

begin
    read (Amount, Tobacco, Card);
    if (Amount <= 100) and (Tobacco = 0) and (Card = 1) then
        writeln ( ' Approve charge')
    else
        writeln (' Check with credit department')
end.
```

As an exercise, see if you can rewrite this program using nested
if statements.

The syntax diagram for the **case** statement is shown in Figure 4.6.

Figure 4.6 Syntax
diagram for **case**
statement.

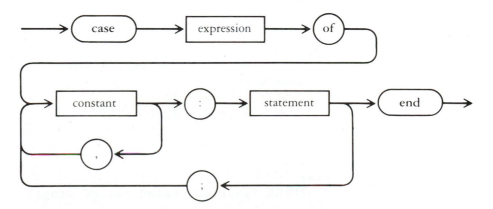

Consider the following set of nested **if** statements

```
if a=1 then
    x := x+1
else
    if a=3 then
        x := x+3
    else
        if a=4 then
            z := x
        else
            if a=5 then
                z := z + x
```

The **case** statement offers a simpler way to perform all of these tests:

```
case a of
    1 : x := x + 1;
    3 : x := x + 3;
    4 : z := x;
    5 : z := z + x
end
```

When the **case** statement is executed, the **selector expression** is evaluated. In our example, the variable a is the selector expression. The value of the selector expression must be one of the **case labels** listed in the body of the statement. In the example above, a must be 1, 3, 4, or 5. The **case** statement will execute *one and only one* of the alternative statements, depending on the value of the selector expression. If a is 1, then x : = x + 1 will be executed; if a is 3, then x : = x + 3 will be executed; if a is 4, then z : = x will be executed; if a is 5 then z : = z + x will be executed. The value of the selector expression cannot be any value other than those listed. If it is a value other than one of the case labels, the result of executing the **case** statement is *undefined*—that is, there is just no telling what will happen.

To avoid this situation, we can use an **if** statement with the **case** statement.

```
if (a>0) and (a<6) and (a<>2) then
    case a of
        1 : x := x + 1;
        3 : x := x + 3;
        4 : z := x;
        5 : z := z + x
    end
else
    {CASE label evaluated out of range}
```

More than one case label may appear in a case label list, but a given label may appear on only one list. The following is a valid **case** statement:

```
case a of
   1, 2 : x := x + 1;
   3, 6 : ;
      4 : z := z + x
end
```

Here, the permissible values of a are 1, 2, 3, 4, and 6. The assignment $x := x + 1$ will be executed if a is 1 or 2; the assignment $z := z + x$ will be executed if a is 4; nothing will be executed if a is 3 or 6. The null statement is associated with the case labels 3 and 6. Any of the statements in the body of the **case** statement can, of course, be compound statements.

The **case** statement also can be used in situations where we are working with a large range of possible values. For example, a professor awards letter grades on an examination based on the following cutoff values:

Letter Grade	Lowest Numerical Value
A	90
B	80
C	70
D	60
F	Below 60

We might think, at first glance, that we have to list all the possible numerical grades (we are assuming that they are integers from 0–100) in the case labels. However, this is not necessary. We can reduce considerably the number of labels needed by using division. Let us assume that the student's grade is assigned to the variable grade. The following **case** statement would print out the appropriate letter grades:

```
case grade div 10 of
            10, 9 : writeln('A');
                8 : writeln('B');
                7 : writeln('C');
                6 : writeln('D');
   5, 4, 3, 2, 1, 0 : writeln('F');
end
```

Note the indentation convention that we have been following with **case** statements: we vertically align **case** and **end**, and we indent the case labels and the statements. The **case** statement is one of the few places in a Pascal program where the reserved word **end** appears without a matching **begin**.

SELF-TEST 4

1. If a boolean expression uses boolean operators such as **and** and **or**, as well as relational operators, why must it use parentheses?

2. Which of the following boolean expressions are logically equivalent? *p* and *q* are two boolean variables.

(a) p < > q

(b) (p **and not** q) **or** (**not** p **and** q)

(c) **not** (p = q)

(d) (p **or** q) **or not** (p **and** q)

3. Rewrite each of the following statements in an equivalent form, without compound conditions.

(a)
```
if (x<y) or (w<z) then
    writeln ('Made it')
else
    writeln ('Did not make it')
```

(b)
```
if ((a>=b) or (c=5)) and (d=1) then
    writeln ('Made it')
else
    writeln ('Did not make it')
```

(c)
```
if ((a>=b) and (c=5)) or (d=1) then
    writeln ('Made it')
else
    writeln ('Did not make it')
```

(d)
```
if ((a>=b) and (c=5)) and (d=1) then
    writeln ('Made it')
else
    writeln ('Did not make it')
```

4. Rewrite the following as a single **if . . . then . . . else** statement.

```
if a <> 13 then
    if x > 7 then
        if w < 45 then
            b := b - 5
        else
            b := b + 5
    else
        b := b + 5
else
    b := b + 5
```

5. Determine if the following **case** statements are valid. If a statement is not valid, state why.

(a)
```
case Number of
   1,2 : a := 4;
     2 : a := 6;
     3 : a := 7;
     0 : a := 8
end
```

(b)
```
case a=b of
    true : a := 5;
    false : begin
               a := 6;
               write (a+b)
            end
end
```

(c)
```
case x*y-4 of
   0 : writeln (x);
   1 : x:=5;
   3 : case x of
          1 : y := 0;
          7 : y := y + 1
       end
end
```

(d)
```
case sqr(x) of
    1 : writeln('One');
    4 : writeln('Two');
    9 : writeln('Three');
   16 : writeln('Four')
end
```

Answers

1. Boolean expressions using boolean operators **and** or **or** must use parentheses because of the priority of these operators.

2. The logically equivalent expressions are a, b, and c.

3.

(a)
```
if x<y then
     writeln ('Made it)
else
     if w<z then
          writeln ('Made it)
     else
          writeln ('Did not make it')
```

(b)
```
if a>=b then
   if d=1 then
      writeln('Made it')
   else
      writeln('Did not make it')
else
   if c=5 then
      if d=1 then
         writeln('Made it')
      else
         writeln('Did not make it')
   else
      writeln('Did not make it')
```

(c) **if** a>=b **then**
    if c=5 **then**
      writeln('Made it')
    else
      if d=1 **then**
        writeln('Made it')
      else
        writeln('Did not make it')
  else
    if d=1 **then**
      writeln('Made it')
    else
      writeln('Did not make it')

(d) **if** a>=b **then**
    if c=5 **then**
      if d=1 **then**
        writeln('Made it')
      else
        writeln('Did not make it')
    else
      writeln('Did not make it')
  else
    writeln('Did not make it')

4. **if** (a<>13) **and** (x>7) **and** (w<45) **then**
    b := b - 5
  else
    b := b + 5

5. (a) Not valid. A case label can only be used once. 2 is used twice.
(b) Valid (c) Valid (d) Valid

     We will now look at the use of selection in the solution of a real problem.

APPLICATION

Income Tax Computation

The problem is to write a computer program that computes the tax of a single taxpayer, given the taxable income. To compute the tax, we will use the tax rate schedule in Table 4.3. This is an abbreviated schedule for the purpose of our problem. It would not be difficult to extend the program to handle the full tax schedule—that is, taxable incomes above $15,000.

The first outline of the algorithm is:

```
begin
   Input taxable income
   Compute tax
   Output tax
end.
```

APPLICATION

Income Tax Computation (*continued*)

The first statement, Input taxable income, needs no additional elaboration. The last statement, Output result, needs a little explanation.

Table 4.3 Tax rate schedule

Taxable Income		Tax Rate	
Not over $2,300		0	
Over—	But Not Over		of the Amount Over—
$2,300	$3,400	14%	$2,300
$3,400	$4,400	$154 + 16%	$3,400
$4,400	$6,500	$314 + 18%	$4,400
$6,500	$8,500	$692 + 19%	$6,500
$8,500	$10,800	$1,072 + 21%	$8,500
$10,800	$12,900	$1,555 + 24%	$10,800
$12,900	$15,000	$2,059 + 26%	$12,900

We will only be able to output the result if the income is less than $15,000 (the largest value in our tax rate schedule). We will use a boolean variable, Possible, to determine if we were able to compute the tax. If the computation was possible, we will output the result. The first statement becomes:

```
read (Income)
```

The last statement becomes:

```
if Possible then
    writeln (' Income Tax: $ ',Tax :7:2)
```

The statement "compute tax" needs additional elaboration. It requires that we use the information in the tax rate table to do the computation. To do this we will have to determine the range within which the income falls, and then use the appropriate tax calculation. This can be done by using nested **if . . . then . . . else** statements.

Note that we initialize the boolean variable Possible to true. If we fail
to compute the tax, we set it to false.

```
Possible := true;
if Income <=2300 then
  Tax := 0
else
  if Income <= 3400 then
    Tax := 0.14 * (Income - 2300)
  else
    if Income <= 4400 then
      Tax := 154 + 0.16 * (Income - 3400)
    else
      if Income <= 6500 then
        Tax := 314 + 0.18 * (Income - 4400)
      else
        if Income <= 8500 then
          Tax := 692 + 0.19 * (Income - 6500)
        else
          if Income <= 10800 then
            Tax := 1027 + 0.21 * (Income - 8500)
          else
            if Income <= 12900 then
              Tax := 1555 + 0.24 * (Income - 10800)
            else
              if Income <= 15000 then
                Tax := 2059 + 0.26 * (Income - 12900)
              else
                begin
                  writeln ('Income too large for program');
                  Possible := false
                end
```

We can now put everything together to obtain the full program.

```
program Incometax (input, output);

{********************************
 * Program to compute Federal   *
 * Income Tax for taxable Incomes *
 * up to $15,000                *
 ********************************}

var
    Income   : real;    {Taxable income}
    Tax      : real;    {Income tax}
    Possible : boolean; {Variable to indicate if
                         tax computation is possible}
```

APPLICATION   **Income Tax Computation (***continued***)**

```
begin

    {Input income}

    read (Income);

    {Compute tax}

    Possible := true;
    if Income <=2300 then
      Tax := 0
    else
      if Income <= 3400 then
        Tax := 0.14 * (Income - 2300)
      else
        if Income <= 4400 then
          Tax := 154 + 0.16 * (Income - 3400)
        else
          if Income <= 6500 then
            Tax := 314 + 0.18 * (Income - 4400)
          else
            if Income <= 8500 then
              Tax := 692 + 0.19 * (Income - 6500)
            else
              if Income <= 10800 then
                Tax := 1027 + 0.21 * (Income - 8500)
              else
                if Income <= 12900 then
                  Tax := 1555 + 0.24 * (Income - 10800)
                else
                  if Income <= 15000 then
                    Tax := 2059 + 0.26 * (Income - 12900)
                  else
                    begin
                      writeln ('Income too large for program');
                      Possible := false
                    end;
    if Possible then
      writeln (' Income Tax: $ ', Tax :7:2)
end.
```

Given the following input:

13421

the output will be:

Income Tax: $ 2194.46

Given the input:

16790

the output will be:

Income too large for program

APPLICATION

Computation of the Day of the Year

We want a program that will compute the day of the year given the month, day of the month, and year. For example, if the input to the program is:

2   7   1983

the output should be:

2/7/1983 is day 38 of 1983

The initial attempt at the algorithm is:

begin
    Input month, day, year
    Compute day of year
    Output day of year
end.

Expanding "Compute day of year," we use a **case** statement to compute the day of the year:

```
case Month of
    1  : DayOfYear := Day;
    2  : DayOfYear := 31 + Day;
    3  : DayOfYear := 59 + Day;
    4  : DayOfYear := 90 + Day;
    5  : DayOfYear := 121 + Day;
    6  : DayOfYear := 151 + Day;
    7  : DayOfYear := 182 + Day;
```

APPLICATION

Computation of the Day of the Year (*continued*)

```
      8  : DayOfYear := 212 + Day;
      9  : DayOfYear := 242 + Day;
     10  : DayOfYear := 273 + Day;
     11  : DayOfYear := 303 + Day;
     12  : DayOfYear := 334 + Day
end
```

This solution, however, is incomplete. We failed to take leap years into consideration. The following code needs to be added after the **case** statement:

```
if year mod 4 = 0 then
   if year mod 100 <> 0 then
     if month > 2 then
         DayOfYear := DayOfYear + 1
```

We can now put everything together to obtain the following program:

```
program YearDay (input, output);


{********************************
* Program to compute the day of *
* the year, given the month,    *
* day of the month, and year.   *
********************************}

var
    Day        : integer;
    Month      : integer;
    Year       : integer;
    DayOfYear  : integer;
    Valid      : boolean;

begin

    read (Month, Day, Year);

    { validate the month and compute the day of year}

    Valid := (Month >0) and (Month < 13);
    if not Valid then
        writeln (' Illegal month. Please correct')
    else
```

APPLICATION

**Computation
of the
Day of the
Year**
(*continued*)

```
begin
  case Month of
    1  : DayOfYear := Day;
    2  : DayOfYear := 31 + Day;
    3  : DayOfYear := 59 + Day;
    4  : DayOfYear := 90 + Day;
    5  : DayOfYear := 121 + Day;
    6  : DayOfYear := 151 + Day;
    7  : DayOfYear := 182 + Day;
    8  : DayOfYear := 212 + Day;
    9  : DayOfYear := 242 + Day;
   10  : DayOfYear := 273 + Day;
   11  : DayOfYear := 303 + Day;
   12  : DayOfYear := 334 + Day
  end {of CASE}

  {Check if it is a leap year and make adjustment}

  if Year mod 4 = 0 then
    if Year mod 100 <> 0 then
      if Month > 2 then
          DayOfYear := DayOfYear + 1;

  write (Month :3,' / ',Day :4,' / ', Year :5,
        ' is day ');
  writeln (DayOfYear :4, ' of ', Year :5)
end {of ELSE}
end.
```

**4.7
COMMON
ERRORS**

Selection statements provide a programmer with many potential error sources. Perhaps the most common error involves the placement
of semicolons in the **if . . . then . . . else** statement. A semicolon
should *not* appear just before the **else**. Such a semicolon will be detected as a syntax error. A more subtle error and, therefore, more difficult to find, is illustrated in the following example:

```
if x<0 then;
    writeln ('The number is negative');
read(x)
```

This is yet another case of a misplaced semicolon, but this one is not a
syntax error. Here the statement writeln ('The number is negative')
will be executed whether $x < 0$ is true or false. Because of the extra
semicolon immediately following the **then**, the compiler thinks that

the **then** clause of the **if . . . then** statement consists of the null statement. The same error would occur if an **else** were erroneously followed by a semicolon.

Remember to use **begin** . . . **end** pairs around each compound statement. Omitting either a **begin** or an **end** may be detected as a syntax error. Omitting both, on the other hand, may cause the program to execute incorrectly. Be especially careful when changing programs. You may introduce the need for **begin** . . . **end** pairs when you modify structures in such a way that compound actions are now used where single statements were present earlier.

Boolean expressions are also often responsible for many errors. The most common errors with boolean expressions involve a lack of understanding of the precedence rules of the boolean operators **not**, **and**, and **or**. If you use parentheses with these operators you should be able to avoid trouble most of the time. You also must remember that these operators must have boolean operands. The expression

```
if x <> (5 or 8) then
```

is not valid because 5 and 8 are not boolean variables. The correct expression is:

```
if (x <> 5) or (x <> 8) then
```

Using **not** can be quite tricky. The expression:

```
if (not Found) and (not Finished) then
```

is *not* equivalent to the expression:

```
if not (Found and Finished) then
```

It is, however, equivalent to:

```
if not (Found or Finished) then
```

A more subtle error assumes that two **if . . . then** statements with logically opposite conditions are equivalent to a single **if . . . then . . . else** statement. For example, the pair of statements

```
if Number >= 40 then
   Number := 0;
if Number < 40 then
   Number := 5;
```

is *not* equivalent to

```
if Number >= 40 then
   Number := 0
else
   Number := 5;
```

The **case** statement is also often the source of run-time errors. This occurs when the selector expression evaluates to a value that is not one of the case labels. Some Pascal compilers provide a special label called **else** or **otherwise**. The action associated with this label is taken when the selector expression is evaluated to a value not matching one of the case labels. This, however, is not a standard feature. To minimize run-time errors with **case** statements, use **if . . . then . . . else** statements to check for ranges on selector expressions whenever possible.

4.8 CHAPTER REVIEW

Pascal statements are normally executed in sequence until the delimiter **end.** is reached. Sometimes a Pascal program must alter this order of execution, particularly when it is necessary to choose from several alternative operations.

We use the **if . . . then . . . else** statement in Pascal to choose which of two alternative operations should be performed, based on the truth value of a condition. If the condition is true, then one statement is executed. If the condition is false, then the other statement is executed.

Conditions may be either true or false. Variables that may assume either of the values true or false are called boolean variables or logical variables. To declare a variable to be of type boolean we say:

```
var
   variablename : boolean
```

The value of a boolean variable may be output from a Pascal program, but a boolean variable may not be included in the input list of a read or readln statement.

Relational operators are used in comparisons. Pascal has seven relational operators, six of which are:

Operator	Meaning
=	is equal to
< >	is not equal to
<	is less than
>	is greater than
< =	is less than or equal to
> =	is greater than or equal to

Relational operators are given a lower priority than arithmetic operators; so, in expressions involving both types of operators, all arithmetic computations are performed before any of the relational operators are used.

The **if** statement may occur without an **else**. Such a statement is called an **if . . . then** statement. The **if . . . then** statement is useful when you want to perform an action if a certain condition is true and simply bypass that action if the condition is false.

In many instances in the Pascal language, multiple statements need to be treated as a single statement unit. To facilitate this, the reserved words **begin** and **end** are used to bracket a group of statements. The whole group is called a **compound statement**.

Pascal provides the **empty statement**, or **null statement**, to make the use of semicolons more flexible. A semicolon inserted after a statement, but not separating that statement from a following statement (because there is no following statement), is considered to be separating from an empty statement.

When an **if . . . then . . . else** statement occurs within another **if . . . then . . . else** statement, we say that one statement is **nested** within the other. Since making decisions based on the outcome of other decisions is common, nested **if . . . then . . . else** statements occur frequently. Indentation, to improve readability, is particularly important when statements are nested.

Conditions and boolean variables can be combined using boolean operators, namely **and**, **or**, and **not**. The precedence of all operators we have presented up to this point, including boolean operators, is:

1. **not**
2. *, /, **div**, **mod**, **and**
3. +, −, **or**
4. =, < >, <, >, < =, > =

Because of the precedence rules of boolean operators, parentheses always should enclose arithmetic and relational expressions used with boolean operators.

When there are more than two actions from which to choose, we can use the **case** statement. When the **case** statement is executed, the selector expression is evaluated. Based upon its value, whichever one statement has the appropriate value in its case-label-list is executed. If the selector expression evaluates to a value that does not appear in the case-label-list, then the result of executing the **case** statement is undefined.

**4.9
EXERCISES**

4.1. Fill in the blanks in each of the following:

(a)   Decision making is accomplished with the _____ statement.

(b)   A condition may have one of two values: either _____ or _____.

(c)   The **else** portion is performed when the condition tested in an **if** statement is _____.

(d)   Variables that can only take on the values true or false are often called _____ variables or _____ variables.

(e)   If the variable test has the value true then the statement writeln (test) outputs _____.

(f)   Boolean variables usually arise from the evaluation of expressions that involve_____.

(g)   Relational operators are given a (lower/higher) _____ priority than arithmetic operators.

(h)   When the reserved words **begin** and **end** are used to bracket a group of statements, the whole group is called a _____ statement.

(i)   In Pascal, an **else** is always associated with the _____ **if**.

(j)   **and**, **or**, and **not** are called _____ operators.

(k) When the value of the selector expression does not match one of the labels in a **case** statement, the result of executing the **case** statement is _____.

(l)   The **case** statement is one of the few examples in Pascal in which the reserved word **end** appears without a matching _____.

4.2. Answer each of the following true or false. If your answer is false, state why.

(a) In Pascal, statements are always executed in sequence until the **end.** is reached.

(b) Suppose a program contains the statement a : = b/c, and during the execution of the program, c will become equal to zero and stay zero. This will cause a serious error and the program will terminate execution.

(c) When the condition in an **if . . . then . . . else** is evaluated and the condition is true, the **then** portion is performed and the **else** portion is bypassed.

(d) Boolean variables cannot be used in the input list of a read or readln statement.

(e) The second operation to be performed in the following expression:

3 **mod** 2 > (6 − 2 ∗ 4) **div** 7

is **div**.

(f) The value of x after the following correct Pascal statement is performed

x : = 3 + 2 < = 35 **div** 7

is true.

(g) The **if . . . then . . . else** statement in Pascal is flexible in the sense that either the **else** or the **then** may be omitted in simpler decision-making situations.

(h) The **begin . . . end** brackets in Pascal facilitate the insertion of multiple statements in places where normally only one statement is allowed.

(i) The null statement has no effect and is ignored by Pascal.

(j) The logical **and** operation causes a boolean expression such as "a **and** b" to be true only when both boolean variables a and b are true.

(k) Because of the precedence of boolean operators, parentheses should always enclose arithmetic and relational expressions used with boolean operators.

(l) The third operation to be performed in the following:

(7 **mod** 2 > = 9 **div** 8) **and** (3 ∗ 8 > = 16 − 5)

is > = .

(m) The value of the following expression is true:

11 < = 92 **or** 15 > = 5

(n) The purpose of indentation is to improve readability.

4.3. Describe the function(s) performed by each of the following statements:

(a) ```
if a = 1 then
    writeln (' a is equal to 1')
else
    writeln (' a is not equal to 1')
```

(b) ```
x := a + b <= c mod d
```

(c) ```
if HoursWorked > 40.00 then
    Overtime := HoursWorked - 40.00
else
    Overtime := 0
```

(d) ```
if DayOfYear = 170 then
    writeln (' This must be June')
```

(e) ```
if DayOfYear = 200 then
begin
    writeln (' This must be July');
    Month := 7;
    writeln (' We should go swimming')
end
```

(f) ```
if (Sex = 1) or (Sex = 2) then
    writeln (' code is correct')
else
    writeln (' code is incorrect')
```

(g) ```
if (Sex = 1) or (Sex = 2) then
    if Sex = 1 then
        writeln (' female')
    else
        writeln (' male')
else
    writeln (' code is incorrect')
```

(h) ```
if Sex = 1 then
    writeln (' female');
if Sex = 2 then
    writeln (' male');
if (Sex <> 1) and (Sex <> 2) then
    writeln (' code is incorrect')
```

Note: Carefully compare and contrast the Pascal code in parts (g) and (h).

```
(i) if a = 5 then
       if b = 6 then
           writeln (' 7')
       else writeln (' 8')
```

```
(j) if a = 1 then
       if b = 1 then
           if c = 1 then
               if d = 1 then
                   writeln (' someone likes 1s')
```

```
(k) if (a=1) and (b=1) and (c=1) and (d=1) then
       writeln (' someone likes 1')
```

Note: Carefully compare and contrast the Pascal code in parts (j) and (k).

```
(l) if a=1 then if b=1 then if c=1 then if d=1 then
    writeln (' Someone does not like indentation')
```

```
(m) case Sex of
       1 : writeln (' female')
       2 : writeln (' male')
    end
```

```
(n) case Celebration of
       1 : writeln (' Christmas');
       2 : writeln (' Easter');
       3 : writeln (' Thanksgiving');
       4 : writeln (' Summer Vacation')
    end
```

```
(o) case Grade div 10 of
       9,10 : writeln (' excellent');
          8 : writeln (' good');
          7 : writeln (' satisfactory');
          6 : writeln (' pass');
        4,5 : writeln (' failed - should work harder');
    0,1,2,3 : writeln (' hopeless')
    end
```

4.4. What does each of the following Pascal statements print?

```
(a) writeln (3 > 4)
```

```
(b) writeln (7 <= 11)
```

```
(c) writeln (17 <> 2*2*2*2+1)
```

(d) **writeln (true and** true, true **and false)**

(e) **writeln (false and** true, false **and false)**

(f) **writeln (true or** true, true **or false)**

(g) **writeln (false or** true, false **or false)**

(h) **writeln (not** true, **not** false)

(i) **writeln (false or** true **or** false **or false)**

(j) **writeln (true and** false **and** true **and** true)

(k) **writeln (true and** false **or** true)

(l) **writeln (not** true **or** true **and not** true)

4.5 Write Pascal statements to accomplish each of the following tasks:

(a) Determine if an exam grade (0 to 100) is greater than or equal to 60. If it is, print the message "passed," otherwise print the message "failed."

(b) Declare the variables *a*, *b*, and *c* to be boolean.

(c) A boolean variable Rain has the value true if it is raining and false if it is not raining. Test the variable and print a message to tell whether or not it is raining.

(d) Using only a single write statement, print the message "true" if *x* is equal to *y*, otherwise print the message "false."

(e) The real variable Hours contains a number from 0 to 100. Write a nested **if . . . then . . . else** construction to print the messages indicated below:

Hours	Message
$0 <= Hours <= 30$	excessive absence
$30 < Hours <= 50$	normal
$50 < Hours <= 70$	excessive overtime
$70 < Hours <= 100$	crazy

(f) The lengths of the sides of a triangle are in real variables *a*, *b*, and *c*. For *a*, *b*, and *c* to actually be correct, the sum of any two must be (strictly) greater than the third. Write a single **if . . . then . . . else** to determine if *a*, *b*, and *c* truly represent a triangle. If yes, then print "triangle," otherwise print "not a triangle."

(g) A positive integer is stored in p. Use a **case** statement to print a message telling whether the number is odd or even.

4.6. Write a program that reads three numbers and prints the largest of the three numbers.

4.7. Write a program that reads four numbers and prints the largest of the four numbers. Considering the limited subset of the Pascal language with which you are familiar, comment on the feasibility of preparing a program to read 10 numbers and print the largest of the 10 numbers.

4.8. Write a Pascal program that calculates a person's gross pay based on the hours worked each day of the week. The program reads 7 numbers that represent the hours worked on Monday, Tuesday, Wednesday, Thursday, Friday, Saturday, and Sunday, respectively. The program also reads an eighth number representing the person's hourly salary. The following rules apply:

(a) Any and all hours worked on weekends are paid at double-time (i.e., twice the person's hourly rate).

(b) The first 40 hours worked during the week (i.e., Monday through Friday) are compensated at straight-time, which is equal to the person's base salary times hours worked.

(c) Any hours worked in excess of 40 hours during the week are compensated at time-and-one-half, which is 1.5 times the person's hourly rate.

Your program should read the data for one employee and determine and print the gross pay due that employee for the week.

Try your program with the following sets of data:

```
8  8  8  8  8  0  0  5.00
10 10 10 10 10  0  0  4.00
8  8  8  8  0  0  0  4.50
0  0  0  0  0  8  8  6.00
8  8  8  8  8  8  8  6.50
10 10 10 10 10  8  0  6.25
```

4.9. One of the most popular gambling games in casinos throughout the world is the game of craps. The rules vary somewhat, but the basic game goes something like this:

Roll two dice (each of which contains six faces valued 1, 2, 3, 4, 5, 6). Calculate the sum of the faces showing on the two dice. If the sum is 2, 3, or 12, then the person loses. If the sum is 7 or 11, then the person wins. If the sum is 4, 5, 6, 8, 9, or 10 then the person neither wins nor loses but must roll again. The goal on the next and all subsequent rolls is to match the 4, 5, 6, 8, 9, or 10 (i.e., the roller's "point") to win; if a 7 is rolled after the first roll, then the person loses.

We will see the game of craps again in this book. For now, we are concerned with only the first roll. Write a Pascal program that reads a pair of integers representing the faces of two dice. Calculate the sum of the faces showing on the two dice. Write a **case** statement to handle the decision-making operations necessary on the first roll: **if** the person rolls 2, 3, or 12 **then** write the message "you lose." **If** the person rolls 7 or 11 **then** write "you win," and **if** the person rolls 4, 5, 6, 8, 9, or 10 **then** write "your point is (sum of the two dice)—roll again."

4.10. The quadratic equation

$$ax^2 + bx + c = 0$$

when solved for x has two roots, namely:

x = (−b + sqrt (b * b − 4 * a * c)) / (2 * a)

and

x = (−b − sqrt (b * b − 4 * a * c)) / (2 * a)

A simple program to determine the roots of a quadratic equation might read a, b, and c and then calculate the two roots according to the above formulas. For many possible sets of values for a, b, and c this would work well, but several combinations of a, b, and c could cause serious problems.

For example, suppose your program reads the value 0 for a. Most computer systems would consider this to be a serious error and would probably terminate execution in drastic fashion, preventing completion of the program's calculations. Thus, **if** statements are needed in a program such as this to prevent calculations that might lead to trouble.

Another potential problem is the calculation of

sqrt (b * b − 4 * a * c)

The quantity in parentheses is called the discriminant, and it is critical to the calculation of the roots of the quadratic equation. If the discriminant is zero, then both formulas above yield the same results, and the equation has two identical roots. If the discriminant is negative, then the roots are imaginary because of the calculation of the square root of a negative quantity. This problem is interesting because it reveals the subtleties that are often involved in developing computer programs to solve numerical problems. The message is: be careful!

Write a Pascal program that reads three real numbers (a, b, and c) and determines and prints the two roots of the quadratic equation for which a, b, and c are coefficients. If a is zero, then print the message "not a quadratic equation." If the discriminant is zero, then print the message "both roots are identical" and print the root. If the discriminant is negative, then print the message "the roots are imaginary." Run your program with several sets of input data to test these various cases.

4.11. Write a Pascal program that reads a date as three variables, namely month (1–12), day (1–31), and year (e.g., 1985), and prints the date, as in:

January 31, 1984

Use the **case** statement to convert the month number to the month name.

4.12. A palindrome is a number (or word or sentence) which reads the same forward as backward. For example, each of the following is a palindrome:

787
123454321
able was I ere I saw elba

and, if we ignore blanks,

a man a plan a canal panama

Write a Pascal program that reads a five-digit integer and determines if it is a palindrome.

4.13. A common data processing application of computers is in billing systems. When a customer hasn't paid a bill, computerized billing systems are designed to repeatedly request payment in increasingly harsh words. A customer who has let payment slip 30 days may be politely reminded that the bill is due. A customer whose bill is 120 days old may be threatened with legal action if the bill is not paid immediately. "Dunning" is the process of making repeated and insistent demands upon a debtor for payment of a debt.

Write a Pascal program that reads two numbers, namely the amount owed by a debtor and the number of days that this amount owed is past due. Your program should print a dunning message that indicates the severity of the indebtedness. If the amount is less than 30 days old, then be very polite in requesting payment. If the amount is 30–59 days old, then ask if the debtor has overlooked the payment and apologize for bothering the debtor. If the amount is 60–89 days old, then remind the debtor that credit is a privilege not to be abused and easily can be lost. If the amount is 90 days old, or older, then threaten legal action if the bill is not paid within 72 hours of receipt of the notice.

5. Repetition

The programs we have written so far probably appear trivial to you in one important way: they can only process one set of values for a given execution. For example, we were able to compute the gross income for only one employee. If we wished to calculate the gross income for two or more employees we would have to run the program two or more times! It would be much better if we could provide our program with a list of employees, whose gross salaries we desire to compute, and let the program automatically process the whole list. In short, we would like some or all of the actions of the program to be executed more than once, but with different data items.

The steps of an algorithm or program that are executed more than once are called a **loop**: a series of steps that are *iterated* or *executed repetitively.* We often need to iterate the execution of some steps of an algorithm for two reasons:

1. We need to perform the same operations on different data.
2. We need to repeat a group of operations in order to solve the problem.

The situation we described with the gross salary program falls into the first category. We are interested in repeating the program with different data for each employee. We will see examples of the second category later where we start with a single value and repeat computations until we obtain the desired result.

In computer programming there are two forms of loops: the **conditional loop,** or *indeterminate loop,* and the **counter-controlled loop.** A conditional loop is repeated as long as, or until, some condition is true. A counter-controlled loop is repeated a given number of times, while the iterations are counted.

Suppose you want to write a program to compute the average of ten numbers. Our first attempt at the algorithm might look like:

```
begin
    Input the numbers
    Compute the average
    Output the average
end.
```

Although the algorithm will work, it requires that we declare ten variables, one for each of the numbers to be averaged, input the values of all the variables first, and finally compute and output the average. This is not only unnecessary, but it would become intolerable if we attempted to generalize our program to average one thousand numbers.

A much better approach takes advantage of the fact that we do not need to have all the numbers available at once. All we need to do is keep a running total of the numbers we are to average. To calculate the average, we divide the total by the number of values we have. This suggests that we input one number at a time and add that number to the total until we have read all the numbers. Then we divide the total by ten to obtain the average. The algorithm to do this is:

begin
    Initialize total to 0
    Initalize count to 0
    repeat
        Input a number
        Add number to total
        Add 1 to count
    until count is equal to 10
    Compute average
    Output average
end.

In pseudocode, the conditional loop is expressed by bracketing the actions to be repeated with the words **repeat** and **until**. This algorithm requires that the three actions,

Input number
Add number to total
Add 1 to count

be repeated until the condition,

count is equal to 10

is true. The three actions are known as the *body of the loop* and the condition is called the **termination condition.** First, the actions of the body are executed, then the condition is evaluated. If the condition is true, the statement execution leaves the loop and continues by processing the statements following the loop. If the condition is false, the statements in the body are executed again. Note that we not only have to keep a running total, but also we must count the numbers as they are read in. This is to make sure that we input exactly ten numbers. Also note that in order to accumulate the total correctly and to count properly the numbers being input, we must first *initialize* both to zero.

The repeat . . . until Statement

Pascal provides a conditional repetition statement equivalent to the one we used in our algorithm. It has the general form:

repeat
    statement1;
    statement2;
       .
       .
       .
    statementn
until boolean expression

The reserved words **repeat** and **until** are used to bracket the body of the loop. Thus, the statements of the loop are a compound statement. This is an example of a compound statement where we do not use **begin** and **end** to set off the statements. To reflect the fact that the body of the loop is a compound statement, the **repeat . . . until** statement is indented by vertically aligning **repeat** and **until**. The boolean expression following **until** is the termination condition of the loop. Figure 5.1 shows the syntax diagram for a **repeat . . . until** statement.

    The flow of control through the loop is:

1. Execute the compound statement that makes up the body of the loop.

Figure 5.1 Syntax diagram for **repeat** . . . **until**

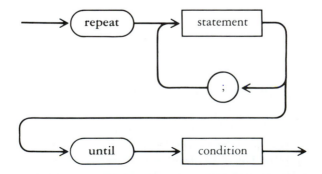

2. Evaluate the boolean expression. If the result is true, terminate the loop and continue execution with the statement following it. If the boolean expression is false, execute the body of the loop again.

An important property of the **repeat . . . until** loop is that the *body is executed at least once.* This is true because the termination condition is tested at the bottom of the loop. Figure 5.2 shows a flowchart illustrating the flow of control through a **repeat . . . until** loop.

Figure 5.2 Flow of control through a **repeat** . . . **until** loop

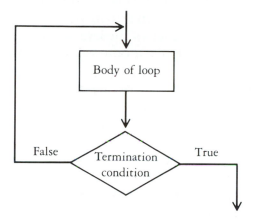

We can now code our algorithm into Pascal:

EXAMPLE 5.1 Program to Compute the Average of Ten Numbers Using repeat . . . until

```
program Average (input, output);
{**************************
 * Program to compute the  *
 * average of ten numbers. *
 **************************}
var
    Number, Total, Mean : real;
    Count : integer;

begin
    {Initialize count and total}

    Count := 0;
    Total := 0.0;

    repeat
        read (Number);
        Total := Total + Number;
        Count := Count + 1
    until Count = 10;
```

**EXAMPLE 5.1
Program to
Compute the
Average of Ten
Numbers Us-
ing repeat . . .
until**
(*continued*)

```
{compute and output average}

    Mean := Total / 10.0;
    writeln (' The average is ',Mean :8:2)
end.
```

Now, let us consider another example of a program using a **repeat
. . . until** loop. The problem is to find the largest of 100 integers in
the input file. The approach is to inspect one value at a time as it is being read and to keep track of the largest value seen *so far* as we move
through the input file. Each new value is compared against the current largest value. If it is larger, it becomes the new candidate for the
largest. If the new value is not larger than the largest so far, we keep
the current largest and read in the next value. As the initial candidate
for the largest value we will use the first value read.

**EXAMPLE 5.2
Program to
Find the Larg-
est Integer**

```
program Largest (input, output);

{****************************************
* Program to find the largest integer *
* in a file containing 100 integers.   *
****************************************}

var
    Number, Largest, Count : integer;

begin
    {Initialize count and largest}

    Count := 0;
    Largest := -maxint;

    {Read one number at a time and compare to current
    value of largest. If number is larger than
    largest then replace the value of largest with
    the value of number}

    repeat
        read (Number);
        Count := Count + 1;
        if Number > Largest then
            Largest := Number
    until Count >= 100;
```

**EXAMPLE 5.2
Program to
Find the Larg-
est Integer**
(*continued*)

```
{output largest value}

    writeln (' The largest value is: ' Largest :8)
end.
```

The while . . . do Statement

Conditional loops in Pascal can also be constructed using the **while
. . . do** statement, whose general form is

while boolean expression **do**
    statement

Note that the **while . . . do** statement allows for the repetition of a
single statement based on the truth value of a boolean expression,
the *condition for repetition*. The statement is repeated *while* the
boolean expression remains true. When the boolean expression becomes false, processing continues with the execution of statements
following the **while . . . do** structure.

    When we wish to repeat more than one action, we must use a
compound statement. In this case, the **while . . . do** statement has
the following form:

while boolean expression **do**
    begin
        statement1;
        statement2;
           .
           .
           .
        statementn
    end

The syntax diagram for the **while . . . do** statement is shown in Figure 5.3.

    The **while . . . do** statement is executed as follows:

1. Evaluate the boolean expression. If the value is true, execute the
   body of the loop. If the value is false, execute the statement following the body.
2. After executing the body of the loop return to evaluate the boolean expression.

Figure 5.3 Syntax
diagram for
while . . . **do** loop

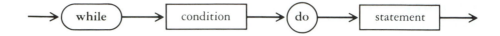

Figure 5.4 illustrates the flow of control for a **while . . . do** statement.

In contrast to the **repeat . . . until** statement, the boolean expression for a **while . . . do** statement is evaluated at the *top* of the loop rather than at the bottom. Thus, the body of a **while . . . do** statement need not necessarily be executed at all; that is, if the boolean expression is initially false, then program execution will skip over the loop entirely and proceed with the next statement. The boolean expression for a **repeat . . . until** loop specifies the *termination condition,* while the boolean expression for a **while . . . do** loop specifies the *condition for repetition.* The following program segments illustrate this difference:

```
{multiply the integers from 1 to 5}
Product := 1;
Count := 1;
repeat
   Product := Product * Count;
   Count := Count + 1
until Count > 5
```

Rewriting the above **repeat . . . until** loop as a **while . . . do** loop, we have:

```
{multiply the integers from 1 to 5}
Product := 1;
Count := 1;
while Count <= 5 do
   begin
      Product := Product * Count;
      Count := Count + 1
   end
```

The boolean expression for the **repeat . . . until** loop

```
Count > 5
```

specifies the condition for terminating the loop; that is, when the expression is true, the repetition is terminated. On the other hand, the boolean expression for the **while . . . do** loop

```
Count <= 5
```

Figure 5.4 Flow of control for **while** . . . **do**

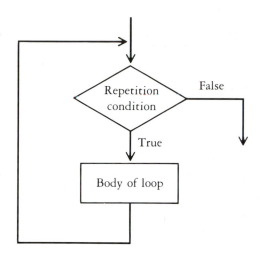

specifies the condition for repeating the loop; that is, while the expression is true, the loop is repeated. The conditions are logically opposite. Thus, we could have expressed any one of them as **not** the other. For example, Count < = 5 could have been written as **not** (Count > 5) and the **while . . . do** loop could thus be written as:

```
{multiply the integers from 1 to 5}
Product := 1;
Count := 1;
while not(Count > 5) do
   begin
      Product := Product * Count;
      Count := Count + 1
   end
```

The first version, using the boolean expression, Count < = 5, is, however, preferred because it is easier to understand.

In general, any conditional loop can be written either as a **repeat . . . until** loop or as a **while . . . do** loop. Many programming languages provide only one of these statements. The advantage of having both statements is that it allows us to use the one which is more natural for a particular problem. Let us now rewrite our program to compute the average of ten numbers using the **while . . . do** statement instead of the **repeat . . . until.** In this case, neither statement appears to have a clear advantage over the other. In most applications, however, the **while . . . do** statement is more useful than the **repeat . . . until** because it allows for the possibility that the loop should not be executed at all.

EXAMPLE 5.3 Program to Compute the Average of Ten Numbers Using while . . . do

```pascal
program Average (input, output);

{**************************
* Program to compute the  *
* average of ten numbers. *
**************************}

var
    Number, Total, Mean : real;
    Count : integer;

begin
    {Initialize count and total}

    Count := 0;
    Total := 0.0;

    while Count < 10 do
      begin
          read (Number);
          Total := Total + Number;
          Count := Count + 1
      end;

    {compute and output average}

    Mean := Total/10.0;
    writeln (' The average is ',Mean :8:2)
end.
```

The Use of Loops to Input Data

Consider the following problem: Write a computer program to compute the average of an arbitrary set of numbers. What differentiates this problem from the previous one is that we do not know in advance how many numbers we are to average. In the previous problem we knew that we had exactly ten numbers. Thus we were able to count the values we were reading to determine when we had input all the data. In this situation, however, how are we to determine that all the values have been read and it is time to quit reading and to compute the average?

A common way to solve this problem is to use a **sentinel** to indicate the end of data. The data values for the program are prepared in the usual way, but a special value, which cannot be confused with an actual data value, is added to the end of the data. This value, which is called a **sentinel** or **flag**, is there to indicate the end of the data. For example, if we assume that our program will only be required to average non-negative numbers (an acceptable assumption if we are considering such numbers as grades on a test, but clearly not acceptable when computing the average daily temperature in January), then we can place a negative value, such as -1, at the end of our data as a sentinel. The data for the program might appear as:

78 67 98 57 0 65 100 23 -1

All the values except the -1 are actual data values and are to be used in computing the average. The -1 is the sentinel and should not be used in the computation of the average.

The algorithm to compute the average is going to have to use the input value of a number to control the loop. In other words, we will continue to input and process values until we input the value of the sentinel. The following is a possible algorithm to do this using a **repeat . . . until** loop:

begin
    Initialize total to 0
    Initialize counter to 0
    repeat
        Input number
        Add number to total
        Add 1 to counter
    until number equals -1
    Compute average
    Output averge
end.

Unfortunately, this algorithm is *incorrect*. To see this, suppose that the input consists of:

$2 -1$

The first value read is 2. This value is added to the total and 1 is added to the counter. The termination condition is now tested. Since "number" has a value of 2 the termination condition (number equals -1) is "false". Therefore, control returns to the top of the loop and the entire body of the loop is executed again. The value -1 is read as the current value of "number". It is added to the total and 1 is added to the counter. When the bottom of the loop is reached, the termination condition is tested again. This time it is found to be true. The average is computed and printed. This average, however, is incorrect since the sentinel value was counted and included in the total. The problem arises because we input a value and did the computations before we tested for termination. We have to rearrange the steps of the algorithm in such a way that we test for termination before we count the value or add it to the total. This can be done by reading the first value before we enter the loop and then reading the remaining values just before we test for the termination of the loop.

begin
   Initialize total to 0
   Initialize counter to 0
   Input number
   repeat
     Add number to total
     Add 1 to counter
     Input number
   until number $= -1$
   Compute average
   Output average
end.

By repeating the steps we carried out with the first algorithm, convince yourself that this algorithm will indeed work correctly.

We are now ready to code the algorithm into Pascal (Example 5.4). Note the use of the **const** definition to define the sentinel. This makes it easier to change the program to use other sentinel values if we have to. We, of course, could have used the **while . . . do** loop to design our algorithm. We will leave it as an exercise for you to rewrite the program with the **while . . . do** statement instead of the **repeat . . . until** statement. Note also that the above program will

**EXAMPLE 5.4
Program to
Compute the
Average of
Several Non-
Negative Numbers**

```
program Mean (input, output);

{*************************************
 * Program to compute the average    *
 * of an arbitrary set of non-negative *
 * numbers. A sentinel of -1 is used  *
 * to indicate the end of data.       *
 *************************************}
```

**EXAMPLE 5.4
Program to
Compute the
Average of
Several Non-
Negative Num-
bers**
(*continued*)

```
const
    Sentinel = -1;
var
    Number, Total, Average : real;
    Counter : integer;

begin
    {initialize counter and total}

    Total := 0.0;
    Counter := 0;

    {input first value and enter loop}

    read (Number);
    repeat
        Total := Total + Number;
        Counter := Counter + 1;
        read (Number)
    until Number = Sentinel;
    Average := Total/Counter;
    writeln (' The average is : ',Average :8:2)
end.
```

still output incorrect results if the sentinel appears as the first input value.

Let us now consider the problem we raised at the beginning of this chapter: We want to write a program that computes the gross wages for an arbitrary number of employees. We will assume that for each employee we have the employee number, the hourly wage, and the hours worked. We wish to compute the employee's gross wages based on a 40-hour week; that is, for the first 40 hours worked each employee receives the normal hourly rate and for hours worked beyond 40 the employee receives time-and-a-half. This is what we did in Example 4.5 with a single employee. Here, we do not know how many employees we have, but it certainly could be more than one. To indicate the end of the data, we placed an "extra employee" at the end of the data. This extra employee has an identification number of

0000, earns 0.0 hourly wage, and worked 0 hours: obviously a sentinel. The data for our program look like this:

0001	4.86	40
0012	5.75	43
0834	3.95	38
6491	6.45	41
.	.	.
.	.	.
.	.	.
7812	2.79	54
0000	0.00	0

The Pascal program to compute and print the gross salaries for all the employees is shown in Example 5.5.

Assume the input file contains:

0001	4.86	40
0012	5.75	43
0834	3.95	38
6491	6.45	41
7812	2.79	54
0000	0.00	0

Then the output of this program appears as:

EMPLOYEE	SALARY
1	194.00
12	255.88
834	150.10
6491	267.67
7812	170.19

The Use of eof

Sentinels are used to determine when the end of the input data is reached. It is, however, often difficult to find an "impossible" data value to serve as a sentinel. For example, if we wanted to generalize the program to compute the average of a set of numbers so that it would work with negative numbers, we could no longer use − 1 as a sentinel. We could not use another symbol such as $ or * for a sentinel either, since the read procedure is looking for a real number. The $ or * would result in a type error.

Fortunately, Pascal provides us with a "built-in" sentinel, the boolean function **eof**. A more detailed definition of eof will be found

**EXAMPLE 5.5
Program to
Compute the
Gross Salary
for a Group of
Employees**

```pascal
program Grosspay (input, output);

{******************************************
* Program to compute the gross pay for    *
* an unknown number of employees. The     *
* program inputs each employee's id       *
* number, hourly rate, and hours worked.  *
* An id number of 0000 is used to         *
* indicate the end of data.               *
******************************************}

const
    Sentinel = 0;

var
    IdNumber : integer;
    Rate, HoursWorked, Overtime, Salary : real;

begin
    {Print headings}

    writeln(' EMPLOYEE      SALARY');
    writeln;

    read (IdNumber, Rate, HoursWorked);
    while IdNumber <> Sentinel do
      begin
          {Determine if overtime is to be paid}

          if HoursWorked > 40 then
            Overtime := HoursWorked - 40
          else
            Overtime := 0;

          {compute salary}

          HoursWorked := HoursWorked - Overtime;
          Salary := HoursWorked * Rate
                        + Overtime * Rate * 1.5;

          {output result}

          writeln (IdNumber :8, Salary :10:2);

          {input next employee}

          read (IdNumber, Rate, HoursWorked)
      end { of WHILE loop }
end.
```

in the chapter on files. For now we simply need to know that eof, which is short for end-of-file, is false as long as there is data to be read and becomes true when the computer encounters the end of the file. To use eof successfully we must understand precisely when it becomes true. Let us, therefore, examine in greater detail how numerical values are input from the standard *input* file. Assume that the statement:

```
read (Number)
```

is repeatedly being executed, and that the input data for a program appear as:

```
12   2   3
1    34  7
9    10  45
```

In the standard input file these values are organized as follows:

12   2   3 \ 1   34   7 \ 9   10   45 \ |

That is, we can think of the values as being arranged in a long list separated by special **end-of-line** characters, which are nonprintable characters used by the system to determine where one line ends and another line begins. We have indicated these characters by the symbol \, for purposes of illustration. At the end of the file there is one more nonprintable character called the **end-of-file** character, which we represented by the symbol | and which the computer system uses to determine the end of the file.

At any point in time, only one character in the input file is accessible to the program. Pascal keeps track of the accessible character by using a variable called a *file window,* which it moves along the file. Before any values are read, the file window contains the first character in the file. In our example it, therefore, contains a blank.

□12   2   3 \ 1   34   7 \ 9   10   45 \ |

If the statement read(Number) is now executed with the above data in the input file, the character in the file window is considered for assignment to the variable Number. However, since we are looking for a numeric value, blanks are ignored and the window moves to the next character. It continues to do so until it encounters the next nonblank character. Here the first nonblank character is the digit 1. Since we are attempting to read an integer, all digits will now be processed until the first character other than a digit is encountered. Thus, the integer 12 is read and assigned to the variable Number. The file window now contains the next available character. This is illustrated below:

12□2   3 \ 1   34   7 \ 9   10   45 \ |

Executing read(Number) again will assign the value 2 to the variable Number. Again, all the blanks will be ignored because we are looking for a numeric value. The file window now contains the next character:

12   2□3 \ 1   34   7 \ 9   10   45 \ |

Yet another read(Number) execution will input the value 3 and position the window as follows:

12   2   3⬚1   34   7 \ 9   10   45 \ |

Note that the file window now contains the end-of-line character. For purposes of input, Pascal treats the end-of-line character as if it were a blank. We will see shortly how this character can also be used to detect the end of a line. The next execution of read(Number) will assign the value 1 to Number and position the window as shown:

12   2   3 \ 1□34   7 \ 9   10   45 \ |

What is in the file window right after the last integer value is assigned to Number? This situation is illustrated below:

12   2   3 \ 1   34   7 \ 9   10   45⬚|

We can see that the file window contains the end-of-line character directly in front of the end-of-file character. *When the file window contains the end-of-file character, eof is true. Otherwise, it is false.* Thus, in our example, eof is not true when the last value is read. This may cause problems when we are using eof as a condition for a loop reading data. Consider the following example:

```
{Warning -- Incorrect use of eof}
Total := 0.0;
Count := 0;
while not eof do
   begin
      read(Number);
      Total := Total + Number;
      Count := Count + 1
   end;
Average := Total / Count
```

This loop will *not* compute the average correctly. Assume that the data values for the program are arranged as follows:

```
12   2   3
1   34   7
9   10   45
```

After the last value, 45, is read, the file window contains the end-of-line character that follows the 45. Consequently, eof is not "true" and the loop will be executed again. No value will be input. What value actually is assigned to Number depends on the particular implementation of Pascal. With some Pascals, the attempt to execute the extra read may result in a run-time error. With other versions, the last value assigned to Number, namely 45, will be used again. With yet other versions, Number will be assigned the value zero. In all cases, however, the average, if it is computed at all, will be computed incorrectly.

The problem of the above loop can be corrected in several ways. One way is to make sure that the last incorrect value is not processed. That is, on most systems, we can handle eof the same way we handled the sentinel value earlier. The first value is input before we enter the loop and all remaining values are input at the bottom of the loop:

```
Total := 0.0;
Count := 0;
read (Number);
while not eof do
   begin
      Total := Total + Number;
      Count := Count + 1;
      read (Number)
   end;
Average := Total / Count
```

The above segment will compute the average correctly.

A better way to avoid potential problems with eof is to use readln instead of read. The data, of course, must be organized appropriately. For example, if data in the input file appear as:

```
12
2
3
1
34
7
9
10
45
```

then the following loop will produce the correct result:

```
Total := 0.0;
Count := 0;
while not eof do
   begin
      readln (Number);
      Total := Total + Number;
      Count := Count + 1
   end;
Average := Total / Count
```

The readln statement works here because it resets the window to the next line (that is, to the first character after the end-of-line character), immediately after it assigns the value in the file window to the variable Number. Thus, when the last value is read, eof is true and control passes to the statement following the loop. The readln statement is especially useful when we need to input more than one value at a time, as in the gross-salary computation example. In such cases, the values to be input together are arranged on a single line and readln is used to input one line at a time.

The function eof returns the value true when the end-of-file character is in the file window and false otherwise. Functions that return boolean values are known as **predicates.** Pascal has three predicate functions, which are described in Table 5.1.

Table 5.1
Predicate
functions

Name	Description	Argument	Value of Function
odd (x)	true if x is odd false otherwise	integer	boolean
eof (f)	end-of-file indicator	file	boolean
eoln (f)	end-of-line indicator	file	boolean

The function odd takes an integer argument and returns a boolean value that is true if the integer is odd and false if the integer is even. The functions eof and eoln, as we just saw, are used to detect the end-of-file marker and the end-of-line marker respectively. The argument to each function is a file. If the file we are working with is the standard input file, then the argument can be omitted. Thus:

| eof | is equivalent to | eof (input) |
| eoln | is equivalent to | eoln (input) |

We will see in the chapter on files how these functions can be used with files other than the standard input file.

SELF-TEST 1

1. How many times will each of the following loops be executed? What will be the output of each of the following program segments?

(a)
```
x := 5;
y := 30;
repeat
    x := x + 5
until x > y;
writeln (x,y)
```

(b)
```
x := 5;
y := 30;
while x < y do
    x := x + 5;
writeln (x,y)
```

(c)
```
x := 5;
y := 40;
repeat
    x := x * 2
until x >= y;
writeln (x,y)
```

(d)
```
x := 5;
y := 40;
while x<=y do
    x := x * 2;
writeln (x,y)
```

(e)
```
x := 5;
y := 30;
repeat
    x := x + 2
until x <= y;
writeln (x,y)
```

(f)
```
x := 5;
y := 30;
while x > y do
    x := x + 2;
```

2. Which of the following statements apply to **repeat . . . until** structures only? To **while . . . do** structures only? To both?

(a) The body of the loop is executed at least once.

(b) The boolean expression controlling the loop is evaluated before the loop is entered.

(c) Must use the **begin . . . end** construction if more than one statement is to be repeated.

(d) The body of the loop may not be executed at all.

(e) Has a condition for termination.

(f) Has a condition for repetition.

3. The program segment below is supposed to sum an unknown number of integers. Will it work? If not, modify it so that it will.

```
Total := 0;
while not eof do
    begin
        read (Number);
        Total := Total + Number
    end
```

4. What does the following program segment do?

```
Counter := 0;
read (Number);
while not eof do
   begin
      if not odd(Number) then
         Counter := Counter + 1;
      read (Number)
   end
```

Answers

1. (a) 6 times, 35 30 (b) 6 times, 35 30 (c) 3 times, 40 40 (d) 4 times, 80 40 (e) 1 time, 7 30 (f) 0 times, 5 30
2. (a) **repeat . . . until** (b) **while . . . do** (c) **while . . . do** (d) **while . . . do** (e) **repeat . . . until** (f) **while . . . do**
3. It will not work properly. The end of the file will not be encountered when the last value is read. Thus an extra value may be added to the total. The correct version is:

```
Total := 0;
read(Number);
while not eof do
   begin
      Total := Total + Number;
      read(Number)
   end
```

4. It counts the even numbers in the input file.

5.3 COUNTER-CONTROLLED LOOPS

In some cases where we use either a **repeat . . . until** statement or a **while . . . do** statement, we can use a third approach that further simplifies the construction of loops. We can do this when we know in advance how many times the loop is to be executed. Consider the following **while . . . do** loop used to print the values of the first ten positive integers:

```
Number := 1;
while Number <= 10 do
   begin
      write (Number :4);
      Number := Number + 1
   end;
writeln
```

The value of the variable Number is used to control the loop. First, the value is initialized to its *initial value,* 1 in this case. The value is then *tested* to see if it is less than or equal to its *final value,* 10. If it is not greater than 10 the body of the loop is executed. The value of Number is *incremented by 1* and the process, except for the initialization, is repeated. A single Pascal statement allows us to combine some of these steps; it is the **for** statement and has the general form:

for controlvariable : = initialvalue **to** finalvalue **do** statement

Using the **for** statement we can rewrite the above program segment as:

```
for Number := 1 to 10 do
   write ( Number :4);
writeln
```

The **for** statement repeatedly executes the statement write (Number) as Number varies from 1 to 10. The initialvalue and final value can be expressions. For example, if *x* is 2 and *w* is 23 then

```
for Number := x + 3 to x * w - 4 do
   write (Number :4);
writeln
```

is equivalent to

```
for Number := 5 to 42 do
   write (Number :4);
writeln
```

The **for** statement provides only for the repetition of a single statement following the word **do.** If we wish to repeat more than one statement, we have to use a compound statement:

```
for controlvariable : = initialvalue to finalvalue do
  begin
    statement1;
    statement2;
       .
       .
       .
    statementn
  end
```

The **for** statement is executed as follows:

1. The control variable is initialized to its starting value.
2. The current value of the control variable is compared to the final value. If the current value is less than or equal to the final value, the body of the loop (the statement following the **do**) is executed.
3. The control variable is incremented by 1.
4. Steps 2 and 3 are repeated until the control variable exceeds the final value.

The **for** loop is useful in problems where we know in advance the initial and final values for the control variable. This is usually the case when working with arrays, the topic of the next chapter. Consider the following additional simple examples:

```
{compute the product of the first
 five positive integers}

Product := 1;
for I := 1 to 5 do
   Product := Product * I;
writeln (Product)
```

Contrast this with the same problem where we used the **while . . . do** and **repeat . . . until** loops.

```
{sum integers from -123 to 426}

Sum := 0;
for I := -123 to 426 do
   Sum := Sum + I;
writeln (Sum)
```

Consider now the following problem: we want to print out the integers 1 to 10 in reverse order. That is, we want to print 10 9 8 . . . 1. To do this we can use the following form of the **for** loop:

```
for Number := 10 downto 1 do
   write (Number :4);
writeln
```

The **downto** form of the **for** statement provides repetition for a sequence of *decreasing* values of the control variable. In this case, the loop will be executed if the initial value is greater than or equal to the final value. We could have used the **downto** form of the **for** loop to compute the product of the first five positive integers as illustrated in a previous example:

```
Product := 1;
for i := 5 downto 1 do
   Product := Product * i;
writeln (Product)
```

Figure 5.5 shows the syntax diagram for the general form of the **for** statement.

The control variable, initial value, and final value must be of type *integer*. We will relax this requirement later, but the important point here is that they *cannot be of type real.* The initial value of the control variable is assigned only once. It changes as the loop is repeated. When the loop terminates, however, the control variable is *undefined.* You may not assume that the control variable has a value that is 1 greater than the final value (or 1 less than the final value if you are using the **downto** form). You should treat the control variable after a **for** loop just as you would treat any undefined variable; that is, assign it a value before you use it.

We can use **for** loops to input data provided the data are properly arranged. To use the **for** loop, we need to know in advance exactly how many values we will input. This may be accomplished by counting the data values and including the count as the first data value. For example, assume we need to average the following values:

78 67 98 57 0 65 100 23

We have 8 values; thus we include 8 as the first entry in our data:

8 78 67 98 57 0 65 100 23

The program to average these numbers appears as Example 5.6.

Figure 5.5 Syntax diagram for **for** statement

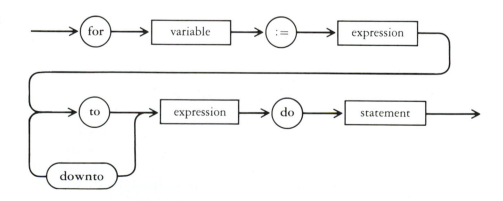

EXAMPLE 5.6 Program to Compute the Average of a Set of Numbers Using a for Statement

```pascal
program Mean (input, output);

{*************************************
* Program to compute the average of *
* a set of real numbers. The count   *
* is the first data value.           *
*************************************}

var
    I, Count : integer;
    Number, Total, Average : real;
begin
    {initialize total}

    Total := 0.0;

    {input the value of count and read that many numbers}

    read (Count);
    for I := 1 to Count do
       begin
           read (Number);
           Total := Total + Number
       end;
    Average := Total/Count;
    writeln (' The average is : ',Average :8:2)
end.
```

SELF-TEST 2

1. What output will the following program segment produce?

```pascal
for i := 1 to 5 do
   begin
      for j := 1 to i do
         write('x');
      writeln
   end
```

2. What output will the following program segment produce?

```pascal
for i := 1 to 6 do
   begin
      for j := 1 to 6 do
         if (i = j) or (i+j = 7)
             write ('1')
         else
             write ('0');
      writeln
   end
```

3. What is wrong with each of the following program segments?

(a) **for** i := 1 **to** 5 **do**
      begin
         i := i + 1;
         write (i)
    end

(b) read (a);
    for i := a **downto** 1 **do**
        writeln (i);
    writeln(i)

Answers

1. x
  xx
  xxx
  xxxx
  xxxxx

2. 100001
  010010
  001100
  001100
  010010
  100001

3. (a) The index to the loop cannot be altered in the loop.   (b) The index variable is not defined once the loop terminates. Thus, the last writeln will result in a run-time error since *i* is undefined.

5.4 ADDITIONAL SCALAR TYPES

Up to this point we have only considered the scalar types *integer, real,* and *boolean.* We now introduce the remaining scalar data types of Pascal. The types we will discuss are *char,* short for character, and *user-defined types.* Both of these types are most useful with loops.

The Type Char

Although we have used boolean variables to control the flow of execution of a program, so far we have worked primarily with numeric values. We used non-numeric character strings to label output in write and writeln statements; however, these character strings are constants and we cannot change their values. It is useful in many situations to have variables that can assume character values. Many applications require the manipulation of character data. For example, a program that prints a customer's charge bill not only must be able to work with numeric data involving charges and payments on account, but must also handle such character data as customer name, address, and so forth.

Pascal provides the standard data type **char.** Elements of the data type char are the individual characters that are represented on a specific computer. A **character constant** consists of a *single* character enclosed in single quotes:

'A'
' ' (blank)
'1'
'*'

The single quotes are necessary so that the computer knows that the 1 is a character instead of an integer, or that the * is a character instead of the multiplication operator. Unfortunately, not all computers use the same character set, although they all generally support the numerals 0–9, the 26 capital letters A–Z, the blank, the usual punctuation marks, and a small number of special symbols such as @, $, +, −, and =. The American Standard Code for Information Interchange (ASCII) and the Extended Binary Coded Decimal Interchange Code (EBCDIC) are the most commonly used character sets. As we saw in Chapter 1, characters are represented inside computer systems by binary digits. This representation can also be interpreted as a number. For example, the EBCDIC representation of the letter *A* is 11000001. Thus, the decimal number associated with *A* is 193. A similar scheme holds with ASCII characters. A partial listing of character representations for ASCII and EBCDIC appears in Table 5.2.

Table 5.2
Character codes

Character	ASCII Code	Decimal Equivalent	EBCDIC Code	Decimal Equivalent
'0'	0110000	48	11110000	240
'1'	0110001	49	11110001	241
'2'	0110010	50	11110010	242
.	.	.	.	.
.	.	.	.	.
.	.	.	.	.
'A'	1000001	65	11000001	193
'B'	1000010	66	11000010	194
'C'	1000011	67	11000011	195
.	.	.	.	.
.	.	.	.	.
.	.	.	.	.

The complete ASCII and EBCDIC character sets are shown in the Appendix B.

Note that the alphabetic characters have the same order as the letters of the alphabet. This is because the decimal equivalent of A is 65 in ASCII and 193 in EBCDIC, the decimal equivalent of B is 66 in ASCII and 194 in EBCDIC, and so on. Thus, A is less than B in both codes, just as you would expect. This makes it possible to use relational operators with character data and obtain meaningful results. For example, the following are valid boolean expressions in Pascal:

Expression	Result
'A' > = 'C'	false
'c' < > 'x'	true
'1' < '2'	true

Note again that 1 and '1' are not the same. In fact, the numerical equivalent of '1' is 49 in ASCII and 241 in EBCDIC. It is important to note that character constants are character strings, but a character string may not be a character constant since character constants are restricted to a single character. Character strings are a more complex data type as we shall see in the next chapter.

Variables of type char are declared in the usual way:

```
var
     Letter, Symbol : char;
```

Thus,

```
Letter := 'A';
Symbol := '+'
```

assign the character values A and ' + ' to the variables Letter and Symbol respectively.

Input of Character Data
If Letter is a variable of type char, the statement

```
read (Letter)
```

reads a *single* character from the standard input file and assigns it to the variable Letter. The operation of reading character data is not the same as the operation of reading numeric data. Recall that read

(Number), where Number is of type integer or real, will skip blanks as it searches the input file for a digit. The statement read(Letter), where Letter is of type char, will not. In fact, the statement read (Number) could make the computer skip over many blanks, including complete blank lines. The statement read(Letter) will *never* skip a blank in the input file. This is because the blank character is just another value of type char.

Another difference between numeric and character data lies in the fact that the form of numeric data is the same in internal assignments (using the assignment statement) and in external assignments (using the read or readln procedures). That is, in the internal assignment

```
Number := 43.5
```

and in the external assignment

```
read (Number)
```

the constant 43.5 is represented the same way. It appears as

43.5

in the input file.

The form of character constants, however, is not the same in internal and external assignments. In the internal assignment

```
Letter := 'A'
```

the constant 'A' is enclosed in single quotes. On the other hand, in the external assignment

```
read (Letter)
```

the character constant to be read is *not* enclosed in quotes in the input file and thus appears as

A

Although the difference in representation appears capricious at first sight, it *is* reasonable and actually works to the programmer's advantage. It certainly would be inconvenient if we had to enclose every single character in quotes!

Let us now look at a simple program that inputs characters. The program in Example 5.7 reads a file containing character data and counts the number of blanks in those data.

**EXAMPLE 5.7
Program to
Count the
Number of
Blank Charac-
ters in an In-
put File**

```pascal
program CountBlanks (input, output);

{**************************
* Program to count blank *
* characters in an input *
* file.                  *
**************************}
const
   Blank = ' ';
var
   Count : integer;
   Ch    : char;
begin
   {initialize count and input first character}

   Count := 0;
   read (Ch);

   {check if blank and read next character until
    the end of the file is encountered}

   while not eof do
      begin
         if Ch = Blank then
            Count := Count + 1;
         read (Ch)
      end;

   writeln (' Number of blank characters: ', Count :6)
end.
```

Note in the above example that we can define constants of type char. The above program also counts end-of-line characters as if they were blanks. We could restrict ourselves to counting the blank characters in a single line of the input file. To do this we have to change

while not eof **do**

in the above program to

while not eoln **do**

When we are reading data of type char, eoln is true when the file window contains the end-of-line character. It is false otherwise. The program in Example 5.8 reads all the characters on a line and outputs each word on a separate line. It assumes that words are separated from each other by a single blank character.

EXAMPLE 5.8 Program to Input a Line of Text and Separate it into Single Words

```
program Words (input, output);

{****************************
 * Program to separate a    *
 * line of text into words. *
 ****************************}
const
   Blank = ' ';
var
   Ch : char;
begin
   while not eoln do
      begin
         {input character}

         read (Ch);

         {if the character is a blank output word
         otherwise place character in output buffer}
         if Ch = Blank then
            writeln
         else
            write (Ch);
      end {of WHILE loop}
end.
```

When this program is provided with the following input:

Now is the time for all good men to come to the aid of their country.

the output will be:

Now
is
the
time
for
all
good
men
to
come
to
the
aid
of
their
country.

User-Defined Types

The data types discussed so far—integer, real, boolean, and char—are all *standard scalar types.* Pascal also allows the programmer to define his or her own data types. This is often very useful in making control structures easier to understand and thus improving the readability of a program. A programmer can define a new scalar type in Pascal in two ways:

1. By enumerating all the values that any variable of the type can assume, or
2. By restricting the range of an existing type.

Enumerated Types

Suppose we need a loop to compute the weekly income of an employee, given the daily income for the days Monday through Friday. One approach may take the following form:

```
Total := 0.0;
for Day := 1 to 5 do
begin
   read (DailyPay);
   Total := Total + DailyPay
end
```

We are assuming, of course, that the appropriate declarations have been made earlier in the program. Specifically, we are assuming that the variable Day was declared as follows:

```
var
   Day : integer;
```

A better approach is to declare Day as:

```
var
   Day : (sunday, monday, tuesday, wednesday,
          thursday, friday, saturday);
```

What this declaration does is *enumerate* all the possible values the variable Day can assume. We can now rewrite the loop as:

```
Total := 0.0;
for Day := monday to friday do
   begin
      read (DailyPay);
      Total := Total + DailyPay
   end
```

The purpose of the loop is clearly more apparent in the second example.

The variable Day in the second illustration is said to be a **user-defined type.** We could have made its type explicit by using a **type** definition to provide the type with its own identifier:

```
type
   Weekday = (sunday, monday, tuesday, wednesday,
               thursday, friday, saturday);
var
   Day : Weekday;
```

The above **type** *definition* provides us with an identifier, or type name, for the new scalar data type Weekday. We can then use this new type to declare variables of that type as we did with the variable Day. The type definition for enumerated scalar types takes the following general form:

```
type
     identifier = (identifierl, identifier2, . . . , identifiern);
```

It should be remembered that when we use a type definition, the identifier we select for the type is *not* a variable name and, therefore, we cannot assign values to it. In the above example, the role played by the identifier Weekday is exactly the same as the role played by the predefined identifiers: integer, real, char, and boolean. In fact, boolean is a predefined enumerated type. Its definition is:

```
type
   boolean = (false, true);
```

We, of course, need not specify this definition; it is provided by the Pascal compiler.

Just as the type identifier is not a variable, neither are the identifiers representing the possible values for the type. We cannot assign values to monday or tuesday, any more than we can assign values to true or 5. The type definition for an enumerated scalar type not only introduces a new type identifier but also does the following:

1. Lists the identifiers denoting the constants of the new type; and
2. Defines the order of the constants.

The *order* in which the values are listed in a type definition establishes the ordering for that type. In the above example, sunday was listed first. This makes sunday less than any other of the listed values.

Similarly, monday is less than any of the values that follow it. Because of this ordering, each identifier that is used to specify a value in a user-defined type can only be listed in one **type** definition. The following two **type** definitions, taken together, are *invalid*:

```
type
   Color = (red, blue, yellow);
   Hue   = (pink, rose, yellow, red);
```

If both definitions were allowed, we could not decide whether yellow < red or red < yellow.

Enumerated scalar data types are for *internal use only.* We can assign and test such values in a progam, but we *cannot output* them using a write or a writeln statement *nor can we input* them using a read or readln statement.

Subrange Types

It is often the case that a variable will assume values of a certain type within a specific range only. For example we may have the following declaration:

```
var
   Year : integer;
```

Yet in the program, the values of year will always be between 1940 and 1980. The declaration

```
var
   Year : 1940..1980;
```

conveys this restriction to the computer. Furthermore, the Pascal compiler generates code to check that no variables outside this range are assigned to Year when the program runs. If such an assignment is attempted, it results in a run-time error and the program halts. This type of checking can be a valuable tool when a program is being run.

Just as with the enumerated data type, we can define subrange types explicitly by using a **type** definition. The general form of a subrange type definition is:

```
type
    identifier = lowestvalue .. highestvalue;
```

The following are all valid examples of subrange **type** definitions:

```
type
   YearRange = 1940 .. 1980;
   Letter    = 'A' .. 'Z';
   Workday   = monday .. friday;
```

The last subrange type definition is only valid if the enumerated type Weekday, as shown earlier, is defined prior to the definition of Workday. Subrange types can be defined for integers, characters, and enumerated types. A subrange of type real is not allowed.

5.5 FUNCTIONS WITH SCALAR PARAMETERS

Pascal has predefined functions that are useful when working with scalar types. These functions are given in Table 5.3.

Table 5.3 Functions with scalar parameters

Name	Description	Argument	Value of Function
succ (x)	Returns a value that is the successor of x in the ordering	Any scalar type except real	Same as parameter
pred (x)	Returns a value that is the predecessor of x in the ordering	Any scalar type except real	Same as parameter
ord (x)	Returns ordinal value of x	Any scalar type except real	Integer
chr (x)	Returns character value corresponding to the integer x	Integer	Char

The functions "succ" and "pred" are used with any scalar type, except real, to obtain the successor or predecessor (if any) of a given value. To see how these functions work consider the following examples:

Expression	Value
pred (3)	2
pred (0)	-1
succ (23)	24
succ (0)	1

The pred and succ functions, when used with integers, can be used to increment or decrement a counter by one. They can be used for equivalent operations with boolean, char, or user-defined types, as the following examples illustrate:

type
```
    MonthType = (jan, feb, mar, apr, may, jun,
                 jul, aug, sep, oct, nov, dec);
```

Expression	Value
pred(feb)	jan
pred(aug)	jul
pred(true)	false
pred('B')	'A'
pred('3')	'2'
succ(feb)	mar
succ(aug)	sep
succ('B')	'C'
succ('3')	'4'

The predecessor of the first value of a given type and the successor of the last value are undefined. The ordering for user-defined types is defined by the order in which the constants of that type are listed. Thus, the following values are *undefined*:

```
pred(jan)
pred(false)
succ(dec)
succ(true)
succ(maxint)
```

User-defined types are considered to be numbered starting with 0 for the first value, 1 for the next value, and so on. The type definition for MonthType has the following numbers associated with it:

type
```
    MonthType = (jan, feb, mar, apr, may, jun,
                  0    1    2    3    4    5
                 jul, aug, sep, oct, nov, dec);
                  6    7    8    9    10   11
```

The numbers, which indicate the order in which the constants of the given type have been defined, are called the *ordinal numbers* of the corresponding constants. In the above illustration, the ordinal number of *jul* is 6 and the ordinal number of *dec* is 11. The predefined Pascal function "ord" returns the ordinal number of its argument. Thus, for the user-defined type MonthType it would return the following values:

Expression	Value
ord(jul)	6
ord(dec)	11
ord(jan)	0

When used with type char, the ord function returns the decimal equivalent of the underlying numeric representation of the character. The following examples illustrate the values that would be returned depending on whether the ASCII or EBCDIC character sets are used:

Expression	Value for ASCII Character Set	Value for EBCDIC Character Set
ord('0')	48	240
ord('1')	49	241
ord('A')	65	193
ord('B')	66	194

The remaining predefined function, chr, is used to convert an ordinal number to its corresponding character:

Expression	Value
chr(49)	'1'
chr(65)	'A'

The above examples assume that the underlying character set is ASCII.

5.6 STRUCTURED PROGRAM-MING

We have now studied all the *control structures* of Pascal. There are three basic control structures, or patterns, through which we control the sequence of execution of statements in a program. These structures are: *sequence, selection,* and *iteration.* They are the basic building blocks of all Pascal programs.

The sequence control structure is illustrated in Figure 5.6. One statement simply follows another in sequence.

In Pascal the prototype of a sequence control structure is a compound statement. We represent such a structure by using **begin . . . end.** Thus, the structure illustrated in Figure 5.6 can be written as:

```
begin
    Statement;
    Statement
end
```

The selection control structure is implemented in Pascal in terms of three language features: the **if . . . then . . . else,** the **if . . . then,** and the **case** statements. The **if . . . then . . . else** selection control structure is illustrated in Figure 5.7.

The **if . . . then** selection control structure is illustrated in Figure 5.8.

Finally, the **case** selection control structure is illustrated in Figure 5.9.

We already have seen how these structures are expressed in pseudocode and in Pascal.

Figure 5.6 Sequence control structure

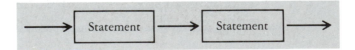

Figure 5.7 if . . . then . . . else selection control structure

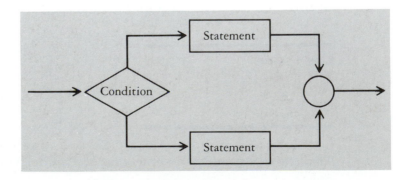

Figure 5.8 if . . . then selection control structure

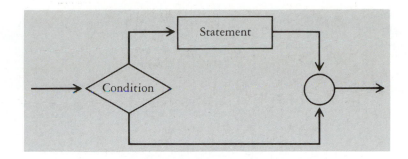

Figure 5.9 case selection control structure

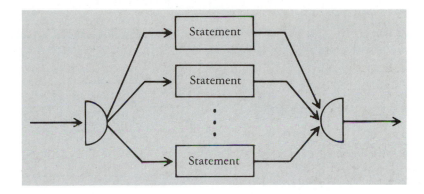

Figure 5.10 while . . . do iteration control structure

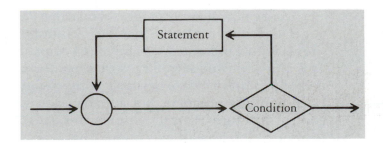

The iteration control structure provides a progammer with a looping or repetition mechanism. As we saw, Pascal has three language features to implement iteration: **while . . . do, repeat . . . until,** and **for . . . to.** The **while . . . do** iteration structure is illustrated in Figure 5.10.

The **repeat . . . until** iteration control structure is illustrated in Figure 5.11.

Finally, the **for . . . to** iteration control structure is shown in Figure 5.12.

Figure 5.11 re-peat . . . until iteration control structure

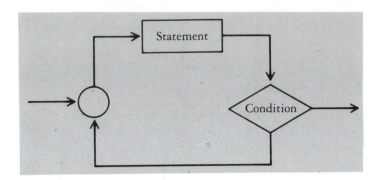

Figure 5.12 for . . . to iteration control structure

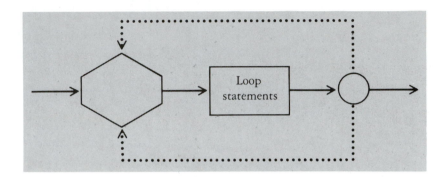

To see how these structures are used in Pascal programs, consider the algorithm presented in flowchart form in Figure 5.13. The entire algorithm presented in Figure 5.13 consists of control structures. This is probably no surprise to you since these control structures are the only means we have available at this point to control the flow of execution in a program. Not all languages, however, have Pascal's control structures. Furthermore, even Pascal allows for other means to control the flow of execution. This is accomplished by using an *unconditional* transfer of control, or the **goto** statement.

The goto Statement

To perform an unconditional transfer of flow of execution, we simply write:

goto statement label

where statement **label** is a label that appears in the program at a certain line of code and is declared previously in a **label** declaration. A

Figure 5.13 Structured flowchart

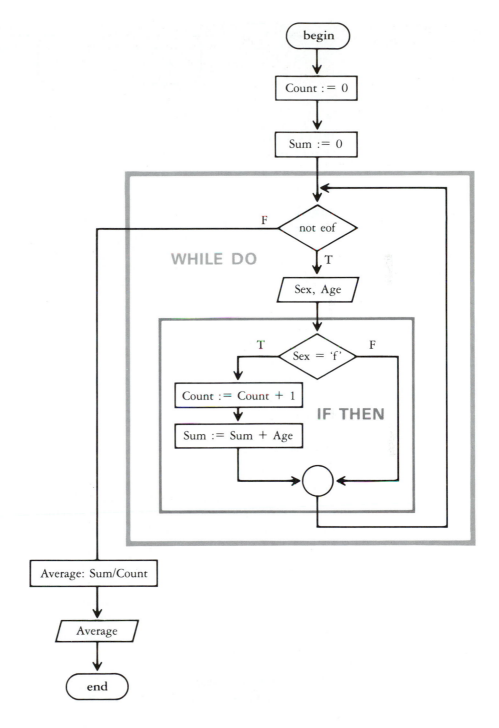

Figure 5.14 Syntax
diagram for **label**
declaration

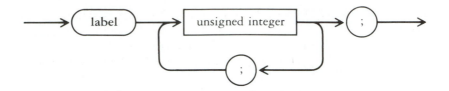

Figure 5.14 Syntax diagram for **label** declaration

label declaration must precede the **const** definition. The syntax diagram for the label declaration is shown in Figure 5.14.

For example, if we want to declare 10 and 5 as statement labels,
we would write:

```
label
   10, 15;
```

Once a label is declared, it can be used to label a statement. For
example,

```
10: x := 34.5
```

attaches the label 10 to the statement x : = 34.5. We can declare and
attach labels to as many statements as we want, as long as each label
is unique. However, labels are only useful with **goto** statements. The
execution of a **goto** statement causes an unconditional transfer of
control to the statement with the label. For example:

goto 10

will cause execution to continue at the statement with label 10.

Labels and **goto** statements appear to be a simple yet powerful
idea. This is indeed true, but the indiscriminate use of **goto** statements easily can lead to programs with very complex flow of control
structures. Such code is sometimes referred to as *spaghetti code,* because that is what its flowchart tends to resemble. In view of the
availability of other Pascal control structures we have described,
goto statements very rarely are *needed* in Pascal programs. Using
goto statements, we can construct any of the three control structures we have studied. For example, the **if . . . then . . . else** structure

```
if Sex = Male then
   NumberMales := NumberMales + 1
else
   NumberFemales := NumberFemales + 1
```

can be constructed with the **goto** statements:

```
if Sex = Male then goto 10
    NumberFemales := NumberFemales + 1;
goto 20;
    10 : NumberMales := NumberMales + 1;
20:
```

Even a quick examination of the code fragment using **goto**s should convince you that the **if . . . then . . . else** structure is to be preferred. Theoretically, we do not need a **goto** statement at all. Any Pascal program can be written using only the sequence, selection, and iteration control structures we have described so far. Where, then, is the **goto** statement useful? There are not too many places in a program. However, one use deals with verification of input data. We *can* use an **if . . . then . . . else** statement to check if data being read is valid. The general structure of the test would be:

```
if data is not valid then
    print an error message
else
    process the data
```

The statement "process the data" may, in fact, be the rest of the program. Thus, we have the awkward situation where most of the program may appear as an **else** clause to an **if . . . then . . . else** statement. A **goto** statement could be used to simplify this situation; for example,

```
if data is not valid then
    begin
        print an error message;
        goto 10
    end;
process the data
        .
        .
        .
    10:
    end.
```

Here we use an **if . . . then** statement to validate the data, and a **goto** statement to avoid making the rest of the program an **else** clause. When an invalid data clause is encountered, we print an error message and transfer flow of control to the end of the program. As a rule, however, **goto** statements make a program more difficult to read and debug. Therefore, they should be avoided.

SELF-TEST 3

1. Consider the following program segment. What will be the output, if the input is:

This is a question about characters, however, it's not difficult.

```
repeat
   read(Letter);
      if Letter <> ',' then
        write(Letter)
      else
        writeln
until Letter = '.'
```

2. What does the following program do? (Assume input begins with a nonblank character.)

```
read(Letter);
while Letter <> ' ' do
   begin
      while Letter <> ' ' do
        begin
            write(Letter);
            read(Letter)
        end;
        read(Letter)
   end;
writeln
```

3. Decide if the following **type** definitions are valid. If a definition is not valid, state why.

(a) `Languages = (BASIC, FORTRAN, COBOL, Pascal, LISP);`

(b) `NorthAmerica = (CANADA, MEXICO, USA);`

(c) `Positives = 1..maxint;`

(d) `Numbers = (1,2,3,4);`

(e) `Negatives = 0..-maxint;`

(f) `Coins = (Penny, Nickel, Dime, Quarter, Penny);`

4. Determine the value of each of the following functions, if possi-

ble. If the function invocation is not valid, state why. Where characters are used, assume ASCII representation.

(a) `ord(false)`

(b) `succ(false)`

(c) `ord('8')-ord('0')`

(d) `pred(succ(5))`

(e) `succ(3.5)`

(f) `chr(65)`

Answers

1. This is a question about characters
     however
         it's not difficult.
2. It reads and prints characters until it encounters two consecutive blanks.
3. (a) Valid (b) Valid (c) Valid (d) Not valid. Digits are not valid identifiers. (e) Not valid. The subrange must be specified in increasing ordinal values. (f) Not valid. Identifiers may not be repeated.
4. (a) 0 (b) True (c) 8 (d) 5 (e) Not valid. Succ does not take real numbers as arguments. (f) A (Assuming ASCII code)

We will now examine some problems in which the programming ideas of this chapter are applied. The first application prints a table of temperatures in Celsius and Fahrenheit. The second application deals with a business problem: balancing a checkbook. The third application deals with a mathematics problem: the computation of the square root of a number.

APPLICATION

Celsius to Fahrenheit Conversion

We want to print, in tabular form, the Celsius temperatures from − 20 to 80 and their Fahrenheit equivalents. To compute the Fahrenheit temperature, given the Celsius temperature, we will use the conversion formula:

$$F = (9/5 * C) + 32$$

The algorithm is straightforward:

begin
    Print headings
    for Celsius temperature = − 20 **to** 80 **do**
        Compute the Fahrenheit equivalent
        Print both temperatures
end.

APPLICATION

**Celsius to
Fahrenheit
Conversion**
(*continued*)

The Pascal program corresponding to the above algorithm is:

```
program Conversion (output);

{*****************************************
* Program to convert temperatures from  *
* -20 degrees to 80 degrees Celsius to  *
* equivalent temperatures in degrees    *
* Fahrenheit.                           *
*****************************************}

const
    Low = -20;
    High = 80;

var
    Fahrenheit : real;
    Celsius    : integer;
begin
    {print headings}

    writeln (' CELSIUS          FAHRENHEIT');
    writeln;

    {compute and print the temperatures}

    for Celsius := Low to High do
        begin
            Fahrenheit := (9/5)*Celsius + 32;
            writeln (Celsius :6, Fahrenheit :16:1)
        end
end.
```

APPLICATION

**Balancing a
Checkbook**

This check-balancing program will input the current balance, the amount of each check, and the amount of each deposit. It will output, in tabular form, the amount of each transaction and the balance after the transaction is applied to the account. Specifically, the input data will appear as follows:

```
256.89
c 12.34
d 450.00
c 23.78
c 120.99
c 378.50
d 500.00
c 45.25
```

APPLICATION

Balancing a Checkbook (*continued*)

The first line is the current balance. The remaining lines are transactions. The type of transaction is identifed by the first character on each line. The letter *c* indicates a check, while the letter *d* indicates a deposit. The second entry on each line indicates the amount of the transaction. Thus, "c 12.34" is a check for $12.34, and "d 450.00" is a $450.00 deposit.

The basic structure of the algorithm is:

```
begin
    Input current balance
    repeat
        Input a transaction
        if the transaction is a check then
            Subtract amount of check from current balance
            Output amount of check and new balance
        else
            Add amount of deposit to current balance
            Output amount of deposit and new balance
    until end-of-file
end.
```

If you examine this algorithm more closely, you will note that we made the assumption that the transaction code is always correct. To convince yourself of this, trace the algorithm with the transaction "a 34.78." Because this transaction is not a check, our algorithm will automatically assume it is a deposit and credit the account with $34.78. In fact, the transaction code *a* is an error, and should be identified as such.

In general, it is good practice when designing algorithms to take into consideration the possibility of bad data. This is called **defensive programming.** Most business programs do extensive error checking. Incorrect data entries, if undetected, can have serious effects on the final result. It is, of course, not always possible to detect certain errors. For example, there is no way we can detect an incorrect transaction amount unless the error is extreme, such as a negative amount or a very large amount. We can easily incorporate the ability to detect bad transaction codes. We have done this in the following algorithm:

```
begin
    Input current balance
    repeat
        Input a transaction
        if the transaction is valid then
            if the transaction is a check then
```

APPLICATION

Balancing a Checkbook
(*continued*)

        Subtract amount of check from current balance
        Output amount of check and new balance
     else
       Add amount of deposit to current balance
       Output amount of deposit and new balance
   else
     Output error message
 until (end-of-file) **or** (invalid transaction)
end.

Note that now we will continue to process transactions until we either reach the end of the data or we encounter a bad transaction. The decision to terminate processing transactions if we encounter a bad one is reasonable here because we are interested in balancing the account, and this cannot be done with any certainty if any bad data are present. However, there are situations when we would simply discard the bad data entry and continue processing the remaining values.

We can now write the Pascal program.

```
program Checkbook (input, output);

{**********************************
* Program to balance a checkbook. *
**********************************}

type
   TransType = (check, deposit, error);

var
   Balance, Amount : real;
   Transaction     : TransType;
   Valid           : boolean;
   Code            : char;

begin
   {Print headings and input current balance}

   writeln (' CODE   AMOUNT   BALANCE');
   writeln;
   readln (Balance);

   {process each transaction until eof
    or an invalid transaction is encountered}
```

APPLICATION

**Balancing a
Checkbook**
(*continued*)

```
repeat
    readln (Code, Amount);
    Valid := true;
    if Code = 'c' then
        Transaction := check
    else
        if Code = 'd' then
            Transaction := deposit
        else
            Transaction := error;

    {Update balance}

    case Transaction of
        deposit : Balance := Balance + Amount;
        check   : Balance := Balance - Amount;
        error   : begin
                        writeln (' Incorrect
                                    transaction code');
                        writeln (Code, Amount :8:2);
                        Valid := false
                  end
    end {case};
    writeln (Code :3, Amount :6:2, Balance :7:2)
until eof or (not Valid)
end.
```

APPLICATION

**Computation
of the Square
Root of a
Number**

Let us now look at an application using a loop that starts with a single value and repeats a set of actions until the desired result is obtained. We will examine a classical mathematics problem: the computation of the square root of a number. There are many algorithms to compute square roots. We will look at one attributed to Sir Isaac Newton. Newton's method makes use of the following approach: if r is an approximation to the square root of a number, x, then $(r + x/r)/2$ is a better approximation. We will repeat the approximation calculation until the difference between the square of the approximation and the number is less than some small predetermined number. Giving special consideration to the fact that the square root of a negative num-

APPLICATION

Computation of the Square Root of a Number
(*continued*)

ber does not exist, and that we do not need to approximate the square root of zero, the algorithm can be written as:

```
begin
  Input number
  if number < 0 then
    Output error message
  else
    if number = 0 then
      Root = 0
    else
      Root = 1
      repeat
        Root = (root + number/root)/2
        Difference = root*root − number
      until absolute value of difference < tolerance
  Output root
end.
```

The corresponding Pascal program is:

```pascal
program SquareRoot (input, output);

{**********************************
* Program to compute the square root *
* of a number using Newton's method. *
**********************************}

const
    Tolerance = 0.0001;


var
    Root, Number, Difference : real;


begin
    {Input number}

    read (Number);

    {test for zero}

    if Number < 0 then
        writeln (' Input error -- Negative value')
```

APPLICATION

Computation of the Square Root of a Number (*continued*)

```
else
    if Number = 0 then
        Root := 0
    else
        begin

            {set initial guess to 1 and iterate}

            Root := 1;
            repeat
                Root := (Number/Root + Root)/2;
                Difference := Root*Root - Number;
            until abs(Difference) < Tolerance
        end;
if Number >= 0 then
    writeln(' The square root of ',Number :8:2,
    ' is ', Root :8:3)
end.
```

When this program is run with an input value of 2, the output will be:

```
The square root of     2.00 is     1.414
```

5.7 COMMON ERRORS

Loops provide even experienced programmers with many opportunities for errors. When considering potential errors with loops, you should look for problems in the following areas:

1. The loop is not entered when it should be.
2. The loop terminates after the wrong number of iterations.
3. The loop never terminates.

To make sure that the loop is entered when it should be, examine the exact circumstances of its first iteration. Make sure that all the necessary variables have been initialized and that the entry condition is met.

The most common errors with loop termination involve *off-by-one* errors. That is, situations where the loop is executed one time too many or one time too few. Trace the execution of the loop through its final few iterations carefully, step by step to correct this error.

Another common error with loops is termination. If the loop fails to terminate, you have an **infinite loop.** This often happens because the required modifications of the variables used to test for repetition or termination do not take place in the body of the loop. Make sure that the exit condition can be met by carefully examining the changes in the values of the variables involved in the control of the loop. A common cause of infinite loops is the incorrect use of **and** and **or** in compound conditions. Be especially wary of loop termination conditions involving tests of exact equality or inequality with real numbers. Often, small numerical errors involving real numbers will cause the loop to fail to terminate.

Another basic error with loops involves the failure to execute all the statements in the loop's body. This occurs if **begin . . . end** pairs are not properly used, or are missing, or a semicolon is misplaced. The loop

```
read(Number);
while Number <> -1 do
   Total := Total + Number;
   read(Number);
writeln (Total)
```

will only repeat the first statement. Because the value of the control variable Number is not altered in the body of the loop, this is an infinite loop. Similarly, the loop

```
read(Number);
while Number <> -1 do;
   begin
      Total := Total + Number;
      read(Number)
   end;
writeln (Total)
```

will execute the null statement forever because of a misplaced semicolon.

One of the most common off-by-one errors involves processing a sentinel value. We discussed these errors earlier in the chapter. It always pays to check carefully the loop's boundary conditions. Be especially careful with end-of-file and end-of-line conditions. Remember that the end-of-line character is read as a blank. Thus, if you have extra blanks in your output, check to see how you have handled eoln.

Attempting to read past the end of the file is a more serious mistake, and will cause premature termination of your program. Make sure that you are correctly checking for the end of the file, especially if you are reading more than one value at a time. There must be enough data in the file to provide every variable in a read or readln statement with a value.

Errors also may occur when declaring user-defined types. Make sure that no identifiers are repeated. Be especially careful with compilers that consider only the first so many characters of an identifier, usually eight. In the following example, there is an error in the type definition because the compiler only uses the first eight characters of an identifier:

```
type
    Counters = (NumberOfStudents, NumberOfGrades);
```

5.8 CHAPTER REVIEW

Most problems that are worth solving on a computer involve repetition. A loop is a series of steps that are iterated or executed repetitively. Looping is used when (1) the algorithm is used to perform the *same* operations on different sets of data, or (2) the algorithm must repeat a group of operations in order to solve the problem.

A conditional loop is repeated as long as or until some condition is true. A counter-controlled loop is repeated a given number of times while the iterations are counted.

One form of conditional looping is provided by the **repeat . . . until** statement whose general form is:

repeat
    statement1;
    statement2;

      .

      .

      .

    statementn
until boolean expression

The reserved words **repeat** and **until** are used to bracket the body of the loop, which may consist of several statements. This is an example of a compound statement where we do not need to use the **begin . . . end** brackets. The boolean expression following **until** is the termination condition of the loop. The flow of control through the loop is:

1. Execute the compound statement that makes up the body of the loop.
2. If the boolean expression is false, then repeat the loop again. If the boolean expression is true, then terminate the loop and continue processing by executing the statements after the loop.

The body of the **repeat . . . until** loop is always executed at least once.

Conditional loops in Pascal can also be constructed using the **while . . . do** statement whose general form is:

while boolean expression **do**
   statement

The **while . . . do** statement provides for the repetition of a single statement based on the truth value of a boolean expression, the condition for repetition. The statement in the body of the **while . . . do** is repeated as long as the boolean expression remains true. When the boolean expression becomes false, processing continues with the statements following the **while . . . do** structure.

To repeat more than one statement with a **while . . . do** we must use a compound statement as the body of the **while . . . do**, bracketed by a **begin . . . end.** The flow of control through the **while . . . do** statement is as follows:

1. Evaluate the boolean expression.
2. If the boolean expression is true, then execute the statement in the body of the **while . . . do** loop and evaluate the boolean expression again. If the boolean expression is false, then continue processing by executing the statements after the loop.

Note that the body of the **while . . . do** may, if the boolean expression is initially false, not be executed at all.

A sentinel value, or flag, may be used to mark the end of a list of data items to be read. This technique is useful when we don't know in advance the exact number of values in the data. Of course, a sentinel must be a value that cannot be confused with a legitimate data value.

Pascal provides a built-in sentinel, the boolean function eof (end of file). The value of eof is false as long as data remain to be read. The value of eof becomes true when the end of the input data is encountered in the form of the end-of-file character. Pascal also provides the boolean function eoln, which can be used to determine when we reach the end of a line. It becomes true when the special end-of-line character is encountered during reading of data values. There is a third boolean function, odd(x), which can be used to determine if the integer "x" is odd.

Counter-controlled loops are implemented in Pascal with the **for** statement whose general form is:

for controlvariable : = initialvalue **to** finalvalue **do** statement

The **for** statement allows us to execute a single statement a specified number of times. If we wish to execute more than a single statement in this manner we must use the **for** statement with a **begin . . . end**.

The **for** statement is executed as follows:

1. The controlvariable is initialized to initialvalue. Note that initialvalue may be an expression that must be evaluated first.
2. The value of controlvariable is compared to the value of finalvalue (which also may be an expression that must be evaluated first). If the value of controlvariable is less than or equal to the value of finalvalue, then the body of the loop is executed. If the value of controlvariable is greater than finalvalue, the body of the loop is bypassed and processing continues with the execution of the statements following the **for** structure.
3. The value of controlvariable is incremented by 1.
4. Steps (2) and (3) are repeated until the value of controlvariable finally exceeds the value of finalvalue.

The **downto** form of the **for** statement provides repetition for a sequence of decreasing values of the control variable.

Pascal provides the standard data type char for variables that can assume character values. Elements of the data type char are the individual characters that are represented on a particular computer. Examples of character constants are '1' or '*'.

Unfortunately, not all computers use the same character set. Characters are represented inside computer systems as groups of binary digits. Each character is represented by a different, fixed-length pattern of bits. The set of character representations used on a particular computer system is called that computer's **character set.** The two most popular character sets in use today are ASCII (American Standard Code for Information Interchange) and EBCDIC (Extended Binary Coded Decimal Interchange Code).

The character sets associate numeric values with the characters in such a way that B is greater than A, C is greater than B, etc. Thus, it is possible to use the relational operators to compare characters. After declaring variables Letter and Symbol as char, assignments such as the following may be made:

```
Letter := 'A';
Symbol := '+'
```

Character data may be read in:

```
read (Letter)
```

This reads the next character in the input stream, even if it is a blank. Blanks are treated as valid characters just as letters, digits, and special symbols.

Pascal also allows the programmer to define his or her own data types in one of two ways:

1. By enumerating all of the values that any variable of the type can assume, or
2. By restricting the range of an existing type.

When we use a **type** definition, the identifier we select for the type is not a variable name, and therefore, we cannot assign values to it. The **type** definition for an enumerated scalar type does each of the following:

1. Introduces a new type identifier.
2. Lists the identifiers denoting the constants of the new type.
3. Defines the ordering of the constants.

The order in which the values (or constants) are listed in a type definition establishes the ordering for that type. Each identifier used to specify a value in a user-defined type can only be listed once in one type definition.

Enumerated scalar data types are for internal use only. We can assign and test such values in a program, but we cannot output them using a write or writeln statement, nor can we input them using a read or readln statement.

Subrange types allow the programmer to specify that a particular data type will consist of a restricted set of values from an enumerated type. Subrange types can be defined for integer types, character types, and enumerated types. A subrange of type real is not allowed.

Pascal has predefined functions that are useful when working with scalar types. These functions are:

1. succ(x)   Returns a value that is the successor of x in the ordering.
2. pred(x)   Returns a value that is the predecessor of x in the ordering.
3. ord(x)   Returns ordinal value of x.
4. chr(x)   Returns character value corresponding to the integer x.

Goto statements are used for conditional branching. Statements with labels attached to them are used with **goto** statements. **Goto**

statements, however, should only be used as a last resort, when no other Pascal statement will do the job well.

5.9 EXERCISES

5.1. Fill in the blanks in each of the following:

(a) A _____ is a series of steps that are iterated or executed repetitively.

(b) The two reasons why we often need to iterate the execution of some steps of an algorithm are _____ and _____.

(c) The two forms of loops in Pascal are the conditional loop and the _____ loop.

(d) Of the two conditional loops, **repeat . . . until** and **while . . . do**, which contains a body that is executed at least once? _____.

(e) The conditon used in the **repeat . . . until** loop controls _____. The condition used in the **while . . . do** statement controls _____.

(f) The **while . . . do** statement is executed as long as the condition remains _____. The **repeat . . . until** statement is executed until the condition becomes _____.

(g) A "special" value that cannot be confused with an actual data value and that is placed after a program's input data to indicate "end of data" is called a(n) _____.

(h) The boolean function _____ is provided by Pascal as a built-in _____ to signal when a program reaches the end of its input data.

(i) The **for . . . do** may be used to control loops when we know in advance _____.

(j) The **for . . . do** statement

```
for i := a to b do
    statement
```

will not execute statement when _____.

(k) The _____ alternate form of the **for . . . do** provides repetition for a sequence of decreasing values of the control variable.

(l) When the following **for . . . do** statement terminates, the value of the control variable, i, is _____.

```
for i := 1 to 10 do
    t := t + i
```

(m) A character constant consists of a single character enclosed in _____.

(n) A program that inputs two character values may use a _____ operator to determine if they are in alphabetical order.

(o) The two ways in which a new type can be defined in Pascal are _____ and _____.

(p)
```
var
    JanuaryDays : 1..31;
```

is an example of _____ in which we limit the range of values that the variable JanuaryDays can assume.

5.2. Answer each of the following true or false. If your answer is false, state why.

(a) A conditional loop always terminates when a condition becomes false.

(b) All compound statements in Pascal must be explicitly bracketed by **begin . . . end.**

(c) If the condition is true upon entry to a **repeat . . . until** statement, then the body statements will not be executed.

(d) In contrast to the **repeat . . . until** statement, the boolean expression for a **while . . . do** statement is evaluated at the top of the loop rather than at the bottom.

(e) A sentinel value must be different from any of the possible valid data values for an application. Therefore, the letter *e* is an appropriate sentinel value in a program that computes class average on a quiz in which the grades range from 0 to 100.

(f) The **for . . . do** statement can count down as well as up.

(g) In Pascal, the control variable in a **for . . . do** loop must be of type integer.

(h) In the ASCII character set, the letter *S* is greater than the letter *Q*.

(i) In the EBCDIC character set, the letter *S* is greater than the letter *Q*.

(j) The statement read(Letter) where Letter has been declared as a char variable will never skip a blank in the input file.

(k) Pascal allows the programmer to define customized data types useful for particular problems.

(l) When we use a **type** definition, the identifier we select for the type is not the identifier for a variable, and therefore, we cannot assign values to it.

(m) Enumerated scalar data types are for internal use only. We can assign and test such values in a program, but we cannot ouput them using a write or writeln statement and we cannot input them using a read or readln statement.

(n) A subrange of type real is not allowed.

5.3. Describe the function(s) performed by each of the following Pascal statements:

(a) `repeat...until`

(b) `while...do`

(c) `for...do`

(d) `Total := Total + Number`

(e) `Count := Count + 1`

(f) `if Number > Largest then`
     `     Largest := Number`

(g)   `Salary := HoursWorked * Rate + Overtime`

(h)   ```
      while not eof do
          begin
              read (Number);
              Total := Total + Number;
              Count := Count + 1
          end
      ```

(i)   ```
      for Number := 1 to 10 do
          write (Number : 4);
      writeln
      ```

(j)   ```
      for i := 5 downto 1 do
          Product := Product * i;
      writeln (Product)
      ```

(k)   ```
      while not eof do
          begin
              if ch = blank then
                  Count := Count + 1;
              read (ch)
          end
      ```

(l)   ```
      var
          Day : (sunday, monday, tuesday, wednesday,
                 thursday, friday, saturday);
      ```

(m)   ```
      type
          Weekday = (sunday, monday, tuesday, wednesday,
                     thursday, friday, saturday);
      ```

(n)   ```
      type
          boolean = (false, true);
      ```

(o)   ```
      var
          Year : integer;
      ```

(p)   ```
      var
          Year : 1950..1985;
      ```

(q)   ```
      type
          Letter = 'A'..'Z';
      ```

5.4. Write Pascal statements to accomplish each of the following tasks:

(a) Initialize the variables Total and Count to zero.

(b) Increment the variable Count by 1.

(c) Add the variable Number into a running total kept in variable Total.

(d) Initialize a variable Counter to 1. Now write a statement that adds Counter to CounterTotal until Counter becomes equal to 50.

(e) Write a compound statement that adds 1 to variable Count and that adds variable Number into a running total being kept in variable Sum.

(f) Write a **while . . . . do** statement that reads a variable Number, adds it into running total Sum. The last number to be read is 17, and it, too, should be added into Sum.

(g) Write a conditional loop that totals 15 numbers of data. The sentinel at the end of the data items is −1. Be careful not to add the sentinel value into the sum of the numbers.

(h) Print the numbers 1 to 15 on the same line using a counter-controlled loop.

(i) Declare the variables Letter, Digit, and SpecialSymbol to be of type char.

(j) Declare the variable Month so that it may assume only the twelve month names.

(k) Declare a new data type called WorkingDay, whose values may be monday, tuesday, wednesday, thursday, or friday.

(l) Declare a variable called Year, whose values may be 1980, 1981, . . . , 1989 only.

5.5. Write a Pascal program that totals the squares of the first 50 positive integers and then prints the result. Thus, your program will produce the following sum:

$$1^2 + 2^2 + \ldots + 50^2$$

5.6. The factorial of a positive integer, n, is defined as:

$$n * (n-1) * (n-2) * \ldots * 1$$

Write a Pascal program that prints the factorials of the positive integers from 1 to 10.

5.7. The factorial of n, written $n!$, can be enormously large, even for relatively small values of n, such as 15 or 20. Most computers only represent a limited range of integers. To represent very large (or very small) values, the programmer must use real numbers instead of integers. The largest real number representable on a computer (be careful, this is not maxint) varies from one computer system to the next. Write a Pascal program to determine the largest factorial your computer can represent. Do this with either a **while . . . do** or **repeat . . . until**, whose condition will never allow it to exit the loop. Calculate and print successively larger factorials until the program terminates because of "overflow"; that is, because the program develops a number larger than the computer can represent.

5.8. The medieval investigator, Leonardo (Fibonacci) da Pisa, proposed the unending sequence of numbers:

1, 1, 2, 3, 5, 8, 13, 21, 34, 55, . . .

in which each term is defined as the sum of its two predecessors. Write a Pascal program to calculate and print the first 30 Fibonacci numbers.

5.9. Fibonacci numbers are more than just a mathematical curiosity; examples of Fibonacci numbers occur in nature and even in classical art and architecture. In the core of daisy blossoms there are sets of clockwise and counterclockwise spirals; there are 21 clockwise and 34 counterclockwise spirals with the ratio 21:34 consisting of adjacent Fibonacci numbers. The opposing spirals in pine cones occur in a 5:8 ratio. Even pineapple "bumps" occur in an 8:13 ratio.

After the number 3 in the Fibonacci sequence, successive numbers occur with a ratio that remains close to 1:1.618 (sometimes called the "golden ratio"). For example:

21: 13 = 1.6154
34: 21 = 1.6190
55: 34 = 1.6176

Write a Pascal program that calculates the ratios between the first 30 pairs of successive Fibonacci numbers.

5.10. In the Fahrenheit temperature scale, water freezes at 32 degrees and boils at 212 degeees. In the Celsius scale, water freezes at 0 degrees and boils at 100 degrees. The formulas for converting one scale to the other are:

Celsius to Fahrenheit
$F = (9/5) * C + 32$

Fahrenheit to Celsius
$C = (5/9) * (F - 32)$

Write a Pascal program that prints a table showing the Fahrenheit temperatures equivalent to Celsius temperatures of 0 to 100 degrees. Write a second Pascal program that shows the Celsius temperatures equivalent to Fahrenheit temperatures of 32 to 212 degrees.

5.11. In the last problem, you probably printed the temperature conversion tables in one long column. This produces a lengthy printout, wastes paper, and produces information that is not compact or easy to use. It is often worth some additional programming time to produce neater and more concise output.

Rewrite the temperature conversion programs to pack the information more tightly onto your printed output. Use a multiple column format (10 columns if you can). A portion of your printout might look something like this:

Celsius	Fahrenheit					
0–9	32.0	33.8	35.6	37.4	39.2	. . .
10–19	50.0	51.8	53.6	55.4	57.2	. . .
20–29	.					
.	.					
.	.					
.						

5.12. When money is deposited in a bank that pays interest once per month, and when the original amount and interest remain on deposit, the interest is said to be compounded. The formula for the amount of money remaining on deposit, P, when an amount, A, is deposited initially and when interest is paid at a monthly rate, I, for N months is:

$$P = A * (1 + I)^N$$

Write a Pascal program that calculates the principal, P, remaining on deposit when $1000.00 is invested at 1% interest per month. Show the principal remaining on deposit at the end of each of the first 30 months.
5.13. Modify the compound interest problem above so that it produces a table showing the principal remaining on deposit at the end of each of the first 30 months for interest rates of 1%, 1.1%, 1.2%, . . . , 1.9% per month. Your printout might look something like this:

Month	Amounts Remaining on Deposit at Monthly Interest Rates:						
	1.0%	1.1%	1.2%	1.3%	1.4%	1.5%	. . .
1	.						
2	.						
.	.						
.	.						
.							
30							

5.14. In mathematics and the sciences, we frequently use the transcendental constant, e, which is approximately equal to 2.7182818. Students of calculus know that the following Maclaurin series can be used to represent e:

$$e = 1 + \frac{1}{1!} + \frac{1}{2!} + \frac{1}{3!} + \frac{1}{4!} + \ldots + \frac{1}{n!} + \ldots$$

Clearly, as n becomes large, the contribution of each additional term becomes very small. Write a Pascal program that will calculate and print values of e derived by using increasing numbers of terms in the Maclaurin series for e. Your output might look something like this:

Number of Terms	Value of Last Term	Approximation of e
1	1	1.0
2	1	2.0
3	0.5	2.5
4	0.1666	2.6666
.	.	.
.	.	.
.	.	.

5.15. Write Pascal programs to produce each of the following patterns. Each of your programs may contain a maximum of three write (or writeln) statements chosen from:

```
writeln
write ('*')
write (' ')
```

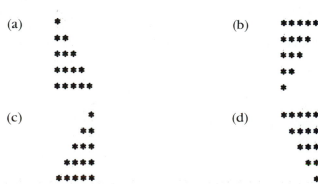

5.16. In the input file there are an unknown number of lines, each containing a student's name (up to 20 letters) and four numbers representing that student's grades (on a 4-point scale) in four courses. These students all took the same four courses.

Your job is to write a Pascal program that will:

(a) Print the student's name and his or her grade point average.

(b) Print "honors" after the GPA if it is 3.5 or higher, and "warning" if it is below 1.5.

(c) Print the average over all students for each course.

For example, if the input file contained:

Cobol, Carl	3.0	2.7	2.0	2.8
Pascal, Blaise	3.7	3.5	4.0	4.0
Fortran, Fred	0.0	1.0	2.5	1.0
Lovelace, Ada	4.0	3.0	3.5	3.5

then your program's output should look something like:

Students	GPA	Special Note
Cobol, Carl	2.625	
Pascal, Blaise	3.800	honors
Fortran, Fred	1.050	warning
Lovelace, Ada	3.500	honors

Course 1 average: 2.675
Course 2 average: 2.550
Course 3 average: 2.925
Course 4 average: 2.825

Your program must print labels for the columns and answers as shown above; you should always try to make computer output self-explanatory.

6. Arrays

6.1 STRUCTURED DATA TYPES

The scalar data types we have used so far are called *simple* data types. Variables of simple data types can only assume a single value of that type at any one point in the program. Thus, a variable of type integer can only be assigned a single value of type integer. Similarly, a variable of type char can only be assigned a single value of type char. Pascal also has *structured* data types. A structured data type is a data type whose value is made up of collections of simpler types. There are many ways to structure or organize simple data types into composites. One way is to arrange the simple data types into lists or tables. The structured type that uses this method of organizing data is called an **array type**, or simply an **array**.

6.2 THE CONCEPT OF AN ARRAY

Consider the following problem: we have test scores for 35 students and wish to obtain the average of all these scores. We also want to determine and print the difference between each score and the average. We cannot approach this task the same way we approached the computation of the average of a set of numbers. When all we needed was the average, we were able to input each number, completely process it by adding it to a running total, and input the next number. When the next number was input, however, the earlier value was lost because the same variable was used to store the new value.

Here, we not only need to compute the average of a set of scores, but we also have to compute the difference between each score and the average. To do this, we either must read all the test scores twice, or save all the scores so that they are available when we need to compute the differences. Using only the Pascal features we have studied so far, we would require separate variable names for each test score. Thirty-five variables, such as Score1, Score2, Score3, . . . , Score35, of the appropriate type could be declared. However, the resulting program would be cumbersome. It would involve reading each score separately, calculating the average, then computing the difference for each score using a separate assignment statement. We would need 35 assignment statements to compute the difference between each score and the average as illustrated in the program fragment below:

```
Difference := Score1 - Average;
writeln (Difference);
Difference := Score2 - Average;
writeln (Difference);
Difference := Score3 - Average;
writeln (Difference);
                .
                .
                .
Difference := Score35 - Average;
writeln (Difference);
```

The situation would, of course, be even worse if we had to perform the same calculations with 200 or 1000 scores.

The fact that the variables Score1, Score2, . . . , Score35 are distinct, forces us to use individual assignment statements to compute each difference even though the computations performed with each variable are exactly the same. Thus, the possibility of using repetition in what appears to be a repetitive situation is precluded by the fact that the variables involved are unrelated to each other.

A better approach is to consider all of these variables as **components** of a single variable called an **array** and to use a *subscript* to differentiate between the components. This is illustrated in Figure 6.1, where we have a single array variable, *Score*, with 35 components or elements.

In the array of Figure 6.1, the single identifier Score is associated with 35 adjacent main storage locations, one location for each component or element of the array. We can select a given component by using a subscript in square brackets. Thus, Score[1] refers to the first component or element of Score, namely 78. Similarly, Score[3] refers to the third component of Score, or 100. The numbers 78, 95, 100, . . . , 65 are the values of the elements. The integers enclosed in the square brackets are the subscripts. The variable Score, whose value is the entire array, is known as an **array variable**. The variables Score[1], Score[2], . . . , Score[35], whose values are the individual components of the array, are known as **subscripted variables**. We

Figure 6.1 The components of the array *Score*

	Score [1]	Score [2]	Score [3]	•••	Score [35]
Score	78	95	100	•••	65

can use subscripted variables in the same way as any variables we have studied so far: that is, they can be used in assignment statements, output statements, input statements, and so forth. For example:

```
Score[1] := 77;
Score[2] := 98;
Score[5] := 2 * Score[1];
Score[12] := Score[2] - Score[1];
writeln (Score[1], Score[12]);
read (Score[4])
```

The assignment statements

```
Score[1] := 77
```

and

```
Score[2] := 98
```

assign the values 77 and 98 to the first and second components of Score. The assignment statements

```
Score[5] := 2 * Score[1]
```

and

```
Score[12] := Score[2] - Score[1]
```

assign the values 154 and 21 to the 5th and 12th components of Score respectively. The statement

```
writeln (Score[1], Score[12])
```

outputs the values 77 and 21 and

```
read (Score[4])
```

assigns a value to the 4th component of Score from the standard input file.

The subscript of a subscripted variable does not have to be a constant. It can be an expression. For example, if i has a value of 4, then

```
Score[i]
```

refers to the 4th component of Score and

```
Score[i+2]
```

refers to the 6th component of the array Score. It is precisely the fact that expressions can be used as subscripts to arrays, as we shall see shortly, that makes arrays useful.

Array Declarations

To declare an array that consists of 35 components, each capable of storing an integer, the following Pascal declaration can be used:

```
var
   Score : array[1..35] of integer;
```

The declaration mentions two data types: the **component data type**, integer in our example, and the **subscript data type**, the subrange type 1..35 in our example.

The general form of an array declaration is:

```
var
   identifier : array [subscript type] of component type;
```

In the declaration, the identifier names the array variable. The subscript type may be either of the two standard types boolean or char, any user-defined enumerated scalar type, or a subrange type. Neither of the standard types integer or real can be used as index types for arrays because this would create arrays with an infinite number of components. A subrange of type integer, however, can be used.

The component type describes each element of the array. It can be any of the scalar types we have studied thus far or, as we will see later, it can even be a structured type. Note that *all components of an array are of the same type*.

The following examples are *valid* array declarations:

```
const
   Min = 1;
   Max = 100;

type
   DaysOfWeek =(sunday, monday, tuesday, wednesday,
                thursday, friday, saturday);
```

```
var
   TestScores  : array[Min..Max] of real;
   LetterCount : array['a'..'z'] of integer;
   DegreeCount : array[-10..10] of integer;
   HoursWorked : array[DaysOfWeek] of real;
   DigitFlag   : array['0'..'9'] of boolean;
   Answers     : array[boolean] of integer;
   Name        : array[1..20] of char;
```

Given the above declarations, some of the possible assignment statements are:

Assignment Statement	Possible Interpretation
TestScores [58] := 79.5	The test score of the 58th student is assigned the value 79.5
LetterCount ['r'] := 0	The counter for the letter 'r' is initialized to 0
HoursWorked[monday] := 8.0	The number of hours worked on Monday is set to 8.0
DigitFlag['4'] := true	The flag indicating that '4' was found is set to true
Answer[true] := Answer[true] + 1	The counter for true answers is incremented by 1
Name[1] := 'S'	The first letter of the name is set to 'S'

When declaring arrays, the **type** definition can also be used. For example, to declare two array variables "Midterm" and "Final" to hold the grades of a group of students, we can use the following statements:

```
const
   ClassSize = 50;

type
   Grades = array[1..ClassSize] of real;

var
   Midterm, Final : Grades;
```

The above variable declaration reserves two arrays, each with 50 components capable of assuming real values.

Array Subscripts

Subscripts are used to differentiate between the individual components of an array. An array component can be referenced by giving the name of the array, followed by a subscript enclosed in square brackets. The subscript may be a constant, a variable, or even an expression. The only restriction is that the type of the expression must correspond to the subscript type in the declaration.

The fact that the index into an array can be an expression allows the same code to refer to different components of an array merely by changing the current value of the subscript variable. The example below illustrates how a 1 could be added to the first 5 components of the array Score by making the subscript, i, assume the values 1 through 5 while the assignment statement Score[i] := Score[i] + 1 is executed repeatedly.

```
for i := 1 to 5 do
   Score[i] := Score[i] + 1
```

Let us trace the execution of this code. We will assume that the array, Score, has the values shown in Figure 6.2(a) prior to the execution of the **for** loop. Figure 6.2(b) shows the step-by-step execution of the **for** loop, and (c) shows the array after execution of the **for** loop.

Figure 6.2 Step-by-step processing of an array

	Score [1]	Score [2]	Score [3]	Score [4]	Score [5]
Score	12	72	398	8	0

a

i	Score [i]	Score [i] + 1
1	12	13
2	72	73
3	398	399
4	8	9
5	0	1

b

	Score [1]	Score [2]	Score [3]	Score [4]	Score [5]
Score	13	73	399	9	1

c

The **for** statement is used to "move through" the array, processing each component the same way, but processing only one component at a time. This is the most common way of using arrays. Here are some additional examples of processing arrays one element at a time. Assuming the following array declaration:

```
var
   Score, Copy : array[1..5] of integer;
```

for statements can be used to:

1. Print values stored in an array, assuming that the values have already been stored:
   for i := 1 **to 5 do**
      writeln (Score[i] :5)

2. Initialize the components of an array to zero:
   for i := 1 **to 5 do**
      Score[i] := 0

3. Sum the values of the components of an array:
   Total := 0;
   for i := 1 **to 5 do**
      Total := Total + Score[i]

4. Copy an array into another array:
   for i := 1 **to 5 do**
      Copy [i] := Score[i]

5. Copy an array into another array in reverse order:
   for i := 1 **to 5 do**
      Copy [6 − i] := Score[i]

It is important to understand the difference between the *subscript* to an array, the *value of the subscript*, and the *value of a component*. The subscript is enclosed in square brackets following the array identifier. Its value is used to select one of the array components for processing. The component is the value that is being processed. In the example above, where we copied one array into another array in reverse order, the subscript of array Copy is [6 − i]; when *i* is 1, its value is 5. Thus, the component of array Copy that is changed when *i* is 1 is the 5th component. This component is assigned the value of the first component of array Score.

If the type of a subscript expression does not agree with the declared subscript type of the array, a compile-time error will result, and an error message indicating an incorrect type will be printed. If the value of a subscript expression is outside the subrange type specified in the array declaration, a run-time error will occur, because there is no such array component. This will result in an error message indicating a value out of range and the termination of execution of your program. For example, if for the array declarations above we attempted the following assignment:

```
Score[i] := 0
```

and the current value of *i* was 6, we would be attempting to assign a value to the 6th component of array Score. Because there is no such component, we have a subscript value out of range.

Most Pascal operators do not act on arrays as a whole, but on their components—the values of the subscripted variables. However, if two arrays have the same structure (that is, the component types and the subscript types are the same), the assignment operator can be used to assign the value of one array variable to another. This can be done without using subscripts. For example, suppose that we have the following declarations:

```
type
    List = array[1..10] of integer;

var
    x, y : List;
```

then we can make the assignment:

```
x := y
```

which is equivalent to:

```
for i := 1 to 10 do
    x[i] := y[i]
```

Note, however, that in most Pascal implementations, the arrays in the following declaration:

```
var
    a : array[1..20] of integer;
    b : array[0..19] of integer;
```

would not be considered to have the same structure. Although they have the same number of integer components, the subscript types are different. Most Pascal compilers would even consider the following two arrays to be of different types.

```
var
  a : array[1..20] of integer;
  b : array[1..20] of integer;
```

With those Pascal compilers, two variables are of the same type only if they are declared with the same *named* type. Thus, if we want to declare array *a* to be of the same type as array *b* we must first name a type and then declare both arrays to be of that type. This could be done as follows:

```
type
  ArrayType = array[1..20] of integer;

var
  a,b : ArrayType;
```

Reading Values into an Array

Values can be assigned to components of an array using a read or a readln statement in the same way as we would assign values to any other variable. In fact, with subscripted variables, as with any other variables, values *must* be assigned, either by an assignment statement or a read or readln statement, before the variables can be manipulated. The declaration statement only reserves the main storage locations for possible use. It does not assign values.

With arrays, we often want to assign values only to some of the components. That is, we may want to fill the array only partially. Just because an array is declared to be a given size does not mean it is necessary to assign values to all of its components. What is important is that we have an array large enough to handle all the possible values we need to process.

To illustrate this, let us return to the problem that we introduced at the beginning of this chapter. We wish to determine the deviation from the average of the scores on a test. We will solve a more general problem and design an algorithm that will process the grades for a class of any size up to 50 students. In order to do this, we declare an array capable of storing 50 grades, even if for a particular execution of the program we only have 35 or 40 grades to process. Our first approximation to the algorithm is:

begin
    Input all the scores
    Compute and output the average
    Compute and output the difference between
        each score and the average
end.

The statement

Input all the scores

is now expanded as follows. Note that we do not use a **for** loop since we do not know how many scores we have. We are assuming that the scores were not counted prior to running the program.

Initialize subscript to 1
Input value of first component of array
while (scores remain to be processed) **and**
        (subscript is less than the class size) **do**
        Increment subscript by 1
        Input value of the array component indexed by the current value of
        subscript
Set the count to subscript

First, the subscript of the array that will hold each score is initialized to 1. The first score is read into the first location of the array. The subscript is incremented by 1 and we continue to input values into consecutive locations of the array until we reach the end of the file. Once all the values have been read, the current value of the subscript tells us how many values have been read.
    The statement

Compute and output the average

can be expanded to:

Initialize total to 0
for index starting at 1 **to** number of values read **do**
   Add consecutive values of array to total
Compute the average
Output the average

Only those components of the array that contain values that were read in the previous step are summed.

Finally, the statement

Compute and output the difference between each score and the average

can be expanded as:

for index starting at 1 **to** number of scores **do**
    Compute the difference between the score and the average
    Output the score and the difference

Assembling all the pieces of the algorithm and translating the algorithm into Pascal, we have the program in Example 6.1.

**EXAMPLE 6.1
Program to
Compute the
Average and
Deviations
from the Average of a Set of
Scores**

```pascal
program Deviations (input, output);

{*****************************************
* Program to compute the average grade  *
* and the deviation of each grade from  *
* the average for a class.              *
*****************************************}

const
    ClassSize = 50;

type
    Class = array[1..ClassSize] of integer;

var
    i, Count : integer;
    Total, Average, Deviation : real;
    Scores : Class;

begin
    {Input the test scores}

    i := 0;
    while (not eof) and (i < ClassSize) do
        begin
            i := i + 1;
            readln(Scores[i]);
        end {While loop};
```

**EXAMPLE 6.1
Program to
Compute the
Average and
Deviations
from the Aver-
age of a Set of
Scores**
(*continued*)

```
Count := i;
{Compute and output the average}

Total := 0;
for i := 1 to Count do
   Total := Total + Scores[i];
Average := Total / Count;
writeln (' Average Grade: ', Average : 10:2);
writeln;

{Compute and output the differences}

writeln ('   GRADE        DEVIATION FROM AVERAGE');
writeln;
for i := 1 to Count do
   begin
      Deviation := Scores[i] - Average;
      writeln ( Scores[i] : 6, Deviation :21:2)
   end {For loop}
end.
```

Given the data (One score per line)

76 80 80 88 86 86 87 80 90 93 90 66

the results are:

Average Grade: 83.50

GRADE	DEVIATION FROM AVERAGE
76	-7.50
80	-3.50
80	-3.50
88	4.50
86	2.50
86	2.50
87	3.50
80	-3.50
90	6.50
93	9.50
90	6.50
66	-17.50

Let us look at another example of a program using arrays. The program in Example 6.2 summarizes the results of an opinion poll. An unknown number of individuals was asked to rate a new product on a scale of 1 to 5.

like very much	like	neutral	dislike	dislike very much
5	4	3	2	1

We wish to summarize the number of responses of each type. The approach is to use an array to count each type of response (Example 6.2).

**EXAMPLE 6.2
Program to
Summarize the
Results of a
Survey**

```
program Survey (input, output);

{***************************
 * Program to summarize the *
 * results of a survey.     *
 ***************************}

type
   Votes = array[1..5] of integer;

var
   Responses : Votes;
   Choice, i : integer;

begin
   {Initialize array for counting}

   for i := 1 to 5 do
      Responses[i] := 0;

   {Input choices and increment corresponding
    array location to count each type of response}

   read (Choice);
```

EXAMPLE 6.2
Program to
Summarize the
Results of a
Survey
(*continued*)

```
while Choice <> -1 do
    begin
        Responses[Choice] := Responses[Choice] + 1;
        read (Choice)
    end;

{Output summary}

writeln(' RESPONSE          FREQUENCY');
writeln;
for i := 1 to 5 do
    writeln ( i :6, Responses[i] :14)
end.
```

Given the input

```
5 3 3 2 2 2 2 5 1 1 5 3 4 3 5 1 4 4 5 4 4 2 5 4 3 2
2 5 5 2 3 2 4 3 2 1 4 3 4 1 1 1 5 5 2 5 4 1 4 1 2 -1
```

the output would appear as:

RESPONSE	FREQUENCY
1	9
2	12
3	8
4	11
5	11

SELF-TEST 1

1. Determine if each of the following declarations is correct. If there is an error, make the necessary corrections.

(a) **type**
      Month = 1..12;
   var
      Budget : **array**[12] **of** real;

(b) **type**
      Colors = (yellow, green, red, white, blue);
   var
      Tint : **array**[1..Colors] **of** boolean;

(c) **type**
```
    Temperature = -20..110;
var
    MinTemp: array[1..31] of Temperature;
```

(d) **const**
```
    LastRow = 20;
var
    Occupied : array[1..LastRow] of boolean;
```

2. Provide the necessary definitions and declarations to create the arrays described below.

(a) Array CapitalLetters has a component for each capital letter, and each component is the number of capital letters counted.

(b) Array GradeReport has a component for each course taken. The courses are: Statistics, Computer Science I, Biology, French, and General Psychology. Each component is the letter grade in the course (A, B, C, D, or F).

(c) Array Elected has a component for each candidate. The candidates are Devine, Devlin, Horgan, Rogers, and Skinner. Each component indicates if the candidate was elected in the previous election.

3. Assume the following declarations have been made:

```
type
    Week = (sunday, monday, tuesday, wednesday,
            thursday, friday, saturday);
var
    Days : array[Week] of integer;
    Alphabet : array['A'..'Z'] of integer;
    Numbers : array[-10..10] of integer;
    WeekDay : Week;
    i : integer;
    j : char;
```

Describe what values are assigned to each of the arrays by the following program segments.

(a) **for** i := -10 **to** 10 **do**
```
    Numbers[i] := sqr(i)
```

(b) **for** WeekDay := sunday **to** saturday **do**
```
    Days[WeekDay] := 0
```

(c) **for** j := 'A' **to** 'Z' **do**
        Alphabet[j] := ord(j)−ord('A') + 1
        {Assume ASCII character set}

4. What will be the output of the following program assuming that
the input consists of the following values?
1 2 3 4 5 6 7 8 9

```
program Question4 (input, output);
var
    x : array[1..20] of integer;
    i,j,k : integer;
begin
    i := 0;
    while not eof do
        begin
            i := i + 1;
            read(x[i])
        end;
    for j := 1 to i div 2 do
        begin
            k := x[j];
            x[j] := x[i−j+1];
            x[i−j+1] := k
        end;
    for j := 1 to i do
        write( x[j]);
    writeln
end.
```

Answers

1. (a) Invalid. Subscript should be [1..12].   (b) Invalid. Subscript
should be [Colors].   (c) Valid   (d) Valid

2. (a) **var**
        CapitalLetters : **array**['A'..'Z'] **of** integer;

   (b) **type**
        Course = (Stat, CompSciI, Bio, French, GenPsych);
      var
        GradeReport : **array**[Course] **of** char;

   (c) **type**
        Candidate = (Devine, Devlin, Horgan,
                     Rodgers, Skinner);
      var
        Elected : **array**[Candidate] **of** boolean;

3. (a) The squares of the values −10 through 10 are assigned to the corresponding components of the array Numbers. That is, the component Numbers[−10] is assigned 100, the component Numbers[−9] is assigned 81, etc. (b) Each component of the array Days is initialized to 0. (c) The components of the array Alphabet are assigned an integer corresponding to their position in the alphabet. That is, Alphabet['A'] is assigned 1, Alphabet ['B'] is assigned 2, etc.
4. The output will be 9 8 7 6 5 4 3 2 1

6.3 SEARCHING AND SORTING ARRAYS

One of the most common applications of computers involves *searching* lists or arrays to determine if a particular value is in the list. There are many reasons why we often need to search arrays. We may simply want to determine if a particular value occurs as a component, we may want to determine where it occurs, or we may want to locate a component to modify or replace it. Many times we need to search one array and retrieve the corresponding component of another array. For example, consider the problem of locating the price of an item in a table. Table 6.1 shows how such data might be arranged in an input file. The first number on each line is the item number, while the second number is the price of that item. Our problem consists of reading the information into two arrays: one to hold the item numbers, another to hold the prices. We then search the item number array for the desired item number and output the corresponding component of the price array.

Arrays may be searched in different ways. Here, we introduce the topic by examining the simplest of these algorithms, the **linear search**. Consider the array illustrated in Figure 6.3. The numbers stored in this array are not arranged in any particular sequence. That is, they are not arranged in either increasing or decreasing sequence.

Table 6.1 Table of item prices

Item	Price
0002	4.75
0009	0.79
0028	6.78
0856	2.98
1198	1.05
1356	9.99
2780	3.75

Figure 6.3 Unsorted array

	a [1]	a [2]	a [3]	a [4]	a [5]	a [6]	a [7]	a [8]	a [9]	a [10]
a	82	38	10	7	85	67	94	31	37	5

In a **linear** or **sequential** search, we search for a value in a list or array by examining each item in order, starting at the beginning of the list or array. When we find the item we are looking for, we stop. For example, we might look for the number 37 in the above array. We start at the first element of the array by examining the value 82. Since this is not the value we want, we go on to the next value and continue examining values in sequence until we arrive at 37 in the ninth location of the array. Of course, it is possible that the data item we are searching for is not in the array. We determine this by reaching the end of the array without finding the value we are looking for. The algorithm for the linear search is straightforward.

```
begin
      Set found to false
      Set index to 1
      while (index is less than or equal to array size)
            and (found is false) do
          if item being searched for is equal to component
                being examined then
              Set found to true
          else
              Increment index by 1
      if found is true then
          Item was found at current value of index
      else
          Item is not in array
end.
```

Using the linear search algorithm we developed, we can now write our program (Example 6.3) to look up the price of an item given the item number. Note we use an item number equal to −1 as a sentinel to indicate the end of the table of item prices.

EXAMPLE 6.3 Program to Look up the Price of an Item

```
program LookUpPrice (input,output);

{***********************************
 * Program to look up the price of *
 * an item given the item number.  *
 ***********************************}
```

**EXAMPLE 6.3
Program to
Look up the
Price of an
Item**
(*continued*)

```
const
   Maxsize = 100;

var
   ItemNumbers      : array[1..Maxsize] of integer;
   Prices           : array[1..Maxsize] of real;
   Item, i, Count : integer;
   Found            : boolean;

begin
   {Input and count item numbers
    and corresponding prices}

   i := 1;
   readln (ItemNumbers[i],Prices[i]);
   while ItemNumber[i] <> -1 do
      begin
         i := i + 1
         readln(ItemNumber[i], Prices[i]);
      end
   Count := i - 1;

   {Input the item number of the item to be found
    and search for the item}

   read (Item);
   Found := false;
   i := 1;
   while (i <= Count) and (not Found) do
      if Item = ItemNumbers[i] then
         Found := true
      else
         i := i + 1;

   {If the item was found output the price
    otherwise print an error message}

   if Found then
      writeln (' Item Number: ',Item :5,
         ' Price: ', Prices[i] :7:2)
   else
      writeln (' Item Number: ',Item :5,
         ' Not in data file.')

end.
```

EXAMPLE 6.3
Program to
Look up the
Price of an
Item
(*continued*)

Given the following input

```
0002   4.75
0009   0.79
0028   6.79
0856   2.98
1198   1.05
1356   9.99
2780   3.75
 − 1   0
1356
```

the output is:

`Item Number:   1356  Price:       9.99`

The program in Example 6.3 does not take advantage of the fact that the item numbers are arranged in increasing order. Since that is the case, our linear search algorithm might be improved as follows:

```
begin
    Set found to false
    Set finished to false
    Set index to 1
    while (index is less than or equal to array size)
            and (found is false) and (finished is false) do
        if item being searched for is equal to component being examined
                then
            Set found to true
        else
            if item being searched for is less than component
                being examined then
                Set finished to true
            else
                Increment index by 1
    if found is true then
        Item was found at current value of index
    else
        Item is not in array
    end.
```

In this algorithm, we introduce another flag called "finished," which we set to true when we encounter a value that is greater than the value we are looking for. Since the elements of the array are arranged in increasing order, all remaining values to be examined are greater than what we are looking for and we might as well terminate the search. We leave the modification of the price look-up program, in order to incorporate the ability to terminate the search without going through the whole array, as an exercise.

The ability to terminate the search without having to examine all the components of an array was predicated on the fact that the array was properly ordered. When the components of an array are sequenced in ascending or descending order, searching algorithms much more efficient than a linear search can be used. Thus, algorithms for rearranging the components of an array into a particular order (i.e., *sorting algorithms*) are as important as algorithms for searching. We need to sort data for many reasons. As we pointed out, searching can be much faster with sorted arrays. Also, we often need to sort data before we print reports to make it easier to interpret the output of a program.

One way to sort an array is to locate the smallest value, move it to the first position of the array, locate the next smallest value, move it to the second position of the array, and so on. That is, we continuously select the smallest remaining value and move it to its appropriate position in the array. This sorting algorithm is called a **selection sort**. The algorithm for the selection sort is:

begin
    Set start to 1
    while (start is less than number of elements in array) **do**
        Beginning at start locate the smallest element of the array
        Interchange the smallest element and the element at start
        Increment start by 1
end.

Expanding the statement

Beginning at start locate the smallest element of the array

we have:

Set location of smallest element of the array to start
for i equals start + 1 to number of elements **do**
    if element at location i is less than
        element at location smallest **then**
      Set location of smallest element to i

The statement

Interchange the smallest element and the element at start

can be explanded into:

Copy the contents of location smallest into a temporary location
Copy the contents of location start into location smallest
Copy the contents of the temporary location into location start

If we put all the pieces together, we can now write the Pascal program in Example 6.4, which inputs a list of integers, sorts the list in ascending order, and prints the result.

EXAMPLE 6.4 Program to Sort a List of Integers in Ascending Order

```pascal
program SelectionSort (input, output);

{*******************************************
* Program to sort a list of integers      *
* in ascending order using the selection  *
* sort algorithm.                          *
*******************************************}

const
    Maxsize = 100;

var
    List : array[1..Maxsize] of integer;
    Start, NumberOfValues, Smallest, Temp, i : integer;

begin
    {Input values}

    i := 1;
    while not eof and (i <= Maxsize) do
      begin
          readln(List[i]);
          i := i + 1
      end;
    NumberOfValues := i - 1;

    {Print array}

    for i := 1 to NumberOfValues do
      write ( List[i] :5);
    writeln;
```

**EXAMPLE 6.4
Program to
Sort a List of
Integers in As-
cending Order**
(*continued*)

```
{sort array}

for Start := 1 to NumberOfValues do
   begin
      {Find location of smallest}

      Smallest := Start;
      for i := Start + 1 to NumberOfValues do
        if List[i] < List[Smallest] then
           Smallest := i;

      {Interchange}

      Temp := List[Smallest];
      List[Smallest] := List[Start];
      List[Start] := Temp;
   end; {For loop}
{Print sorted array}

writeln;
for i := 1 to NumberOfValues do
   write (List[i] :5);
writeln
end.
```

When this program is executed with the following data in the input file

37 34 90 52 77 30 2 12 96 14 (One value per line)

the output is:

37	34	90	52	77	30	2	12	96	14
2	12	14	30	34	37	52	77	90	96

**6.4
CHARACTER
STRINGS**

In our previous examples we have used arrays to process numeric data. As we indicated earlier, however, the component type of an array does not need to be numeric. We can declare and use arrays whose component type is char. The following statement declares the character arrays "Firstname" and "Lastname."

```
var
   Firstname : array[1..12] of char;
   Lastname  : array[1..20] of char;
```

As with the components of other arrays, we can use loops to manipulate characters stored in an array. The following program segment reads 12 characters from the input file and stores them in the array Firstname. It then reads the next 20 characters and stores them in the array Lastname.

```
for i := 1 to 12 do
   read (Firstname[i]);
for i := 1 to 20 do
   read (Lastname[i])
```

Processing character data one character at a time, however, is very tedious because loops have to be used for all manipulations. Fortunately, Pascal has a special type of array to facilitate the manipulation of more than one character at a time.

In Chapter 2 we introduced objects of the form 'Hello.' These objects are **character strings**. Although we have used character strings many times, we never indicated their data type. All character strings are constants of the type:

packed array [1..n] **of** char

where *n* is the length of the string. Thus, 'Hello' is a constant of type:

packed array[1..5] of char

In other words, it is a character string of length 5. The string 'The average is:' is a constant of type:

packed array[1..15] of char

The term **packed** tells the system that the storage used by the array should be minimized by packing the individual components closely together within main storage. Figure 6.4 shows the syntax diagram for the full array type definition.

When we declare an **array**[1..20] **of** char, as we did for Lastname, some computers allocate 32 bits (binary digits) to represent a single character. If the same array is declared **packed array**[1..20] **of** char, the same computers allocate only 8 bits to represent a character, thus saving storage. The effect of packing an array economizes storage, but often at the expense of speed because the system may have to do more work to access a component of an array that has been declared **packed**. In general, the meaning of a program is not

Figure 6.4 Syntax
diagram for **array**
data structure

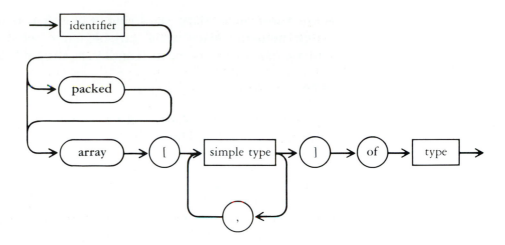

affected by whether we use a packed or nonpacked array. The only possible effect is on storage size and the speed of execution.

There are packed arrays of component types other than char. For example, we can have the declaration:

```
var
    a : packed array[1..30] of boolean;
```

Although packed arrays have, in general, the same operations associated with them as nonpacked arrays, packed arrays of char are special in Pascal and are known as **strings**. They have some special operations associated with them.

Consider the following type definition and variable declaration:

```
type
    String = packed array[1..9] of char;

var
    Name : String;
```

Then we can assign a string of length 9 to the variable name as in the following example:

```
Name := 'Alexander'
```

The constant string 'Alexander' must be *exactly* 9 characters long. The assignment

```
Name := 'Mary'
```

is *not valid* since 'Mary' is a string of length 4. In order to be able to assign the string 'Mary' to the variable name, we would have to pad it with blanks so as to make its length 9, as shown below:

```
Name := 'Mary     '
```

The use of packed arrays greatly facilitates the printing of character strings. As you know, the procedures write and writeln allow the output of constant character strings of any length. For example,

```
writeln ('Hello')
```

prints a string of length 5. We can also output values of packed arrays of characters as if they were constant strings. Thus

```
Name := 'Erika     ';
writeln (' Name : ',Name)
```

outputs two strings, one constant and one the value of a variable:

```
Name :  Erika
```

With most implementations of Pascal, however, it is not possible to read in a value of a string as easily as it can be printed. It must be read in character by character as follows:

```
for i := 1 to 9 do
   read (Name[i])
```

Besides being able to assign strings to packed arrays of characters and being able to use such variables in output lists of write and writeln statements, we can also use them in relational expressions. This is important because it allows us to compare and order character strings. The relational operators =, < >, <, >, < =, and > = can be used with packed character arrays of the same length. Given the following declarations:

```
type
   String = packed array[1..5] of char;

var
   Word1, Word2 : String;
```

and the assignments:

```
Word1 := 'abcd  '
Word2 := 'abcde'
```

the following comparisons are true:

Word1 < Word2
Word1 = 'abcd '
Word2 < > 'abcdf'
Word1 > 'abcd '

The order of two strings is determined by the order of the first two characters that differ. Thus:

'abcd ' < 'abcde' is true because ' ' < 'e'
'abcdf' > 'abcde' is true because 'f' > 'e'

Note that relational operators can only be used with packed arrays of characters of the *same length*. The comparison

'abc' < 'abcde'

is not valid.

Let us look at a program (Example 6.5) involving character strings. The program determines if a character string is a palindrome. You will recall from the exercises of Chapter 4 that a palindrome is a string that reads the same forward as backward. For example, 'radar' is a palindrome. To determine if a string is a palindrome, our program inputs the string, reverses the nonblank characters, and compares the original with the reversed string. If the two strings are equal, the string is a palindrome.

**EXAMPLE 6.5
Program to
Determine If a
String Is a
Palindrome**

```
program Palindrome (input, output);

{*********************************
 * Program to determine if input *
 * string is a palindrome.       *
 *********************************}

const
   StringSize = 80;
```

EXAMPLE 6.5
Program to
Determine If a
String Is a
Palindrome
(*continued*)

```
type
    String = packed array[1..StringSize] of char;
var
    Original, Reverse : String;
    i, Length : integer;
    Ch : char;
begin
    {Initialize original string to blanks}

    for i := 1 to StringSize do
        Original[i] := ' ';

    {Input original string counting characters}

    i := 1;
    while not eoln and (i <= SringSize) do
        begin
            read(Ch);
            Original[i] := Ch;
            i := i + 1
        end; {While loop}
    Length := i - 1;

    {Initialize reverse string to blanks
      and reverse the original string}

    for i :=1 to StringSize    do
        Reverse[i] := ' ';
    for i := 1 to Length do
        Reverse[Length+1-i] := Original[i];

    {Test for palindrome}

    if Original = Reverse then
        writeln (' Palindrome')
    else
        writeln (' Not a palindrome')
end.
```

When the program is executed with the following as input:

madam

the result is:

```
Palindrome
```

SELF-TEST 2

1. Assume the following declarations have been made:

```
type
   ShortString = packed array[1..15] of char;
   LongString  = packed array[1..30] of char;
var
   a,b : ShortString;
   x,y : LongString;
   i   : integer;
   Ch  : char;
```

Determine if any of the following program segments have any errors. If there are errors, correct them.

(a)
```
read(a);
writeln(a)
```

(b)
```
for i := 1 to 30 do
    begin
        read(Ch);
        x[i] := Ch
    end;
writeln(x)
    read(x[i]);
```

(c)
```
for i := 1 to 15 do
    begin
        read(Ch);
        a[i] := Ch;
        write(Ch)
    end;
writeln
```

(d)
```
for i := 1 to 30 do
    begin
        read(Ch);
        x[i] := ch
    end;
y := x;
writeln(y)
```

2. What will be the output of the following program segments, assuming that the following declarations have been made:

```
type
   String = packed array[1..10] of char;
var
   a,b : String;
   i,j : integer;
```

and that the input consists of the following values?

```
ABCDEFGHIJ
0123456789
```

(a)
```
for i := 1 to 10 do
    read (a[i]);
readln;
for i := 1 to 10 do
    read (b[i]);
for i := 1 to 10 do
    write (a[i],b[i]);
writeln
```

(b)
```
for i := 1 to 10 do
    read (a[i]);
readln;
for i := 1 to 10 do
    read (b[i]);
write (a ,b);
writeln
```

(c)
```
for i := 1 to 10 do
    read (a[i]);
readln;
for i := 1 to 10 do
    read (b[i]);
if a <> b then
    writeln (a)
else
    writeln (b)
```

(d)
```
for i := 1 to 10 do
    read (a[i]);
readln;
for i := 1 to 10 do
    read (b[i]);
j := 1;
for i:= 10 downto 1 do
    begin
        write(a[i],b[j]);
        j := j + 1
    end
```

Answers

1. (a) Invalid. A string must be read one character at a time. Corrected version is:

```
for i := 1 to 15 do
        read(a[i]);
    writeln(a)
```

(b) Valid (c) Valid (d) Valid

2. (a) A0B1C2D3E4F5G6H7I8J9 (b) ABCDEFGHIJ0123456789 (c) ABCDEFGHIJ (d) J0I1H2G3F4E5D6C7B8A9

6.5 MULTI-DIMENSIONAL ARRAYS

We often need arrays that correspond to entries in a table rather than a list. For example, the data in the following table

Student	Test			
	1	2	3	4
1	68	75	78	65
2	100	91	87	95
3	85	87	78	96

could be represented as the two-dimensional array in Figure 6.5.

As with one-dimensional arrays, a two-dimensional array is given an identifier that refers to the whole array. To locate a component of a two-dimensional array, two subscripts must be used, one for the row number and one for the column number. For example, assume that the array of Figure 6.5 is named Grades. The component

Figure 6.5 Two-dimensional array

Column Numbers

Row Numbers	1	2	3	4
1	68	75	78	65
2	100	91	87	95
3	85	87	78	96

Grades[1,3] refers to the value in row 1, column 3. That is, the value of Grades[1,3] is 78. Similarly, the value of Grades[3,2] is 87.

Each two-dimensional array used in a program must be declared. The declaration of such an array is similar to that of a one-dimensional array. For example, to declare the array Grades corresponding to Figure 6.5, we can use the declaration:

```
var
   Grades : array[1..3,1..4] of integer;
```

Here, in square brackets after the reserved word **array**, we have two ranges, one for each index. The first index is the row index and ranges from 1 to 3. The second index is the column index and ranges from 1 to 4. We could also have made the declaration by first naming a **type**:

```
type
   Class = array[1..3, 1..4] of integer;
var
   Grades : Class;
```

A two-dimensional array is often processed by using nested loops. As an example, consider the program in Example 6.6 that reads the data corresponding to Figure 6.5 and prints it out. On each line of the input file we have one row of data.

In Example 6.6 one **for** loop is nested inside another. Consider the two loops used to input the values of the array. We have to use two subscripts: *i* for the row number and *j* for the column number. When *i* is 1, the inner loop makes *j* go from 1 to 4. This means that we input the first line of data and store the 4 values in Grades[1,1], Grades[1,2], Grades[1,3], Grades[1,4]. These are the components of row 1 of the table. When *i* is 2, the inner loop again will make *j* go

**EXAMPLE 6.6
Program to
Read and Print
a Two-Dimen-
sional Array**

```pascal
program ReadArray (input, output);

{*****************************
 * Program to read and print *
 * a two-dimensional array.   *
 ****************************}

var
    Grades : array[1..3, 1..4] of integer;
    i, j   : integer;

begin
    {Read array one row at a time}

    for i := 1 to 3 do
        begin
            for j := 1 to 4 do
                read (Grades[i,j]);
            readln
        end;

    {Print array one row at a time}

    for i := 1 to 3 do
        begin
            for j := 1 to 4 do
                write (Grades[i,j] :5);
            writeln
        end
end.
```

through all the values from 1 to 4, thus reading the second line of the input file into the second row of the array. This continues as *i* goes from 1 to 3. In the program of Example 6.6 the output loop could have been eliminated by inserting the write and writeln statements in the appropriate location of the input loop. We leave it as an exercise for you to eliminate the output loop.

It is possible, of course, to declare and use arrays with three or even more dimensions. The declaration

```pascal
var
    ItemsSold : array[1..2, 1..3, 1..4] of integer;
```

could be used to declare an array to store the number of items sold for a two-month period by three salespersons selling four products. The component

ItemsSold[1,2,4]

holds the number of items sold in month 1 by salesperson 2 of product 4. Processing such an array may require up to three nested loops. The following segment computes the total number of items sold by all the salespersons for all the months.

```
Total := 0;
for Month := 1 to 2 do
   for Salesperson := 1 to 3 do
      for Product := 1 to 4 do
         Total := Total + ItemsSold[Month,Salesperson,Product]
```

We are, of course, assuming that all the variables were appropriately declared earlier, and that the array ItemsSold contains the correct values. The assignment statement

```
Total := Total + ItemsSold[Month, Salesperson, Product]
```

is executed a total of 2 * 3 * 4 or 24 times.

Multidimensional arrays can use enormous amounts of main storage. For instance, the seemingly innocuous declaration

```
var
   a : array[1..100, 1..100, 1..100] of real;
```

reserves 100 * 100 * 100 or 1000000 storage locations, each capable of holding a real number. This is more storage than most computers can provide!

Arrays of Arrays

Pascal allows us to have arrays of any type. Until now we have been working with arrays whose base type is a scalar type, such as integer, real, char, boolean, or a user-defined type. Since we can define an array type, we can also have arrays whose components are each another array. For example, consider the following declarations:

```
const
   NumTests = 5;
   NumStudents = 35;
```

```
type
   Student = array[1..NumTests] of integer;
var
   Class : array[1..NumStudents] of Student;
```

The array Class has 35 components of **type** Student. Thus, Class[3] refers to the third component of Class. In other words, it refers to the third student. The type Student, in turn, is an array that can hold 5 test grades. The data for the second test of the third student is stored in Class[3][2]. The first subscript, [3], is used to select the Student, which, in this case, is an array holding 5 integers representing that student's grades. The second subscript [2] is used to select that student's second test.

The above declaration is, of course, equivalent to

```
const
   NumTests = 5;
   NumStudents = 35;
var
   Grades : array[1..NumStudents, 1..NumTests] of integer;
```

The component Grades [3,2] of the array Grades is equivalent to the component Class[3] [2] of the array Class. The only advantage of the Class array over the Grades array is that it allows the assignment of all the grades of a student without using a loop. Thus, to assign the grades of the fifth student to the tenth student we can use the statement

```
Class[10] := Class[5]
```

With Grades we would have to write a loop to assign the 5 values one at a time.

Arrays of Character Strings
A very useful application of arrays, whose elements are other arrays, involves character strings. Recall that in Pascal a character string is a **packed array** of characters. Thus, an array whose elements are character strings can be declared as follows:

```
type
   Name = packed array[1..15] of char;
```

```
var
   Customers : array[1..100] of Name;
```

The array Customers has 100 components, each of which is a character string of length 15. Just as with any array whose elements are another array, we can reference the name of a particular customer by using a single subscript. The component Customers[34] refers to the name of the 34th customer. All operations that can be used with strings can be used with components of the array Customers. The statement

```
Customers[1] := Customers[99]
```

assigns the name of customer 99 to customer 1. The statement

```
writeln (Customers[5])
```

prints the character string that makes up the fifth customer's name. Finally, the boolean expression

```
Customers[34] = Customers[35]
```

compares the equality of the names of the 34th and 35th customers.

Although, as illustrated above, we can process character strings in arrays as single units, we must read such a string into an array one character at a time. That is, for purposes of input we have to treat the array Customers as a two-dimensional array. The following program segment could be used to input the name of 100 customers, where each name is on a separate line of the input file.

```
for i := 1 to 100 do
   begin
      for j := 1 to 15 do
        read (Customers[i,j]);
      readln
   end
```

The program of Example 6.7 illustrates a simple application of string arrays. The program reads the twelve months of the year and prints them in calendar and reverse order.

**EXAMPLE 6.7
Program to
Print the
Months of the
Year**

```
program MonthsOfYear (input, output);

{**********************************
* Program to print the months of   *
* the year in correct and reverse   *
* order.                            *
**********************************}

type
    MonthName = packed array[1..9] of char;

var

    Months : array[1..12] of MonthName;
    i, j   : integer;

begin
    {Input months from standard input
     file one month per line}

    for i := 1 to 12 do
        begin
            {Initialize name to blanks}

            for j := 1 to 9 do
              Months[i,j] := ' ';

            {Input name of month}

            j := 1;
            while not eoln and (j <= 9) do
              begin
                  read (Months[i,j]);
                  j := j + 1
              end; {While loop}
            readln
        end; {For loop}

    {Output months in correct order}

    writeln (' The twelve months in calendar order:');
    writeln;
    for i := 1 to 12 do
        writeln (Months[i]);
```

**EXAMPLE 6.7
Program to
Print the
Months of the
Year**
(*continued*)

```
{Output months in reverse order}

writeln;
writeln (' The twelve months in reverse order:');
writeln;
for i := 12 downto 1 do
    writeln (Months[i])
end.
```

Given the data

January
February
March
April
May
June
July
August
September
October
November
December

the output is:

```
 The twelve months in calendar order:

January
February
March
April
May
June
July
August
September
October
November
December

 The twelve months in reverse order:

December
November
```

EXAMPLE 6.7
Program to
Print the
Months of the
Year
(*continued*)

```
October
September
August
July
June
May
April
March
February
January
```

SELF-TEST 3

1. Find the errors, if any, in each of the following segments. If possible, correct the errors.

(a) **var**
```
    a,b,d[1..10,2..5] : integer;
```

(b) **var**
```
      i,j,k,n : integer;
      a : array[i..j,k..n] of integer;
```

(c) **var**
```
      a : array[10..20,1..5] of real;
    begin
      a[12,3] := 0
    end
```

(d) **var**
```
      a : array[10..20,1..5] of real;
      i : integer;
    begin
      for i := 10 to 20 do
        a[i] := i
```

2. What is the size of each of the following arrays? That is, how many elements can be stored in a variable of each of the following types?

(a) **type**
```
      Area = array[1..10,1..4] of char;
```

(b) **type**
```
      a = array[-3..15] of real;
```

(c) **type**
```
b = array[3..23,'A'..'Z'] of char;
```

(d) **type**
```
c = array[1..5,boolean] of char;
```

3. Assume that the array x is declared as follows:

var
```
x : array[1..2,1..5] of integer;
```

Determine what values will be assigned to the array by each of the following program segments:

(a)
```
for i := 1 to 2 do
    for j := 1 to 5 do
        x[i,j] := i+j
```

(b)
```
for j := 1 to 5 do
    for i := 1 to  2 do
        x[i,j] :=   i+j
```

(c)
```
for i := 1 to 2 do
    for j := 1 to 5 do
        if j <= i then
            x[i,j] := 0
        else
            x[i,j] := 1
```

(d)
```
k := 1;
for i := 1 to 2  do
    for j := 1 to 5 do
        begin
            x[i,j] := k;
            k := k + 1
        end
```

Answers

1. (a) Invalid declaration. Should be:

var
```
a,b,d: array[1..10,2..5] of integer;
```

(b) Invalid declaration. Indices into the array must be constants.
(c) Valid   (d) Invalid assignment statement. Two subscripts are needed.

2. (a) 40   (b) 19   (c) 546   (d) 10

3. (a)

	1	2	3	4	5
1	2	3	4	5	6
2	3	4	5	6	7

(b)

	1	2	3	4	5
1	2	3	4	5	6
2	3	4	5	6	7

(c)

	1	2	3	4	5
1	0	1	1	1	1
2	0	0	1	1	1

(d)

	1	2	3	4	5
1	1	2	3	4	5
2	6	7	8	9	10

We will now examine in greater detail some more complex applications of arrays. Many problems in the social sciences involve the collection and analysis of large amounts of data. One method of summarizing large collections of raw data involves grouping the data into classes and counting the number of values that fall into each class. Such summaries are called **frequency distributions**. These frequency distributions are often displayed graphically as **bar graphs** or **histograms**. Our first applications program constructs a frequency distribution and histogram from a collection of raw data.

APPLICATION

Frequency Distribution

We assume that the input data consist of integers. These may be responses to a questionnaire, test scores, demographic information, and so forth. Our program will be able to handle up to 1000 such data items. If more data need to be processed, the program can easily be modified to accommodate larger amounts of data. The program allows the user to specify how many classes will be used to summarize the data up to a maximum of 20 classes. This information must precede the actual data to be summarized.

The top level of our algorithms is:

begin
    Input the number of classes
    Input data values into an array
    Find the largest and smallest values input
    Compute the class width and initialize class counters
    Classify each input value into its proper class
    Output for each class the lower and upper boundaries, number of values
        in class, and percentage of values in class
    Output the histogram
end.

Input of the number of classes the user wants for the frequency distribution is straightforward. We only need to be concerned with validating the input value. Thus, the first statement of the above algorithm can be expanded to:

Input number of classes
if number of classes is greater than 20 **then**
    Print error message and set the number of classes to 20

To input the data we simply read one value at a time until we reach the end of the file.

APPLICATION

**Frequency
Distribution
(*continued*)**

Initialize subscript to 1
while (subscript is less than or equal to 1000)
            and (data remain to be read) **do**
            Read data value into array at location indexed by subscript
            Increment subscript by 1

We saw earlier how to find the smallest and largest value of an array. Thus, the third statement of our algorithm is not difficult to expand.

Initialize smallest to first component of the array
Initialize largest to first component of the array
for i equals 2 **to** number of elements in array **do**
   if element at location i is less than smallest **then**
      Set smallest to element at location i
   if element at location i is greater than largest **then**
      Set largest to element at location i

To compute the class widths we divide the difference between the largest and smallest values by the number of classes. We will use an array to count the frequencies in each class. Thus, to initialize the counters we initialize the array to zero.

Set the width to (largest − smallest) divided by number of classes
   for i equals 1 **to** number of classes **do**
      Set the ith element of frequency array to 0

To read each input value into its proper class we use two nested loops. The outer loop moves through all the input values. The inner loop compares the input values against successive lower class boundaries, starting with the last class. If a value falls into a given class, then the appropriate frequency is incremented by 1.

for i equals 1 **to** number of values **do**
   Set j to the number of classes
   Compute the lower bound for the jth class
   while (the ith input value is less than the current lower bound) **do**
      Decrement j by 1
      Compute the lower bound for the jth class
   Increment the jth element of the frequency array by 1

To output the frequencies and percentages we use a loop.

Print headings
for i equals 1 **to** number of classes **do**

Compute lower and upper bound
Compute percentage
Print lower bound, upper bound, frequency, and
   percentage

Finally, to output the histogram we use nested loops. The outer
loop moves through the frequency array while the inner loop prints
asterisks. The number of asterisks printed is equal to the frequency.

for i equals 1 **to** number of classes **do**
   for j equals 1 **to** value of ith element of frequency array **do**
      Print an asterisk

We can now put all the pieces together and write the complete
Pascal program.

```pascal
program Distribution (input, output);

{********************************
* Program to tabulate data into *
* a frequency distribution and  *
* print the distribution and a  *
* histogram.                    *
********************************}

const
   Maxsize = 1000;

var
   Scores :array[1..Maxsize] of integer;
   Frequency : array[1..20] of integer;
   NumClass, Smallest, Largest, Total, i, j : integer;
   Width, Low, High, Percent : real;

begin
   {Input the number of classes}

   read (NumClass);
   if NumClass > 20 then
      begin
         writeln (' Too many classes specified');
         writeln (' The number is set to 20');
         NumClass := 20
      end;
```

APPLICATION

Frequency Distribution (*continued*)

```
{Input data values into array}

i := 1;
while (not eof) and (i <= Maxsize) do
   begin
      read (Scores[i]);
      i := i + 1
   end;
if i > Maxsize then
   Total := i - 1
else
   Total := i - 2;


{Find the smallest and largest values}

Smallest := Scores[1];
Largest := Scores[1];
for i := 2 to Total do
      if Scores[i] < Smallest then
         Smallest := Scores[i]
      else
         if Scores[i] > Largest then
            Largest := Scores[i];

{Compute class width and initialize counters}

Width := (Largest - Smallest) / NumClass;
for i := 1 to NumClass do
   Frequency[i] := 0;

{Classify each input value into its proper class}

for i := 1 to Total do
   begin
      j := NumClass;
      Low := Smallest + (j-1) * Width;
      while Scores[i] < Low do
        begin
           j := j - 1;
           Low := Smallest + (j-1) * Width
        end;
      Frequency[j] := Frequency[j] + 1;
   end;
```

APPLICATION

**Frequency
Distribution**
(*continued*)

```
{Output frequency table}

writeln('-------------------------------------------');
writeln(' CLASS    CLASS BOUNDARIES  FREQ.  PERCENT');
writeln('-------------------------------------------');
for i := 1 to NumClass do
   begin
      Low := Smallest + (i-1)*Width;
      High := Low + Width;
      Percent := (Frequency[i]/Total)*100;
      writeln(i :4, Low :14:3, High:9:3,
         Frequency[i] :12, Percent :13:3)
   end;
writeln('-------------------------------------------');

{Output the histogram}

writeln;
writeln;
writeln('              HISTOGRAM');
writeln;
writeln(' CLASS         FREQ.');
for i := 1 to NumClass do
   begin
      write (i :4, Frequency[i] :12);
      write ('        ');
      for j := 1 to Frequency[i] do
        write ('*');
      writeln
   end
end.
```

If this program is provided with the following input

8
1 2 4 6 8 9 2 4 5 8 9 7 7 2 4 6 0 1 2 6 8 4 2 5 5 7 8 8 9

the output will be:

CLASS	CLASS BOUNDARIES		FREQ.	PERCENT
1	0.000	1.125	3	10.714
2	1.125	2.250	4	14.286

(Output continues on the next page.)

APPLICATION

Frequency Distribution (*continued*)

3	2.250	3.375	0	0.000
4	3.375	4.500	4	14.286
5	4.500	5.625	3	10.714
6	5.625	6.750	3	10.714
7	6.750	7.875	3	10.714
8	7.875	9.000	8	28.571

```
                     HISTOGRAM

      CLASS           FREQ.
        1               3      ***
        2               4      ****
        3               0
        4               4      ****
        5               3      ***
        6               3      ***
        7               3      ***
        8               8      ********
```

APPLICATION

Graphing a Function

Let us now look at a simple mathematical application involving a two-dimensional array. We want to write a program to print the graph of a function. The approach we take is to use a two-dimensional array to represent the grid on which the function is to be printed. The algorithm takes the following form:

begin
    Initialize grid to blanks
    Insert axes
    Compute and insert values of functions
    Print grid
end.

The above steps can easily be expanded using loops. These loops can be seen in the next Pascal program. Note that this program plots two functions on the same coordinate system. The first function is $Y = -X - 3$, the second is $Y = X^2 - 16$. The functions are only plotted for integral values of X.

APPLICATION

Graphing a
Function
(*continued*)

```
program Graph (output);

{*******************************
 * Program to plot the integral *
 * values of Y = -X - 3 and      *
 * Y = X*X - 9                    *
 * (X ranges from -29 to +29).    *
 *******************************}

const
    LowX = -29;
    HighX = 29;
    LowY = -15;
    HighY = 15;
type
    Horizontal = LowX..HighX;
    Vertical = LowY..HighY;

var
    Grid : array[Horizontal,Vertical] of char;
    X : Horizontal;
    Y : Vertical;

begin

    {Initialize grid}

    for X := LowX to HighX do
        for Y := LowY to HighY do
            Grid[X,Y] := ' ';

    {Insert axes}

    for X := LowX to HighX do
        Grid[X,0] := '-';
    for Y := LowY to HighY do
        Grid[0,Y] := '|';

    {Insert values of functions}

    for X := LowX to HighX do
        begin
            Y := X*X - 9;
            if (Y >= LowY) and (Y <= HighY) then
                Grid[X,Y] := '*';
            Y := -X - 3;
```

APPLICATION

Graphing a Function (*continued*)

```
            if (Y >= LowY) and (Y <= HighY) then
               Grid[X,Y] := '*'
      end;

   {print grid}

   for Y := HighY downto LowY do
      begin
         for X := LowX to HighX do
            write (Grid[X,Y]);
         writeln
      end
end.
```

The output of the program looks like:

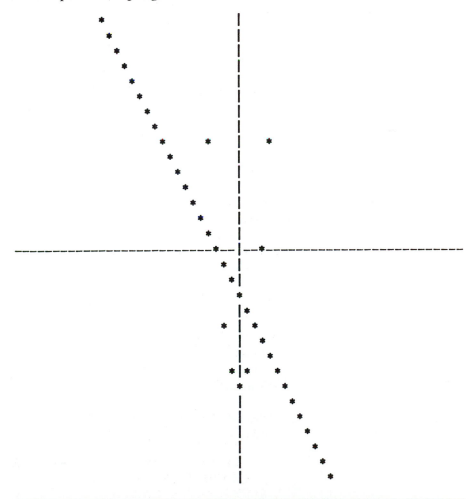

6.6
COMMON
ERRORS

When it comes to programming difficulties, arrays can be relied on to be difficult for a beginner. Although it is not difficult to work with a single element of an array, it is another matter to process an entire array systematically and correctly. So do not be discouraged if you experience real problems when working with arrays.

When using arrays the most common problem involves the use of subscripts outside the allowed range. Such errors are most often caused by incorrect subscript expressions, or loop indices that do not terminate properly. One of the most common of such errors occurs when searching arrays. The following program segment is intended to find the value of Number in the array NumberList, which is declared as NumberList : **array**[1..100] **of** integer.

```
read (Number);
Location := 1;
while NumberList[Location] <> Number do
   Location := Location + 1
```

This segment will work perfectly as long as the value of Number is somewhere in NumberList. However, if the value is not in NumberList a run-time error will occur when Location reaches the value of 101 and we attempt to examine the 101st component of NumberList.

If we insert a check to ensure that Location never exceeds 100, we may not cure the problem. The following code still results in the same difficulty.

```
read (Number);
Location := 1;
while (Location <= 100) and
       (NumberList[Location] <> Number) do
   Location := Location + 1
```

This is because Pascal evaluates compound conditions completely, even when there is no logical need to do this, before it returns a value of true or false.

Of course we can solve the problem by using a boolean variable such as Found.

```
read (Number);
Location := 1;
Found := false;
```

```
while (Location <= 100) and (not Found) do
   if NumberList[Location] = Number then
      Found := true
   else
      Location := Location + 1
```

An incorrect subscript will not always cause a run-time error. It may simply give you incorrect results. If you get incorrect results in a program involving arrays, it is always wise to take a look at the subscripts. This can be done easily by inserting diagnostic output statements into your program, which print the values of the subscripts.

Another common source of problems with arrays involves algorithms in which we are examining pairs of adjacent locations. For example, assume that for every value of *Location* in our previous example we want to compare NumberList[Location] to NumberList [Location + 1] or NumberList[Location − 1]. Nothing is particularly difficult about writing a loop to do this. However, we should remember that not every component has a component preceding it or following it. You should always double check the subscripts at loop boundaries.

With packed arrays of characters, a common error is to attempt to assign or to compare constants of the wrong length to string variables. Make sure that the number of characters in the constant string equals the number of components in the array. Also remember that character strings must be read one character at a time, although they can be printed as a whole.

The errors encountered in using multidimensional arrays are similar to those encountered using one-dimensional arrays. The most frequent errors are due to out-of-range subscripts. These errors are, in fact, more common with multidimensional arrays because more subscripts, as well as nested loops, are used. With multidimensional arrays additional care must be taken to use the subscripts in a manner consistent with the array declaration. Interchanging row and column subscripts may not only result in run-time errors due to subscripts out of range, but most certainly will lead to incorrect results.

6.7 CHAPTER REVIEW

In addition to simple data types such as scalars, Pascal has **structured data types**: data types whose values are made up of collections of simpler types.

One way to organize simple data types into structures is to arrange them into lists or tables. Such a structure is called an **array**. An array is simply a collection of adjacent main-storage locations, each capable of storing values of the same type. For example, the declaration

```
var
   Test: array[1..50] of integer;
```

reserves storage for any array called Test consisting of 50 locations, each capable of storing an integer.

The **type** definition can also be used to declare an array. The type definition and variable declaration below also reserve 50 main storage locations, each capable of storing an integer.

```
type
   Grades = array[1..50] of integer;
var
   Test: Grades;
```

To refer to an individual **component** or element of an array we use the expression

array identifier [arithmetic expression]

like any ordinary variable identifier. The arithmetic expression may be a constant, a variable, or a more complex expression, as long as its value is of the same type as the subscript type. For example, the expression Test [5] refers to the 5th component of the array Test and the expression

```
writeln(Test[5])
```

prints the current value of that component.

There are many methods of working with the components of an array. Most of them involve moving through the array component by component. This movement is usually done using a **for . . . do**, **while . . . do,** or **repeat . . . until** loop. We can process an array using a **for . . . do** loop as follows:

for Index: = InitialPosition **to** FinalPosition **do**
   Process the component at position "Index"

It is possible to refer to an entire array at one time. The expression x: = y is valid if *x* and *y* are both arrays of the same type.

The component type of an array need not be a numeric value. One common and useful class of arrays is called character strings. In Pascal a character string is of the type

packed array [subscript type] **of** char

The **packed** option of the array definition is used to conserve storage. Strings, which are **packed arrays** of characters, can be compared by using relational operators, and they can be output without loops by using the write or writeln statements. We can also assign string constants to string variables as long as the string constant has exactly the same number of characters as the array has elements. Strings, however, must be read from the input file one character at a time using a loop.

Multidimensional arrays can be declared by specifying two or more subscript types. The declaration

```
var
    Grades: array[1..5, 1..10] of integer;
```

reserves storage locations to store a table consisting of 5 rows and 10 columns. Each of the 50 locations of this array is capable of storing an integer.

Elements of multidimensional arrays are referenced by expressions using as many subscripts as there are dimensions. The expression

```
Grades [3,7]
```

references the component in row 3 and column 7 of the array Grades. Processing multidimensional arrays usually involves nested loops.

Pascal also allows us to structure multidimensional arrays by constructing arrays whose components are other arrays. The declaration

```
type
    Row = array[1..10] of integer;
var
    Table: array[1..5] of Row;
```

gives us an array called Table consisting of components of type Row, which in turn are arrays of integers. The above declaration gives us a two-dimensional array consisting of 5 rows, each capable of storing 10 integers. The notation Table[3][5] can be used to refer to the 5th component of the 3rd row. This notation is equivalent to Table [3,5].

The most common of the arrays, whose components are other arrays, are arrays of strings.

**6.8
EXERCISES**

6.1. Fill in the blanks for each of the following:

(a) A _____ data type is a data type whose values are made up of collections of simpler types.

(b) The process of reserving storage for an array is called _____ the array.

(c) A variable whose value is the entire array is known as a(n) _____ _____.

(d) An array declaration mentions two data types: the _____ data type and the _____ data type.

(e) The subscript type in the declaration of an array cannot be either the standard type _____ or the standard type _____.

(f) If the value of a subscript expression is outside the subrange type specified in the declaration a(n) _____ error will occur.

(g) The only Pascal operator that can act on arrays as a whole is the _____ operator.

(h) An algorithm for rearranging the components of an array in a particular order is called a _____.

(i) By defining character strings as **packed array** we have three advantages. We can use _____ operators to compare entire strings. We can _____ the entire string at once. We can assign a _____ string to a string variable.

(j) A **packed array** of characters _____ be input as an entire string using the read or readln statements.

(k) The number of values that can be stored in an array declared as:

```
a:  array[1..10,1..6,1..8] of ...
```

is _____.

(l) In the following definitions,

```
type
    Row = array[1..18] of integer;
var
    Table : array[1..25] of row;
```

the component type of the array Table is _____.

(m) In the above question the component type of array Row is _____.

(n) Given the definition and declaration,

type
   String = **packed array**[1..10] **of** char;
var
   Names : **array**[1..50] **of** String;

the type of the variable Names[5] is _____. The type of the variable Names[5][1] is _____.

(o) How many storage locations are reserved by the following array declaration _____?

var
   a : **array**[2..8,-5..4,-1..7] **of** char;

(p) In a double-subscripted array, the first subscript is the _____ _____ by convention.

6.2. Answer each of the following true or false. If your answer is false, state why.

(a) When an array is declared, the type of the components, as well as the type of the subscript, must be specified.

(b) The type of an array subscript can be any scalar type.

(c) In the array declaration,

X : **array** [Low..High] **of** ...

the number of variable locations reserved in main storage is High − Low + 1.

(d) If an array is declared, it does not define any of the values of its components.

(e) If a component of an array is used in an expression, the value of the subscript variable and of the component variable referred to by the subscript must be defined.

(f) If a component of an array variable is used in a read statement, the subscript variable must be defined, but the component referred to by the subscript need not be defined.

(g) The subscript of an array may be any valid expression whose type is of the subscript type.

(h) Given the declaration,

var
   x : **array**[1..44] **of** char;

a valid subscripted variable is x[2.5].

(i) The identifier chosen by a programmer for an array variable must con-
form to the same rules as identifiers for scalar variables.
(j) A programmer can declare an array variable to have the same name as a
scalar variable declared in the same block of the program.
(k) The arrays declared as

```
var
    a : array[1..10] of char;
    b : array[0..9] of char;
```

are of the same type.
(l) If two arrays, x and y, are of the same type, then the assignment statement x: = y is valid provided y is defined.
(m) Given the declaration,

```
var
    a : array[1..10] of integer;
```

the statement write(a) will print all the values of a.
(n) Character strings must be compared character by character.
(o) Given the declaration,

```
var
    Letters: packed array[1..16] of char;
```

the statement writeln(Letters) is valid.
(p) Given the declaration in Exercise 6.2(o) of Letters, the statement
readln (Letters) is valid.
(q) Pascal allows us to have arrays of arrays.
(r) Given the declaration,

```
type
    Line = packed array[1..60] of char;
var
    Page : array[1..40] of Line;
```

Page[2,4] refers to the same component as Page[2][4].
(s) Given the above declaration of Page, we would require one loop to print
Page.
(t) Given the above declaration of Page, we would require two nested loops
to read Page.

6.3. Describe the function(s) performed by each of the following Pascal
statements:

```
(a) var
        List = array[1..20] of integer;
```

(b) **type**
    ClassList = **array**[1..50] **of** integer;
  var
    Midterm, Final : ClassList;

For questions (c) through (h), use the above declarations.

(c) **for** i:=1 **to** 50 **do**
    Midterm[i] := 0;

(d) **for** i:=1 **to** 50 **do**
    Final[i] := Midterm[i];

(e) Final := Midterm

(f) writeln(Midterm[5] : 5)

(g) **for** i:=1 **to** 50 **do**
    Final[i] := Final[i]/100

(h) **for** i:=1 **to** 50 **do**
    read(Final[i])

(i) Sum:=0;
  for i:= 1 **to** 50 **do**
  Sum := Sum + Final[i]

(j) **for** i:=1 **to** 50 **do**
    writeln(' Average: ',(Midterm[i]+Final[i])/2 :5:2)

For questions (k) through (n), use the following declaration:

type
  Alpha = **packed array**[1..20] **of** char;
var
  Name, Address : Alpha;

(k) **for** i:= 1 **to** 20 **do**
    read(Name[i])

(l) writeln(Name)

(m) Address := '37 Pleasant Street   '

(n) **if** Name >= 'S   ' **then**
    writeln ('Name in latter part of Alphabet')

For questions (o) through (p) use the following declaration:

```
type
   BoardStatus = (black,white,empty);
var
   Board : array[1..8,1..8] of BoardStatus;
```

(o) ```
    for i := 1 to 8 do
        for j := 1 to 8 do
            Board[i,j] := empty
    ```

(p) ```
    for i := 1 to 8 do
        for j := 1 to 8 do
            case Board[i,j] of
                black : writeln('Position',i:2,j:2, 'black');
                white : writeln('Position',i:2,j:2, 'white');
                empty : writeln('Position',i:2,j:2, 'empty')
            end
    ```

6.4. Let List be an array of 30 integers. Write a program to read a collection of up to 30 integers and do the following:

(a) Print all the integers read in.

(b) Print only the integers in odd locations (i.e., 1,3,5,etc.).

(c) Replace each element in the array with the sum of all the elements up to and including that element.

6.5. A company pays its salespeople on a commission basis. The salespeople receive $50 per week plus 10% of their gross sales for that week. For example, a salesperson who sells $500 worth of merchandise in a week receives $50 plus 10% of $500 for a total of $100.

Write a program that determines how many salespeople earned salaries in each of the following ranges (use an array to count):

$ 50 – $ 99.99
$100 – $199.99
$200 – $299.99
$300 – $399.99
$400 – $499.99
$500 and over

6.6. One of the techniques used by cryptographers to break codes is to use the frequency with which different characters appear in an encoded text. Write a program to examine text and count the frequency of occurrence of each character in it. You may assume that only the 26 letters of the English alphabet are of interest. Punctuation is to be ignored. Your program should print the alphabet, together with the frequency of occurrence of each letter.

6.7. Write a program that will determine the largest and second-largest component of an array containing no more than 100 real numbers. The data values are to consist of an integer specifying the number of real numbers to be read, followed by the elements to be read.

6.8. Write a program that reads a list of integers and prints it in the same order in which it was read. It should, however, not print duplicate values. Thus, given the list,

2 3 45 5 6 78 12 45 2 6 9

it should print:

2 3 45 5 6 78 12 9

6.9. Let *x* be an array declared as:

var
    x : **array**[1..100] **of** integer;

(a) Write a program to read up to 100 integers and store them in array *x*.
(b) Find and print the largest value of *x*. Assume the largest value is unique.
(c) Find and print the location of the largest value. Assume the largest value is unique.
(d) Find and print the location of the largest value. Assume the largest value may not be unique.

6.10. The production costs and quantity of each product are stored in the following form:

Product	Quantity	Costs per Unit		
		Direct Materials	Direct Labor	Overhead
1	3000000	3.00	5.00	4.00
2	255000	6.00	7.00	4.50

Write a program that uses two arrays, a one-dimensional array to store the quantity, and a two-dimensional array to store the costs.
(a) Print the above information in a clean tabular form.
(b) Compute and print total costs for direct materials, direct labor, and overhead based on the costs and quantities given.
(c) Compute and print the total cost for all units of each product produced.

6.11. In the text, you studied an algorithm for the selection sort, where we located the smallest value and moved it to the front of the array. Another approach is to copy successive smallest values into a second array and to replace each value we copy by some value that is clearly not one of the original data values.

Write a program that sorts an array by copying values into a second array. Each time a value is copied it should be replaced by maxint.

6.12. Another common sorting algorithm is called the *bubble sort*. It sorts an array by comparing adjacent values and interchanging them if they are out of sequence. Moving through the array once, inspecting adjacent values for the possibility of an interchange, is considered one pass. If $n - 1$ passes are made through an array containing n values, the array will be sorted. The algorithm can be written as:

```
begin
    for index starting at 1 to n − 1 do
        Begin with the first pair of elements
    for each pair do {Perform pass}
        if pair is out of order then
            interchange
        Move to the next pair
end.
```

(a) Write a program that reads a set of integers into an array, prints the array, sorts it in ascending order using the bubble sort, and prints it again.
(b) When using the bubble sort, we often do not need to make the maximum of $n - 1$ passes. There is an easy way to tell if an array is completely sorted. If a pass finds every consecutive pair in order and does not make any interchanges, then the array is already sorted. We can modify the above algorithm to take advantage of this information. Simply set a boolean variable Sorted to true before making a pass, and set it to false whenever an interchange is made. At the end of the pass, if Sorted is still true the array is sorted.

Modify your algorithm of part (a) to incorporate this feature.

6.13. Write a program that reads a sentence with no punctuation other than a period at the end, and which prints the sentence with the words in reverse order. For example, if the original sentence is,

This is a sentence.

it should come out as:

sentence a is This.

6.14. A tic-tac-toe board can be numbered as follows:

```
  1  |  2  |  3
─────┼─────┼─────
  4  |  5  |  6
─────┼─────┼─────
  7  |  8  |  9
```

It can be represented by the following array:

```
type
    Entry = (X, O, Empty);
var
    Board : array[1..9] of Entry;
```

Write a program that keeps track of a tic-tac-toe game played by two play-ers. Your program should:

(a) Initialize the board.
(b) Request a move from a player.
(c) Validate the move. A player, for example, is not allowed to move into a not empty location.
(d) Continue playing the game until one of the players wins or the game is a draw.

6.15. A magic square is an N by N array of integers 1 through N. The sum of the values of each row, each column, and the main diagonals are equal. Write a program that reads the size of a square, then each row, and verifies if the square is a magic square. Assume that the size of the square is 10 or less. For example, given the data,

```
  4
 16   9   2   7
  6   3  12  13
 11  14   5   4
  1   8  15  10
```

your program should determine that this is a 4 by 4 magic square.

6.16. Data on the age, sex, and marital status of a group of students in the entering class of a small college are stored as follows:

Student ID	Age	Sex (1 = Male 2 = Female)	Marital Status (1 = Single 2 = Married)
1001	19	1	1
1011	20	2	2
0110	18	2	1

Tabulations of the students' marital status, sex, and age are needed. The results are to be presented as follows:

Table 1

Age	Single		Married	
	Male	Female	Male	Female
18 and under				
19 or 20				
21 and over				

Table 2

Age	Single	Married
18 and under		
19 or 20		
21 and over		

Table 3

Age	Male	Female
18 and under		
19 or 20		
21 and over		

Write a program to create a three-dimensional array to store the tabulated data. The subscripts of the array should indicate the age group, sex, and marital status respectively. Print the above tables.

7. Procedures and Functions

**7.1
USER-DEFINED
FUNCTIONS**

The predefined functions of Pascal which we studied in earlier chapters, make operations that are not easily possible with the usual operators available to a programmer. In addition, programmers can define their own functions to extend the capabilities of the language even further. As an example, let us assume that we need a function to compute the third power, or cube, of a number. We can design this function by using the **function definition** given in Example 7.1.

A function definition has the same structure as a program, except it is introduced by a **function heading** instead of a program heading. The reserved word **function** starts the function heading. It is followed by an identifier that names the function. In our example, the identifier that names the function is Cube. It is by this name that the function will be called in the rest of the program. The portion of the heading enclosed in parentheses is the **formal parameter list** of the function. The term **formal parameter** describes a variable that is used by the function. When the function is invoked, the formal parameter is assigned the value whose cube we desire. The function does its calculations using this value as input data, and then returns the result to the calling program. The parameter list, (x: real), identifies the formal parameter x and specifies its type—real in our example. The type of the value that the function returns is specified following the parameter list. In our example, Cube returns a real number.

**EXAMPLE 7.1
Function to
Cube a Real
Number**

```
function Cube(x: real): real;

{Function returns the cube of a real number x}

begin
  Cube := x*x*x
end; {of Cube function}
```

In general, there can be any number of parameters of different types, including no parameter at all. The body of the function, bracketed by **begin** and **end** statements, describes the actions and/or computations to be performed on the input values when the function is executed. To communicate the result of the computations back to the main program, this result must be assigned to the function name. In our example, the body of the function consists of the single statement

```
Cube := x*x*x
```

which computes the cube of x and assigns the result to Cube. This can then be communicated to the portion of the program that called the function.

Let us now see how a user-defined function works. Example 7.2 illustrates the definition and use of a user-defined function in a program.

Note that the function definition comes after the variable declarations. Also note, the reserved word **end** that terminates the function definition is followed by a semicolon instead of a period. Only the program is terminated by a period. The general form of a function definition is:

function identifier (formal parameter list): result-type;
Local variable declaration section
begin
    function body
end;

Note that the body *must* have at least one statement that assigns a value to the function name. This value is returned as the function result. The local variable declaration section of the function is used to declare variables used only by the function, and nowhere else in the program. We will see examples of such declarations later.

Function Parameters

The purpose of a function definition is to *describe* computations to be done on the data in the formal parameter list. It is important to note that no computations are done as a result of writing out the function definition. The actual execution of the statements in the body of the function only occurs when the function is invoked in the calling program. In the above example, the statement

**EXAMPLE 7.2
Program to
Illustrate a
Function
Definition and
Invocation**

```
program UseOfAFunction (input, output);

{****************************************
* Program illustrating the definition  *
* and use of a function to compute the *
* cube of a number                     *
****************************************}

var
  a, b : real;

function Cube(x: real): real;

  {Function returns the cube of a real number x}

  begin
      Cube := x*x*x
  end; {of Cube function}

begin {Main program}

  a := Cube(1.23);
  while not eof do
      begin
          readln (b);
          if Cube(b) > a then
              writeln (b :8:3, Cube(b) :10:3)
      end {While loop}
end.
```

```
a := Cube(1.23)
```

invokes the function Cube. This statement causes the function Cube to be executed. At the start of execution, the constant 1.23 is assigned to the formal parameter, x. When the function terminates execution, the result, 1.860867, is assigned to a. The expression

```
Cube(1.23)
```

is called the **function designator**, and the constant 1.23 is called the **argument** or **actual parameter** of the function. To invoke a function we use the function designator in an expression. When execution of a program reaches the function designator: (1) the value of

Figure 7.1 Flow of control for program with a function

```
program UseOfAFunction (input, output);
var
    a, b : real;

function Cube (x: real) : real;
    {Function returns the cube
    of a real number x}

    begin
              Cube := x*x*x
    end; {of Cube function}

    begin {Main} {EXECUTION STARTS HERE}
    a := Cube (1.23); {CONTROL IS TRANSFERRED TO FUNCTION CUBE}
    {CONTROL RETURNS HERE}
    readln (b);

    writeln (a :8:3, b :8:3, Cube (b) :10:3)
    end.
```

the actual parameter is assigned to the formal parameter, (2) the statements of the function are executed, and (3) the result is returned as the value of the function. This value can then be used in the program. The actual flow of control for the Cube program is illustrated in Figure 7.1.

As Figure 7.1 illustrates, in addition to the invocation

```
a := Cube(1.23)
```

the program invokes the function Cube in one more place. The line

```
writeln (a :8:3, b :8:3, Cube(b) :10:3)
```

invokes the function Cube with the current value of *b* as the actual parameter. It then outputs the values of *a* and *b* as well as the value of the function (the cube of *b*).

We have said that a user-defined function can have more than one formal parameter. Consider the function in Example 7.3, which finds the larger of two integers.

The function designator:

```
Larger (4,5)
```

invokes the function Larger with 4 and 5 as the actual parameters. The number of actual parameters in the function designator must be the same as the number of formal parameters in the function defini-

EXAMPLE 7.3
Function to
Find the
Larger of Two
Numbers

```
function Larger(a, b :integer): integer;

{Function to find the larger of a and b}

begin
   if a > b then
       Larger := a
   else
       Larger := b
end; {of function Larger}
```

tion. The correspondence between actual and formal parameters is determined by the order of the parameters in each list. That is, the first actual parameter will always correspond to the first formal parameter, the second actual parameter to the second formal parameter, and so on. Thus, when the function designator,

Larger (4,5)

is executed, the constant 4 is assigned to *a* and the constant 5 is assigned to *b*. The actual parameter in a function designator can be any expression whose type is the same as that of the corresponding formal parameter. For example, the following are all valid invocations of the function Larger:

Function Designator	Value
Larger (4,5)	5
Larger (4,3 − 2)	4
Larger (3 * 2,75 **div** 4)	18
Larger (12,sqr (4))	16
Larger (2,Larger (3,1))	3

In the last two examples, one of the actual parameters is itself a function designator. When an expression contains nested calls to functions, the inner call is executed first and the result of that call is used as an actual parameter in the execution of the outer call.

The formal parameter list of a function definition can contain structured as well as scalar parameters. The program in Example 7.4 includes a function that uses an array parameter.

**EXAMPLE 7.4
Program to
Input an Array
and Find the
Smallest Value
in It**

```
program SmallValue (input, output);

{*******************************
* Program to read an array and *
* locate the smallest value in *
* the array.                   *
*******************************}

type
  ListType = array[1..50] of integer;
var
  List    : ListType;
  Counter : integer;

function LocSmall(x : ListType;
                  First, Last: integer) : integer;

  {Function to locate the position of the smallest
   value in an array between positions First and Last}

  var
    Small, i : integer; {"Small" is used to keep track
                         of the location of the current
                         smallest value as "i" moves
                         through the array "x"}

  begin {Function LocSmall}

    {Initialize Small to first location of array}

    Small := First;

    {Scan the rest of the array to determine if any
     values are smaller than the value at location
     "Small"}

    for i := First + 1 to Last do
        if x[i] < x[Small] then
        Small := i;
    LocSmall := Small;
  end; {of FUNCTION LocSmall}

  begin { Main program}

    {Input and count values in data file}
```

**EXAMPLE 7.4
Program to
Input an Array
and Find the
Smallest Value
in It**
(*continued*)

```
Counter := 0;
while not eof do
    begin
        Counter := Counter + 1;
        readln (List[Counter])
    end;

{Find and print location of smallest value}

writeln('The location of the smallest value is: ',
    LocSmall(List,1,Counter) :4)
end.
```

The function LocSmall has three formal parameters. The first formal parameter, *x*, is of type ListType. The other two formal parameters, First and Last, are of type integer. When declaring formal parameters, *only named data types are allowed in the parameter list.* That is, we can only have parameters whose type is any of the standard types (real, integer, char, boolean) or a user-defined type, such as ListType used in Example 7.4. Thus, the heading for LocSmall

```
function LocSmall(x: array[1..50] of integer;
                  First, Last: integer): integer;
```

is *not valid* since the type specification for *x* is not a named type. When you need to use an array in the formal parameter list of a function, you should first define a named array type and then use that type to specify any formal parameters.

The function LocSmall also contains a declaration of the variables small and *i*, which are used by the function. Since these variables are declared inside the function, they are considered **local variables.** Storage for them is allocated only when the function is invoked. A local variable is not defined outside the body of the function, and it does not retain its value from one execution of the function to the next. It comes into being when the function begins its execution and disappears when the function terminates execution. The variables declared in the parameter list are also local variables and exist only when the function is executing.

When the program of Example 7.4 is executed with the following data:

```
12
34
11
9
45
34
325
4
343
5
6
7
1
78
89
56
```

the output is:

The location of the smallest value is: 13

The ability to define functions and to invoke them at any point in a program is a very powerful programming tool. First, it allows a programmer to write a group of statements only once, as a function, and then specify their execution at many points in the program. This saves on coding and reduces the chances of making errors. Second, the use of functions makes the design of algorithms easier. For example, the main program of Example 7.4 could have been written without having to worry about how to find the location of the smallest value in the array. Once the main algorithm is written and tested, the programmer can then go on to write the required functions. This permits a programmer to concentrate on one task at a time. We can think of the functions as *subprograms* that the main program uses. Thus, a complex problem can be broken down into subproblems, and these subproblems can be solved independently. We have done this throughout the text: when designing our algorithms, we first outlined the subproblems and then separately refined each of them. This approach is called **top-down programming.** Although we have used top-down programming in the design of our algorithms, up to now we have coded these algorithms into single, often complex progams. User-defined functions, by allowing us to think of the subproblems as subprograms, make it possible for us to carry the top-down approach into the coding of programs.

While functions can be used to create subprograms, they have a major limitation. Although we can pass a function any number of values via the parameter list, the function always returns exactly one value as a result. Frequently, we wish to use a subprogram that does not return any value, but instead performs a set of operations, such as printing a table, or we wish it to return several values. A **procedure** provides us with a subprogram capable of returning several values, or no values at all. We will discuss procedures in the next section.

SELF-TEST 1

1. Which of the following **function** headings are valid and which are invalid?

(a) **function** One(a, b :integer);

(b) **function** ThisOne(x:char): integer;

(c) **function** OneMore(a: char):0..10;

(d) **function** YetAnother: real;

2. Assume the following definitions and declarations:

```
const
    MaxSize = 100;
type
    String = packed array[1..MaxSize] of char;
var
    Line1, Line2 : String;
    a, b, c : integer;
    Letter : char;
    z : real;
```

The heading for **function** Index is:

```
function Index (s1, s2 : String;
                Start: integer) : integer;
```

Which of the following expressions are valid and which are not? If an expression is not valid, explain why.

(a) `a := Index(Line1,Line2,1)`

(b) `writeln(Index(Line1,Line2,b))`

(c) `read(Index(Line1,line2,c))`

(d)
```
repeat
    b := b + 1
until  Index(Line1,Line2,b) = 0
```

(e) `c := Index(Line1,a,Line2)`

(f) `a := Index(Line1,Line2,z)`

3. Consider the following functions:

```
function Secret (x : integer): integer;
var
    i, j : integer;
begin
    i := 2 * x;
    if i > 10 then
        j := x div 2
    else
        j := x div 3;
    Secret := j - 2
end {of FUNCTION Secret};
```

```
function Another (a,b : integer):integer;
var
    i,j : integer;
begin
    j := 0;
    for i := a to b do
        j := j + i;
    Another := j
end {of FUNCTION Another}
```

What will be the output of each of the following program segments?

(a)
```
x:= 10;
writeln (Secret(x))
```

(b)
```
x := 5;
y := 8;
writeln (Another(x,y))
```

(c)
```
x := 10;
k := Secret(x);
writeln(x,k,Another(x,k))
```

(d) `x := 5;`
    `y := 8;`
    `writeln(Another(y,x))`

Answers

1. (a) Not valid. The function must have a type associated with the value it returns.   (b) Valid   (c) Not valid. The type of the function must be a named type.   (d) Valid

2. (a) Valid   (b) Valid   (c) Not valid. Function expressions cannot be used in read statements.   (d) Valid   (e) Not valid. The types of the actual parameters do not agree with the corresponding types of the formal parameters.   (f) Not valid. The types of the actual parameters do not match the types of the corresponding formal parameters.

3. (a) 3   (b) 26   (c) 10 3 0   (d) 0

7.2 PROCEDURES

The general form of the definition of a procedure is:

procedure identifier (formal parameter list);
Local variable declaration section
begin
procedure body
end;

The first line of the procedure definition is the **procedure heading.** The identifier following the reserved word **procedure** names the procedure. The formal parameter list specifies the formal parameters and their types. Any identifiers declared in the declaration section of the procedure are local to the procedure. That is, they are defined only when the procedure is being executed. Finally, the procedure body describes the operations to be performed by the procedure. If the procedure has no parameters, then the formal parameter list and its parentheses are omitted from the procedure heading.

The differences between procedure and function definitions are: first, we do not specify in the procedure heading a type for the procedure itself. This is not necessary because the procedure need not return any values at all, or it may return many values of different types. We shall see shortly that a procedure uses the parameter list to return, as well as receive, values. Second, it is not required and, in fact, *not permitted* to assign a value to the procedure name in the body of the procedure. *The procedure name is used only for identifying the procedure.* Finally, the reserved word **procedure,** instead of **function,** is used in the procedure heading.

EXAMPLE 7.5 Procedure to Compute the Cube of a Number

```
procedure Cube (x :real; var xcube :real);

{procedure to compute the cube of a real number
 "x" and return the value in "xcube"}

begin
  xcube := x*x*x

end; {of PROCEDURE Cube}
```

As an example, consider the **procedure definition** in Example 7.5, which is equivalent to the previously defined **function** Cube.

The procedure Cube has two parameters. The parameter x represents the real number to be cubed. The parameter xcube represents the result of cubing x, and its value is returned by the procedure. The reserved word **var** in front of xcube indicates that xcube is a **variable parameter** or a **pass-by-reference parameter.** Variable parameters are used by a procedure to return values to the program that invokes it. The parameter, x, is not preceded by the word, **var,** and therefore, is called a **pass-by-value parameter**, or simply a **value parameter.** Value parameters are used only to pass values to procedures.

The program of Example 7.6 shows how the procedure Cube is declared and invoked in a program.

The main program contains two *procedure calls* that invoke the procedure Cube. The procedure call,

```
Cube(1.23,a)
```

invokes the procedure Cube and passes the value 1.23 to the procedure by assigning it to the formal parameter, x. The procedure computes the cube of x and assigns the result to the actual parameter, a. The procedure is again invoked by the procedure statement:

```
Cube(b,c)
```

Here, the value of b is passed to the procedure, which computes the cube of that value and returns it as the value of the variable, c. Note that *procedure calls are written as independent statements, whereas function designators are always written as components of expressions.* To understand how values are passed to a procedure and

EXAMPLE 7.6
Program Illustrating Definition and Invocation of a Procedure

```pascal
program CubeANumber (input, output);

{***************************************
* Program to input a list of          *
* numbers cube them and output all     *
* numbers whose cube is greater than  *
* the cube of 1.23.                    *
***************************************}

var
  a,b,c : real;

procedure Cube (x :real; var xcube :real);

  {Procedure to compute the cube of a real number
   "x" and return the result in "xcube"}

  begin {PROCEDURE Cube}
      xcube := x*x*x
  end; {of PROCEDURE Cube}

begin {Main program}

  Cube(1.23,a);

  while not eof do
      begin
          readln (b);
          Cube (b,c);
          if c > a then
              writeln (b :8:3, c :10:3)
      end {WHILE loop}
end.
```

returned by the procedure, let us now examine the parameter mechanism in greater detail.

Procedure Parameters

Let us compare the procedure call,

Cube (1.23,a)

with the procedure heading,

procedure Cube (x :real; **var** xcube :real);

The correspondence between the actual parameters of the procedure call and the formal parameters of the procedure heading is:

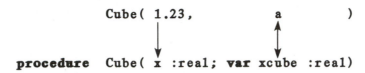

The actual parameter 1.23 corresponds to the formal parameter *x*, which is a *pass-by-value* parameter. The actual parameter *a* corresponds to the formal parameter xcube, which is a *pass-by-reference* parameter. Value parameters are used to pass data into the procedure. They cannot be used to pass results out of the procedure. This is why we drew the arrow in only one direction when we diagrammed the correspondence between the actual and formal parameters.

When data values are communicated from the calling program to a procedure using pass-by-value parameters, these values are assigned to the corresponding formal parameters. Conceptually, value parameters provide a mechanism to input values into the procedure. A formal parameter that is a value parameter is distinct from the corresponding actual parameter. It is a new variable with its own identifier and storage location in main storage. When a procedure is called, the computer assigns the corresponding actual parameter values to the appropriate pass-by-value formal parameters. When the procedure terminates, the storage allocated to the pass-by-value parameter is reclaimed and the formal pass-by-value parameter no longer exists.

In the procedure call

```
Cube(1.23,a)
```

the value of the constant 1.23 is assigned to *x*. The procedure then does all of its computations using x. Similarly, when the procedure call

```
Cube(b,c)
```

is executed, the value of b is assigned to x. The procedure then does its computations with x. The value of b remains unchanged even if x is changed within the procedure. In fact, it is still unchanged when the procedure terminates, and x ceases to exist. It is precisely because pass-by-value parameters obtain their values by an assignment of the value of the actual parameter to the corresponding formal parameter that they are called pass-by-value parameters. Since assignments are used to communicate values to pass-by-value parameters, actual parameters corresponding to pass-by-value formal parameters can be constants, variables, or expressions. If an expression is used as an actual parameter, it is first evaluated, then its value is assigned to the formal parameter. The predefined functions and the user-defined functions that we have studied thus far all used pass-by-value parameters.

The formal parameter xcube in the procedure heading is a pass-by-reference, or variable, parameter. The reserved word **var** preceding the variable identifier is used to designate pass-by-reference parameters. Pass-by-reference parameters can be used to pass data into or out of the procedure. When pass-by-reference parameters are used, the values of the actual parameters are *not* assigned to the corresponding formal parameters. Instead, we can regard the actual and formal parameters as synonyms; that is, as different identifiers for the same variable. When pass-by-reference parameters are used, no new variables are created. Instead, for the duration of the procedure, a main storage location, which already exists and whose identifier is the corresponding actual parameter, is given yet another name—the pass-by-reference parameter identifier. Thus, whatever happens to the pass-by-reference parameter will automatically happen to the corresponding actual parameter. As an illustration, consider the following program segment using the procedure Cube, which we defined earlier.

```
        .
        .
        .
b := 2.0;
Cube(b,c);
writeln(b :5:2, c :5:2);
        .
        .
        .
```

Let us assume that the variable *c* is not assigned a value earlier in the program. Before the above segment is executed, the values of the variables are:

Variable	Value
b	?
c	?

When

```
b := 2.0
```

is executed, 2.0 is assigned to *b* and the values of the variables become:

Variable	Value
b	2.0
c	?

The procedure call

```
Cube(b,c)
```

is now executed. This results in the following actions:

1. The value of *b* is assigned to *x*.
2. A correspondence is set up between *c* and xcube.
3. Control passes to the procedure Cube.
4. The procedure computes the cube of *x* and assigns the result to xcube. Since xcube and *c* are synonyms (that is, two different names for the same location in main storage) the cube of 2.0, or 8.0, is assigned to *c* automatically when it is assigned to xcube.
5. The procedure terminates and control returns to the statement following the procedure statement.

At this point in the program the values of the variables are:

Variable	Value
b	2.0
c	8.0

The values 2.0 and 8.0, therefore, will be printed by the writeln statement. The variables x and xcube no longer exist at this point of the program because they are local to the procedure Cube, and exist only when the procedure is executing.

Because pass-by-reference or variable parameters communicate by equating the identifiers of the corresponding variables, the actual parameters corresponding to pass-by-reference formal parameters *must* be variables. They cannot be constants or expressions. Generally, we use pass-by-value parameters to pass values to a procedure and pass-by-reference parameters to return results. We could, of course, use pass-by-reference parameters both to pass values to procedures and to return results. However, since pass-by-reference parameters will automatically change corresponding actual parameters, if the formal parameters are changed, they should not be used when the values of the actual parameters need to be protected.

When passing a large data structure to a procedure, pass-by-reference parameters are sometimes used to save space and processing time. A pass-by-value parameter requires that the actual parameter be assigned to the formal parameter. That is, the value of the actual parameter must be copied into the formal parameter. In the case of an array, this would necessitate copying the entire array into the formal parameter. This takes both time and storage. If the formal parameter is a pass-by-reference parameter, then only one copy of the array exists, with both the formal and actual parameters referring to that copy.

To get a better understanding of the parameter-passing mechanism used by procedures, consider the following additional examples. A parameter list can contain identifiers of parameters of any given type. Parameter lists are much like ordinary variable declarations, except that the list is enclosed in parentheses and **var** is used only with pass-by-reference parameters. The headings below illustrate various parameter lists.

```
procedure PrintName (Name : String);


procedure Swap (var First,Second : integer);


procedure Find (List : ListType;{Array to be searched}
                Key : integer   {Value being sought in array}
                var Found : boolean; {Flag to indicate if
                                        value sought is found}
                var Location:integer);{Subscript of array
                                        where "Key" is located}
```

Procedure PrintName has one pass-by-value parameter. It is passed a character string, which it prints in a fancy format. Thus, it does not return anything. Procedure Swap, on the other hand, has two pass-by-reference parameters. This is necessary because the procedure interchanges the values of the parameters and returns them interchanged. Finally, the procedure Find has both pass-by-value and pass-by-reference parameters. Note how comments are used in the parameter list to document the parameters. The order in which the parameters are listed is arbitrary. Pass-by-value and pass-by-reference parameters can be declared in any order desired. The order in which parameters are declared should be based on readability. Whatever makes for the most readable heading and call should be used.

Let us consider one more example of a program involving procedures. The program in Example 7.7 is the same as the sorting program in Example 6.4, but it uses procedures to print the array and to swap values. It also uses a function to locate the smallest value in the array. Here we use a pass-by-reference parameter to pass the array. This saves space and execution time. We could also have used a pass-by-value parameter to pass the array if storage and execution time were of no concern and if we wanted to make sure that the original array was protected.

**EXAMPLE 7.7
Program to
Sort an Array
Using Proce-
dures**

```
program Sort (input, output);

{****************************
* Program to sort an array  *
* of integers in ascending  *
* order using the selection *
* sort.                      *
****************************}
```

EXAMPLE 7.7   **Program to Sort an Array Using Procedures** (*continued*)

```
const
  MaxSize = 100;
type
  List = array[1..MaxSize] of integer;
var
  Numbers         : List;     {Array to be sorted}
  NumberOfValues  : integer;  {Number of values in array}
  Start           : integer;  {Location of first unsorted element}
  Small           : integer;  {Location of smallest value}
  i               : integer;  {Read loop index}

procedure Swap( var x,y : integer);

  {*******************************
   * procedure to swap "x" and "y"*
   ******************************}

  var
      Temp : integer; {Temporary location used for
                          swapping}

  begin {Swap}
      Temp := x;
      x  := y;
      y  := Temp
  end; {of Swap}

function LocSmall(x : List;
                  First, Last: integer): integer;

  {Function to locate the position of the smallest
   value in an array between positions First and Last}

  var
      Small, i : integer; {"Small" is used to keep track
                             of the location of the current
                             smallest value as "i" moves
                             through the array "x"}

begin {Function LocSmall}

    {Initialize Small to first location of array}

    Small := First;
```

EXAMPLE 7.7   **Program to Sort an Array Using Procedures** (*continued*)

```
{Scan the rest of the array to determine if any
 values are smaller than the value at location
 "Small"}

for i := First + 1 to Last do
    if x[i] < x[Small] then
    Small := i;
    LocSmall := Small
end; {of FUNCTION LocSmall}

procedure Print( var a :List; Length :integer);

{**********************************************
 * Procedure to print an array of size "Length" *
 **********************************************}


var
    i : integer;
begin
    for i := 1 to Length do
        write (a[i] :5);
    writeln
end; {of Print}

begin {Main program}

  {Input and count values}

  i := 1;
  repeat
      read (Numbers[i])
      i := i + 1;
  until eof or (i > MaxSize);
  if i > MaxSize then
      writeln (' WARNING -- input values may be lost');
  NumberOfValues := i - 1;

  {Print array}

  Print(Numbers, NumberOfValues);

  {sort array}
```

EXAMPLE 7.7   **Program to Sort an Array Using Procedures** (*continued*)

```
Start := 1;
while Start < NumberOfValues do
    begin
        Small := LocSmall(Numbers,Start,NumberOfValues);
        Swap(Numbers[Start],Numbers[Small]);
        Start := Start + 1
    end;

{print array}

Print (Numbers, NumberOfValues)
end.
```

SELF-TEST 2   1. Which of the following **procedure** headings are valid and which are invalid?

(a) **procedure** `One( a, b :integer);`

(b) **procedure** `ThisOne(x:char):integer;`

(c) **procedure** `OneMore(`**var** `a: char);`

(d) **procedure** `YetAnother(a:0..10);`

(e) **procedure** `ThatOne;`

(f) **procedure** `(`**var** `x, y :real);`

2. Assume the following definitions and declarations:

```
const
    MaxSize = 100;
type
    String = packed array[1..MaxSize] of char;
var
    Line1, Line2 : String;
    a : integer;
    Letter : char;
```

The heading for **procedure** "Concatenate" is:

```
procedure Concatenate(var s1, s2: String);
```

Which of the following expressions are valid and which are not? If an expression is not valid, explain why.

(a) `a :=Concatenate(Line1,Line2)`

(b) `writeln(Concatenate(Line1,Line2))`

(c) `Concatenate(Line2,Line1)`

(d) `Concatenate(Line2,letter)`

(e) `Concatenate(Line1,Line1)`

(f) `Line1 := Concatenate(Line1,Line2)`

3. Suppose that for each of the following **procedure** definitions we execute the same main program:

```
begin {Main program}
    x := 1;
    y := 2;
    ProcA(x,y);
    writeln(x,y)
end {of Main Program}.
```

What is printed, given the following definitions of ProcA?

(a) **procedure** ProcA(r,s :integer);
```
    begin
        r := 10;
        s := 20
    end;
```

(b) **procedure** ProcA(**var** r,s : integer);
```
    begin
        r := 10;
        s := 20
    end;
```

(c) **procedure** ProcA(r :integer
                    var s :integer);
```
    begin
        r := 10;
        s := 20
    end;
```

(d) **procedure** ProcA(**var** r :integer; s : integer);
    begin
      r := 10;
      s := 20
    end;

4. What will the following program print?

```
program Question4 (output);
var
   x,y :  integer;

procedure Guess(a : integer;var b :integer);
begin
   a := a + 5;
   b := b + a
end {of PROCEDURE Guess};

begin {Main Program}
   x := 1;
   y   :=  2;
   Guess(x,y);
   write (x,y);
   Guess(x,x);
   writeln(x,y)
end.
```

Answers

1. (a) Valid   (b) Not valid. Procedures are not typed.   (c) Valid
(d) Not valid. Parameter types must be named types.   (e) Valid
(f) Valid
2. (a) Not valid. Procedure calls are not parts of expressions.
(b) Not valid. Procedure calls cannot be used as expressions in
writeln statements.   (c) Valid   (d) Not valid. Actual and formal parameter types do not agree.   (e) Valid   (f) Not valid. Procedure
calls are not parts of expressions.
3. (a) 1 2   (b) 10 20   (c) 1 20   (d) 10 2
4. 1 8
   7 8

**7.3
BLOCK
STRUCTURES**

In Chapter 2 we saw that a Pascal program consists of a program
heading and a body called a *block*. The block contains the definitions, declarations, and statements of the program. This is also true

for procedures and functions. That is, a procedure or function consists of a procedure or function heading and a block. The block for a procedure or function, just as the block for a program, contains the definitions, declarations, and statements of that procedure or function. Figure 7.2 shows the procedure heading and the block of the procedure Swap, which we used earlier.

In Pascal all definitions and declarations apply *only to the block containing the definitions and declarations.* When we declare a variable in a block, we can only refer to it in that block. In the procedure Swap the variable Temp is declared in the block of that procedure. It is only meaningful to refer to it in that procedure. That part of the program in which it is meaningful to refer to an identifier is called the **scope** of the identifier. Thus, we say that the scope of Temp is procedure Swap.

The program of Example 7.7 consists of four blocks. One block consists of the program itself; that is, it begins right after the program heading and ends with the **end.** of the program. The other three blocks are the two procedures and the function we defined in the program. They each begin right after the respective procedure or function headings and end with the respective **end**s of the statement parts of the procedures and function. This is illustrated in Figure 7.3, where we have drawn boxes to represent each of the blocks.

Because the two procedures and the function are inside the block of the main program, any identifier declared in the main program may be referenced anywhere in either of the procedures or the

Figure 7.2 Structure of a **procedure**

Procedure Heading

```
procedure Swap( var x,y : integer);


{*******************************
* Procedure to swap "x" and "y"*
*******************************}
```

Block

```
var
    Temp : integer;

begin {Swap}
    Temp := x;
    x := y;
    y := Temp
end; {of Swap}
```

Figure 7.3 Block structure of sort program

program Sort (input, output);

```
const
   MaxSize = 100;
type
   List : packed array[1 . . MaxSize] of integer;
var
   Numbers : List;
   Start, Small, NumberOfValues, i : integer;

   procedure Swap        (var x, y : integer);

      var
         Temp : integer;
      begin {Swap}
         . . .
      end; {of Swap}


   function Smallest      (var a :List;
                           First,
                           Size :integer)
                                     :integer;

      var
         i, LocSmall : integer;
      begin { Smallest}
         . . .
      end; {of Smallest}


   procedure Print        (var a :List;
                           Length :integer);

      var
         i : integer;
      begin {Print}
         . . .
      end; {of Print}

   begin {Main program}
      . . .
   end.
```

function. There is an exception to this, which we will discuss shortly. Because identifiers declared in the main program can be referenced by any procedure or function defined in the main program,
they are called **global** identifiers. The scope of global identifiers is
the whole program. Some of the global identifiers are: MaxSize, List,
Small, and NumberOfValues.

Identifiers that are declared in a procedure or function are **local**
identifiers and can be referenced only in that procedure or function.
The scope of each of these identifiers is the procedure or function
within which it is declared. It is not possible to reference Temp in the
main program or in a procedure or function other than Swap.

The identifier i, although declared in the main program, *cannot*
be used in either the procedure Print or the function Smallest. This is
because in Print and in Smallest we have a local declaration of i. Although it is not valid to declare a variable more than once in a given
block, multiple declarations are possible as long as each declaration
is in a different block. When a variable is declared more than once, in
separate blocks, the resulting variables are distinct. Each reference to
i in Smallest manipulates the i local to Smallest. A reference to i in
Print results in a manipulation of the i declared in Print. Any other
reference to i would result in manipulating the global variable i.

Nested Procedures

The definitions and declarations in a block include not only definitions of constants and types and the declarations of all the variables
in a block, but also definitions of procedures and functions. As procedures and functions themselves have blocks, we can nest procedures and functions within other procedures and functions. The diagram in Figure 7.4 illustrates such nesting.

The scope rules we saw earlier apply to nested structures as well;
that is, the scope of an identifier is the block in which it is declared,
unless it is redeclared inside another block. Thus, the identifier b is
global to the whole program and can be referenced in all the procedures, as well as the main program. The identifier a is declared in the
main program and thus can be used in it, as well as any procedure
where it is not redeclared. Because it is redeclared in procedure p1,
its scope is the main program and procedure p3, but not procedure
p1. The identifier a, declared in procedure p1, has the same scope as
identifiers c and d, which are declared in the same procedure. The
scope of all three identifiers is p1 and p2. Finally, the scope of e and f
is procedure p2 only, and the scope of g is procedure p3 only.

Figure 7.4 Nested block structure

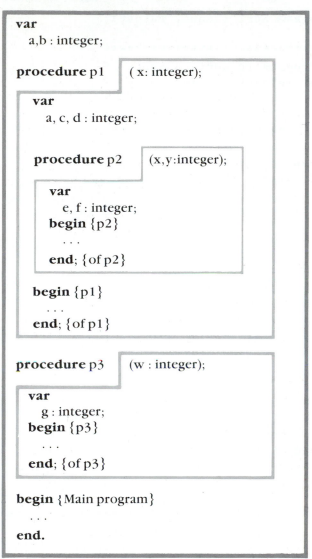

program Prog (input, output);

```
var
   a,b : integer;

procedure p1    ( x: integer);

   var
      a, c, d : integer;

   procedure p2    (x,y:integer);

      var
         e, f : integer;
      begin {p2}
         . . .
      end; {of p2}

   begin {p1}
      . . .
   end; {of p1}


procedure p3    (w : integer);

   var
      g : integer;
   begin {p3}
      . . .
   end; {of p3}

begin {Main program}
   . . .
end.
```

A final note about the scope of variables is in order. Since global variables can be referenced anywhere in the main program, including any procedures or functions defined in the program, we do not actually need parameters to communicate with procedures. We could instead use global variables. The program of Example 7.7 could have been written as in Example 7.8.

EXAMPLE 7.8   **Program to Sort Array Using Global Variables**

```
program Sort (input, output);

{***************************
 * Program to sort an array  *
 * of integers in ascending  *
 * order using the selection  *
 * sort.                     *
 ***************************}

const
  MaxSize = 100;
type
  List = array[1..MaxSize] of integer;
var
  Numbers : List;
  Start, Temp, Small, LocSmall, NumberOfValues, i : integer;

procedure Swap;

  {******************************
   * Procedure to swap two values *
   ******************************}

  begin {Swap}
      Temp := Numbers[Small];
      Numbers[Small] := Numbers[Start];
      Numbers[Start] := Temp
  end; {of Swap}

function Smallest :integer;

  {*****************************************
   * Function to find the location of the  *
   * smallest value in an array containing *
   * "Size" values starting at location    *
   * "First"                               *
   *****************************************}

  begin { Smallest}
      LocSmall := Start;
      for i := Start + 1 to NumberOfValues do
          if Numbers[i] < Numbers[LocSmall] then
              LocSmall := i;
      Smallest := LocSmall
  end; {of Smallest}
```

EXAMPLE 7.8 **Program to Sort Array Using Global Variables** (*continued*)

```pascal
procedure Print;

   {********************************
   * Procedure to print an array. *
   ********************************}

   begin
       for i := 1 to NumberOfValues do
           write (Numbers[i] :5);
       writeln
   end; {of Print}

begin {Main program}

   {Input values}

   i := 1;
   repeat
       read (Numbers[i]);
       i := i + 1
   until eof or (i > MaxSize);
   if i > MaxSize then
       begin
           writeln(' WARNING -- Data values',
                       '  may have been lost');
           NumberOfValues := i-1
       end
   else
           NumberOfValues := i-2;
   {Print array}

   Print;

   {Sort array}

   Start := 1;
   while Start < NumberOfValues do
       begin
           Small := Smallest;
           Swap;
           Start := Start + 1
       end;
   {print array}

   Print
end.
```

In Example 7.8, we wrote the procedures Swap and Print, as well as the function Smallest, without using parameters. Such parameterless procedures and functions communicate with the rest of the program through global variables. The disadvantage of this approach is that we must know exactly what the environment of a procedure or function is before we can write it. For example, we must know what the identifiers are for all data used by the main program. We need this information in order to be able to access the variables of interest and to avoid accidentally changing other variables. Changes of global variables by procedures or functions are called *side effects* and can lead to errors that are very difficult to detect. If we use parameters and local variables, we are able to write procedures and functions without undue concern about naming variables and about potential side effects. Thus, we almost invariably use parameters and local variables in designing our procedures and functions. The result is programs with procedures and functions relatively independent of each other and the main program. Such programs are called **modular** programs, and they can be created one module or subprogram at a time. Consequently, they are easier to read, to understand, and to modify.

Forward Declaration

In the example of Figure 7.4, it would be illegal for the main program to invoke procedure p2. The name of a procedure is an identifier just like any other identifier in a program. Thus, p2 can only be referenced in the block in which it is defined, procedure p1. Only procedure p1 and procedure p2 can reference procedure p2. The procedures p1 and p3 are defined in the main program and, thus, should be able to reference each other. But, in fact, only procedure p3 can reference procedure p1. Procedure p1 cannot reference procedure p3 because the definition of p3 follows that of p1. A procedure must be declared before it can be called. We can summarize the procedure calls for Figure 7.4 as follows:

Procedure	Can Call
Main Program	p1, p3
p1	p1, p2
p2	p1, p2
p3	p1, p3

Figure 7.5 The **forward** declaration

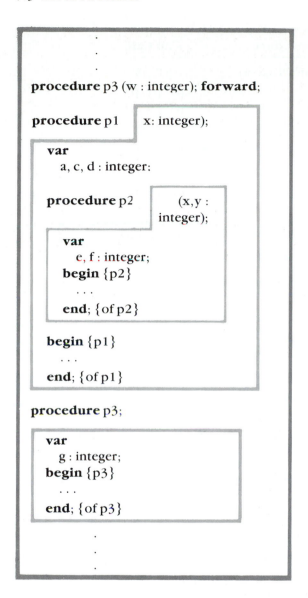

```
        .
        .
        .

procedure p3 (w : integer); forward;

procedure p1    x: integer);

   var
     a, c, d : integer:

   procedure p2    (x,y :
                     integer);

      var
        e, f : integer;
      begin {p2}
        . . .

      end; {of p2}

   begin {p1}
     . . .

   end; {of p1}

procedure p3;

   var
     g : integer;
   begin {p3}
     . . .

   end; {of p3}

        .
        .
        .
```

If we wish to reference p3 from p1, we can either reverse the order of the declarations or use a **forward** declaration. Figure 7.5 illustrates a **forward** declaration. Note that the body of the procedure is replaced by the reserved word **forward**. When the procedure is defined later in the program, a shortened heading is used.

The procedures p1 and p2 can now reference procedure p3, even though the definition of procedure p3 follows that of procedures p1 and p2. Procedure p3, however, still cannot reference p2 because p2 is defined inside procedure p1. We can now summarize which procedure can call which for Figure 7.5 as follows:

Procedure	Can Call
Main Program	p1, p3
p1	p1, p2, p3
p2	p1, p2, p3
p3	p1, p3

SELF-TEST 3   1. The block structure of a program is illustrated below.

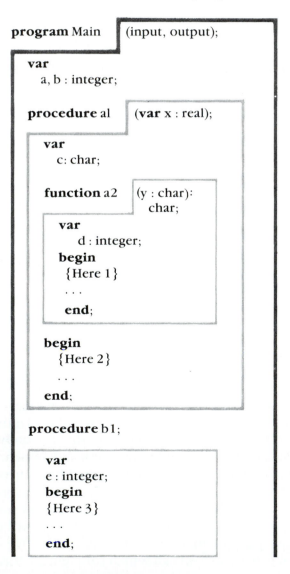

```
program Main    (input, output);

    var
      a, b : integer;

    procedure a1    (var x : real);

       var
         c: char;

       function a2    (y : char):
                        char;
          var
            d : integer;
          begin
           {Here 1}
            . . .
          end;

       begin
         {Here 2}
          . . .
       end;

    procedure b1;

       var
       e : integer;
       begin
       {Here 3}
        . . .
       end;
```

```
begin {Main}
  {Here 4}
  . . .
end.
```

Which variables can be referenced at the following locations in the program?

(a) Here 1   (b) Here 2

(c) Here 3   (d) Here 4

2. Which subprograms can the following call?

(a) main program   (b) procedure a1

(c) function a2   (d) procedure b1

3. How could the above structure be modified to allow procedure a1 to call procedure b1?

Answers

1. (a) a, b, c, d, x, y   (b) a, b, c, x   (c) a, b, e   (d) a, b
2. (a) a1, b1   (b) a1, a2   (c) a2   (d) a1, b1
3. To allow procedure a1 to call procedure b1, either b1 must be defined before a1 or a **forward** declaration for b1 should be used.

7.4 RECURSION

You will note that in the example in Section 7.3 a procedure can call itself. As an illustration of such a procedure, consider Example 7.9.

**EXAMPLE 7.9
Program to
Illustrate
Recursive
Calls**

```
program RecursiveSum (input,output);

{*************************************
 * Program to illustrate a function *
 * calling itself.                  *
 *************************************}

type
  NumberList = array[1..10] of integer;
var
  Numbers : NumberList;
  i : integer;

function Sum(var NumArray : NumberList; Last :
 integer):integer;
```

EXAMPLE 7.9
Program to
Illustrate
Recursive
Calls
(*continued*)

```
{**********************************
* Function that sums the components *
* of an array by adding the "Last"  *
* component to the sum of the        *
* remaining components.              *
**********************************}

begin

    {If there is only one component
     then the sum is equal to value
     of that component.}

    if Last = 1 then
        Sum := NumArray[Last]
    else
        {There is more than one element.
         The sum is the last element plus
         the sum of the other elements
         in the array.}

        Sum := NumArray[Last] + Sum(NumArray,Last-1);
end {of FUNCTION Sum};

begin {Main Program}

  {Read the elements of the array}

  for i := 1 to 10 do
      read(Numbers[i]);

      {Compute and print the sum}

      writeln (' Sum: ';Sum(Numbers,10): 5)
end.
```

Given the data

1 2 3 4 5 6 7 8 9 10

the output will be:

Sum: 55

The program in Example 7.9 reads and sums an array. It does this by invoking the function Sum, which, in turn, invokes itself. A procedure or function that calls itself is said to be **recursive**. When the function Sum is first called in the main program, it is passed the array to be summed, and the constant "10" indicates that there are ten elements in the array. When the function is first entered, the value of the parameter Last is compared to 1, the value of the index of the first location of the array. If Last is, in fact, equal to 1, then we know that there is only one value to be summed, and we can set the sum to that value and return from the function. If, on the other hand, Last is not equal to 1, we invoke the function again, but this time with Last − 1 as the second parameter. The sum of the values in the array is then set to the sum of Last − 1 values plus the value at location Last. To see what actually happens with these repeated calls to the function Sum, we have inserted some writeln statements in our program and then executed it again. The revised program is shown in Example 7.10.

EXAMPLE 7.10 Recursive Program with Trace

```
program RecursiveSum (input,output);

{***********************************
* Program to illustrate a function *
* calling itself. The function     *
* includes output statements to    *
* permit tracing program execution.*
***********************************}

type
  NumberList = array[1..10] of integer;
var
  Numbers : NumberList;
  i : integer;

function Sum(var NumArray : NumberList;
                  Last : integer):integer;

  {***********************************
  * Function that sums the components *
  * of an array by adding the "Last"  *
  * component to the sum of the       *
  * remaining components.             *
  ***********************************}
```

EXAMPLE 7.10   Recursive Program with Trace (*continued*)

```
var
    Total : integer;

begin

    writeln (' Now entering Function Sum. Last:',Last: 5);

    {If there is only one component
     then the total is equal to value
     of that component.}

    if Last = 1 then
        Total := NumArray[Last]
    else
        {There is more than one element.
         The total is the last element plus
         the sum of the other elements
         in the array.}

        Total:=  NumArray[Last] + Sum(NumArray,Last-1);

        writeln(' Now returning from function Sum.',
                ' Total: ',Total:5);

        {Set Sum to Total and return value}

        Sum := Total
    end {of FUNCTION Sum};

begin {Main Program}

  {Read the elements of the array}

  for i := 1 to 10 do
      read(Numbers[i]);

  {Compute and print the sum}

  writeln (Sum(Numbers,10): 5)
end.
```

Given the same input as the previous example, the output will be:

```
Now entering Function Sum. Last:    10
Now entering Function Sum. Last:     9
Now entering Function Sum. Last:     8
Now entering Function Sum. Last:     7
Now entering Function Sum. Last:     6
Now entering Function Sum. Last:     5
Now entering Function Sum. Last:     4
Now entering Function Sum. Last:     3
Now entering Function Sum. Last:     2
Now entering Function Sum. Last:     1
Now returning from Function Sum. Total:     1
Now returning from Function Sum. Total:     3
Now returning from Function Sum. Total:     6
Now returning from Function Sum. Total:    10
Now returning from Function Sum. Total:    15
Now returning from Function Sum. Total:    21
Now returning from Function Sum. Total:    28
Now returning from Function Sum. Total:    36
Now returning from Function Sum. Total:    45
Now returning from Function Sum. Total:    55
      55
```

Note that we make ten calls to the function before returning for the first time. The first call is made with the value of 10 for the parameter Last. This call is made in the main program. It, in turn, generates the call with the value of 9 for Last. That call generates one with the value of 8 for Last, and so on. This process continues until the call with 1 for the parameter Last is generated. At that point the function is able to return a value for the sum without generating an additional call. Once it has the sum for Last equals 1, it can compute the sum for Last equals 2, and so on. The function returns values from all the calls in the opposite order in which the calls were made. The first call it returns from is Sum(Numbers,1). This is the last call that was made. When it returns from this call, it also returns the value of 1 for Sum (Numbers,1). It then returns from Sum(Numbers,2) with a value of 2 + Sum(Numbers,1) which is 2 + 1, or 3, as we have the value of Sum(Numbers,1). This returning process continues until the function finally returns from the first call we made, the one in the main program, with a value of 55. Note that in this version of the program, we used a local variable Total. This is because the statement:

```
writeln(' Now returning from function Sum.',
        ' Sum : ',Sum :5);
```

is not permitted. The identifier Sum is not the name of a variable. It is the name of a function. If it is used on the right side of an assignment statement or in an expression, such as in the output list of a writeln statement, it is considered to be a function call and requires a list of parameters that generate yet another recursive call.

The function Sum could, of course, be written without using recursion. Example 7.11 shows the iterative counterpart of our recursive function.

The nonrecursive definition of the function Sum is certainly simpler. Note that here, again, we need the local variable Total. The statement:

```
Sum := Sum + NumArray[i]
```

is not permitted again because Sum is the name of a function and not a variable.

We can illustrate the first-called-last-returned nature of recursive calls by writing a recursive procedure that reads a string of characters and prints it backward. Example 7.12 (p. 338) shows such a program. The procedure ReverseAndPrint reads a single character and checks to see if the end of the line has been reached. If there are more characters, it calls itself to read another character. When it reaches the end of the line it prints a character and returns. The character printed will be the one read in the last invocation of the procedure, which continues to print characters until they are all printed. However, since it will print them in the reverse order in which they were read, the line will be printed backward.

A function or procedure is recursive if it is defined in terms of itself. Many such definitions exist in mathematics. For example, recall that the factorial of a non-negative integer is defined as:

$$n! = \begin{cases} 1 & \text{if } n = 0 \\ n * (n - 1)! & \text{if } n > 0 \end{cases}$$

Note that the above recursive definition includes two parts:

1. A definition of the function in terms of itself.
2. A concrete value for the function at some point. The definition of the function in terms of itself must also lead to the concrete value if repeated often enough.

EXAMPLE 7.11
Iterative Version of Function to Sum an Array

```pascal
program IterativeSum (input,output);

{*************************************
 * Program to illustrate the iterative *
 * version of a recursive function.    *
 *************************************}

type
  NumberList = array[1..10] of integer;
var
  Numbers : NumberList;
  i : integer;

function Sum(var NumArray : NumberList;
             Last : integer):integer;

  {*************************************
   * Function that sums the components *
   * of an array by using a loop.      *
   *************************************}

  var
      Total, i : integer;

  begin

      {Initialize Total and sum all values in array}

      Total := 0;
      for i := 1 to 10 do
          Total := Total + NumArray[i];

      {Set Sum to Total and return value}

      Sum := Total
  end {of FUNCTION Sum};

begin {Main Program}

  {Read the elements of the array}

  for i := 1 to 10 do
      read(Numbers[i]);

  {Compute and print the sum}

  writeln (' Sum: ';Sum(Numbers,10): 5)
end.
```

**EXAMPLE 7.12
Using Recursion to Print
a String
Backward**

```
program Backward  (input,output);

{*********************************
* Program to illustrate the order *
* in which calls and returns are  *
* made by reading a string        *
* recursively and printing it in  *
* reverse order.                  *
*********************************}

procedure ReverseAndPrint;

   {*****************************
   * Recursive procedure to     *
   * read a line of characters  *
   * and print it in reverse    *
   * order.                     *
   *****************************}

   var
      Character : char;

   begin
      {Read a character and continue
       reading as long as the end of the
       line is not reached }

      read (Character);
      if not eoln then
         ReverseAndPrint;
      write(Character)
   end {of PROCEDURE ReverseAndPrint};

begin {Main Program}

  ReverseAndPrint;
  writeln
end.
```

Given the following line of input:

This sentence will come out backward.

the output will be:

```
.drawkcab tuo emoc lliw ecnetnes sihT
```

It is to this type of problem that recursion can be applied successfully. This is because:

1. The solution is easy to specify for certain special conditions, called the **stopping states.** (In our example, the stopping state is the value of 1 for $n!$.

2. For any other condition there is a well-defined set of rules that eventually leads to a stopping state. These are the **recursion steps.** (In our example, for $n > 0$ we have a rule that allows us to redefine the problem with a smaller n. This eventually leads to a definition of the problem with a value of 1 for $n!$, and thus we reach the stopping state.)

A Pascal function to compute the factorial of n, given the above definition of factorial, is provided in Example 7.13.

Here again, we can easily write an iterative version of the function Factorial using a **for . . . do** loop. When we have the choice of

**EXAMPLE 7.13
Recursive
Function to
Compute the
Factorial of n**

```
function Factorial(n : integer): integer;

{*****************************
 * Recursive function to     *
 * compute the factorial of  *
 * a non-negative integer "n" *
 *****************************}

begin

  {Validate n}

  if n < 0 then
      begin
          writeln(' Invalid parameter -- Negative');
          Factorial := 0
      end
  else
      {Compute Factorial}

      if n = 0 then
          Factorial := 1
      else
          Factorial := n * Factorial(n-1)
end {of Function Factorial};
```

an iterative or recursive approach, which should be used? In most cases it turns out that the iterative approach is superior. The computer takes much more time and uses much more storage in setting up recursive calls and returns than it does in executing loops. In our examples we used recursion to illustrate the concept, not to write the most efficient program. However, recursion is very useful when you cannot see a straightforward solution to a problem, but you can see a way to transform the problem into a simpler or smaller one. Recursion also is useful when the problem is initially stated in recursive terms. Some mathematical problems are of this nature. An example of a function particularly well suited to a recursive definition is Euclid's algorithm for computing the greatest common divisor of two positive integers.

$$
GCD(m,n) = \begin{cases} n & \text{if } n \le m \text{ and } m \bmod n = 0 \\ GCD(n,m) & \text{if } m < n \\ GCD(m, m \bmod n) & \text{otherwise} \end{cases}
$$

where the notation GCD (m,n) stands for the greatest common divisor of m and n.

A Pascal program implementing this algorithm is shown in Example 7.14.

As a final example of recursion, we will consider a sorting algorithm (Example 7.15, p. 344). The sort is called a **quicksort.** It functions by selecting an element of the array to be sorted, called the **pivot,** and placing the pivot in its final position in the array. As the pivot's position is being found, the other elements are moved so that all the elements to the left of the pivot are less than it, and all the elements to the right of the pivot are greater than it. The array is thus split into two pieces. These pieces are then sorted by making recursive calls to the sorting algorithm. The recursion stops when we find that the portion of the array we are sorting has only one element.

The algorithm can be described as follows:

begin
    if array to be sorted has more than one element **then**
        select the pivot.
        Rearrange array to place pivot in correct location.
        Sort array to left of pivot.
        Sort array to right of pivot.
end.

**EXAMPLE 7.14
Euclid's Algo-
rithm for the
Greatest Com-
mon Divisor**

```
program Euclid (input,output);

{*************************
* Program to Illustrate *
* Euclid's algorithm.   *
*************************}

var
  x,y : integer;

function GCD (m,n : integer):integer;

  {**************************
  * Function to compute     *
  * the greatest common     *
  * divisor of two          *
  * integers.               *
  **************************}

  begin
      if (n <= m) and (m mod n = 0) then
          GCD := n
      else
          if m < n then
              GCD := GCD(n,m)
          else
              GCD := GCD(n,m mod n)
  end {of FUNCTION GCD};

begin {Main Program}

  x := 72;
  y := 20;
  writeln(' GCD(',x:1,',',y:1,')=',GCD(x,y):1)
end.
```

The output of this program will be:

```
GCD(72,20)=4
```

We begin by developing the function to select the pivot. This function returns the position of the pivot. If the array has only one element, it returns a 0.

```
function Pivot(i,j : integer): integer;

{*****************************
 * Function to select pivot  *
 * for Quicksort. It selects *
 * the first element of the  *
 * array.                    *
 *****************************}

begin
  if i >= j then
      Pivot := 0
  else
      Pivot := i
end;
```

Although we selected the first element of the array to be sorted as the pivot value, other means of selecting the pivot value are also used. For example, the larger of the first two values is often used as the pivot.

Once the pivot value has been selected, we need an algorithm to place the pivot in the correct location. To do this we use two indices into the array: one index, L, moving from left to right; the other, R, moving from right to left. At all times the values to the left of L are less than the pivot, while the values to the right of R are greater than or equal to the pivot. To achieve this, L moves past any element that is less than the pivot. It stops moving when it reaches an element greater than or equal to the pivot. If L moves past R, then we are done, and the pivot is positioned. If L stops to the left of R, R begins to move from right to left. R moves past any value greater than or equal to the pivot. When R stops, the value at L is swapped with the value at R, and L resumes its motion. The complete sort for pivot = 4 is illustrated below.

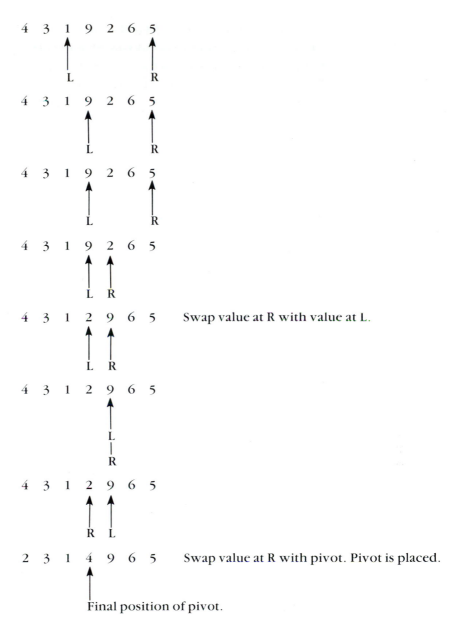

In order to sort the rest of the array, repeat the process with arrays to left and right of the pivot. The complete Quicksort algorithm is coded in Example 7.15.

Note how we invoke the Quicksort algorithm recursively with the two parts of the array to the left and right of the pivot value once the value is positioned.

EXAMPLE 7.15
Quicksort

```pascal
procedure Quicksort (First, Last: integer);
{************************************
* Procedure to sort the elements of *
* A from A[First] to A[Last]. A is  *
* a global variable.                *
************************************}

var
  PivIndex : integer;
  L, R : integer;

function Pivot(i,j : integer): integer;

  {****************************
  * Function to select pivot  *
  * for Quicksort. It selects *
  * the first element of the  *
  * array.                    *
  ****************************}

  begin
      if i >= j then
          Pivot := 0
      else
          Pivot := i
  end;

procedure Swap (var x, y : integer);

  {******************************
  * Procedure to swap two values. *
  ******************************}

  var
      Temp : integer;
  begin
      Temp := x;
      x := y;
      y := Temp
  end;

begin {Quicksort}

  {Select pivot}
```

EXAMPLE 7.15
Quicksort
(*continued*)

```
    PivIndex := Pivot(First,Last);

    if PivIndex <> 0 then
        begin
            {Initialize L and R for scan}

            L := PivIndex + 1;
            R := Last;

            {Scan until L > R}
            repeat
                while (A[L] <= A[PivIndex]) and (L<=R) do
                    L := L + 1;
                while A[R] > A[PivIndex] do
                    R := R - 1;
                if R > L then
                    Swap(A[L],A[R])
            until L>R;
            Swap(A[PivIndex], A[R]);
            Quicksort(First, R-1);
            Quicksort(R+1,Last)
        end
end;
```

SELF-TEST 4

1. Consider the following function:

```
function Mystery (a : integer):integer;
begin
  if a < 0 then
      writeln ('Error')
  else
      if a = 0 then
          Mystery := 0
      else
          Mystery := a + Mystery(a-1)
end {of FUNCTION Mystery};
```

What is the output of the function using the following actual parameters?

(a) 0   (b) − 1
(c) 5   (d) 10

2. Rewrite the above function as an iterative function.
3. The *n*th Fibonacci number is defined recursively as follows:

If *n* is 1 or 2, then the *n*th Fibonacci number is 1.
If *n* is 3 or more, then the *n*th Fibonacci number is the sum of the two previous Fibonacci numbers.

Write a recursive function to compute the *n*th Fibonacci number.

Answers

1. (a) 0   (b) Error   (c) 15   (d) 55

2.
```
function Mystery (a : integer):integer;
var
   Sum,i : integer;
begin
   Sum := 0;
   if a < 0 then
       writeln ('Error')
   else
       for i := 1 to a do
             Sum := Sum + i;
   Mystery := Sum
end {of FUNCTION Mystery};
```

3.
```
function Fibonacci(n :integer):integer;
begin
   if (n=1) or (n=2) then
       Fibonacci := 1
   else
       Fibonacci := Fibonacci(n-1) + Fibonacci(n-2)
end {of FUNCTION Fibonacci};
```

Let us now examine in greater detail how we can use procedures and functions to design and code programs.

APPLICATION

Simulation of a Dice Game

Computers are often used to simulate various processes. In many simulations, events appear to occur at random. For this reason, one of the requirements of almost any simulation program is some facility for generating random numbers. We will now examine a program that simulates the game of craps, a dice game.

APPLICATION

Simulation of a Dice Game (*continued*)

In the game of craps, a player rolls two dice. We know that each die has six faces, and these faces have one, two, three, four, five, or six spots respectively. After the dice have been tossed, the sum of the number of spots on the top faces is obtained. If the sum is 7 or 11 on the first throw, the player wins. If the sum is 2, 3, or 12 the player loses. If the sum is 4, 5, 6, 8, or 10, then that sum becomes the player's "point." To win, the player must continue to roll the dice until he makes his point. If the player rolls a 7 before he makes his point he loses.

We can design an algorithm to play the game as follows:

begin
    Roll die1
    Roll die2
    Compute the sum of the two rolls
    Print the sum
    if the sum is equal to 7 or 11 **then**
        Declare the player the winner
    else
        if the sum is equal to 2, 3, or 12 **then**
            Declare the player the loser
        else
            The sum becomes the point
            while player is not winner or player is not loser **do**
                begin loop
                    Roll die1
                    Roll die2
                    Compute the sum of the two rolls
                    Print the sum
                    if the sum is equal to **7 then**
                        The player is the loser
                    else
                        if the sum is equal to the point **then**
                            The player is the winner
                end loop
            if player won **then**
                Declare player the winner
            else
                Declare player the loser
end.

In order to simulate the toss of a die, we need to be able to select an integer between 1 and 6 at random. An algorithm that performs

APPLICATION

Simulation of a
Dice Game
(*continued*)

such a selection is called a **random number generator.** There are various techniques for generating sequences of random numbers. A commonly used approach is called the **linear congruential method.** In this approach, successive values in the sequence of random numbers are generated by the following relation:

$$X_{n+1} = (a * x_n + c) \textbf{ mod } m$$

The initial value x is known as the **seed,** the constant a is the **multiplier,** the constant c is the **increment,** and the constant m is the **modulus**. To see how this algorithm works, consider the following example. The values of the constants are $a = 2, c = 3, m = 10,$ and $x = 1$.

$$x_0 = 1$$
$$x_1 = (2 * 1 + 3) \textbf{ mod } 10 = 6$$
$$x_2 = (2 * 6 + 3) \textbf{ mod } 10 = 5$$
$$x_3 = (2 * 5 + 3) \textbf{ mod } 10 = 3$$
$$x_4 = (2 * 3 + 3) \textbf{ mod } 10 = 9$$
$$x_5 = (2 * 9 + 3) \textbf{ mod } 10 = 1$$
$$x_6 = (2 * 1 + 3) \textbf{ mod } 10 = 6$$

The above example illustrates how the sequence of random numbers generated in this fashion will eventually repeat, although judicious choices of the constants a, c, x_0, and m will allow for the generation of fairly long lists before the numbers start repeating themselves.

The numbers generated by this algorithm are, of course, not truly random, because we can always compute the value of x_{n+1} from the value of x_n. The numbers are, therefore, more correctly called **pseudorandom numbers.** We will use the following constants in our algorithm:

$$a = 13077$$
$$c = 6925$$
$$m = 32768$$

Given the above equation for generating sequences of pseudorandom numbers, it is easy to write a Pascal pseudorandom number generator. Our function computes a random number in the range from 0 to 1. It assumes the existence of a global variable, Seed, which is used to start the sequence. In an application of the function, the initial value of Seed will be supplied by the user.

APPLICATION

**Simulation of a
Dice Game**
(*continued*)

```
var
   Seed : 0..65535;

function Random :real;

{***********************************************
* Function to compute pseudo-random numbers.  *
* It returns a real number in the interval     *
* 0 to 1. It also alters the value of seed,    *
* a global variable.                           *
***********************************************}

const
   a = 13077;
   c = 6925;
   m = 32768;
begin
   {Compute the new value of Seed}

   Seed := (Seed*a+c) mod m;

   {Divide by the value of the modulus
    to set the random number in the range
    0 to 1}

   Random := Seed/32768.0
end;
```

The last line of the function guarantees that the value returned is in the range from 0 to 1. In order to simulate the toss of a die, we need to rescale the number returned by our random number generator so that it yields one of the integers 1, 2, 3, 4, 5, or 6. We can do this by multiplying and shifting the range of the random numbers as follows:

The function Random yields a number in the range:
   $0 < \text{Random} < 1$
Multiplying by 6, we have:
   $0 < 6 * \text{Random} < 6$
Adding 1, we have:
   $1 < 6 * \text{Random} + 1 < 7$
Finally, if we use the trunc function, we obtain the expression:
   trunc $(6 * \text{Random} + 1)$
whose possible values are the integers 1, 2, 3, 4, 5, 6. This is the result we are looking for.

APPLICATION

Simulation of a Dice Game (*continued*)

We can now write our simulation for the game of craps.

```pascal
program Craps (input,output);

{*****************************************
 * Program to simulate the game of craps *
 *****************************************}

var
   Die1, Die2, Total, Point : integer;
   Seed : 0..65535;
   Lost, Won : boolean;

function TossDie : integer;

   {*****************************************
    * Function to simulate tossing a        *
    * six-sided die. The function uses      *
    * a function "Random" which generates   *
    * a random number in the range          *
    * 0 < Random <1.                        *
    *****************************************}

   var
       Die : 1..6;

   function Random : real;

       {********************************
        * Function to generate a random *
        * number from the interval 0 to *
        * 1. The random numbers are      *
        * uniformly distributed in the   *
        * interval.                      *
        ********************************}

       const
           a = 13077;
           c = 6925;
           m = 32768;
       begin
           Seed := (Seed*a+c) mod m;
           Random := Seed/32768.0
       end { of Function Random};
```

APPLICATION

Simulation of a Dice Game
(*continued*)

```
begin { Function TossDie}
    TossDie := trunc( 6.0*Random+1)
end {of Function TossDie};

begin {of Main Program}

{Input initial value of seed to initialize
 the random number generator}

write (' Enter a positive integer :');
readln( Seed);

{Toss both dice}

Die1 := TossDie;
Die2 := TossDie;
Total := Die1 + Die2;
writeln (' Player rolled ',Die1:1,' + ',
         Die2:1,' = ',Total:1);

{Determine if Player won or lost on
 first toss or needs to toss again}

if (Total = 7) or (Total = 11) then
    writeln (' Player wins.')
else
    if (Total = 2) or (Total = 3) or (Total = 12) then
        writeln (' Player loses.')
    else
        begin
            {Player must toss again}

            Point := Total;
            Lost := false;
            Won := false;

            {Continue tossing until player wins or
             loses}
            repeat
                Die1 := TossDie;
                Die2 := TossDie;
                Total := Die1 + Die2;
                writeln (' Player rolled ',Die1:1,' + '
                         ,Die2:1,' = ',Total:1);
```

APPLICATION

Simulation of a Dice Game (*continued*)

```
                         if Total = 7 then
                             Lost := true
                         else
                             if Total = Point then
                                 Won := true
                  until Won or Lost;

                  {Check if player won or lost and
                   print appropriate message}

                  if Won then
                      writeln (' Player wins.')
                  else
                      writeln (' Player loses.')
            end
      end {Main Program}.
```

Two sample executions of the program follow:

```
Enter a positive integer : 78
Player rolled 3 + 1 = 4
Player rolled 6 + 3 = 9
Player rolled 1 + 2 = 3
Player rolled 4 + 5 = 9
Player rolled 6 + 6 = 12
Player rolled 5 + 5 = 10
Player rolled 4 + 5 = 9
Player rolled 6 + 1 = 7
Player loses.

Enter a positive integer : 12345
Player rolled 5 + 4 = 9
Player rolled 2 + 2 = 4
Player rolled 5 + 5 = 10
Player rolled 3 + 1 = 4
Player rolled 2 + 6 = 8
Player rolled 3 + 6 = 9
Player wins.
```

APPLICATION

Computation of the Median of a Set of Scores

Assume that we have two sets of examination scores for the same class. In order to assign grades, we would like to obtain some statistics on each test. Specifically, we would like the median on each test and on the composite scores of both tests.

The data in the input file appear as:

```
78   86
89   85
97   91
 .    .
 .    .
 .    .
```

The first data item on each line is the grade on the first examination for a given student. The second item is the grade on the second examination for the same student. There are less than 50 students.

We first develop the algorithm for the main program assuming that we have the following procedures:

1. Procedure to sort an array.
2. Procedure to compute the median.
3. Procedure to print an array.

The main algorithm has the following general form:

begin
    Input the grades on both tests into two arrays.
    Using the sort procedure, sort a copy of the first array.
    Using the print procedure, print the sorted array.
    Using the median procedure, compute and print the median.
    Using the sort procedure, sort a copy of the second array.
    Using the print procedure, print the sorted array.
    Using the median procedure, compute and print the median.
    Compute the average on the two tests for each student.
    Using the sort procedure, sort the array containing the averages.
    Using the print procedure, print the sorted array.
    Using the median procedure, compute and print the median.
end.

We can diagram the relationship between the main program and the procedures as in Figure 7.6.

APPLICATION

Computation of the Median of a Set of Scores (*continued*)

Figure 7.6 Calling hierarchy

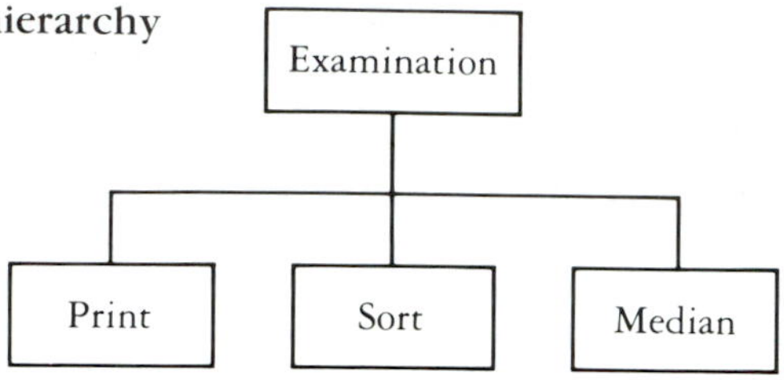

The diagram illustrates the calling hierarchy of the procedures in the main program. It shows that the main program, Examination, can call or invoke the procedures Print, Sort, and Median. At this stage in the development of the algorithm we are not concerned with the internal structure of the procedures. We assume that we will be able to write them later, and proceed now with the development of the algorithm for the main program. Coding our algorithm into Pascal we have:

```
program Examination (input, output);

{**********************************************
* Program to input grades on two tests       *
* for a group of students. Sort each         *
* test, compute the median and print it,      *
* compute the average on both tests,          *
* sort the averages and compute and print    *
* the median of the averages.                 *
**********************************************}

const
   ClassSize = 50;
type
   Class = array[1..ClassSize] of real;
var
   Test1, Test2 : Class;
   i, Largest, Start, Count, Middle : integer;
   Temp, Median : real;

begin
   {Input grades on both tests}

   i := 1;
   while (not eof) and (i <= ClassSize) do
```

APPLICATION

Computation of the Median of a Set of Scores
(*continued*)

```
begin
    readln ( Test1[i], Test2[i]);
    i := i + 1
end;
Count := i - 1;

{Copy test1 into temporary}

Temporary := Test1;

{Sort temporary array}

Sort(Temporary, Count);

{Print sorted array}

Print(Temporary, Count);

{Compute the median and print it}

Median(Temporary, Count, Med);
writeln ('Median for test 1: ',med :7:2);

{Copy test2 into temporary}

Temporary := Test2;

{Sort temporary array}

Sort(Temporary, count);

{Print sorted array}

print(Temporary, Count);

{Compute the median and print it}

Median(Temporary, Count, Med);
writeln ('Median for test 2: ',med :7:2);

{Compute the averages}

for i := 1 to count do
    Temporary[i] := (Test1[i] + Test2[i]) / 2;
```

APPLICATION

**Computation
of the Median
of a Set of
Scores**
(*continued*)

```
{sort the averages}

Sort(Temporary, Count);

{Print sorted array}

Print(Temporary, Count);

{Compute the median and print it}

Median(Temporary, Med);
writeln ('Median for averages of both tests: ',med :7:2)
end.
```

We can use the sorting algorithm of Example 7.7 to develop the procedure to sort an array. The sorting procedure itself makes use of two subprograms as illustrated by the calling hierarchy in Figure 7.7.

We now are ready to code the sort procedure together with the procedure swap and the function smallest.

```
procedure Sort (var x : Class; Size : integer);

{******************************
* Procedure to sort an array  *
* of integers in ascending    *
* order using the selection   *
* sort                        *
******************************}

var
  Start, Small : integer;

procedure Swap( var x,y : integer);
```

Figure 7.7 Calling
hierarchy for
procedure sort

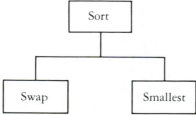

APPLICATION

Computation of the Median of a Set of Scores (*continued*)

```
{*******************************
* procedure to swap two values *
*******************************}

var
  Temp : integer;
begin {swap}
  Temp := x;
  x := y;
  y := Temp
end; {of swap}


function Smallest (var a :Class;
                     First, Size :integer) : integer;

{*****************************************
* Function to find the smallest value   *
* in an array containing "size" values  *
* starting at location "first"          *
*****************************************}

var
  i, LocSmall : integer;

begin { smallest}
  LocSmall := First;
  for i := First + 1 to Size do
      if a[i] < a[LocSmall] then
          LocSmall := i;
  Smallest := LocSmall
end; {of smallest}


begin {Sort procedure}

  Start := 1;
  while Start < Size do
      begin
          Small := Smallest(x, Start, Size);
          Swap(x[Start], x[Small]);
          Start := Start + 1
      end
end; {of Sort}
```

APPLICATION

**Computation
of the Median
of a Set of
Scores**
(*continued*)

The procedure to compute the median uses the sorted array to obtain the "middle" score. If the array has an even number of entries the two middle values are averaged.

```
procedure Median(var y : Class;
                     Number :integer;
                     var Med :real);

{*****************************
* Procedure to compute the  *
* median of  a set of scores *
*****************************}

var
  Middle : integer;

begin {Procedure median}
  Middle := (Number + 1) div 2;
  if odd(Number) then
      Med := y[Middle]
  else
      Med := (y[Middle] + y[Middle + 1]) / 2
end; {of Median}
```

Finally, we write the procedure to print the array.

```
procedure Print(var x :Class; Number :integer);

{******************************
* Procedure to print an array *
******************************}

var
  i : integer;

begin {procedure print}
  for i := 1 to Number do
      write ( x[i] :6:2);
  writeln
end; {of print}
```

We can now put everything together, which gives us the following program.

APPLICATION

**Computation
of the Median
of a Set of
Scores**
(*continued*)

```pascal
program Examination (input, output);

{*********************************************
* Program to input grades on two tests      *
* for a group of students, sort each        *
* test, compute the median and print it,    *
* compute the average on both tests,        *
* sort the averages and compute and print   *
* the median of the averages.               *
*********************************************}

const
  ClassSize = 50;
type
  Class = array[1..ClassSize] of real;
var
  Test1, Test2 : Class;
  i, Largest, Start, Count, Middle : integer;
  Temp, Median : real;

procedure Sort (var x : Class; Size : integer);

{*****************************
* Procedure to sort an array *
* of integers in ascending   *
* order using the selection  *
* sort                       *
*****************************}

var
  Start, Small : integer;

procedure Swap( var x,y : integer);

{*****************************
* procedure to swap two values *
*****************************}

var
  Temp : integer;
begin {Swap}
  Temp := x;
  x := y;
  y := Temp
end; {of swap}
```

APPLICATION

**Computation
of the Median
of a Set of
Scores**
(*continued*)

```
function Smallest (var a :Class;
                      First, Size :integer) : integer;

{****************************************
 * Function to find the smallest value  *
 * in an array containing "size" values *
 * starting at location "first"         *
 ****************************************}

var
  i, LocSmall : integer;

begin { smallest}
  LocSmall := First;
  for i := First + 1 to Size do
      if a[i] < a[LocSmall] then
          LocSmall := i;
  Smallest := LocSmall
end; {of Smallest}



begin {Sort procedure}

  Start := 1;
  while Start < Size do
      begin
          Small := Smallest(x, Start, Size);
          Swap(x[Start], x[Small]);
          Start := Start + 1
      end
end; {of Sort}

procedure Median(var y :Class;
                    Number :integer;
                    var Med :real);

{***************************
 * Procedure to compute the  *
 * median of a set of scores *
 ***************************}

var
  Middle : integer;
```

APPLICATION

Computation of the Median of a Set of Scores
(*continued*)

```pascal
begin {Procedure Median}
  Middle := (Number + 1) div 2;
  if odd(Number) then
      Med := y[Middle]
  else
      Med := (y[Middle] + y[Middle + 1]) / 2
end; {of median}

procedure Print(var x :Class; Number :integer);

{*******************************
* Procedure to print an array *
*******************************}

var
  i : integer;

begin {procedure Print}
  for i := 1 to Number do
      write ( x[i] :6:2);
  writeln
end; {of Print}

begin
  {Input grades on both tests}

  i := 1;

  while (not eof) and (i <= ClassSize) do
      begin
          readln ( Test1[i], Test2[i]);
          i := i + 1
      end;
  Count := i - 1;

  {Copy test1 into temporary}

  Temporary := Test1;

  {Sort temporary array}

  Sort(Temporary, Count);

  {Print sorted array}
```

APPLICATION

**Computation
of the Median
of a Set of
Scores**
(*continued*)

```
Print(Temporary, Count);

{Compute the median and print it}

Median(Temporary, Count, Med);
writeln ('Median for test 1: ',Med :7:2);

{Copy test2 into temporary}

Temporary := Test2;

{Sort temporary array}

Sort(Temporary, Count);

{Print sorted array}

Print(Temporary, Count);

{Compute the median and print it}

Median(Temporary, Count, Med);
writeln ('Median for test 2: ',Med :7:2);

{Compute the averages}

for i := 1 to Count do
    Temporary[i] := (Test1[i] + Test2[i]) / 2;

{sort the averages}

Sort(Temporary, Count);

{Print sorted array}

Print(Temporary, Count);

{Compute the median and print it}

Median(Temporary, Count, Med);
writeln ('Median for averages of both tests: ',Med :7:2)
end.
```

APPLICATION

Computation of the Median of a Set of Scores (*continued*)

Given the input

```
87   79
65   87
98   95
91   100
76   65
95   95
75   69
67   56
```

the program produces the desired result.

```
65.00  67.00  75.00  76.00  87.00  91.00  95.00  98.00
Median for test 1:    81.50
56.00  65.00  69.00  79.00  87.00  95.00  95.00 100.00
Median for test 2:    83.00
59.50  70.50  76.00  77.00  83.00  95.00  95.50  96.50
Median for averages of both tests:   79.50
```

7.5 COMMON ERRORS

When defining procedures and functions, make sure that you place these definitions in the correct location: between the variable declarations and the start of the statement section. Also remember that a given procedure or function may not reference a variable unless the variable has been declared in that procedure or function.

When calling procedures or functions, a common error is not to match properly the actual and formal parameters. Make sure that the parameter lists not only have the same number of variables, but also have these variables sequenced in the same way.

Another common error involving procedures is to fail to declare a reference parameter when a value needs to be returned. Remember that a procedure can return values only through a pass-by-reference parameter. Failure to declare a parameter as pass-by-reference may result in your procedure performing its function correctly, but failing to pass its results back to the calling program. On the other hand, if you use pass-by-reference parameters when you do not need to, you may alter values of variables that should not be changed, and cause an undesirable side effect that may be very difficult to isolate. Be wary. Declare all variables needed by a procedure or function within that procedure or function. Also remember that expressions and constants can only correspond to pass-by-value formal parameters. Variables can correspond to both pass-by-value and pass-by-reference formal parameters.

When writing procedures and functions, remember that the value or values that the procedure or function returns must be assigned to the appropriate variable. In a function, make sure that the function is assigned its value. In a procedure, make sure that the variable or variables that are used to return the values are assigned these values in the procedure.

Recursion presents its own problems. One common problem is to create recursive calls when they are not desired. Such calls are often created by using the procedure or function name on the right side of an assignment statement. For example, in the following, the function calls itself recursively without end:

```
function PosCount: integer;
var
    Number : integer;
begin
    read(Number);
    while not eof do
        begin
            if Number > 0 then
                PosCount := Poscount + 1;
            read(Number)
        end {of WHILE loop}
end {of FUNCTION PosCount};
```

Infinite recursion errors can also occur because of an incorrectly designed recursive algorithm. When writing a recursive function or procedure, make sure that you have included the appropriate conditions that will allow for the termination of recursive calls; that is, conditions that do not generate new recursive calls. Also, if the function name is used on the right side of an assignment statement, it often will result in a confusing error condition. For example, the following function:

```
function Power (x:real; n:integer): real;
begin
    if n = 0 then
        Power := x
    else
        begin
            Power := Power(x,n-1);
            writeln( Power)
```

```
      end
end {of FUNCTION Power};
```

will result in a compilation-time error. The writeln statement, which was inserted for debugging purposes, will cause an error because the reference to Power will be interpreted as a recursive call. Because Power in the output list fails to have the correct number of parameters, the error is a syntax error, and the program will fail to compile. Finally, be careful not to create a situation in which you have unplanned, indirect recursion. This will occur if function or procedure *a* calls function or procedure *b*, which in turn calls function or procedure *a*.

7.6 CHAPTER REVIEW

Procedures and functions are used to implement programs in a modular fashion. They are also useful in writing programs where certain actions need to be repeated in more than one place. These actions can be specified once, as a procedure or function, and then repeated as many times as desired by invoking the procedure or function at different points in the program.

Functions are used when we need to compute a single value. They are created in a Pascal program by using function definitions. The general form of a function definition is:

function identifier (formal parameter list): result-type;
Local variable declaration section
begin
   function body
end;

The identifier provides the function name. The formal parameters and their types are specified in the formal parameter list. The type of the result is specified by "result-type." The local variable declaration section of the function is used to declare variables used by the function. The function body describes the computations performed by the function. The body must have at least one statement that assigns a value to the function name. This value is returned as the function result.

The purpose of a function definition is to describe computations to be done on the data in the formal parameter list. The execution of the statements in the body of the function only occurs when the function is invoked in the program.

Functions are invoked by using their names with actual parameters in the appropriate places in the program. Remember that a function invocation is an expression that returns a single value. When the function is called, the returned value must be correctly utilized; that is, assigned to a variable of the appropriate type, or printed, or passed to another function, etc.

When a function is invoked, the actual parameters in the invocation must match the formal parameters in the definition in (1) number, (2) type, and (3) position.

Procedures provide us with subprograms capable of returning several values or no value at all.

The general form of a procedure definition is:

procedure identifier (formal parameter list);
Local variable declaration section
begin
    procedure body
end;

The first line of the procedure definition is the **procedure heading.** The identifier following the reserved word **procedure** names the procedure. The formal parameter list specifies the formal parameters and their types. Any identifiers declared in the procedure are local to the procedure. Finally, the procedure body describes the operations to be performed by the procedure. If the procedure has no parameters, then the formal parameter list and the parentheses are omitted from the procedure heading.

Procedure calls are always written as independent statements. Function calls are always written as part of an expression.

By using parameters, we can use different data with a procedure or function each time it is called. Procedures obtain and return values through their parameter lists. Communication through the parameter list reduces the possibility of undesirable side effects. There are two types of parameters in Pascal: pass-by-value and pass-by-reference parameters. Pass-by-value parameters are used only for passing values to the procedure or function. They transmit actual parameters to a procedure or function by assigning the value of the actual parameter to the formal parameter. Although the value of the formal parameter may be altered by the procedure or function, the actual parameter remains unchanged.

Pass-by-value parameters are declared as follows:

parameter1, parameter2, . . . , parametern: type;

Pass-by-reference parameters transmit values to and from a procedure by equating the identifiers of the actual and formal parameters so that they both refer to the same main-storage location. As the value of the formal parameter is altered, the actual parameter is changed correspondingly. To return values, a procedure must use pass-by-reference parameters. They provide two-way communication of data between the procedure and the calling program. Pass-by-reference parameters are declared as follows:

var parameter1, parameter2, . . . , parametern : type;

In Pascal all definitions and declarations apply only to the block containing the definitions and declarations. An identifier declared in a given block can be used anywhere in that block, unless it has been redeclared in an inner block. When a variable is declared more than once in different blocks, the resulting variables are distinct. Thus, a procedure may reference any identifier declared in the main program or in a procedure or function that contains the procedure or function doing the referencing. Identifiers declared in the main program are **global** to the whole program and may be referenced by any procedure or function in the main program. Identifiers declared in a procedure or function are local to that procedure or function and may be referenced only in that procedure or function, or in any wholly contained procedure or function. If an identifier is redeclared in a nested procedure or function, a reference to that identifier will always result in the manipulation of the *local*, rather than the *global*, variable.

In Pascal, an identifier can be referenced only if it has been declared earlier in the program. Therefore, a procedure cannot call another procedure that is declared below it in a program unless a **forward** declaration is used.

In Pascal, any procedure or function can call itself. This is called **recursion.** Recursion is useful when we are dealing with problems that can be reduced to a problem that is the same as the original one but contains fewer elements. Recursion can successfully be applied to problems with the following characteristics:

1. The solution is easy to specify for a few special cases, called the *stopping states.*
2. There are well-defined steps for eventually reaching a stopping state for any given situation in the problem.

7.7
EXERCISES

7.1. Fill in the blank in each of the following:

(a) The reserved word _____ starts the function heading.

(b) The portion enclosed in parentheses is the _____ _____ _____ of the function heading.

(c) The parameter list of a function specifies the _____ input data to the function.

(d) Parameters used in the function definition are called _____ parameters.

(e) Function definitions in a program are placed _____ the variable declarations.

(f) A function is invoked by using an expression called the function _____.

(g) Parameters used in the function invocation are called _____ parameters.

(h) A function returns exactly _____ value(s).

(i) A function returns its value by assigning it to the _____ _____.

(j) The first line of a procedure definition is the _____ _____.

(k) How many values can a procedure return? _____.

(l) The formal parameters of a procedure may be of two types: _____ parameters and _____ parameters.

(m) _____ parameters are used to pass data into the procedure.

(n) Actual parameters that correspond to _____ formal parameters may be constants, variables, or expressions.

(o) To return values to its calling program, a procedure uses _____ parameters.

(p) Actual parameters that correspond to _____ formal parameters must be variables.

(q) When the value of a formal pass-by-reference parameter is altered in a procedure, the value of the corresponding actual parameter (is/is not) _____ changed.

(r) When the value of a formal pass-by-value parameter is altered in a procedure, the value of the corresponding actual parameter (is/is not) _____ changed.

(s) A procedure or function consists of a heading and a _____.

(t) Variables declared in a procedure or function are called _____ variables.

(u) Variables declared in the main program are called _____ variables.

(v) When an identifier is declared twice, once in the main program and once in a procedure or function, references to the identifier in the procedure or function will always refer to the _____ identifier.

(w) A direct assignment to a global variable from a procedure or function is called a _____ _____.

(x) Calling a procedure by another procedure before it is defined is permitted if there is a _____ declaration for the procedure being called.

(y) Functions and procedures may include _____ calls to themselves.

7.2. Answer each of the following true or false. If your answer is false, state why.

(a) In a function definition, the portion of the heading enclosed in parentheses is the actual parameter list.

(b) A function can return as many values as the programmer wishes.

(c) The function heading requires that we specify the type of the variable returned by the function.

(d) The parameter list specifies the input values to the function.

(e) When a function is invoked, the formal parameters and actual parameters need only agree in number.

(f) Only named data types are allowed in formal parameter lists.

(g) A local variable retains its value from one execution of a function to the next.

(h) When a procedure is invoked, the procedure name is used in an expression.

(i) Call-by-value parameters are used by procedures to return values to the calling program.

(j) A procedure must return at least one value.

(k) Although it is not usually done, the formal parameters of a function can be call-by-reference parameters.

(l) Call-by-value parameters are sometimes used to save time and storage when large structures are being passed to a procedure or function.

(m) Once an identifier has been declared anywhere in a program, it cannot be declared again.

(n) Global identifiers always take precedence over local ones.

(o) Progams can be written that do not use parameter lists to communicate between procedures and functions.

(p) Procedures and functions cannot call themselves because this would lead to infinite loops.

(q) A special declaration is required in order to have a recursive function or procedure.

7.3. Describe what each of the following statements does.

(a) **function** Tails (Coin :integer):boolean;

(b) **if** Tails(1) **then**
```
      Coin1 := Coin1 + 1
```

(c) **procedure** Clock (Hours :integer; Minutes: integer);

(d) Clock(12,5)

(e) **procedure** Follows (**var** a,b:integer); **forward**;

7.4. For each of the following, determine what the output of each program segment will be.

(a) **program** QuesA (input, output);
```
   var
      x,y,z : integer;
   function SubA (a,b :integer):integer;
      begin
```

```
        SubA := a+b
    end;
begin {Main}
    x:=1;
    y:=2;
    z:=SubA(x,y);
    writeln(z);
    writeln(SubA(z,y))
end. {of QuesA}
```

(b)
```
program QuesB (input, output);
var
    x,y,z : integer;
function SubB (a,b :integer):integer;
    begin
        SubB := a div b
    end;
begin {Main}
    x:=1;
    y:=2;
    if x<=y then
        z:=SubB(x,y)
    else
        if SubB(y,x)>0 then
            z:=SubB(y,x)
        else
            z:= SubB(x,x);
    writeln(z)
end. {of QuesB}
```

(c)
```
program QuesC (input, output);
var
    x,y,z : integer;
procedure SubC(a,b: integer; var c: integer);
    var
        x :integer;
    begin
        x:=a + 1;
        a:=a - 1;
        b:=5 * b;
        c:=a + b
    end;
begin {Main}
    x:=1;
    y:=2;
```

```
            z:=3;
            writeln(x,y,z);
            SubC(x,y,z);
            writeln(x,y,z)
         end.{of QuesC}

(d)   program QuesD (input, output);
      var
            x,y,z : integer;
      procedure SubD(var a:integer; b:integer;
                        var c:integer);
         var
            x :integer;
         begin
            x:=a + 1;
            a:=a - 1;
            b:=5 * b;
            c:=a + b
         end;
      begin {Main}
         x:=1;
         y:=2;
         z:=3;
         writeln(x,y,z);
         SubD(x,y,z);
         writeln(x,y,z);
         SubD(x,x,x);
         writeln(x,y,z)
      end.{of QuesD}
```

7.5. What is the difference between formal and actual parameters?

7.6. Write a procedure that is passed a variable Letter of type char and N of type integer and prints Letter N times on a line.

7.7. Write a function that will count the number of times a particular character appears in a character string.

7.8. Write a procedure to center a title. The procedure is passed a string 80 characters long. The title to be centered is located in the first n characters of the string. The procedure should return a line 130 characters long with the title centered as nearly as possible. That is, the number of blanks before and after the title should be equal within one.

7.9. In the game of Hangman, a player attempts to guess a secret word by guessing one letter at a time. Each time an incorrect guess is made, an additional part of a hanging man is drawn. When a predetermined number of wrong guesses is made, usually six, the drawing is complete and the player loses the game.

Write a procedure that is passed the number of wrong guesses and draws part of the hanging man. In other words, your procedure should draw six figures, each succeeding one incorporating the previous one. The final figure may look something like the following:

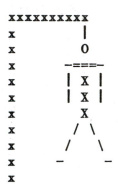

```
xxxxxxxxxx
x          |
x          0
x        -===-
x        | X |
x        | X |
x          X
x         / \
x        /   \
x       -     -
x
```

7.11. One of the oldest forms of secret codes is a translation code. The use of such a code is attributed to Julius Caesar. In a translation code, the letters are simply shifted a fixed number of places as shown below.

English A B C D E F G H I J K L M N O P Q R S T U V W X Y Z
Code   D E F G H I J K L M N O P Q R S T U V W X Y Z A B C

(a) Write a procedure that receives a line of English text and the size of the displacement and produces the corresponding coded message.
(b) Write a procedure to decode a message given the size of the displacement.
(c) Write a procedure to break such a code by trying different displacements.

7.12. A slightly more difficult code to break is a general substitution code. In a general substitution code the letters are scrambled in some random pattern as shown below:

English A B C D E F G H I J K L M N O P Q R S T U V W X Y Z
Code   J Y E T D P U F R I B N G H X A Z V Q W L O C S K M

(a) Write a procedure that receives a line of English text and the key to the code and produces an encoded messge.
(b) Write a procedure that decodes a message given the message and the key.
(c) To make such messages even more difficult to decode, letters are often regrouped so as to destroy any information about word length. Modify your encoding procedure so that it returns the encoded string with letters regrouped into "words" consisting of five letters each.

7.13. For tax purposes, business assets can be depreciated by using one of three different methods. The simplest approach is called *straight-line depreciation*. Using this method, the value decreases the same amount each year over the total period. Thus, if an item is depreciated over a five-year period, 1/5 of the total value is depreciated each year.

A second method uses *double-declining balance depreciation*. In this method, the depreciation allowed each year is the current value times $2/n$ where n is the number of years over which the item is to be depreciated.

A third method, known as *sum-of-the-digits* method, works as follows. First, the sum of the numbers from 1 to n is obtained, where n is the number of years over which the item is to be depreciated. Then, the depreciation allowed in the ith year is the original value times $(n - i) + 1$ divided by the sum of the digits.

Write three functions to compute the depreciation of an item using each of the above methods. Use them in a program that inputs the value of an item and the number of years over which it is to be depreciated and prints the amount of depreciation for each year.

7.14. Write a function that simulates the tossing of a coin. Your function should use the random number generator described in the text. Make your program toss a coin 100 times, and count the number of times each side appears. Print the result.

7.15. Computers increasingly are being used as instructional tools. Write a Pascal program that will assist an elementary school student in practicing addition. Your program should use the random number generator to provide two positive one-digit integers, and should print each question in the following format:

HOW MUCH IS x + y ?

where *x* and *y* are the two digits generated at random.

The student then types in an answer. Your program checks the answer for correctness and prints the appropriate message to tell the student if the answer is correct or not. If the answer is incorrect, the student is allowed to try one more time. If it is incorrect after the second attempt, the student is provided with the correct answer.

The program presents ten problems. At the end of a session it tells the student how well he or she did.

7.16. Modify the program of the previous problem to allow the student to select the operation (addition, subtraction, multiplication, or division) or a random combination of all the operations. Be careful that subtractions always result in positive answers and that divisions do not involve fractions.

7.17. Write a progam using recursion that will print out all the possible ways of making change from a dollar bill. This requires all combinations of halves, quarters, dimes, nickels, and pennies. Your output should look like:

Halves	Quarters	Dimes	Nickels	Pennies
2	0	0	0	0
1	2	0	0	0
1	1	2	1	0
1	1	2	0	5
1	1	1	3	0
1	1	1	2	5
.	.	.	.	.
.	.	.	.	.
.	.	.	.	.

Your progam will include a recursive procedure called Change, declared as follows:

procedure Change(Balance, Level : integer);

where balance is the remaining balance, and level is the denomination that is currently being worked on; that is, level 1 would correspond to halves and level 5 to pennies. The procedure Change will recursively make change amounting to the balance using only denominations at a level equal to, or higher than, the level with which it is called. Without the level parameter, it is difficult to write Change in such a way that it does not produce duplicate outputs. When you reach level 5, the balance is simply the number of pennies.

Be especially aware of the possibility that your program may recurse forever. You are strongly urged to include debugging writeln statements to prevent a runaway program.

8. Modular Design

In Chapter 3 we examined the algorithm design process in detail for simple programs. Since then, we have learned how to design progressively more complex algorithms. We will now see how a complex algorithm can be decomposed into smaller functional parts called **modules** and how we can use these modules to facilitate the design and testing of large programs.

A module is any part of a larger, more complex system that performs a well-defined specific task. When we think of any complex system—be it a piece of machinery or a program—we can understand it more readily if we see it as being composed of functionally distinct components. For example, we can think of an automobile as consisting of a body, power train (engine and transmission), cooling system, suspension system, and so on. Each of these components is a module.

When designing a car, we can design it in terms of these modules, and then design the modules themselves in terms of other modules. For example, the power train, as we have stated, consists of the engine and the transmission. The engine itself can be subdivided further into components.

In programming, this process of subdivision may continue until a given module can be expressed in terms of the simple instructions available in a given language. The modules form a **hierarchy** as shown in Figure 8.1.

The module at Level 1 represents the whole system (for example, the car). The modules at Level 2 are the major components of the system (the power train, the brake system, etc.). The modules at Level 3 are the building blocks from which Level 2 modules are constructed (the engine, the transmission, and so on).

When the system under consideration is a computer program, the Level 1 module represents the main program. Modules at Level 2 and below represent procedures and functions.

The hierarchical organization of a program lends itself well to **top-down design**. Using this method, we first design the module at Level 1; that is to say, the main program. We do this in terms of the mod-

Figure 8.1 Module
hierarchy

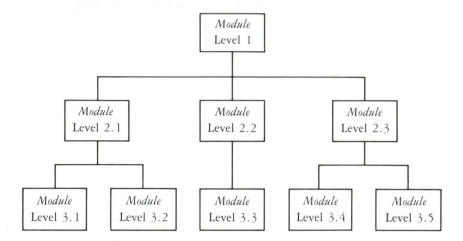

ules at Level 2; that is, we imagine that we have at our disposal the procedures and functions at Level 2, and we design the module at Level 1 using these yet-to-be-written building blocks. While we work on the algorithm for the main program, we do not worry about how the modules at Level 2 eventually will perform their functions. All we care about is what functions they will perform, and how they will interface with the main program.

Once the top-level module has been designed and tested (we will discuss testing later in the chapter), we begin work on the modules at Level 2. Here, again, we proceed one module at a time and design each module in terms of needed modules at Level 3. Again, we are not concerned by the details of any of the other modules, not even with other modules at the same level. In a large program different people probably would work on the other modules anyway.

Proceeding this way, we design the program in top-down fashion. At any point in the process we are concerned about the design of only one module in terms of its immediately subordinate modules. As an example of this top-down modular approach, let us consider a Pascal program to play the game of tic-tac-toe. The main program, called Tic, will form the Level 1 module. We can design this module as follows:

```
begin { TIC Module }
    repeat
        Print headings
        Initialize variables
        repeat
            if computer's turn then
```

```
            Make computermove
            Display board
                    else
            Obtain person's move
                    Change players
                    Increment move counter
            until (movecounter > 9) or (game is won)
            if there is no winner then
                    Declare a draw
            Inquire about playing again
            if answer is 'yes' then
                    Set repeat game flag to true
            else
                    Set repeat game flag to false
        until repeat game flag is false
end. {TIC Module}.
```

In designing this module we made some decisions about the way the game is to be played. For example, we allowed the human player to repeat the game as many times as desired without having to restart the program. The entire module consists of a loop that repeats the game until a repeat flag becomes false. The value of the flag is, of course, controlled by the player and is changed at the bottom of the loop.

The playing of the game itself is controlled by another loop, which plays the game either until someone wins or until nine moves are made. When a game ends, we check to see if we have a winner or if the game is a draw. After printing the appropriate message, we inquire if the game is to be played again.

This algorithm suggests that we could use the following Level 2 modules:

Initialize (Board,MoveCounter,Winner,First). This module sets the playing board to empty, the move counter to 1, and the boolean variable, "Winner," which tells us if we have a winner, to false. It also determines who moves first. These values are returned to the Level 1 module.

ComputerMove (Board,Winner). This module computes and makes the move for the computer. It records the move on the playing board. This module also determines if we have a winner and sets the boolean variable Winner to the appropriate value.

Display(Board). This module displays the playing board.

PersonMove(Board). This module obtains and validates a move from the person playing the game, enters the move on the playing board, and returns the updated board.

Using these modules, we can now diagram the hierarchy for our program as developed so far. This is pictured in Figure 8.2. The main program, module "Tic," also can now be coded, assuming that we have the Level 2 modules Initialize, ComputerMove, PersonMove, and Display (Example 8.1). For simplicity, we will assume that the standard input file is a terminal keyboard and that the standard output file is either a CRT or a terminal print element.

Figure 8.2 First two levels of program TicTacToe

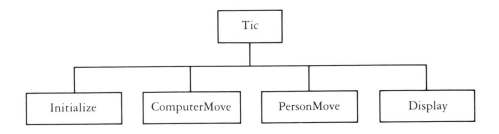

EXAMPLE 8.1 Top Level Module for Program TicTacToe

```pascal
program TicTacToe (input,output);

{*****************************************
* Program to play Tic-tac-toe.          *
* Top level module only.                *
*****************************************}

type
    BoardEntry = (empty, x, o);
    Board = array[1..9] of BoardEntry;
    Mover = (Person, Computer);
var
    i            : integer;
    PlayBoard    : Board;
    WeHaveWinner : boolean;
    MoveCounter  : integer;
    Player       : Mover;
    PlayAgain    : boolean;
    Answer       : packed array[1..3] of char;

begin { Module TIC }
    repeat
```

**EXAMPLE 8.1
Top Level
Module for
Program
TicTacToe**
(*continued*)

```
{ Print headings }

writeln;
writeln(' TIC - TAC - TOE ');
writeln;

{ Initialize variables }
        Initialize (PlayBoard, MoveCounter, WeHaveWinner,
                    Player);

        {Play game until someone wins or 9 moves are made}

        repeat
           if Player = Computer then
              begin
                 ComputerMove(PlayBoard,WeHaveWinner);
                 Display(PlayBoard)
              end
           else
              PersonMove(PlayBoard);

           { Change players and increment move counter }

           if Player = Computer then
              Player := Person
           else
              Player := Computer;
           MoveCounter := MoveCounter + 1
        until (MoveCounter > 9) or (WeHaveWinner);

        { Check for draw }

        if not WeHaveWinner then
           writeln (' It is a draw');

        { Inquire about playing again }

        writeln;
        write(' Do you want to play again (yes or no)? ');
        i := 1;
        while not eoln and (i <= 3) do
           begin
              read (Answer[i]);
              i := i + 1
           end;
        readln;
        writeln;
```

```
            if (Answer[1] = 'y') or (Answer[1] = 'Y') then
                PlayAgain := true
            else
                PlayAgain := false
        until not PlayAgain
end. { TICTACTOE }
```

Notice that at this point we have focused our attention on the flow of the game without any concern about how the computer will make moves, or how we will determine if we have a winner, or any of the other details of the game. Having written the Level 1 module, we should now test it. By far the best way to test a program, or any other system, is to test it at each step of its construction.

8.3
TOP-DOWN
TESTING

Our approach to testing is to start with the top-level module and test it first. Then we test Level 2 modules, and so on, until all the program modules are tested. Modules are tested in the same order they are designed and written. This is called **top-down testing**. In this approach, every module is tested in the same environment in which it will be used in the finished program. There is, however, a problem. How can we test the module at Level 1 when the modules at Level 2, which are called by the Level 1 module, have not yet been written? The answer is to replace the yet-to-be-written modules with stubs. A **program stub** or **stub** is a "dummy" module that takes the place of its actual counterpart while a module at a higher level is being tested. What a stub does depends on what function the module it is replacing performs. Consider the following example, where we have added some lower-level modules and stubs to the module Tic.

In Example 8.2 the module Initialize is completely written. The modules ComputerMove, PersonMove, and Display are stubs. The current structure of the program TicTacToe is shown in Figure 8.3.

Figure 8.3 First two levels of program TicTacToe with stubs

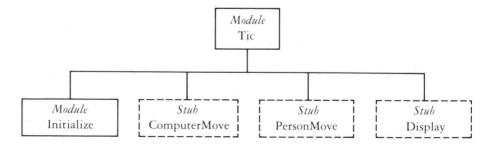

EXAMPLE 8.2
Top-Level
Module with
Stubs for
Lower-Level
Modules

```pascal
program TicTacToe (input,output);

{*****************************************
* Program to play Tic-tac-toe.          *
* Includes main program and stubs for   *
* all level 2 modules.                   *
*****************************************}

type
    BoardEntry = (empty, x, o);
    Board = array[1..9] of BoardEntry;
    Mover = (Person, Computer);
var
    i              : integer;
    PlayBoard      : Board;
    WeHaveWinner: boolean;
    MoveCounter    : integer;
    Player         : Mover;
    PlayAgain      : boolean;
    Answer         : packed array[1..3] of char;

procedure Initialize(var PBoard : Board;
                     var MoveCounter : integer;
                     var Winner : boolean;
                     var First : Mover);

    {*************************************
    * Module  INITIALIZE  to initialize *
    * variables for Tic-tac-toe game.   *
    *************************************}

    var
        i : integer;
        Answer : char;
    begin { INITIALIZE}
        for i := 1 to 9 do
            PBoard[i] := empty;
        Winner := false;
        MoveCounter := 1;

        { Determine who moves first }

        writeln(' Who moves first?');
        writeln(' 1 means you, 2 means the computer.');
        writeln;
```

EXAMPLE 8.2
Top-Level
Module with
Stubs for
Lower-Level
Modules
(*continued*)

```
      readln(Answer);
      while (Answer <> '1') and (Answer <> '2') do
         begin
            writeln(' 1 or 2 please');
            writeln(' Who moves first?');
            writeln(' 1 means you, 2 means the computer');
            writeln;
            readln(Answer)
         end;
      if Answer = '1' then
         First := Person
      else
         First := Computer
   end {of INITIALIZE};

   procedure ComputerMove(var PBoard : Board;
                              var Winner : boolean);

      {*************************************
       * Stub for module   COMPUTERMOVE    *
       *************************************}

      var
         CMove : integer;
         Ch    : char;

      begin {COMPUTERMOVE}

         write (' Enter computer''s move: ');
         readln (CMove);
         writeln;
         PBoard[CMove] := o;
         write (' Is there a winner ? ');
         readln (ch);
         writeln;
         if Ch ='y' then
            Winner := true
         else
            Winner := false
      end {of COMPUTERMOVE stub};

   procedure PersonMove(var PBoard : Board);

      {*****************************
       * Stub for module   PERSONMOVE  *
       *****************************}
```

**EXAMPLE 8.2
Top-Level
Module with
Stubs for
Lower-Level
Modules**
(*continued*)

```
var
    PMove : integer;

begin { PERSONMOVE }
    write (' Enter person''s move : ');
    readln(PMove);
    writeln;
    PBoard[PMove] := x
end { PERSONMOVE stub };

procedure Display(PBoard : Board);

{*****************************
* Stub for module  DISPLAY  *
*****************************}

begin { DISPLAY }
    writeln(ord(PBoard[1]):2,ord(PBoard[2]):2,
            ord(PBoard[3]):2);
    writeln(ord(PBoard[4]):2,ord(PBoard[5]):2,
            ord(PBoard[6]):2);
    writeln(ord(PBoard[7]):2,ord(PBoard[8]):2,
            ord(PBoard[9]):2);
end { of DISPLAY stub };

begin { MAIN program - Module TIC }
    repeat

        { Print headings }

        writeln;
        writeln(' TIC - TAC - TOE ');
        writeln;

        { Initialize variables and print headings}

        Initialize (PlayBoard, MoveCounter,
                    WeHaveWinner, Player);

        {Play game until someone wins or 9 moves are made}

        repeat
            if Player = Computer then
                begin
                    ComputerMove(PlayBoard,WeHaveWinner);
                    Display(PlayBoard)
                end
```

**EXAMPLE 8.2
Top-Level
Module with
Stubs for
Lower-Level
Modules**
(*continued*)

```
      else
        PersonMove(PlayBoard);

      { Change players and increment move counter }

      if Player = Computer then
        Player := Person

      else
        Player := Computer;
      MoveCounter := MoveCounter + 1
  until (MoveCounter > 9) or (WeHaveWinner);

  { Check for draw }

  if not WeHaveWinner then
              writeln (' It is a draw');

  { Inquire about playing again }

  writeln;
  write(' Do you want to play again (yes or no)? ');
  i := 1;
  while not eoln and (i <= 3) do
      begin
        read (Answer[i]);
        i := i + 1
      end;
  readln;
  writeln;
  if (Answer[1] = 'y') or (Answer[1] = 'Y') then
        PlayAgain := true

      else
        PlayAgain := false
  until not PlayAgain
end. { TICTACTOE }
```

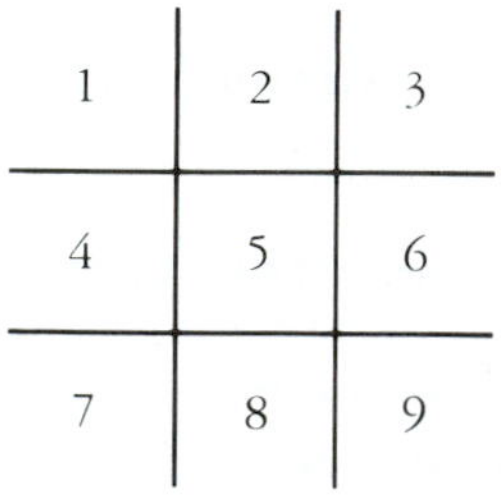

Figure 8.4 Position numbers for tic-tac-toe board

1	2	3
4	5	6
7	8	9

**EXAMPLE 8.2
Top-Level
Module with
Stubs for
Lower-Level
Modules**
(*continued*)

We can now test the top-level module. Below is a sample run. For this, and subsequent runs the positions on the tic-tac-toe board are numbered as shown in Figure 8.4.

```
TIC - TAC - TOE

Who moves first?
1 means you, 2 means the computer.

1
  Enter person's move : 1

  Enter computer's move: 5

  Is there a winner ? no

  1 0 0
  0 2 0
  0 0 0

  Enter person's move : 9

  Enter computer's move: 3

  Is there a winner ? no

  1 0 2
  0 2 0
  0 0 1

  Enter person's move : 7

  Enter computer's move: 4

  Is there a winner ? no

  1 0 2
  2 2 0
  1 0 1

  Enter person's move : 8

  Enter computer's move: 2
```

**EXAMPLE 8.2
Top-Level
Module with
Stubs for
Lower-Level
Modules**
(*continued*)

```
Is there a winner ? yes

1 2 2
2 2 0
1 1 1

Do you want to play again (yes or no)? yes


TIC - TAC - TOE

Who moves first?
1 means you, 2 means the computer.

2

    Enter computer's move: 5

    Is there a winner ? no

    0 0 0
    0 2 0
    0 0 0

    Enter person's move : 1

    Enter computer's move: 3

    Is there a winner ? no

    1 0 2
    0 2 0
    0 0 0

    Enter person's move : 7

    Enter computer's move: 4

    Is there a winner ? no

    1 0 2
    2 2 0
    1 0 0

    Enter person's move : 6
```

EXAMPLE 8.2
Top-Level
Module with
Stubs for
Lower-Level
Modules
(*continued*)

```
Enter computer's move: 8

Is there a winner ? no

1 0 2
2 2 1
1 2 0

Enter person's move : 2

Enter computer's move: 9

Is there a winner ? no

1 1 2
2 2 1
1 2 2

It is a draw
Do you want to play again (yes or no)? no
```

To conserve space, we tested the Level 1 module by playing the game only twice. This exercises the program's repeat option and tests to see if a draw and a win are handled correctly. Of course, other combinations of options also should be tested. For example, we should test to see if the program runs correctly when the person makes the first move and the game is a draw. We only tested a draw with the computer moving first.

Ideally, we should use enough test cases to cause the module being tested to follow every possible path through its algorithm. Except for extremely simple modules, however, this is not practical. If a module contains as few as ten **if . . . then . . . else** structures, there are over 1000 different paths through its algorithm! Repetition complicates matters even further. Testing goals, therefore, are usually somewhat more modest. We simply include enough test cases to cause every decision path to be taken. This insures that all the code is exercised at least once, even if this is not done under all possible combinations of conditions.

Let us now consider the stubs in greater detail. The Display stub prints the board, certainly not in the form we will eventually want to see it, but with enough detail to allow us to keep track of the moves being made. The PersonMove stub requests a move from the human player and enters the move into the playing board. This module is almost in its final form. We will have to add code to validate the move because, at the moment, nothing prevents the player from making a move into an already-occupied board position or into a position not on the board at all.

The ComputerMove stub will need the most work. At the moment, it obtains the values it needs from the keyboard. When fully written, it will have to generate these values internally. That is, the algorithm will have to select the computer's move and determine if the game is won.

8.4 LOWER-LEVEL MODULE DESIGN AND TESTING

Once the top-level module has been tested, we proceed to the lower-level modules. It is now time to design and code the ComputerMove module. First, we have to decide how the computer will make its moves. There are many algorithms for selecting moves in tic-tac-toe. The approach we use here resembles the way a person decides what move to make. As a result, the program will play the game "intelligently," although it will not be unbeatable. To play intelligently the program uses a point system to determine which square on the board constitutes a good move.

The points are computed using the following algorithm:

1. We note that there are eight playing rows on the board: three horizontal rows, three vertical rows, and two diagonals.
2. If a row contains both an X and an O, it is said to be blocked.
3. Based on the contents of each row, point values are assigned according to the following table. The values are chosen to reflect the importance of making a move into a row based on the current contents of that row.

Contents of Row	Points
Blocked	0
Empty	1
1 X	9
1 O	10
2 Xs	100
2 Os	1000

4. To assign a value to a position, we add up the values of all the rows containing that position.

For example, if the game board is:

```
X  |   |
---+---+---
   | X |
---+---+---
O  | O |
```

the rows and their values are:

Row	Value	Reason
123	9	1 X
456	9	1 X
789	1000	2 Os
147	0	Blocked
258	0	Blocked
369	1	Empty
159	100	2 Xs
357	0	Blocked

A row is described in terms of the board positions that make it up. For example, row 123 is made up of positions 1, 2, and 3. This is the top row of the board.

Given the above board, the corresponding position values are:

Position	Value	Row Points
1	109	9 + 0 + 100
2	9	9 + 0
3	10	9 + 1 + 0
4	9	9 + 0
5	109	9 + 0 + 100 + 0
6	10	9 + 1
7	1000	1000 + 0 + 0
8	1000	1000 + 0
9	1101	1000 + 1 + 100

As you can see, position 9 has the greatest value. Thus, the computer will play position 9 and win.

From the description of the algorithm for the computer's move, we can now design the ComputerMove module:

```
begin{ COMPUTERMOVE Module }
    Set board values to zero
    Set PersonWin flag to false
    Evaluate all eight playing rows
if PersonWin flag is true then
    Declare person the winner
    Set the winner flag to true
else
    Find unoccupied location with maximum board value
    Make move
    if computer won then
        Declare the computer the winner
        Set the winner flag to true
end {of COMPUTERMOVE Module}
```

In order to implement this algorithm, we will need a procedure to evaluate each row based on the contents of that row. The procedure "RowValues" will require the following heading:

```
procedure RowValues (Pos1,Pos2,Pos3 : integer;
                     PlayBoard : Board;
                     var Values : PositionValues;
                     var WinFlag : boolean) ;
```

This procedure is passed the three positions that constitute a playing row, the playing board, and the values associated with all the positions. It examines the contents of the playing row and computes the corresponding row value. If the person won, the procedure sets "WinFlag" to true; otherwise, it updates the value of the positions constituting the row.

We are now ready to code the ComputerMove procedure and to use a stub for RowValues.

EXAMPLE 8.3 Module to Select Computer's Moves

```
procedure ComputerMove(var PBoard : Board;
                       var Winner : boolean);

    {****************************************
     * Module  COMPUTERMOVE.  This          *
     * procedure examines the rows of the   *
     * Tic-tac-toe board and selects a      *
     * move for the computer.               *
     ****************************************}
```

EXAMPLE 8.3 Module to Select Computer's Moves (*continued*)

```pascal
type
    PositionValues = array[1..9] of integer;

var
    BoardValues        : PositionValues;
    i, Start, Maximum : integer;
    PersonWin          : boolean;


procedure RowValues(Pos1,Pos2,Pos3 : integer;
                    PlayBoard : Board;
                    var Values : PositionValues;
                    var WinFlag : boolean);


{*******************************
 * Stub for  ROWVALUES  Module. *
 *******************************}


var
    ch        : char;
    RowValue  : integer;

begin {ROWVALUES}

    writeln (' Did person win?');
    readln (ch)
    if ch = 'y' then
        WinFlag := true
    else
        begin
            {Person did not win. Obtain row value}

            writeln (' Enter value for row:',
                    Pos1:3, Pos2:3, Pos3:3);
            readln (RowValue);

            {Adjust the value of each postion on the row}

            Values[Pos1] := Values[Pos1] + RowValue;
            Values[Pos2] := Values[Pos2] + RowValue;
            Values[Pos3] := Values[Pos3] + RowValue
        end
end {of ROWVALUES stub};
```

EXAMPLE 8.3
Module to
Select Com-
puter's Moves
(*continued*)

```
begin { COMPUTERMOVE Procedure }

   {Set board values to zero}

   for i := 1 to 9 do
      BoardValues[i] := 0;

   {Set PersonWin flag to false}

   PersonWin := false;

   {Evaluate all eight playing rows}

   RowValues(1,2,3,PBoard,BoardValues,PersonWin);
   RowValues(4,5,6,PBoard,BoardValues,PersonWin);
   RowValues(7,8,9,PBoard,BoardValues,PersonWin);
   RowValues(1,4,7,PBoard,BoardValues,PersonWin);
   RowValues(2,5,8,PBoard,BoardValues,PersonWin);
   RowValues(3,6,9,PBoard,BoardValues,PersonWin);
   RowValues(1,5,9,PBoard,BoardValues,PersonWin);
   RowValues(3,5,7,PBoard,BoardValues,PersonWin);

   {Check for win by person}

   if PersonWin then
      begin
         writeln (' You win ');
         Winner := true
      end
   else
      begin

         {Find unoccupied location with maximum
          board value}

         Start := 1;
         while PBoard[Start] <> empty do
           Start := Start + 1;
         Maximum := Start;
         for i := Start+1 to 9 do
           if (BoardValues[i]>BoardValues[Maximum]) and
               (PBoard[i]=empty) then
              Maximum := i;

         {Make move}
```

EXAMPLE 8.3 Module to Select Computer's Moves (*continued*)

```
        writeln (' My move is ',Maximum:2);
        PBoard[Maximum] := o;

        {Check if computer won}

        if BoardValues[Maximum] >= 1000 then
          begin

            writeln;
            writeln(' I win!!!');
            Winner := true
          end
      end
end {of COMPUTERMOVE Procedure};
```

We replace the ComputerMove stub in the main program with this code, and then the entire program is tested. The hierarchical diagram for the code developed so far is shown in Figure 8.5. Below is a partial test run of the program in its present stage of development.

Figure 8.5 Hierarchical diagram for program TicTacToe with Computer Move module

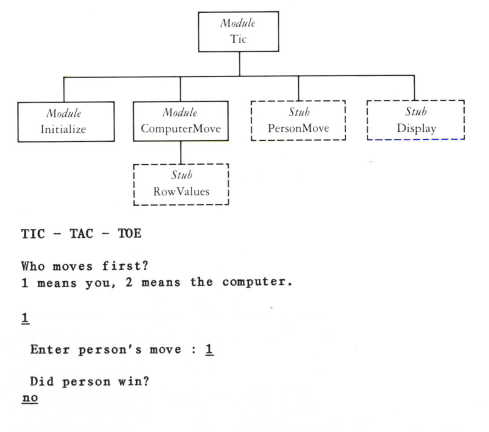

```
TIC - TAC - TOE

Who moves first?
1 means you, 2 means the computer.

1

  Enter person's move : 1

  Did person win?
no
```

**EXAMPLE 8.3
Module to
Select Com-
puter's Moves**
(*continued*)

```
 Enter value for row: 1   2   3
9
 Did person win?
no
 Enter value for row: 4   5   6
1
 Did person win?
no
 Enter value for row: 7   8   9
1
 Did person win?
no
 Enter value for row: 1   4   7
9
 Did person win?
no
 Enter value for row: 2   5   8
1
 Did person win?
no
 Enter value for row: 3   6   9
1
 Did person win?
no
 Enter value for row: 1   5   9
9
 Did person win?
no
 Enter value for row: 3   5   7
1
 My move is 5

 1 0 0
 0 2 0
 0 0 0
 Enter person's move : 9
              .
              .
              .
```

The development and testing process is continued until the entire program is developed, coded, and tested. At each step we focus our attention on a single module. The existing modules provide us with a natural testing harness for the newly developed module. The completed program is shown in Example 8.4.

EXAMPLE 8.4
Completed
Program
TicTacToe

```pascal
program TicTacToe(input,output);

{*******************************
 * Program to play Tic-Tac-Toe. *
 *******************************}

type
    BoardEntry = (empty, x, o);
    Board = array[1..9] of BoardEntry ;
    Mover = (Person, Computer);
var
    i             : integer;
    PlayBoard     : Board;
    WeHaveWinner  : boolean;
    MoveCounter   : integer;
    Player        : Mover;
    PlayAgain     : boolean;
    Answer        : packed array[1..3] of char;

procedure Initialize(var PBoard : Board;
                     var MoveCounter : integer;
                     var Winner : boolean;
                     var First : Mover);


    {*************************************
     * Module  INITIALIZE  to initialize *
     * variables for Tic-tac-toe game.   *
     *************************************}


    var
        i : integer;
        Answer : char;

    begin { INITIALIZE Procedure}
        for i := 1 to 9 do
            PBoard[i] := empty;
        Winner := false;
        MoveCounter := 1;

        { Determine who moves first }

        writeln(' Who moves first?');
        writeln(' 1 means you, 2 means the computer.');
        writeln;
        readln(Answer);
```

EXAMPLE 8.4
Completed
Program
TicTacToe
(*continued*)

```
    while (Answer <> '1') and (Answer <> '2') do
      begin
        writeln(' 1 or 2 please');
        writeln(' Who moves first?');
        writeln(' 1 means you, 2 means the computer');
        writeln;
        readln(Answer);
      end;
    if Answer = '1' then
      First := Person
    else
      First := Computer
  end {of INITIALIZE Procedure};

procedure ComputerMove(var PBoard : Board;
                       var Winner : boolean);

  {************************************
   * Module  COMPUTERMOVE.  This       *
   * procedure examines the rows of the *
   * Tic-tac-toe board and selects a   *
   * move for the computer.            *
   ************************************}

type
  PositionValues = array[1..9] of integer;

var
  BoardValues        : PositionValues;
  i, Start, Maximum : integer;
  PersonWin          : boolean;

procedure RowValues(Pos1,Pos2,Pos3 : integer;
                    PlayBoard : Board;
                    var Values : PositionValues;
                    var WinFlag : boolean);

  {*********************************************
   * Module ROWVALUES evaluates a playing row  *
   * given the playing board and the positions *
   * constituting the row. It returns the value *
   * of each position and a flag indicating if  *
   * the contents of the row being evaluated    *
   * result in a won game.                      *
   *********************************************}
```

**EXAMPLE 8.4
Completed
Program
TicTacToe**
(*continued*)

```
var
    NumberOfx, NumberOfo : integer;
    RowValue              : integer;

begin {ROWVALUES Procedure }

    { count the Xs and Os in the playing row}

    NumberOfx := 0;
    NumberOfo := 0;
    case PlayBoard[Pos1] of
        empty : ;
        x       : NumberOfx := NumberOfx + 1;
        o       : NumberOfo := NumberOfo + 1;
    end;
    case PlayBoard[Pos2] of
        empty : ;
        x       : NumberOfx := NumberOfx + 1;
        o       : NumberOfo := NumberOfo + 1;
    end;
    case PlayBoard[pos3] of
        empty : ;
        x       : NumberOfx := NumberOfx + 1;
        o       : NumberOfo := NumberOfo + 1;
    end;

    { Check to see if person won }

    if NumberOfx = 3 then
        WinFlag := true
    else
        begin
            {Person did not win. Obtain row value}

            RowValue := 0;
            if (NumberOfo = 2) and (NumberOfx = 0) then
                RowValue := 1000;
            if (NumberOfx = 2) and (NumberOfo = 0) then
                RowValue := 100;
            if (NumberOfo = 1) and (NumberOfx = 0) then
                RowValue := 10;
            if (NumberOfx = 1) and (NumberOfo = 0) then
                RowValue := 9;
            if (NumberOfx = 0) and (NumberOfo = 0) then
                RowValue := 1;
```

EXAMPLE 8.4
Completed
Program
TicTacToe
(*continued*)

```
                         {Adjust the value of each position on the row}

                         Values[Pos1] := Values[Pos1] + RowValue;
                         Values[Pos2] := Values[Pos2] + RowValue;
                         Values[Pos3] := Values[Pos3] + RowValue
                      end
               end {of ROWVALUES Procedure};

         begin { COMPUTERMOVE Procedure }

            {Set board values to zero}

            for i := 1 to 9 do
               BoardValues[i] := 0;

            {Set PersonWin flag to false}

            PersonWin := false;

            {Evaluate all eight playing rows}

            RowValues(1,2,3,PBoard,BoardValues,PersonWin);
            RowValues(4,5,6,PBoard,BoardValues,PersonWin);
            RowValues(7,8,9,PBoard,BoardValues,PersonWin);
            RowValues(1,4,7,PBoard,BoardValues,PersonWin);
            RowValues(2,5,8,PBoard,BoardValues,PersonWin);
            RowValues(3,6,9,PBoard,BoardValues,PersonWin);
            RowValues(1,5,9,PBoard,BoardValues,PersonWin);
            RowValues(3,5,7,PBoard,BoardValues,PersonWin);

            {Check for win by person}

            if PersonWin then
               begin
                  writeln (' You win ');
                  Winner := true
               end
            else
               begin

                  {Find unoccupied location with maximum
                   board value}

                  Start := 1;
                  while PBoard[Start] <> empty do
                     Start := Start + 1;
```

**EXAMPLE 8.4
Completed
Program
TicTacToe**
(*continued*)

```
Maximum := Start;
for i := Start+1 to 9 do
  if (BoardValues[i]>BoardValues[Maximum]) and
        (PBoard[i]=empty) then
     Maximum := i;

{Make move}

writeln (' My move is ',Maximum:2);
PBoard[Maximum] := o;

{Check if computer won}

if BoardValues[Maximum] >= 1000 then
      begin
         writeln;
         writeln(' I win!!!');
         Winner := true
      end
   end
end {of COMPUTERMOVE Procedure};

procedure PersonMove(var PBoard : Board);

   {******************************
   * Module PERSONMOVE   accepts *
   * and validates move by person *
   ******************************}

var
   PMove     : integer;
   Move      : char;
   ValidMove : boolean;

begin { PERSONMOVE Procedure}
   ValidMove := false;
   while not ValidMove do
      begin
         writeln;
         write (' Enter your move : ');
         readln(Move);
         writeln;
         readln(Move);

         {Convert move to integer}
```

EXAMPLE 8.4
Completed
Program
TicTacToe
(*continued*)

```
                        PMove := ord(Move)-ord('0');
                        if (PMove > 0) and (PMove < 10) then
                          if PBoard[PMove] = empty then
                              begin
                                 ValidMove := true;
                                 PBoard[PMove] := x
                              end
                          else
                              writeln (' Position ',Move,' occupied')
                        else
                          writeln(' The positions are numbered 1-9.')
                          writeln(' Try again')
                    end
end { PERSONMOVE Procedure };

procedure Display(PBoard : Board);

    {***************************
    * Module  DISPLAY  displays *
    * Tic-tac-toe board.        *
    ***************************}


    function Symbol(Entry : BoardEntry):char;

        {*************************
        * Function to generate a *
        * printable symbol to    *
        * display moves on       *
        * Tic-tac-toe board.     *
        *************************}

    begin {SYMBOL Function}

        case Entry of
           x : Symbol := 'X';
           o : Symbol := '0';
        empty : Symbol := ' '
           end {of CASE}
    end {of Symbol Function};


begin { DISPLAY Procedure}
    writeln;
    writeln (' ',Symbol(PBoard[1]),' | ',Symbol(PBoard[2])
             ,' | ',Symbol(Pboard[3]));
```

EXAMPLE 8.4
Completed
Program
TicTacToe
(*continued*)

```
      writeln ('---|---|---');
      writeln (' ',Symbol(PBoard[4]),' | ',Symbol(PBoard[5])
              ,' | ',Symbol(Pboard[6]));
      writeln ('---|---|---');
      writeln (' ',Symbol(PBoard[7]),' | ',Symbol(PBoard[8])
              ,' | ',Symbol(Pboard[9]));
end { of DISPLAY Procedure};

begin { MAIN program - Module TIC }
   repeat

      { Print headings }

      writeln;
      writeln(' TIC - TAC - TOE ');
      writeln;

      { Initialize variables }

      Initialize (PlayBoard, MoveCounter, WeHaveWinner,
                  Player);

      {Play game until someone wins or 9 moves are made}

      repeat
         if Player = Computer then
           begin
              CompMove(PlayBoard,WeHaveWinner);
              Display(PlayBoard)
           end
         else
           PersonMove(PlayBoard);

         { Change players and increment move counter }

         if Player = Computer then
           Player := Person
         else
           Player := Computer;
         MoveCounter := MoveCounter + 1
      until (MoveCounter > 9) or (WeHaveWinner);

      { Check for draw }

      if not WeHaveWinner then
         writeln (' It is a draw');
```

EXAMPLE 8.4
Completed
Program
TicTacToe
(*continued*)

```
        { Inquire about playing again }

    writeln;
    write(' Do you want to play again (yes or no)? ');
    i := 1;
    while not eoln and (i <= 3) do
        begin
           read (Answer[i]);
           i := i + 1
        end;
    readln;
    writeln;
    if (Answer[1] = 'y') or (Answer[1] = 'Y') then
        PlayAgain := true
    else
        PlayAgain := false
    until not PlayAgain
end. { TICTACTOE }
```

Figure 8.6 Hierarchical diagram for program TicTacToe

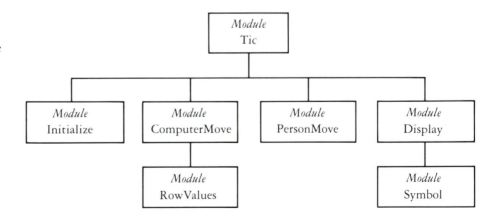

The hierarchical diagram for the completed tic-tac-toe program is shown in Figure 8.6. Part of a test run of the completed program follows. A complete test run would be more involved, because more options would be exercised.

```
TIC - TAC - TOE

Who moves first?
1 means you, 2 means the computer.
```

EXAMPLE 8.4
Completed
Program
TicTacToe
(*continued*)

1

Enter your move : <u>1</u>

My move is 5

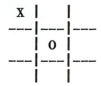

Enter your move : <u>9</u>

My move is 3

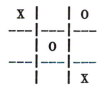

Enter your move : <u>7</u>

My move is 4

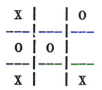

Enter your move : <u>8</u>

You win

```
X |   | O
---|---|---
O | O |
---|---|---
X | X | X
```

Do you want to play again (yes or no)? <u>yes</u>

**EXAMPLE 8.4
Completed
Program
TicTacToe**
(*continued*)

```
TIC - TAC - TOE

Who moves first?
1 means you, 2 means the computer.

1

    Enter your move : 2

    My move is  5

        |  X  |
    ---|---|---
        |  O  |
    ---|---|---
        |     |


    Enter your move : 1

    My move is  3

    X | X | O
    ---|---|---
        |  O  |
    ---|---|---
        |     |


    Enter your move : 7

    My move is  4

    X | X | O
    ---|---|---
    O | O |
    ---|---|---
    X |     |

    Enter your move : 5

    Position 5 occupied

    Enter your move : 6
```

EXAMPLE 8.4
Completed
Program
TicTacToe
(*continued*)

```
My move is  8

X | X | O
---|---|---
O | O | X
---|---|---
X | O |

Enter your move : 9

It is a draw

Do you want to play again (yes or no)? no
```

Many important system and applications programs use character and string manipulations extensively. As an interesting and fun example of string processing we will design a program that translates a Pascal-like program where all the reserved words are in Spanish to standard Pascal.

APPLICATION

Translation
from Spanish
to English

Suppose we have the following Spanish Pascal program. The program is not entirely in Spanish; only the reserved words and predefined identifiers are.

```
PROCEDIMIENTO Example (introduce, producion);

{*************************************
* This PROGRAM reads three numbers   *
* from the input file. The sum and   *
* the average are calculated and     *
* the results are printed.           *
*************************************}

PALABRA
     x1, x2, x3 : flotar;
     Average    : flotar;
     Sum        : flotar;

PRINCIPIO

     { read the three numbers from the input file }

     lee (x1, x2, x3);
```

APPLICATION

**Translation
from Spanish
to English**
(*continued*)

```
{ compute the sum and average }

Sum := x1 + x2 + x3;
Average := Sum / 3;

{ Print the results }

escribe (' The numbers are: ',x1 :7:2, x2 :7:2,
         x3 :7:2);
escribe (' The sum of the numbers is: ', Sum : 9:2);
escribe (' The average is: ', Average :9:2);
escribeln
FIN.
```

We would like to translate this program into standard Pascal so that we could compile it and execute it using our standard Pascal compiler. In order to do this, we will need a dictionary that provides us with the English equivalents of our Spanish terms. The following dictionary will be used:

Spanish	English Equivalent
escribe	write
fin	**end**
flotar	real
integra	integer
introduce	input
lee	read
misma	**const**
palabra	**var**
principio	**begin**
procedimiento	**program**
producion	output

The first version of the algorithm for the top-level module, which reads the dictionary and performs the translation, is:

begin { Translate Module}
   Input dictionary and count the number of entries
repeat

APPLICATION
_____

**Translation
from Spanish
to English**
(*continued*)

Input line of text to be translated
    for every Spanish entry in dictionary **do**
    Find position of word in line to be translated
    while Spanish word is still in line **do**
      Insert English word at appropriate position
      Delete corresponding Spanish word
    Print translated line
  until the end of the file is reached
end.

As we examine this algorithm, we can suggest the following modules:

Readstring (**var** S: String);   This module reads a line of text and returns it as a character string.

Writestring (S: String);   This module prints a character string in a field width equal to the length of the string, ignoring trailing blanks.

Delete (**var** S: String; Start, Span : integer);   This module starting at position "Start," deletes "Span" number of characters from string "S." Characters to the right of the ones deleted are moved forward to fill the hole created by the ones being deleted.

Insert (**var** S,T: String; P: integer);   This module inserts string "T" into string "S" at location "P." Characters in "S" originally to the right of "P" are shifted to the right of the string being inserted.

Locate (**var** S, T :String; Start:integer):integer;   This module locates the first occurrence of string "S" in string "T" starting at location "Start" of "S."

Clear (**var** S: String);   This module initializes a character string to blanks.

Length (**var** s: String); integer;   This module obtains the length of a string. For purposes of length, trailing blanks are not significant.

FirstBlank (S: String; Start:integer): integer;   This module finds the position of the first blank in a given string starting at location "Start." Because strings containing nothing but blanks are considered to have length zero, we need special routines to handle blanks.

The above modules, designed to manipulate strings, will make the translation job easier. Note that the way we are manipulating

APPLICATION

Translation from Spanish to English (*continued*)

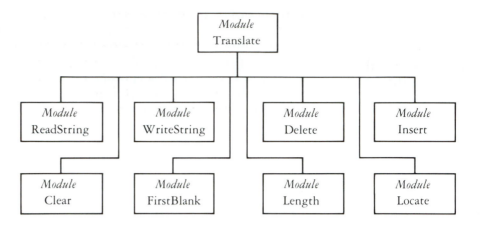

Figure 8.7 Hierarchy for first two levels of translation program

character strings in this program may change the length of a string. By considering trailing blanks in a string as not significant, we treat the strings in a way that allows their lengths to be altered. The interrelationship between the modules is shown in Figure 8.7.

Instead of designing and coding the top-level module and using stubs for the lower-level modules, here we take a different approach. We will design, code, and test the lower-level modules first; so, we will not write the top-level module as such. Instead, we will design and write a module that will call and exercise the lower-level module being tested. A module written to exercise a lower-level module is called a **driver**. The program below illustrates a driver designed to test the module Length.

```
program Test(input,output);

{**********************************
 * Program to test modules to     *
 * input, output, clear, and      *
 * compute the length of a string. *
 **********************************}

const
   Stringmax= 75;

type
   String = packed array[1..Stringmax] of char;

var
   Line : String;
```

APPLICATION

Translation from Spanish to English (*continued*)

```
function Length(var s:String):integer;

    {**********************************
     * Function to compute the length of *
     * a string. Trailing blanks are not *
     * significant and are ignored.      *
     **********************************}

    var
        i     : integer;
        Blank : boolean;
    begin
        i := Stringmax;
        Blank := true;

        {Scan string from rear until a
         non-blank character is found}

        while (i>0) and Blank do
            if s[i] = ' ' then
                i := i - 1
            else
                Blank := false;
        Length := i
    end;

procedure Clear(var S:String);

    {*****************************
     * Procedure to clear a string *
     * to blanks. Stringmax is a   *
     * global constant.            *
     *****************************}

    var
        i : integer;
    begin
        for I:=1 to Stringmax do
            S[i] := ' '
    end;

procedure ReadString(var S : String);

    {**********************************
     * Module to input a line of text. *
     **********************************}
```

APPLICATION

**Translation
from Spanish
to English**
(*continued*)

```
var
   i : integer;
begin
   Clear(S);
   i := 0;
   while (not eoln) and (i<Stringmax) do
      begin
         i := i + 1;
         read(S[i])
      end;
   readln
end;

procedure WriteString(S : String);

   {*******************************
   * Procedure to print a string *
   * S using a field width equal *
   * to the string length.       *
   *******************************}

   begin
      write(S:Length(S))
   end;

begin   {Driver module to test ReadString, Length,
   and WriteString modules}

   while not eof do
      begin
         ReadString(Line);
         WriteString(Line);
         writeln(' Length: ',Length(Line) :3)
      end
end.
```

Given the following input:

short
this is a longer string
    This string has leading blanks

the output will be:

short Length: 5
this is a longer string Length: 23
    This string has leading blanks Length: 34
Length: 0

APPLICATION

**Translation
from Spanish
to English**
(*continued*)

The complete translation program is:

```
program Translate(input,output);

{********************************
* Program to translate "Spanish" *
* Pascal programs to "English"   *
* Pascal programs.               *
********************************}

const
    Stringmax= 75;

type
    String = packed array[1..Stringmax] of char;

var
    English, Spanish : array [1..20] of String;
    Line, Sentinel   : String;
    DictSize, Pos, i : integer;
    Engl, Span       : integer;
    Blank            : boolean;

function Length(var s:String):integer;

    {************************************
    * Function to compute the length of *
    * a string. Trailing blanks are not *
    * significant and are ignored.       *
    ************************************}

    var
        i     : integer;
        Blank : boolean;
    begin
        i := Stringmax;
        Blank := true;

        {Scan string from rear until a
         non-blank character is found}

        while (i>0) and Blank do
            if s[i] = ' ' then
                i := i - 1
            else
                Blank := false;
        Length := i
    end;
```

```
procedure Clear(var S:String);

    {*****************************
    * Procedure to clear a string *
    * to blanks. Stringmax is a   *
    * global constant.            *
    *****************************}

    var
        i : integer;
    begin
        for i:=1 to Stringmax do
            S[i] := ' '
    end;

function Locate(var S,T :String; Start:integer):integer;

    {*********************************
    * Function to locate string S    *
    * in target string T. The        *
    * function returns the position  *
    * of the first character of the  *
    * first occurrence of S in T.    *
    * If S is not in T it            *
    * returns 0. The search begins   *
    * at location Start of T.        *
    *********************************}

    var
        i,j           : integer;
        SizeS, SizeT  : integer;
        Uneq          : boolean;
    begin
        {Compute the lengths of both strings}

        SizeS := Length(S);
        SizeT := Length(T);

        {Validate Start}

        if Start<1 then
            Start:=1;

        {Check if remainder of T is long enough to
         contain S}

        if (Start+SizeT>SizeS+1) or (SizeT=0) then
            Locate:=0
```

```
    else
        begin
            i:=Start-1;
            repeat
                i:=i+1;
                j:=0;
                repeat
                    j:=j+1;
                    Uneq:=T[j]<>S[i+j-1];
                until Uneq or (j=SizeT);
            until (not Uneq) or (i=SizeS-SizeT+1);
            if Uneq then
                Locate:=0
            else
                Locate:=j


        end
end;
procedure ReadString(var S : String);

    {****************************
    * Procedure to input a line. *
    ****************************}

    var
        i : integer;
    begin
        Clear(S);
        i := 0;
        while (not eoln) and (i<Stringmax) do
            begin
                i := i + 1;
                read(S[i])
            end;
        readln
    end;
procedure WriteString(S : String);

    {****************************
    * Procedure to print a string *
    * S using a field width equal *
    * to the string length.       *
    ****************************}

    begin
        write(S:Length(S))
    end;
```

APPLICATION

**Translation
from Spanish
to English**
(*continued*)

```
procedure Delete(var S :String; Start,Span:integer);

    {**********************************
    * Procedure to delete Span number *
    * of characters from string S      *
    * starting at location Start.      *
    **********************************}

    var
        i, Limit, SizeS : integer;
    begin
        SizeS := Length(S);
        Limit:=Start+Span;
        if Start<1 then
            Start:=1;
        if Limit>SizeS+1 then
            Limit:=SizeS+1;
        Span:=Limit-Start;
        if Span>0 then
            begin
              for i:=0 to SizeS-Limit do
                  S[Start+i]:=S[Limit+i];
              for i:=SizeS-Span+1 to SizeS do
                  S[i]:=' '
            end
    end;

procedure Insert(var S,T : String; P:integer);

    {*****************************************
    * Procedure to insert the string S into  *
    * the string T at position Start.        *
    * Characters are shifted to the right     *
    * as necessary. If resulting string       *
    * is too long it is truncated. Attempts   *
    * to insert S beyond end of T produce     *
    * no results.                             *
    *****************************************}


var
    i,j          : integer;
    SizeS, SizeT : integer;
begin
    SizeS := Length(S);
    SizeT := Length(T);
```

APPLICATION

**Translation
from Spanish
to English**
(*continued*)

```
    if SizeT>0 then
        if (p>0) and (p<=SizeS+1) then
            begin
                if SizeS+SizeT<=Stringmax then
                    SizeS:=SizeS+SizeT
                else
                    SizeS := Stringmax;
                for i:=SizeS downto p+SizeT do
                    S[i]:=S[i-SizeT];
                if SizeS<p+SizeT then
                    j:=SizeS
                else
                    j:=p+SizeT-1;
                for i:=p to j do
                    S[i]:=T[i-p+1];
            end
        else
            writeln('Insert error: non-contiguous string')
end;

function FirstBlank (S :String; Start :integer): integer;

    {**************************************
    * Function to locate the position of *
    * the first blank in a string. If no *
    * blank is present the function      *
    * returns a zero.                    *
    **************************************}

    var
        i     : integer;
        Blank : boolean;
    begin

        i := Start;
        Blank := false;
        while (i<Length(S)) and not Blank do
            if S[i] <> ' ' then
                i := i + 1
            else
                Blank := true;
        if Blank then
            FirstBlank := i
        else
            FirstBlank := 0;
    end;
```

```
begin    {TRANSLATE module}

   {Initialize sentinel string}

   Clear (Sentinel);
   Sentinel[1] := '$';

   {Initialize counter and input first line
    from dictionary}

   DictSize := 1;
   ReadString(Line);
   repeat
      {Locate first blank character}

      Pos := FirstBlank(Line,1);

      Clear(Spanish[DictSize]);
      for i := 1 to Pos-1 do
         Spanish[DictSize][i] := Line[i];
      Delete (Line,1,Pos);

      {Remove leading blanks}

      while FirstBlank(Line,1) = 1 do
         Delete(Line,1,1);

      English[DictSize] := Line;
      DictSize := DictSize + 1;
      ReadString(Line)
   until Locate(Line,Sentinel,1) > 0;

   DictSize := DictSize - 1;

   {Input text and translate }

   repeat
      ReadString(Line);

      {Translate}
      for i := 1 to DictSize do
         begin
            Pos := Locate(Line,Spanish[i],1);
            while Pos > 0 do
```

APPLICATION

**Translation
from Spanish
to English**
(*continued*)

```
            begin
                Engl := Length(English[i]);
                Span := Length(Spanish[i]);
                Insert(Line,English[i],Pos);
                Delete(Line,Pos+Engl,Span);
                Pos := Locate(Line,Spanish[i],1)
            end
        end;
        WriteString(Line);
        writeln;
    until eof
end.
```

Given the input:

```
escribe         write
FIN             END
flotar          real
integra         integer
introduce       input
lee             read
MISMA           CONST
PALABRA         VAR
PRINCIPIO       BEGIN
PROCEDIMIENTO   PROGRAM
producion       output
$               $
PROCEDIMIENTO Example (introduce, producion);

{**********************************
* This PROGRAM reads three numbers *
* from a data file. The sum and the *
* average are calculated and the    *
* results are printed.              *
**********************************}

PALABRA
    x1, x2, x3 : flotar;
    Average    : flotar;
    Sum        : flotar;

PRINCIPIO

    { read the three numbers from the input file }

    lee (x1, x2, x3);
```

APPLICATION

**Translation
from Spanish
to English**
(*continued*)

```
{ compute the sum and average }

Sum := x1 + x1 + x3;
Average := Sum / 3;

{ Using the write statement, print the results }

escribe (' The numbers are: ',x1 :7:2, x2 :7:2,
          x3 :7:2);
escribe (' The sum of the numbers is: ', Sum : 9:2);
escribe (' The average is: ', Average :9:2);
escribeln
FIN.
```

the output will be:

```
PROGRAM Example (input, output);

{************************************
* This PROGRAM reads three numbers  *
* from a data file. The sum and the *
* average are calculated and the    *
* results are printed.              *
************************************}

VAR
    x1, x2, x3 : real;
    Average    : real;
    Sum        : real;

BEGIN

    { read the three numbers from the input file }

    read (x1, x2, x3);

    { compute the sum and average }

    Sum := x1 + x2 + x3;
    Average := Sum / 3;

    { Using the write statement, print the results }

    write (' The numbers are: ',x1 :7:2, x2 :7:2,
            x3 :7:2);
    write (' The sum of the numbers is: ', Sum : 9:2);
    write (' The average is: ', Average :9:2);
    writeln
END.
```

**8.5
CHAPTER
REVIEW**

A module is any part of a larger, more complex system that performs a well-defined specific task. We can think of a module as made up of other modules, and these in turn as made up of yet other modules, until we no longer need to subdivide a given module but can instead express it in terms of the instructions available in a given language. In short, the modules of a program form a hierarchy. The module at Level 1 represents the whole system (i.e., the program). The modules at Level 2 are the major components of the system (the procedures and functions used by the program). The modules at Level 3 are the building blocks from which Level 2 modules are constructed (the procedures and functions needed by the Level 2 procedures and functions).

The hierarchical organization of modules lends itself well to top-down design. We first design the module at Level 1, that is to say, the main program. We do this in terms of the modules at Level 2. That is, we imagine that we have the procedures and functions at Level 2 at our disposal and design the module at Level 1 using these yet-to-be-written modules.

Once the top-level module has been designed and tested, we begin work on the modules at Level 2. We proceed one module at a time and design each Level 2 module in terms of the modules it requires at Level 3.

By proceeding this way, we design the program in top-down fashion. At any point in the process we are concerned only about the design of one module in terms of its immediately subordinate modules.

Once a module is designed and coded, we test it. One approach to testing is to start with the top-level module and test it first. Then we test Level 2 modules, and so on, until all the modules are tested. That is, modules are tested in the same order in which they are designed and written. This is called top-down testing. In this approach, every module is tested in the same environment in which it will be used in the finished program.

To test a higher-level module without its lower-level modules, we replace the yet-to-be-written modules with stubs. A *program stub* or *stub* is a dummy module that takes the place of the actual module in order to test a module at a higher level.

When testing a module, ideally, we should use enough test cases to follow every possible path through its algorithm. Except for extremely simple modules, however, this is not practical. Testing goals are usually somewhat more modest. We simply include enough test cases to cause every decision path to be taken. This insures that all the code is exercised, even if not all possible combinations of conditions are tested.

The development and testing process continues until the entire program is developed, coded, and tested. At each step we focus our attention on a single module. The existing modules provide us with a natural testing harness for any newly developed module.

Sometimes, instead of designing and coding the top-level module and of using stubs for the lower-level modules, we design, code, and test the lower-level modules first. In order to do this, we use a module that calls and exercises the module being tested. Such a module is called a *driver*.

The top-down approach is to be preferred in most cases. With any approach, however, the importance of thinking the problem through carefully cannot be overemphasized.

8.6 EXERCISES

8.1. Fill in the blanks in each of the following:

(a) The design approach that identifies major program functions first is called _____.

(b) Basic program functions are subdivided into smaller and smaller subfunctions that are called _____.

(c) A set of logically related program statements performing a single function is called a _____.

(d) The technique of testing higher-level modules before designing lower-level modules is called _____.

(e) A _____ takes the place of a lower-level module when a higher-level module is being tested.

(f) A _____ takes the place of a higher-level module when a lower-level module is being tested.

(g) When testing a module, ideally, one should include enough test cases to _____.

8.2. Answer each of the following true or false. If your answer is false, state why.

(a) The identification of basic program functions is the first step in top-down design.

(b) In program design, modules are usually implemented as procedures and functions.

(c) Testing every path through the algorithm of a module is not practical and is almost never done.

(d) Higher-level modules cannot be tested until all lower-level modules are written.

(e) A module should perform as many functions as possible.

(f) Modules are usually tested when the entire program is written.

(g) The use of stubs should be avoided as much as possible because they are discarded and, therefore, waste time and effort.

8.3. In what way does the use of global variables work against good modular design?

8.4. Consider the initial decomposition of the algorithm to solve the following problem:

Find the lowest common multiple for each pair of several pairs of numbers.

begin {Lowest Common Multiple Module}
    while pairs remain to be processed **do**
        Find the lowest common multiple of the current pair of numbers
        Print the lowest common multiple
end.

(a) What, if any, lower-level modules suggest themselves for this algorithm?
(b) Code the top-level module and the required stubs.
(c) Test the top-level module.
(d) Complete the development of the entire algorithm.

8.5. Consider the initial decomposition of the algorithm to solve the following problem:

Write a program to allow two players to play tic-tac-toe against each other. The program should alternately request moves from each player, validate each move, and display the board with all moves recorded on it. It should also determine if there is a winner or if the game is a draw.

begin { Tic-tac-toe }
    Print headings
    Initialize variables
    repeat
        if first player's turn **then**
            Request move from player 1
            Display board
            Determine if player 1 won
        else
            Request move from player 2
            Display Board
            Determine if player 2 won
        Change players
        Increment move counter
    until (movecounter > 9) **or** (game is won)
    if there is no winner **then**
        Declare a draw
    else
        Declare appropriate player the winner
end.

(a) What, if any, lower-level modules suggest themselves for this algorithm?
(b) Code the top-level module and the required stubs.
(c) Test the top-level module.
(d) Complete the development of the entire algorithm.

8.6. The program to play tic-tac-toe given in the text has certain draw-backs. One major drawback is that the computer, when moving first, will always make the same move. Modify the program so that the computer will make its first move at random. When doing this, give careful consideration to which modules will require modification and which modules will remain intact.

8.7. Use the development strategy illustrated in this chapter to design the first-level module for the following problem:

Write a program which removes all comments from a Pascal program by substituting a blank for each comment, but otherwise leaves the program unchanged.

8.8. Modify the translation program given in this chapter to add the following features:
(a) Comments are not to be translated.
(b) Constant strings are also not to be translated.

Incorporate any additional modules into the existing program, if necessary.

8.9. Design, code, and test a *Text Formatter*. This program should accept character strings and formatting instructions as input and should produce formatted text as output. All formatting commands begin with a period in column 1. Commands appear on a line by themselves. The program should implement the following commands:

.lm n	Set the left margin to column n.
.rm n	Set the right margin to column n.
.i n	Indent n spaces.
.c	Center the next line between the left and right margins.
.s n	Skip n lines.
.f	Fill command. This command adds successive words from the original text until the addition of one more word will exceed the right margin.
.nf	Disengage the fill command.

For example, given the following input text:
.lm 10
.rm 40
.c
Formatting Example

```
.s 3
.f
.i 5
```
This part of the text will
be filled.
That is,
words will be added to lines until
a
word will not
fit within the right margin.
```
.s 2
.nf
```
This part
of the text
will not be filled.

The output of your program should appear as

Formatting Example

This part of the text
will be filled. That is,
words will be added to lines
until a word will not fit
within the right margin.

This part
of the text
will not be filled.

Design your program in such a way as to make it easy to add additional formatting commands without having to redesign the program.

9. Sets

9.1
THE CONCEPT
OF A SET

Consider the following problem: Information on a questionnaire is recorded as in Figure 9.1. We need a way of representing this information so that we can easily add or delete interests, determine if a particular person is interested in a particular topic, compare the interests of different individuals, and otherwise work with the data.

One approach is to represent this information in a boolean array as follows:

```
type
    Areas = (Music, Theater, Art, Baseball, Football,
             Basketball, Hiking, Swimming, Politics,
             Camping);
var
    Interests : array[Areas] of boolean;
```

Using the boolean array, Interests, we can store the data on the questionnaire as in Figure 9.2.

With this method of representation, we can add an interest by changing a false to a true or delete an interest by changing a true to a false. We can also determine if a person has a particular interest by examining the appropriate location of the array for a true or a false entry.

Boolean arrays are a convenient way to represent this kind of data. Pascal, however, has an even more convenient way to do this—

Figure 9.1 Sample interest questionnaire

Interests (Please check as many as applicable)

Music	Theater	Art	Baseball	Football	Hiking	Politics
			×		×	

Figure 9.2 Boolean array representation of interest questionnaire

	Music	Theater	Art	Baseball	Football	Hiking	Politics
Interests	false	false	false	true	false	true	false

the structured data type known as a **set**. Pascal, in fact, is the only general purpose language with this capability.

A set, in mathematics, is any collection of abstract objects. In mathematics, it is represented by curly braces containing the list of the objects that constitute the collection. For example, the set of odd positive integers less than 10 is represented by

$\{1, 3, 5, 7, 9\}$

in mathematics. In Pascal, curly braces are used for comments; so, square brackets are used to represent sets. Thus, the above set would be denoted as:

```
[1, 3, 5, 7, 9]
```

The objects that belong to a set are called its **elements**. The elements of the above set are 1,3,5,7,9. What makes sets useful, as we shall see shortly, is the fact that operations such as adding elements to a set or deleting elements from it, are easy to perform. It is also very easy, in Pascal, to determine if a particular object is or is not an element of a given set.

9.2 SET DECLARA-TIONS

A **set** type can be defined as follows:

type
   Set-type = **set of** Base-type;

The syntax diagram for the definition of a set type is shown in Figure 9.3. As an example, consider

```
type
   Digits = set of 0..9;
```

where "Digits" is the set-type identifier and the subrange type "0..9" is the base type of all sets of type Digits. A variable declared to be of type Digits, the set type, is a set whose elements are chosen from 0..9, the base type. For example, suppose we declare

var
   Numb : Digits;

Then some possible values of "Numb" are:

[1,2,3] [1,3,5,7,9] [8] [ ]

Figure 9.3 Syntax
diagram for **set**
definition

The notation [ ] denotes the **empty** or **null set**: that is, the set that has no elements. Every set type includes the null set as a possible value, regardless of the base type. The set that contains all possible values of the base type is known as the **universal set**. For the base type Digits, the universal set is:

[0..9] or [0,1,2,3,4,5,6,7,8,9]

Consider the following type definitions and variable declaration:

```
type
    Countries = (Canada, USA, Mexico);
    NAContinent = set of Countries;
var
    NorthAmerica : NAContinent;
```

Then the possible values of the variable "NorthAmerica," whose values are "**set of** Countries" are:

```
[ ]   [Canada]   [USA]   [Mexico]   [Canada, USA]
[Canada, Mexico]   [USA, Mexico]    [Canada, USA, Mexico]
```

In fact, NorthAmerica can have only these values. The eight values represent all constants of type NAContinent and are known together as the **power set** of NAContinent. The number of possible values that a set variable can take on—that is, the number of values in the power set—is determined by the number of values in the base type. The base type must be a simple scalar type other than real or integer. However, *subranges* of integers may be used.

For efficiency, some Pascal compilers impose limits on the number of elements in the base type of a set. The limit on the number of elements for which reasonably efficient implementations of sets are possible is usually determined by the word length in the hardware of the computer that is used. For this reason, many implementations allow for base types of no more than 64 values. Because of such restrictions, sets of char are not allowed on some systems. The restriction of the number of elements in the base type of a set often causes problems in enumerating even small sets. For example, if a compiler allows only up to 64 elements in the base type, then the set [1,100] is invalid, in spite of the fact that it has only two elements. This is because the base type of such a set must be "**set of** 1..100" and the subrange "1..100" is too large. It is even possible that only integers within particular subranges are allowed on a particular system. That is, a subrange such as "0..63" might be permitted, whereas subranges such as "95..100" or "−5..0" might not. Unfortunately, these restrictions vary from compiler to compiler. Before using sets in a program you should try to find out what the limits of your particular system are.

SELF-TEST 1

1. List all sets of the types "Color" and "Choice" where:

```
type
    Color = (Red, White, Blue);
    Choice = (a, b, c, d);
```

2. Identify the universal sets in problem 1.

3. Determine which of the following declarations of sets are valid and which are not.

(a) **var**
```
        Grades : set of 'A'..'D';
```

(b) **var**
```
        Digits = set of 0..9;
```

(c) **type**
```
        Colors = (Yellow,Green,Red);
    var
        Mixture : set of Yellow;
```

(d) **type**
```
        Flowers = (Iris,Mum,Rose);
    var
        Bouquet : set of Flowers;
```

(e) **type**
```
        Name=packed array[1..20] of char;
    var
        Family : set of Name;
```

(f) **type**
```
        Rank = (Lieutenant, Captain, Major, Colonel,
                General);
        Officers = set of Rank;
    var
        Staff : Officers
```

Answers

1. The sets of type "Color" are: [ ], [Red], [White], [Blue], [Red, White], [Red,Blue], [White,Blue], [Red,White,Blue]. The sets of type "Choice" are [ ], [a], [b], [c], [d], [a,b], [a,c], [a,d], [b,c], [b,d], [c,d], [a,b,c], [a,b,d], [a,c,d], [b,c,d], [a,b,c,d].

2. The universal set of type "Color" is [Red,White,Blue]. The universal set of type "Choice" is [a,b,c,d].

3. (a) Valid   (b) Not valid. Should use : instead of = .   (c) Not Valid. "Yellow" is not a type.   (d) Valid   (e) Not valid. A structured type cannot be the base type of a set.   (f) Valid

9.3 SET CONSTRUCTORS

Before a set can be manipulated, it must be assigned a value. The general form of the set assignment statement is:

set-identifier : = set expression;

The set expression can be a constant of the appropriate set type, another set identifier, or it may specify one or more operations on sets. The simplest type of assignment statement consists of an identifier on the left side of the assignment operator and a set constant on the right side. Set constants are created by means of **set constructors**. Examples of set constructors are:

```
[15]
[1,2,3]
[3*2,4+5,7]
['A'..'R']
['A'..'Z','0'..'9']
```

A set constructor is an expression that is evaluated before its value is assigned to a set variable. Thus, it may contain arithmetic expressions, as above. It may also contain variables. For example, if a, b, and c have the values 1, 2, and 3 respectively, then the set constructor:

```
[a+b,c mod b, b*c]
```

has the value

```
[3,1,6]
```

Note that the order in which the elements of a set are listed is immaterial. The set

[1,3,6]

is identical to the set

[3,1,6]

The elements may also be specified as subranges:

[1..3]

is equivalent to

[1,2,3]

Given the type definitions and variable declarations below:

```
type
    Areas = (Music, Theater, Art, Baseball, Football,
        Basketball, Hiking, Swimming, Politics,
        Camping);
    Interests = set of Areas;
var
    Sports, Arts : Interests;
```

the following assignment statements are all valid:

```
Sports := [ ];
Sports := [Baseball..Swimming,Camping];
Arts :=[Music, Theater, Art];
Arts :=[Music..succ(Theater)];
```

9.4 SET OPERATORS

One of the reasons for the usefulness of sets in Pascal is the fact that the operations of *union*, *intersection*, and *set difference* are available as primitive operations. This makes addition or deletion of elements from sets very straightforward.

The three operators for sets are defined in Table 9.1. If the variables x and y are of type **set** then:

Table 9.1
Set operators

Operator	Meaning	Example
+	Set Union	[1..3] + [4,5] = [1..5]
*	Set Intersection	[1..3] * [2..5] = [2,3]
−	Set Difference	[1..9] − [1..4] = [5..9]

1. $x + y$ is the set of all values that are either in x, or in y, or in both.

2. $x * y$ is the set of all values that are in x and in y.

3. $x - y$ is the set of all values in x but not in y.

The priorities of $+$, $*$, and $-$, when used as set operators, are the same as when they are used as arithmetic operators. Parentheses can be used in set expressions in the same manner as in arithmetic expressions. The following examples provide additional illustrations of set operations.

Expression	Value
`['A','B','C']+['A','D','E']`	`['A','B','C','D','E']`
`[ ] + [1..5]`	`[1..5]`
`[1..5] * [1,4,6]`	`[1,4]`
`[1..5] * [6..9]`	`[ ]`
`[1..5] - [3,5]`	`[1,2,4]`
`['A','B','C'] - ['X','Y']`	`['A','B','C']`
`[1,2]*[1,4]+[3,5]`	`[1,3,5]`
`[1,2]+[1,4]*[3,5]`	`[1,2]`
`[1,2]*([1,4]+[3,5])`	`[1]`

Set union and set difference are particularly useful to add and to delete set elements. Set union is also useful to read the values of a set from an input file. Example 9.1 illustrates a procedure that reads a set. We assume that the data in the input file are represented as on the survey form of our earlier example: one line per questionnaire, with the response to Music in column 1, Theater in column 2, and so on. An X in a given column indicates that the corresponding interest was checked off on the questionnaire.

**9.5
RELATIONAL
OPERATORS
ON SETS**

Pascal provides five relational operators that can be used to check relationships between sets, and the membership of an element in a set. The relational operators are defined in Table 9.2.

All of the operators in Table 9.2 produce boolean results. The operators "$=$" and "$<>$" are used to test for set equality and inequality, respectively. Two sets are equal if they each contain exactly the same elements. The order of the elements is irrelevant. The operators "$<=$" and "$>=$" are used to test set inclusion. If a and b are sets of the same type, then $a<=b$ tests whether a is a **subset** of b.

**EXAMPLE 9.1
Procedure to
Read a Set**

```
type
    Areas = (Music, Theater, Art, Baseball, Football,
        Basketball, Hiking, Swimming, Politics,
        Camping);
    Interests = set of Areas;

procedure ReadInterests (var intofpers : Interests);

var
    Index      : Areas;
    Ch         : char;

begin
    {Initialize set of interests}

    intofpers := [ ];

    {Input set of interests}

    for Index := Music to Camping do
        begin
            read (Ch);
            if Ch = 'X' then
                intofpers := intofpers + [Index]
        end {of FOR loop}
end {of PROCEDURE};
```

Table 9.2
Set relational
operators

Operator	Meaning	Examples
=	Set equality	[2,3] = [3,2] is true
		[3,5] = [3,4] is false
< >	Set inequality	[2,3] < > [3,2] is false
		[3,5] < > [3,4] is true
< =	Set inclusion	[1..6] < = [1..8] is true
	(Subset of)	[1..6] < = [2..8] is false
> =	Set containment	[1..6] > = [4,5] is true
	(Superset of)	[2..6] > = [1..5] is false
in	Set membership	4 **in** [1..5] is true
	(is an element of)	'X' **in** ['A', 'E', 'I', 'O', 'U'] is false

Set *a* is a subset of *b* if every element of *a* is also an element of *b*. The operator $>=$ is used to test set containment. Set *a* contains *b*, or *a* is a **superset** of *b*, if every element of *b* is also an element of *a*.

Note that $=$, $<>$, $<=$, and $>=$ are used with operands of the same set type. The fifth operator, **in**, is used to test the presence of an individual element in a set. The first operand must be a scalar type, the base type, and the second operand must be the associated set type. If *X* is a value of the base type and *a* is a value of the corresponding set type then:

X **in** *a* is true if *X* is an element of *a*, false otherwise

The **in** operator is commonly used to control the flow of execution in programs involving sets. For example,

```
if Letter in ['A','E','I','O','U'] then
   Vowelcount := Vowelcount + 1
```

or

```
while Letter in ['A','E','I','O','U'] do
   begin
      write (Letter);
      read (Letter)
   end
```

The **in** operator is also used to simplify complex boolean expressions. For instance, suppose that we want to test whether an integer variable, Number, is one of the following values: 1, 3, 4, 6, or 9. One way to do this is to use the following **if . . then** statement, with the compound condition:

```
if (Number=1) or (Number=3) or (Number=4) or (Number=6)
   or (Number=9) then
```

A simpler **if . . then** statement that gives the same result is:

```
if Number in [1,3,4,6,9] then
```

Some care must be taken when using the **in** operator to simplify boolean expressions. Correct use of the **in** operator requires that the scalar operand on the left-hand side of **in** be a value that is of the base type of the set on the right-hand side of the **in**.

The boolean operator, **not**, can be used with the relational operators for sets. It should be remembered, however, that **not** must precede a boolean expression. Thus, the expression

not (3 in [1..5])

is valid, and its value is false. In this example, the boolean expression that is the operand of **not** is "(3 **in** [1..5])." The expression

3 not in [1..5]

on the other hand, even though it appears to be "better" English, is not valid because "**in**[1..5]" is not a boolean expression.

The relational operators for sets all have the same precedence level, and that precedence level is the same as for the arithmetic relational operators. Thus, all relational operators have a precedence level lower than the set operators *, +, and −. In the expressions

[2..5]+[2,6,9] <= [1..6]*[2,4,7]

and

3 in [2...9]*[1..4]

the set expressions involving *, +, and − are evaluated before the relational operators are applied.

Here are some simple examples of how relational operators can be used. The Example 9.2 illustrates a procedure that isolates the distinct digits in an integer. The procedure accepts a positive integer, Number, as a parameter and returns a set consisting of the distinct digits found in the integer. The procedure uses the **mod** operator to extract a digit from Number. It then checks to see if that digit has been extracted earlier. If it is a new digit, then it is added to the set of distinct digits.

EXAMPLE 9.2
Procedure to
Extract Digits
from an
Integer

```
type
     DecDigits = set of 0..9;

procedure ExtractDigits (Number :integer;
                              var Digits : DecDigits)

var
    Digit : 0..9;
begin
    {Initialize the set of digits to the null set}
```

EXAMPLE 9.2
Procedure to
Extract Digits
from an
Integer

```
        Digits := [ ];
      repeat
         {Extract a digit from the number}

         Digit := Number mod 10;

         {Test if digit is new}

         if not (Digit in Digits) then
           Digits := Digits + [Digit];

         {Remove rightmost digit from number}

         Number := Number div 10
      until Number = 0
    end {of PROCEDURE}
```

The Example 9.3 illustrates how the membership operator, **in**, can be used to output a set. A set cannot appear in the output list of a write or writeln statement. To print a set we have to print each element individually. We do this by testing every value of the base type for membership. If the test succeeds, we print the value and delete it from the set before testing for the next value.

EXAMPLE 9.3
Procedure to
Print a Set

```
type
   DecDigits = set of 0..9;
procedure PrintSet (Digits : DecDigits);

var
   Digit : 0..9;

begin
   {Initialize base type to first value}

   Digit := 0;

   {While set is not empty do}

   while Digits <> [ ] do
      begin
        {If base value is in set print it}

        if Digit in Digits then
```

**EXAMPLE 9.3
Procedure to
Print a Set**
(*continued*)

```
        begin
           write (Digit :3);

           {Delete printed value from set}

           Digits := Digits - [Digit]
        end;

     {Obtain next value of base type}

        Digit := Digit + 1;
     end { of WHILE loop}
  end {of PROCEDURE};
```

SELF-TEST 2

1. Give the following assignments, where *A*, *B*, *C*, and *D* are sets:

```
A := [1..20]
B := [1,3,5,7,9,11,13,15,17,19]
C := [1..10,12,15,17]
D := [2,3,5,7,11,13,17,19]
```

evaluate each of the following expressions:

(a) **A+B**
(b) **A*B**
(c) **A+B*C**
(d) **(A+B)*C**
(e) **A+B*C+D**
(f) **A-D**
(g) **A*B+C-D**
(h) **A*B-C*D**
(i) **(A*(B-C)+D)**

2. Assume the set variables *A*, *B*, *C*, and *D* have been assigned the values shown in problem 1. Evaluate each of the following expressions:

(a) **A=B**
(b) **C>=A**
(c) **C-D <> [1,4,6,8,10,12,15]**
(d) **7 in C**
(e) **not(13 in A)**
(f) **B*D <= C**

3. Consider the following set declarations:

```
var
   Letters : set of 'A'..'Z';
   Digits  : set of '0'..'9';
   Characters : set of char;
   Symbol : char;
```

Determine which of the following expressions are valid:

(a) **Character - Symbol**
(b) **Character - [Symbol]**
(c) **[Letters] <= [Digits]**
(d) **Letters * Digits**

Answers

1. (a) A   (b) B   (c) C   (d) C   (e) A   (f) [1,4,6,8,9,10,11,
12,14,15,16,18,20]   (g) [1,4,6,8,9,10,12,15]   (h) [1,9,11,13,15]
(i) D

2. (a) False   (b) False   (c) True   (d) True   (e) False   (f) False

3. (a) Invalid. "Symbol" is not a **set of** char.   (b) Valid   (c) Invalid. "Letters" and "Digits" are not elements of sets. They are also not sets of the same type.   (d) Invalid. "Letters" and "Digits" are not sets of the same type.

APPLICATION

Selection of a Mailing List

As our first example of an application of sets, let us return to our questionnaire about interests. Let us assume that the interests included on the questionnaire are Music, Theater, Art, Baseball, Football, Basketball, Hiking, Swimming, Politics, and Camping. We would like to generate a mailing list from these questionnaires that consists of all the individuals who satisfy the following criteria:

1. The individuals must be interested in Music, Theater, and Art.
2. The individuals must not be interested in Hiking, Swimming, and Camping.
3. Any interests in Baseball, Football, Basketball, or Politics are irrelevant.

We saw earlier how a set of interests for an individual can be read from the input file. What we need now is to design a program to print a name and address under the conditions we just specified. We will design a function that takes a set of interests as input and returns a boolean value that indicates whether the set satisfies the above three criteria.

The first step in testing for the criteria is to eliminate from the set of interests of a given person those interests that are irrelevant. Thus, if "PersInt" is the set of interests being considered, we would like to eliminate from that set the following values: Baseball, Football, Basketball, and Politics. This can be done in two different ways. The simplest way is to compute the following set difference:

PersInt - [Baseball, Football, Basketball, Politics]

Another approach is to compute the following set intersection:

PersInt * [Music, Theater, Art, Hiking, Swimming, Camping]

APPLICATION

**Selection of a
Mailing List**
(*continued*)

Note that the second set in the intersection is the set of all relevant interests. This set can be obtained by taking the union of all interests we want to be checked with all the interests we want not to be checked. That is, it is the union:

[Music, Theater, Art] + [Hiking, Swimming, Camping]

Once we have eliminated the interests that are irrelevant, we can determine if the person under consideration should be included in our mailing list by using the following **if..then** statement:

if PersInt * [Music,Theater,Art,Hiking,Swimming,Camping] =
          [Music,Theater,Art] **then**
          Print person's name and address

We can now write the complete program.

```
program PrintLabels (input, output);

type
    Areas = (Music, Theater, Art, Baseball, Football,
        Basketball, Hiking, Swimming, Politics,
        Camping);
    Interests = set of Areas;

var
    PersInt : Interests;
    Name : packed array[1..20] of char;
    Address : packed array[1..20] of char;
    i : integer;

procedure ReadInterests (var IntOfPers : Interests);
    var
        Index    : Areas;
        Ch       : char;

    begin
        {Initialize set of interests}

        IntOfPers := [ ];

        {Input set of interests}

        for Index := Music to Camping do
```

```
            begin
              read (Ch);
              if Ch = 'X' then
                 IntOfPers := IntOfPers + [Index]
            end {of FOR- loop}


      end {of PROCEDURE ReadInterests};

function Selected (IntOfPers : Interests) : boolean;

    var
       Positive    : Interests;
       Negative    : Interests;

    begin
       {Initialize appropriate sets}

       Positive := [Music, Theater, Art];
       Negative := [Hiking, Swimming, Camping];

       {Determine if person is selected}

       Selected := IntOfPerson * (Positive + Negative) =
                                 Positive

    end {of FUNCTION Selected};

    begin {Main PROGRAM}

       while not eof do
          begin
             for i := 1 to 20 do
               read (Name[i]);
             for i := 1 to 20 do
               read (Address[i]);
             ReadInterests (PersInt);
             if Selected (PersInt) then
               writeln (Name: 21, Address: 21);
             readln
          end { of WHILE loop}

    end {of PROGRAM}.
```

APPLICATION

**Eratosthenes'
Sieve**

We will now write a program to print all the prime numbers between 1 and some arbitrary positive integer, Largest. To obtain the primes, we will use an algorithm known as *Eratosthenes' Sieve*. The algorithm can be described as follows:

1. Start with a set of all the consecutive integers from 1 to Largest.

2. Delete from that set all multiples of 2. They certainly are not prime numbers.

3. Find the next integer remaining in the set larger than the one whose multiples were just deleted and delete all of its multiples. They cannot be primes.

4. Repeat step 3 until the integer whose multiples were just deleted is greater than or equal to the square root of Largest. This termination condition for deleting non-primes is based on the fact that the two factors in a product cannot both be greater than the square root of the product.

5. The elements still in the set after we terminate the deleting process are all the primes between 1 and Largest.

Using this algorithm, we can readily write a program that uses sets to find primes. The major limitation of sets in the program that follows is the restriction on the range of the base types allowed by most compilers. Thus, we can only use the program for relatively small values of Largest.

```
program Eratosthenes (output);

{*********************************
 * Eratosthenes' Sieve to compute *
 * all prime numbers from 2 to a   *
 * given positive integer.         *
 *********************************}

const
   Largest = 64;
type
   Numbers = set of 2..Largest;
var
   Sieve : Numbers;
   I, Prime : 2..Largest;
begin
   {Initialize Sieve}
```

APPLICATION

Eratosthenes'
Sieve
(*continued*)

```
Sieve := [2..Largest];

{Initialize the first prime to 2}

Prime := 2;
repeat
   {Remove all multiples of prime still in the set}

   for I := succ(Prime) to Largest do
       if (I in Sieve) and (I mod Prime = 0) then
           Sieve := Sieve - [I];
   {Locate smallest element of set greater than Prime}

   Prime := succ(Prime);
   while not (Prime in Sieve) do
       Prime := succ(Prime);
until Prime >= sqrt(Largest);

{Print the set of primes}

for I := 2 to Largest do
   if I in Sieve then
       write (I :4);
   writeln
end.
```

The output of the above program is:

```
2 3 5 7 11 13 17 19 23 29 31 37 41 43 47 53 59 61
```

APPLICATION

Lexical
Analyzer

An interesting application of sets is in the design of **scanners**, or **lexical analyzers**. A scanner or lexical analyzer is part of a compiler. It is that part of the compiler that is used to break down a program into its individual symbols. Let us examine how a simple scanner can be written for a small subset of Pascal. The scanner will isolate each symbol and output it on a separate line. We will distinguish among four different kinds of symbols or **tokens**:

1. *Integer constants*. Only unsigned integers are allowed.
2. *Identifiers*. We will follow Pascal's rules for formation of valid identifiers.

APPLICATION

**Lexical
Analyzer**
(*continued*)

3. *Arithmetic Operators*. We will only allow the following operators: $+$, $-$, $*$, and $/$. That is, we will allow real number arithmetic operators. All other symbols, except the assignment operator, will be considered invalid.

4. *Assignment Operator*. We allow the standard Pascal assignment operator, $:=$.

To further simplify the problem, we will require that tokens be separated by one or more blanks. Note that the scanner is capable only of isolating the tokens, and of determining if a given token is valid. It cannot determine if an expression is syntactically correct. In a real compiler these tokens would be passed to a syntax analyzer for the next stage of compilation.

Sets are particularly useful in this kind of character-by-character analysis of the units of a program.

Our analytical program uses two procedures and a function. The first procedure reads a single line from the input file and counts the number of characters on that line. The maximum size of an input line is 80 characters.

The second procedure isolates the tokens in the line read in by the first procedure. A token is any string of characters delimited by blanks. This second procedure skips over blanks until it encounters a nonblank character. It then copies all nonblank characters into an output string, called token, until it encounters another blank.

Finally, the function determines if the token isolated by the previous procedure is valid and returns a code indicating the type of token. The structure of the program is illustrated in Figure 9.4. The main program, with its procedures and functions, is listed below.

```
program Scanner (input, output);

{***********************************************
* Program to isolate symbols or tokens of a    *
* Pascal arithmetic assignment statement.      *
* The valid tokens of an assignment statement  *
* are:                                         *
*   Identifier      Valid Pascal identifier    *
*   Integer         String of digits 0..9      *
*   Arithmetic      +,-,*,/                     *
*    Operators                                  *
*   Assignment      :=                          *
*    Operator                                   *
***********************************************}
```

Figure 9.4 Hierarchical diagram for Scanner

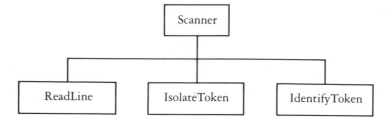

APPLICATION

Lexical Analyzer (*continued*)

```
const
    LineSize = 80;

type
    CodeLine = packed array [1..LineSize] of char;
    TokenType = (Identifier, Number,
                 Operator, Assignment, Error);

var
    SourceLine : CodeLine;
    Size : integer;
    Token : Codeline;
    Success : boolean;
    Location : integer;
    I : integer;

procedure ReadLine (var InputLine : Codeline;
                    var Length : integer);


    {*************************************
     * Procedure to input a line of code *
     *************************************}


    var
        I : integer;

    begin
        I := 1;
        while (not eoln) and (I <= LineSize) do
            begin
                read (InputLine[I]);
                I := I + 1
            end {of WHILE Loop};
```

APPLICATION

**Lexical
Analyzer**
(*continued*)

```
'if I > LineSize then
     Length := I-1
else
     Length := I-2;
readln
end {of PROCEDURE ReadLine};

procedure IsolateToken (var SourceLine, Token :CodeLine;
                        var Loc, Length :Integer;
                        var Found :boolean);


{*****************************
 * Procedure to isolate token *
 * in input line. All tokens  *
 * are separated by blanks.   *
 *****************************}

var
    I,J : integer;
    Finished : boolean;
begin
    {Initialize output string to blanks}

    for I := 1 to LineSize do
       Token[I] := ' ';

    {Locate first non-blank character starting at
     position Loc}

    I := Loc;
    Found := false;
    if I <= Length then
       begin
         {Skip blanks}

           while (not Found) and (I<=Length) do
              if SourceLine[I] <> ' ' then
                 Found := true
              else
                 I := I + 1;

           {If a non-blank character is found
             extract token}
```

APPLICATION

Lexical
Analyzer
(*continued*)

```
                      Loc := I;
                      Finished := false;
                      while not Finished and (I<=Length) do
                          if SourceLine[I] = ' ' then
                              Finished :=true
                          else
                              {Copy token into output string}

                              begin
                                  J := I - Loc + 1;
                                  Token[J] := SourceLine[I];
                                  I := I + 1
                              end
              end;
          Loc := I
   end {of PROCEDURE IsolateToken};

   function IdentifyToken (UnknownToken : CodeLine) :
                               TokenType;

   {***************************
   * Function to identify and *
   * validate a token.        *
   ***************************}

   var
      I : integer;

   begin
      I := 1;

      {Determine if token is an identifier}

      if UnknownToken[I] in ['A'..'Z'] then
        begin
          repeat
              I := I + 1
          until not(UnknownToken[I] in
                  ['A'..'Z','0'..'9']);
          if UnknownToken[I] = ' ' then
              IdentifyToken := Identifier
          else
              IdentifyToken := Error
        end
      else
```

APPLICATION

**Lexical
Analyzer**
(*continued*)

```
{Determine if token is an integer}

if UnknownToken[I] in ['0'..'9'] then
  begin
      repeat
         I := I +1
      until not(UnknownToken[I] in ['0'..'9']);
      if UnknownToken[I]=' ' then
         IdentifyToken := Number
      else
         IdentifyToken := Error
  end
else


  {Determine if token is an arithmetic operator}

  if UnknownToken[I] in ['+','-','*','/'] then
      if UnknownToken[I+1] = ' ' then
         IdentifyToken := Operator
      else
         IdentifyToken := Error
  else


      { Determine if token is an assignment
        operator}

  if UnknownToken[I] = ':' then
      begin
         I := I+ 1;
         if UnknownToken[I] <> '=' then
            IdentifyToken:= Error
         else
            if UnknownToken[I+1] = ' ' then
               IdentifyToken := Assignment
            else
               IdentifyToken := Error
      end
  else
      IdentifyToken := Error


end {of FUNCTION IdentifyToken};
```

APPLICATION

**Lexical
Analyzer**
(*continued*)

```
begin {Main Program}

    {Write Headings}
    writeln( 'TYPE OF TOKEN                TOKEN');
    writeln( '--------------                -----');
    writeln;

    {Process input file until there is no more data}

    while  not eof do
        begin
            ReadLine(SourceLine,Size);
            Location := 1;
            IsolateToken(SourceLine,Token,Location,Size,
                        Success);

            {Process input line as long as tokens can
             be extracted}

            while Success do
              begin
              case IdentifyToken(Token) of
                  Identifier : write ('Identifier           ');
                  Number     : write ('Integer              ');
                  Operator   : write ('Arithmetic Operator');
                  Assignment : write ('Assignment Operator');
                  Error      : write ('Illegal symbol       ')
              end {of CASE statement};

              {Print token}

              I := 1;
              while Token[I] <> ' ' do
                  begin
                      write (Token[I]);
                      I := I + 1
                  end;
              writeln;
              IsolateToken(SourceLine,Token,Location,Size,
                          Success);
            end {of WHILE success loop}
        end {of WHILE NOT eof loop}
end.
```

Given the input

SUM : = FIRST + SECOND / 5
                DIFFERENCE : + 3RD − SECOND2

APPLICATION

Lexical
Analyzer
(*continued*)

the program will produce the following output:

```
TYPE OF TOKEN                TOKEN
-------------                -----

Identifier                   SUM
Assignment Operator          :=
Identifier                   FIRST
Arithmetic Operator          +
Identifier                   SECOND
Arithmetic Operator          /
Integer                      5
Identifier                   DIFFERENCE
Illegal symbol               :+
Illegal symbol               3RD
Arithmetic Operator          -
Identifier                   SECOND2
```

9.6 COMMON ERRORS

One of the most common errors with sets involves an attempt to give the set a value as it is being defined. It is not unusual to see the following incorrect code:

```
var
    Operators : set of ['+', '-', '*', '/'];
```

What is desired here is to define a set, and then assign a variable of that set type the value $['+', '-', '*', '/']$. The definition and assignment must be done separately.

```
var
    Operators : set of char;
begin
    Operators := ['+', '-', '*', '/'];
```

A common, related error is one that is not an error with sets at all, but is instead an error with user-defined scalar types.

```
type
    Operators = ('+', '-', '*', '/');
    OpSet = set of Operators;
```

The problem here is the invalid definition of the enumerated type, Operators. The constants must be identifiers. They cannot be characters.

The failure to initialize a set before using it is yet another common error. When writing a loop that constructs a set consisting of all the characters on a line, do not forget to initialize the set to the null set first, as shown below:

```
Letters := [ ];
while not eoln do
   begin
      read(ch);
      Letters := Letters + [ch]
   end
```

Confusing a set with an *element* of that set is another common error. In the above lines of code, the statement:

```
Letters := Letters + [ch]
```

is correct. On the other hand,

```
Letters := Letters + ch
```

is incorrect.

9.7 CHAPTER REVIEW

A set is a collection of abstract objects. In mathematics, it is represented by curly braces containing a list of the objects that constitute the elements of the set. In Pascal, square brackets are used to represent sets. An example of a set in mathematics is:

$\{2,4,6,8\}$

In Pascal, the same set is represented as:

```
[2,4,6,8]
```

The above set consists of the positive even integers greater than 0 and less than 10. Although there are no restrictions on the elements of a set in mathematics, in Pascal the elements must be of the same base type. The base type of a set can be any scalar or subrange type. However, the number of values of the base type may be severely restricted by a particular compiler.

A **set** type can be declared as follows:

```
type
   settype = set of base type;
```

For example,

```
type
   Digits = set of 1..9;
var
   DigitSets : Digits;
```

First, we defined a data type, Digits, to consist of any set formed from the base type, 1..9. Then, we declared the variable DigitSets to be of that type; that is, DigitSets can be assigned values either of type Digits, or sets formed from the values 1..9.

A set variable can also be declared directly without using a type definition. The above declaration could have been made as:

```
var
   DigitSets : set of 1..9;
```

Set constructors are used to build constants of type **set** and assign these values to set variables. The general form of an assignment statement for sets is:

set identifier : = set constructor expression

The set constructor expression can be a set constant, a set identifier, or one or more operations on sets. The elements of a set in a set constructor expression can be enumerated, specified by subranges, specified by values of arithmetic expressions involving constants or variables, or can be specified by a combination of all of these techniques.

Operators for sets are defined in Table 9.1. The priorities of +, *, and −, when used as set operators, are the same as when these are used as arithmetic operators. Parentheses can be used in set expressions in the same manner as in arithmetic expressions.

Pascal provides five relational operators that can be used to check relationships between sets and the membership of an element in a set. The relational operators are defined in Table 9.2. All relational operators for sets produce boolean results. Relational expressions involving sets are often used to simplify complex boolean expressions.

**9.8
EXERCISES**

9.1. Fill in the blanks for each of the following:

(a) The objects that belong to a set are called its _____.

(b) The notation [ ] denotes the _____ or the _____ set.

(c) The set containing all possible values of the base type is known as the
_____ set.

(d) If the base type of a set contains the elements 1,2, then the sets that can
be formed from this base type are _____, _____, _____, _____, _____,
_____, _____, and _____.

(e) If the base type of a set contains 2 elements, then the number of distinct
sets that can be constructed from it is _____.

(f) The collection of all possible sets that can be constructed from a given
base type is known as the _____.

(g) The set union operator is_____.

(h) The set intersection operator is_____.

(i) The set operator(s) with a higher precedence than set difference is
(are)_____.

(j) The operator for set equality is _____.

(k) The operator to determine if a set is a subset of another set is_____.

(l) The operator to determine if an object is an element of a set is _____.

(m) The precedence of the relational operators for sets is the same as the
precedence for the relational operators for _____.

9.2. Answer each of the following true or false. If your answer is false, state
why.

(a) Set notation in Pascal is the same as in mathematics; that is, curly braces
are used to list the elements of a set.

(b) The null set is a subset of every set.

(c) In Pascal the base type of sets can be any other valid Pascal data type.

(d) The expression [2..1] is valid and is equivalent to [ ].

(e) The set [2,3,5] is identical to the set [2,5,3].

(f) If a and b are sets, then $a + b$ is the set of all values in a and in b.

(g) If a and b are sets, then $a - b$ is the set of all values in b but not in a.

(h) [1..2] * ['A'..'Z'] is a valid Pascal expression and is equal to the null set.

(i) The union of the null set with any other set always yields the other set as
a result.

(j) The relational operator, **in**, can be used interchangeably with the subset
operator.

(k) If a and b are sets, then $a > = b$ is true if every element of b is an element of a.

(l) Given that X is an element of the base type of sets a and b, then X **in** $a +$
b is equivalent to X **in** $(a + b)$.

(m) Given that a, b, and c are sets of the same base type, then $a - b * c$ is
equivalent to $a - (b * c)$.

(n) Set operations are often used to eliminate more complicated tests involving compound conditions on boolean expressions.

(o) Given that X is an element of the base type of sets a and b, then X **in** $(a$
$+ b)$ is equivalent to $(X$ **in** $a)$ **or** $(X$ **in** $b)$.

(p)   Given that X is an element of the base type of sets a and b, then X **in** $(a - b)$ is equivalent to $(X$ **in** $a)$ **and not** $(X$ **in** $b)$.

9.3. Describe the function(s) performed by each of the following Pascal statements:

(a) **type**
```
      LetterSet = set of char;
```

(b) **type**
```
      DaysOfWeek = (Sunday, Monday, Tuesday, Wednesday,
                    Thursday, Friday, Saturday);
      Week = set of DaysOfWeek;
```

(c) **var**
```
      Letters : set of char;
```

(d) **var**
```
      Letters : LetterSet;
```

(e) **var**
```
      Month : array[1..4] of Week;
```

(f) `Letters := [];`

(g) `Letters := ['A'..'Z'];`

(h) `Letters := Letters - ['A','E','I','O','U'];`

(i) **for** `I := 1` **to** `4` **do**
```
      Month[I] := [Sunday..Saturday];
```

(j) `Letters := [];`
```
    for I := 'A' to 'Z' do
      Letters := Letters + [I];
```

(k) `Numbers := [1..50];`
```
    for I := 1 to 50 do
      if I mod 2 = 0 then
        Numbers := Numbers - [I];
```

(l) `Numbers := [1..50];`
```
    for I := 1 to 25 do
      if Numbers * [2*I] <> [] then
        Numbers := Numbers - [2*I];
```

(m) **if** Week * [Sunday,Saturday] <> [] **then**
    writeln (' Weekend included')
  else
    writeln (' Weekend excluded');

(n) **if** [Sunday,Saturday] <= Week **then**
    writeln (' Weekend included')
  else
    writeln (' Weekend excluded');

(o) **if** Letter **in** ['A','E','I','O','U'] **then**
    writeln (' Vowel');

(p) **if** Ch **in** ['A'..'Z'] **then**
  repeat
    write (Ch);
    read (Ch)
  until not (Ch **in** ['A'..'Z','0'..'9']);

(q) Vowels := ['A','E','I','O','U'];
  if Ch **in** Vowels **then**
  case Ch **of**
    'A' : {code for 'A'};
    'E' : {code for 'E'};
    'I' : {code for 'I'};
    'O' : {code for 'O'};
    'U' : {code for 'U'};
  end {of CASE statement}
  else
    {Code for other values of Ch}

9.4. Rewrite the following statements using sets:

(a) (Ch >= 'A') **and** (Ch <= 'Z')

(b) (Day = Monday) **or** (Day = Wednesday)
  or (Day = Thursday)

(c) (Ch >= 'A') **and** (Ch <= 'Z') **or** (Ch >= '0')
  and (Ch <= '9')

(d) `(Number1 = 2)` **and** `(Number2 = 4)` **or** `(Number1 = 5)`
   and `(Number2 = 8)`

(e) `((Number1 >= 0)` **and** `(Number1 <= 9))` **and** `((Number2 >= 0)`
   and `(number2 <= 9))`

9.5. Assume that

```
W := []
X := [0]
Y := [1,2,3,4,5]
Z := [0,2,4,6,8]
```

Evaluate each of the following expressions:

(a) `X+Y-Z`

(b) `(X+Y)*(W+Z)`

(c) `W+X <= Z`

(d) `X <= Y-Z`

(e) `X <= Z-Y`

(f) `3 in (Y-X)`

9.6. Given the definitions:

type
```
   WeekDays = (Sunday, Monday, Tuesday, Wednesday,
                Thursday, Friday, Saturday);
   WeekSet = set of Weekdays;
```

var
```
   Day : Weekdays;
```

(a) Write a program that prints the values of any set of type WeekSet.
(b) Write an assignment statement to assign the appropriate values to the variables Week and Weekend.
(c) Write a boolean expression that determines whether a value of Day is a working day.

9.7. Write a program that reads two sentences, each terminated by a period, and prints a list of the letters that appear in the first sentence but not in the second.

9.8. A real estate agency wants to keep track of property descriptions as follows:

```
const
   NumberOfListings = 30;
type
   Descriptors = (CornerLot, NearSchools, NearShopping,
                  NearTransportation, ShadedLot);
   Property = set of Descriptors;
   Listings = array[1..NumberOfListings] of Property;
   Address = packed array[1..20] of char;
   AddressList = array[1..NumberofListings] of Address;
var
   PropAddr : AddressList;
   PropDescr : Listings;
   CustInterests : Property;
```

The input data are arranged as follows:

Columns	Description
1–20	Property Address
21–24	Descriptors (an X in the corresponding column indicates the presence of the corresponding descriptor)

For example, the data on a typical property might appear as:

37 Pleasant Street   xxx

This property is not a corner lot, is not near schools, is near shopping, is near transportation, and is on a shaded lot.

     You are to write a program that reads the list of currently active properties and their descriptors. It then reads a line representing the description of a property that a particular client would be interested in. Finally, it produces a list of all properties satisfying the client's requirements.

9.9. Modify the program of problem 8.8 to allow a client to specify desirable, as well as undesirable, descriptors. That is, a client should be able to specify the characteristics he would like to see in a property listing, as well as those he does not want to see. Your program should print a listing of all the properties that include all the desirable characteristics but exclude the undesirable ones. You may want to increase the list of possible descriptors.

9.10. Write a function that, given a set, returns the cardinality (number of elements) of the set.

9.11. One way to implement sets is to use boolean arrays. For example, sets with base type "1..7" can be represented by

array[1..7] of boolean;

By setting appropriate locations of such an array to true or false, it is possible to keep track of the elements of sets represented in this fashion. For example, the set [1,3,6] can be represented as:

true	false	true	false	false	true	false
1	2	3	4	5	6	7

Given the **type** definition:

const
   Maxsize = 10;
type
   BaseType = 1..Maxsize;
   ArraySet = **array**[BaseType] **of** boolean;

we can write a procedure for set union as follows:

procedure SetUnion (S1,S2 : ArraySet; **var** S3 : ArraySet);

```
{*************************************
* Procedure to compute the union of *
* sets S1 and S2 and store the      *
* result in S3.                     *
*************************************}

var
   I : BaseType;

begin
   for I := 1 to Maxsize do
      S3[I] := S1[I] or S2[I]
end {of PROCEDURE SetUnion};
```

Write Pascal procedures to implement set intersection and set difference for sets represented by boolean arrays.

9.12. We can implement the relational operators for sets by designing predicate functions. For example, the relational operator **in** can be implemented as:

```
function ElementOf( S : ArraySet; X : BaseType): boolean;

{********************************
* Function to check if X is an *
* element of set S.            *
********************************}

begin
    ElementOf := S[X]
end {of FUNCTION ElementOf};
```

Write Pascal functions to implement the relational operators ($=$, $<>$, $<=$, and $>=$) for sets represented by boolean arrays. Your functions should take two sets (boolean arrays) of the same type as input parameters, and should return a boolean value.

10. Records

10.1
THE CONCEPT
OF A RECORD

Arrays and sets consist of components of the same base type. However, a data structure that is able to store data of different types has many useful applications. For example, when working with an individual's payroll information we may need to store and manipulate the following variables:

```
Name : packed array[1..20] of char;
IDNumber : integer;
GrossPay : real;
```

It would be useful to group this information under a single identifier so that it could be manipulated as a single entity. In computer science, a structure that allows us to group and to manipulate different data types as a single entity is called a **record**. More formally, a record is a structure consisting of a fixed number of components, called **fields.** Unlike arrays and sets, the components of a record need not be of the same type. Also, unlike arrays, the components of a record each have their own identifier.

10.2
RECORD
DEFINITIONS

The payroll information above can be structured into a record as follows:

```
type
   PayrollRecord = record
      Name     : packed array[1..20] of char;
      IDNumber : integer;
      GrossPay : real
   end;
```

The reserved words **record** and **end** are used to bracket the definition. Once a record type has been defined it can be used to declare record variables:

```
var
   EmployeeInfo : PayrollRecord;
```

As with other structures, a record variable can be declared directly without first defining a named record type.

457

```
var
   EmployeeInfo : record
      Name     : packed array[1..20] of char;
      IDNumber : integer;
      GrossPay : real
   end;
```

In this case, however, variables of the same type as "Employee Info" cannot be declared elsewhere in the program. The use of type identifiers, such as "PayrollRecord," is often necessary when more than one variable of the same type is needed.

As another example of a record type, consider the representation of a date. We can think of it as a single record consisting of three fields: a user-defined variable for the month, and two integers—one for the day and one for the year.

```
type
   MonthType = (January, February, March, April, May,
                June, July, August, September, October,
                November, December);
   Date = record
      Month : MonthType;
      Day   : 1..31;
      Year  : integer
   end;

var
   Today, Birthday : Date;
```

The variables "Today" and "Birthday" are of type "Date," and each is capable of storing all the components of this structure, as illustrated in Figure 10.1. Any variable of type Date is allocated storage space for all the fields of Date; that is, the storage space for a user-defined type and for two integers.

The general form for a record type definition is:

```
type
   RecordType = record
      Field1 : Type1;
      Field2 : Type2;
            •
            •
            •
      Fieldn : Typen
   end;
```

Figure 10.1
Record variable of
type date

Month	Day	Year
November	11	1971

Figure 10.2 Syntax
diagram for **record**
declaration

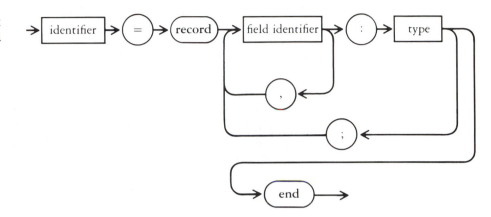

The syntax diagram for the declaration of a record is shown in Figure
10.2. The identifier "RecordType" is associated with the record
structure being defined. Each field is provided with its own identifier
and data type.

Here are some additional examples of record type definitions:

```
type
    PhoneDirectoryEntry = record
        Name : packed array[1..20] of char;
        Address : packed array[1..30] of char;
        PhoneNumber : packed array[1..8] of char
    end;

    Person = record
        Name           : packed array[1..20] of char;
        Sex            : (Male, Female);
        Age            : integer;
        MaritalStatus : (Single, Married, Divorced,
                         Widowed)
    end;

    Characteristics = (NearSchool, NearShopping,
                       NearTransportation, CornerLot,
                       ShadedLot);
    Listing = record
        Location : packed array[1..30] of char;
        YearBuilt      : 1800..1982;
```

```
        NumberOfRooms  :  1..20;
        Baths          :  1..6;
        Taxes          :  real;
        Construction   :  (Frame, AluminumSiding,
                           VinylSiding, Brick,
                           Stone, Masonry);
        Descriptors    :  set of Characteristics;
        LotSize        :  real;
        Price          :  real
    end;
```

The record type "PhoneDirectoryEntry" has three fields. Each field is a character string of different length. The record type "Person" has four fields. Note that the type of a user-defined field can be specified in the record definition, as with fields "Sex" and "Marital-Status" of the record type "Person." A user-defined field can also be specified as a named type, as we did with the field "Month" of the record type "Date." The record type "Listing" describes the listing of a home by a realtor. It consists of nine fields. In particular, note the field "Descriptors," which is a set. Fields of records are not restricted to scalar types. As we shall see later, they can even be records themselves.

10.3 ASSIGNMENT OF VALUES TO RECORDS

Given the above record type definitions, we can now declare record variables. For example, variables of type "Person" can be declared as:

```
var
    Myself, Yourself : Person;
```

Fields of a record are the components of a record variable and are referenced by specifying the variable name, followed by the field identifier, separated by a period. Such expressions are called **field designators.** A field designator names a location corresponding to the designated component of the record variable. The assignment statements

```
Myself.Name := 'Kenneth Programmer  ';
Myself.Sex := Male;
Myself.Age := 25;
Myself.MaritalStatus := Single
```

assign values to the fields, also called components, of the record My-self. These assignment statements are similar to statements used to assign values to array variables. The statement

```
Numbers[15] := 30
```

assigns a value of 30 to the fifteenth component of an integer array, Numbers. Contrast this to the assignment statement

```
Myself.Age := 25
```

which assigns the value 25 to the "Age" component of the record My-self. The record identifier Myself corresponds to the array identifier Numbers, and the field identifier Age corresponds to the array index 15. There is, however, a major difference between the way we may designate a component of a record and a component of an array. The index of an array can be computed as the program executes. That is, we can use index variables, whose values can change as the program executes, to designate components of arrays. We cannot do this with the components of records. The fields of a record that a program will access at any time must be specified when the program is written.

Field designators can be used like any other identifiers. Thus,

```
writeln (Myself.Name)
```

prints:

Kenneth Programmer

The expression

```
read (Yourself.Age)
```

reads a value for the field Age of the record variable Yourself from the standard input file. Finally, the expression

```
Difference := Myself.Age - Yourself.Age
```

computes the difference between the two ages.

A field may itself be an array, and hence its components may be subscripted. For example, to read the value of the field "Name," we have to use the loop

```
for i := 1 to 20 do
   read (Myself.Name[i])
```

Just as with arrays, the value of a complete record variable can be assigned to another record variable of the same type by using a single assignment statement. The assignment statement

```
Yourself := Myself
```

is equivalent to:

```
Yourself.Name := Myself.Name;
Yourself.Sex := Myself.Sex;
Yourself.Age := Myself.Age;
Yourself.MaritalStatus := Myself.MaritalStatus
```

To read or write a record may require fairly lengthy procedures, depending on the number and type of fields involved. The procedure in Example 10.1 reads a record of type Person.

EXAMPLE 10.1
Procedure to
Read a Record

```
procedure ReadPerson (var Per : Person);

{*****************************
* Procedure to read a record *
* of type Person.            *
*****************************}

var
   i : integer;
   Ch : char;

begin
   {Read the name}

   for i := 1 to 20 do
      read (Per.Name[i]);

   {Read the sex}

   read (Ch);
   if Ch = 'm' then
      Per.Sex := Male
   else
      Per.Sex := Female;

   {Read the age}
```

EXAMPLE 10.1
Procedure to
Read a Record
(*continued*)

```
    read (Per.Age);

    {Read the marital status}

    read (Ch);
    if Ch in ['s', 'm', 'd', 'w'] then
        case Ch of
            's' : Per.MaritalStatus := Single;
            'm' : Per.MaritalStatus := Married;
            'd' : Per.MaritalStatus := Divorced;
            'w' : Per.MaritalStatus := Widowed
        end {of Case statement}
    else
        writeln (' Error in marital status code');
    readln;
end {of procedure ReadPerson};
```

We are, of course, assuming that the records in the input file appear as

```
Kenneth Programmer  m25s
Martha Algorithm       f  28m
    .
    .
    .
```

where the name appears in the first twenty columns, the sex is indicated as 'm' for male and 'f' for female in column 21, the age is an integer in columns 22–23, and the marital status is indicated by the appropriate character in column 24.

Here is another example of the use of records. We can define a rational number as the following record:

```
type
    Fraction = record
        Numerator, Denominator : integer
    end;
```

Using this record structure for rational numbers, we can easily implement the usual mathematical operations. We first write a procedure to input a rational number from the standard input file, where the number consists of two integers—one for the numerator and the other for the denominator. Next, we write procedures that multiply and add rational numbers. Procedures to perform the operations of subtraction and division, as well as reducing a rational number to its lowest terms, are also easy to develop and are left as an exercise. Records are, of course, not necessary in the representation of rational numbers. Such a representation, however, has certain advantages. It makes the program easier to read and allows us, in some cases, to deal with a rational number as a single entity. Note, in Example 10.2, how we pass complete records to procedures and how, by using the appropriate fields, we can work with the numerators and denominators independently.

EXAMPLE 10.2 Procedures to Perform Rational-Number Arithmetic

```pascal
program Rationals (input,output);

{*******************************
* Program to perform rational *
* number arithmetic.          *
*******************************}

type
   Fraction = record
      Numerator, Denominator : integer;
   end;

var
   a,b,c :Fraction;

procedure ReadFraction(var x :Fraction);

   {********************************
   * Procedure to read a fraction. *
   ********************************}

   begin
      read (x.Numerator,x.Denominator);
   end {of procedure ReadFraction};

procedure MultiplyFractions( x,y :Fraction;
                             var Product :Fraction);

   {*******************************************
   * Procedure to multiply two fractions     *
   * x and y and return the fraction         *
   * Product as a result.                    *
   *******************************************}
```

**EXAMPLE 10.2
Procedures to
Perform Ra-
tional-Number
Arithmetic**
(*continued*)

```
begin
    Product.Numerator := x.Numerator * y.Numerator;
    Product.Denominator := x.Denominator * y.Denominator
end {of procedure MultiplyFractions};

procedure AddFractions (x,y : Fraction;
                        var Sum :Fraction);

    {************************************
    * Procedure to add two fractions    *
    * x and y and return the fraction   *
    * Sum as a result.                  *
    ************************************}

    begin
        Sum.Numerator := x.Numerator*y.Denominator +
            y.Numerator*x.Denominator;
        Sum.Denominator := x.Denominator*y.Denominator
    end {of procedure AddFractions};

begin {MAIN Program}

    ReadFraction(a);
    readln;
    ReadFraction(b);
    readln;
    MultiplyFractions(a,b,c);
    writeln (a.Numerator :1,'/',a.Denominator :1,' * '
            ,b.Numerator :1,'/',b.Denominator :1,' = '
            ,c.Numerator :1,'/',c.Denominator :1);
    AddFractions(a,b,c);
    writeln (a.Numerator :1,'/',a.Denominator :1,' + '
            ,b.Numerator :1,'/',b.Denominator :1,' = '
            ,c.Numerator :1,'/',c.Denominator :1);
end{of program}.
```

Given the input

```
1   2
1   3
```

the output will be:

```
1/2 * 1/3 = 1/6
1/2 + 1/3 = 5/6
```

Arrays of Records

A common structure in Pascal programs is an array of records. For example, given our earlier definition of the record type, Listing, we can now declare the variable "HousesFor Sale" as:

```
var
    HousesForSale : array[1..20] of Listing;
```

The variable HousesForSale is an array whose components are records of type Listings. Just as with the array variables we studied earlier, to reference any value stored in this array, it is necessary to specify the array component by giving its subscript. Since each array element is a record, we must also specify the field identifier in order to reference a particular field. Thus, to print the value of the field "Location" of the fifth element of the array HousesForSale we write:

```
writeln (HousesForSale[5].Location)
```

To read the locations of all 20 houses from the input file, assuming the proper arrangement of data, we write:

```
for i := 1 to 20 do
   begin
      for j := 1 to 30 do
         read (HousesForSale[i].Location[j]);
      readln
   end
```

The index of the outer loop, i, counts the houses. The index of the inner loop, j, counts the number of characters specifying the location of each house.

The with Statement

When we assigned values to the fields of the record variable Myself, you probably noticed the verbosity of the statements. We had to write the identifier Myself over and over again. This is certainly tedious. It would be nice to be able to write the record identifier once and then to manipulate the field identifiers without having to repeat the record identifier each time. Pascal provides us with just this capability: the **with . . . do** statement. By using the **with** statement we can simplify the assignment statements

```
Myself.Name := 'Kenneth Programmer   ';
Myself.Sex := Male;
Myself.Age := 25;
Myself.MaritalStatus := Single;
```

to:

```
with Myself do
   begin
      Name := 'Kenneth Programmer  ';
      Sex := Male;
      Age := 25;
      MaritalStatus := Single
   end
```

By writing the record identifier Myself between the reserved words **with** and **do**, we specify that the scope of the record variable Myself is the compound statement that follows and that the field identifiers of the record variable can be used as if they were simple variable identifiers. The general form of the **with** statement is:

```
with Record Identifier do
   Statement
```

The statement that is the body of the **with** statement can be a compound statement, as was just illustrated. Within the statement, any field of the record variable can be referenced wihout specifying the record identifier.

The **with** statement could have been used in the procedure ReadPerson (illustrated in Example 10.1) not only to save typing, but also to make it more readable. We do this in Example 10.3.

EXAMPLE 10.3 Procedure to Read a Record Using the with Statement

```
procedure ReadPerson (var Per : Person);

{*****************************
* Procedure to read a record *
* of type Person.            *
*****************************}

var
   i : integer;
   Ch : char;
begin
   with Per do
      begin
         {Read the name}

         for i := 1 to 20 do
            read (Name[i]);
```

EXAMPLE 10.3
Procedure to
Read a Record
Using the with
Statement
(*continued*)

```
          {Read the sex}

          read(Ch);
          if Ch = 'm' then
             Sex := Male
          else
             Sex := Female;

          {Read the age}

          read (Age);

          {Read the marital status}

          read (Ch);
          if Ch in ['s', 'm', 'd', 'w'] then
             case Ch of
                's' : MaritalStatus := Single;
                'm' : MaritalStatus := Married;
                'd' : MaritalStatus := Divorced;
                'w' : MaritalStatus := Widowed
             end {of Case statement}
          else
             writeln (' Error in marital status code')
       end {of With Statement};
    readln;
end {of procedure ReadPerson};
```

When using the **with** statement with arrays of records, care must be exercised to place the **with** in the correct position. Consider Example 10.4, which reads an unknown number of records into an array.

EXAMPLE 10.4
Program to
Read and Print
an Array of
Records

```
program ReadRec (input,output);

{*********************************************
* Program to illustrate the use of          *
* WITH statements with arrays of records.   *
*********************************************}

const
   CustNumber = 100;
```

**EXAMPLE 10.4
Program to
Read and Print
an Array of
Records**
(*continued*)

```
type
    Customer = record
        AccountNumber : integer;
        Name : packed array [1..20] of char;
        Address :packed array [1..30] of char;
        Balance : real
    end;
var
    CustList : array[1..CustNumber] of Customer;
    i, j, Count : integer;

begin
    i := 1;
    while not eof do
        begin
            with CustList[i] do
                begin
                    read (AccountNumber);

                    {Read Name}
                    for j := 1 to 20 do
                        read (Name[j]);

                    {Read Address}
                    for j := 1 to 30 do
                        read (Address[j]);

                    read (Balance);
                    readln
                end {of With Statement};
            i := i + 1
        end {of while loop};
    Count := i-1;
    for i := 1 to Count do
        with CustList[i] do
            writeln (AccountNumber :4,Name :21,
                    Address :31,Balance :6:2);
end {of program}.
```

Given the input

011Charles River	755 Commonwealth Ave Boston MA	3.75
013Bertha Crump	123 Fourth Street Peru IND	13.56
019Nick Sing	111 Cummington St Swamp NH	0.50

**EXAMPLE 10.4
Program to
Read and Print
an Array of
Records**
(*continued*)

the program will produce the desired output:

```
11 Charles River      755 Commonwealth Ave Boston MA   3.75

13 Bertha Crump        123 Fourth Street Peru IND      13.56

19 Nick Sing           111 Cummington St Swamp NH       0.50
```

Because we want to manipulate different elements of the array "CustList" each time we change the value of the index *i*, the **with** statement must be nested inside the **while . . . do** loop for reading and inside the **for** loop for printing. If we moved the **with** statement out of the **while . . . do** loop, as follows:

```
i := 1;
with CustList[i] do
   begin
      while not eof do
         begin
            read (AccountNumber);

            {Read Name}
            for j := 1 to 20 do
               read (Name[j]);

            {Read Address}
            for j := 1 to 30 do
               read (Address[j]);

            read (Balance);
            readln;
            i := i + 1
         end {of while loop}
   end {of With statement};
Count := i-1;
```

the program would produce *incorrect* results. Even though the index *i* is changed within the **while . . . do** statement, and thus also within the **with** statement, the array element into which we are reading the data remains CustList[1].

Similarly, if we rearrange the **for** loop, which prints the array, so that the **with** statement is no longer nested inside the **for** statement:

```
with CustList[i] do
   for i := 1 to Count do
      writeln (AccountNumber :4,Name :21,
                  Address :31,Balance :6:2);
```

the loop will not function as intended. Here again, the value of *i* would remain the same for CustList[i].

The **with** statement can also be used with more than one record. The most general form of the **with** statement is shown in the syntax diagram of Figure 10.3. The syntax diagram indicates that more than one record identifier can be listed between the reserved words **with** and **do**. Thus, a statement of the form:

```
with var1,var2,var3 do
   statement
```

is permitted in Pascal. This statement is equivalent to:

```
with var1 do
   with var2 do
      with var3 do
         statement
```

Given the following type definitions and variable declarations,

```
type
   VarType1 = record
      a1 : integer;
      b1 : real
   end;

   VarType2 = record
      a2 : integer;
      b2 : boolean;
      c2 : real
   end;
```

Figure 10.3 Syntax diagram for **with** statement

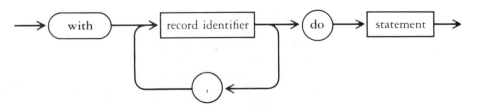

```
var
   x : VarType1;
   y : VarType2;
```

the following **with** statement can be written:

```
with x,y do
   begin
      b1 := c2;
      b2 := true;
      a1 := a2 + 5
   end
```

This statement is short for:

```
with x do
   with y do
      begin
         a1 := c2;
         b2 := true;
         a1 := a2 + 5
      end
```

Since all fields have distinct identifiers, there is no ambiguity in the above **with** statements. However, if the records have fields with the same identifiers, the use of more than one record variable in a **with** statement could lead to errors.

As an example of such an *improper* use of **with**, consider Example 10.5, a modification of the MultiplyFractions procedure we wrote earlier.

EXAMPLE 10.5 Incorrect Use of with Statement

```
procedure MultiplyFractions( x,y :Fraction;
                             var Product :Fraction);

{***************************************
 * Procedure to illustrate the         *
 * INCORRECT use of the WITH statement *
 ***************************************}

begin
   with Product, x, y do
      begin
         Numerator := Numerator * Numerator;
         Denominator := Denominator * Denominator
      end
end {of procedure MultiplyFractions};
```

EXAMPLE 10.5
Incorrect Use
of with
Statement
(*continued*)

Since there are three records with the same field identifiers, Numerator and Denominator, how are we to tell which record variable is associated with which field identifier? We, of course, cannot. The compiler, on the other hand, has no difficulty in making a choice. The choice, in this case, is not what we had in mind when we wrote the procedure. Using Pascal's scope rules, we learn the compiler will associate the field identifiers with the last record listed. Thus, in the above example, the identifiers Numerator and Denominator will be associated with the record y. As a result, the procedure, as written, will yield incorrect results.

The **with** statement should always be used with care, especially with multiple record variables. To correct Example 10.5, you have to decide which of the record variables is to be used with the **with** statement and write out the others as complete field designators. If you decide to use the **with** statement for Product, for example, then you can write the procedure as in Example 10.6.

EXAMPLE 10.6
Correct Use
of with
Statement

```
procedure MultiplyFractions( x,y :Fraction;
                             var Product :Fraction);

{***************************************
 * Procedure to illustrate the         *
 * correct use of the WITH statement   *
 ***************************************}

begin
   with Product do
      begin
         Numerator := x.Numerator * y.Numerator;
         Denominator := x.Denominator * y.Denominator
      end
end {of procedure MultiplyFractions};
```

SELF-TEST 1

1. Write definitions for records to represent the following data:

(a) "EmployeeRecord" has fields for name, id number, gross pay, and net pay.

(b) "TeamRecord" has fields for team name, number of games played, number of games won, number of games lost, number of games tied, and percentage of games won.

(c) "BankAccount" has fields for account number, owner's name, owner's address, current balance, and year-to-date interest accumulated.

(d) "PhoneNumber" has fields for area code, prefix, and number.

2. Consider the following definitions and declarations and state which are valid and which are invalid. Correct the invalid ones.

(a)
```
type
   Rec = record
      Field1 : integer;
      Field2 : integer;
   end;
```

(b)
```
type
   Rec : record
      Field1 : integer;
      Field2 : integer;
   end;
```

(c)
```
type
   Rec = record
      Rec     : integer;
      Field2 : integer;
   end;
```

(d)
```
type
   Rec = record
      Field1 : integer;
      Field1 : integer;
   end;
```

3. Consider the following definitions and declarations:

```
type
   Automobile = record
      Color : packed array[1..10] of char;
      Price : real;
      NumberofCylinders : integer;
      CarType    : (Sedan, HardTop, Convertible);
   end;
var
   CarWanted : Automobile;
   CarsForSale : array[1..30] of Automobile;
```

Which of the following are valid references to fields of records? If a reference is not valid, state why.

(a) `read(CarWanted.CarType)`

(b) `with CarWanted do`
        `read(Price)`

(c) `CarWanted := CarsForSale[1]`

(d) `writeln(CarWanted.Color)`

(e) `with CarWanted, CarsForSale[i] do`
        `writeln(NumberOfCylinders)`

(f) **with** CarWanted **do**
    if Price > CarsForSale[i].Price **then**
      writeln (CarsForSale[i].Color)

Answers

1. (a) EmployeeRecord = **record**
      Name : **packed array**[1..20] **of** char;
      IdNumber : integer;
      GrossPay, NetPay : real
    end;

   (b) TeamRecord = **record**
      Name : **packed array**[1..10] **of** char;
      GamesPlayed , GamesWon, GamesLost,
        GamesTied : integer;
      Percentage : real
    end;

   (c) BankAccount = **record**
      AccountNumber : integer;
      Owner : **packed array**[1..20] **of** char;
      Address : **packed array**[1..20] **of** char;
      Balance, YearToDateInterest : real
    end;

   (d) PhoneNumber = **record**
      AreaCode, Prefix, Number : integer
    end;

2. (a) Valid   (b) Not valid.

                                     type
                                       Rec = **record**
                                           Field1 : integer;
                                         Field2 : integer
                                      end;

    (c) Valid   (d) Not valid.

                                       type
                                         Rec = **record**
                                           Field1 : integer;
                                         Field2 : integer
                                    end;

3. (a) Not valid. User-defined types cannot be printed.   (b) Valid
(c) Valid   (d) Valid   (e) Not valid. Cannot determine the record of
"NumberOfCylinders."   (f) Valid

**10.4
NESTED
RECORDS**

The syntax of a record in Pascal does not exclude a record from becoming a field of another record. Consider the following type definitions:

```
type
   Deductions = record
      FedTax : real;
      StateTax : real;
      SocSec : real
   end;

   EmplRecord = record
      Name : packed array[1..20] of char;
      IDNumber : integer;
      GrossPay : real;
      Taxes : Deductions;
      NetPay : real
   end;

var
   TotDed : Deductions;
   Employee : EmplRecord;
```

The variable "Employee" is a record with five fields. The field "Taxes" is also a record with its own fields. It is a **subrecord** of Employee. In order to access any field of Taxes, we must specify all the variables involved. To assign values to all the fields of Employee, we write:

```
Employee.Name := 'Sam Lipp             ';
Employee.IDNumber := 123456;
Employee.GrossPay := 3132.50;
Employee.Taxes.FedTax := 650.75;
Employee.Taxes.StateTax := 139.17;
Employee.Taxes.SocSec := 133.55;
Employee.NetPay := 2794.03
```

A field of a subrecord of Employee is referenced by field selectors involving two record identifiers. The field selector

```
Employee.Taxes.FedTax
```

references the field "FedTax" of the subrecord "Employee.Taxes." Note that to access a field such as "GrossPay," only one record identifier is used because no subrecords are involved. The field selector

`Employee.Taxes`

references a record of type "Deductions," and hence can be assigned any value of that type. The assignment

`Employee.Taxes := TotDed`

is permitted because "TotDed" is of type Deductions. We assume, of course, that TotDed is defined.

We can use **with** statements with nested records. The following blocks of code using **with** statements are all equivalent to the above assignment statements.

```
with Employee do
   begin
      Name := 'Sam Lipp              ';
      IDNumber := 123456;
      GrossPay := 3132.50;
      Taxes.FedTax := 650.75;
      Taxes.StateTax := 139.17;
      Taxes.SocSec := 133.55;
      NetPay := 2794.03
   end;

with Employee, Taxes do
   begin
      Name := 'Sam Lipp              ';
      IDNumber := 123456;
      GrossPay := 3132.50;
      FedTax := 650.75;
      StateTax := 139.17;
      SocSec := 133.55;
      NetPay := 2794.03
   end;
```

The form you use should emphasize the program's readability regardless of the amount of typing you have to do. As an illustration of nested records, let us look at Example 10.7, a procedure to print an employee's record.

EXAMPLE 10.7 Procedure to Print a Nested Record

```
procedure PrintRecord (var Worker : EmplRecord );

{********************************************
 * Procedure to print an employee record. *
 ********************************************}
```

**EXAMPLE 10.7
Procedure to
Print a Nested
Record**
(*continued*)

```
begin
   with Worker do
      begin
         writeln (' Name :', Name :21);
         writeln (' ID Number :', IDNumber :7);
         writeln (' Gross Pay :', Grosspay :8:2);
         with Taxes do
            begin
               writeln (' Federal Taxes :', FedTax : 8:2);
               writeln (' State Taxes :', StateTax : 8:2);
               writeln (' Soc. Sec. Taxes :', SocSec :8:2)
            end {of With Taxes};
         writeln (' Net Pay :', NetPay :8:2)
      end {of With Worker}
end {of procedure PrintRecord};
```

This procedure illustrates yet another way we can use **with** statements with nested records.

**10.5
VARIANT
RECORDS**

Thus far, each record we have considered has had only fixed fields. That is, once we defined a record type to consist of a number of fields of various types, *all* variables of that record type contained all of those fields. Sometimes is it useful to have records that contain only *some* identical fields. That is, sometimes we may wish to consider two record variables to be of the same record type, even though their structures may differ in some ways, such as having a different number of fields, possibly of different types. To illustrate this, consider again the record Person, which we defined earlier:

```
type
   Status = (Single, Married, Divorced, Widowed);
   Person = record
      Name            : packed array[1..20] of char;
      Sex             : (Male, Female);
      Age             : integer;
      case MaritalStatus : Status of
         Single   : ( );
         Married  : ( SpouseName : packed array[1..20]
                                       of char;
                      SpouseAge   : integer);
         Divorced : ( DivDate : packed array [1..9]
                                    of char);
         Widowed  : ( ExSpName : packed array[1..20]
                                    of char)
   end {of Person Record};
```

In this definition we have made the existence of some fields contingent on the value of another field. All persons have some information in common: Name, Sex, Age, and MaritalStatus. However, depending on the value of MaritalStatus, we see that the remaining information is different. Single persons have no additional information. Married individuals have the spouse's name and age recorded. Divorced individuals have the date of divorce, and widowed persons the name of the former spouse. A record that permits such variations in its structure is known as a **variant record.**

Let us examine the above variant record type definition more closely. The definition consists of two parts: the **fixed part** and the **variant part.** The fixed or invariant part, if it exists, must precede the variant part. In this example, it consists of all the fields listed up to the reserved word **case:** Name, Sex, and Age. The field MaritalStatus is called the **tag field.** Although, in this example, the tag field is an enumerated, user-defined type, it can be any scalar type except real. The tag field is an actual field of the record and is used to store values. It is a **fixed field.**

Following the reserved word **of,** we have a list of the **variant field** declarations, the variant part of the record. The declaration of each variant field consists of a constant of the same type as the tag field, followed by a colon, followed by a list of field declarations in parentheses. The list of field declarations can be empty, signifying that the variant record does not need any additional fields other than those listed in the fixed part. In our example, this occurs when the tag field "MaritalStatus" has a value of Single.

In variant records, the field identifiers must be distinct. The same field identifier cannot occur in two field lists of the variant part, or in both the fixed and variant parts. A record definition can have only one variant part. However, variant parts may be nested; that is, a variant part may itself contain variants. Note that a single reserved word **end** terminates both the variant part and the record definition.

A variable declared to be of the type of a variant record always must contain all the fixed fields, including the tag field. Thus, given the declaration:

```
var
    Myself : Person;
```

references to Myself.Name, Myself.Sex, Myself.Age, and Myself.MaritalStatus are always valid. On the other hand, which variant field can be referenced depends on the value of the tag field. Given the following assignment to the tag field:

```
Myself.MaritalStatus := Married
```

the fields SpouseName and SpouseAge, associated with the tag field value Married, are now accessible, and it is possible to assign values to them. The assignments

```
Myself.SpouseName := 'Dianne Programmer   ';
Myself.SpouseAge := 22
```

are now valid. It is, however, an error to refer to a variant field not associated with the current value of the tag field. Therefore, the assignments

```
Myself.DivDate := '11-Sep-82'
```

and

```
Myself.ExSpName := 'Barbara Programmer   '
```

are *not valid*, because neither of the fields DivDate or ExSpName exists at this time. The **case** statement is used to avoid such errors. The use of this procedure is illustrated in Example 10.8, which prints a record of type Person.

**EXAMPLE 10.8
Procedure to
Print a Variant
Record**

```
procedure WriteVariant( var Per : Person);
{*********************************
* Procedure to write a record of *
* type Person  including the     *
* variant part.                  *
*********************************}

begin
   with Per do
     begin
        {print the fixed part}

        writeln (' Name : ',Name);
        if Sex = Male then
           writeln (' Sex : Male')
        else
           writeln (' Sex : Female');
        writeln (' Age : ',Age :4);

        {print the tag field}
```

EXAMPLE 10.8
Procedure to
Print a Variant
Record
(*continued*)

```
write (' Marital Status : ');
case MaritalStatus of
    Single : writeln (' Single ');
    Married : writeln (' Married ');
    Divorced : writeln (' Divorced ');
    Widowed : writeln (' Widowed ')
end {of Case Statement};

{print the variant part}

case MaritalStatus of
    Single   : ;
    Married  : begin
                    writeln (' Spouse Name :',
                            SpouseName);
                    writeln (' Spouse Age : ',
                            SpouseAge :4)
              end;
    Divorced : writeln ('Divorce Date : DivDate);
    Widowed  : writeln (' Ex-Spouse Name ',
                        ExSpName)
    end {of Case statement}
  end {of With statement}
end {of procedure WriteVariant};
```

We could have used a single **case** statement to print both the tag field and the variant part, but for clarity we separated the task into two **case** statements.

The variant selector in a variant record looks like the **case** control statement. The similarity, however, is only superficial. The case list of a **case** statement describes various actions to be taken that depend on the case label. The field list of the variant part of a record defines the identifiers and the types of the components that correspond to a particular value of the tag field.

Although we stressed the dependence of the variant fields on the value of the tag field, it turns out that the tag field in a variant record is actually optional. It is possible in Pascal to have variant records without tag fields. Although, when such records are defined, they must still contain the tag *type*. The record

```
type
    Alpha = 'A'..'C';
```

```
     VarRecExample = record
       Field1 : packed array[1..20] of char;
       case Alpha of
          'A' : (FieldA : boolean);
          'B' : (FieldB : integer);
          'C' : (FieldC : real)
     end;

var
   SampleRec : VarRecExample;
```

is an example of such a record. In this record, any of the variant fields
can be accessed at any time. However, once a particular variant is
used, any reference to another variant may make any values stored in
the first variant inaccessible. For example, given the following sequence of assignment statements:

```
SampleRec.FieldA := true;
SampleRec.FieldB := 2
```

the statement:

```
writeln (SampleRec.FieldA)
```

may lead to an error because the last variant referenced was variant
B, and variant *A* is, therefore, no longer defined.

Variant records without tag fields are difficult to use. You
should define all your variant records with tag fields, at least until
you find a situation where the tag field clearly is superfluous.

SELF-TEST 2   1. Consider the following definitions and declarations, and state
which are valid and which are not valid. Correct the ones that are not
valid.

(a)
```
type
   Rec = record
      Field1 : record
         Rec : integer;
         Field2 : real
      end;
      Field3 : char
   end;
```

(b)
```
type
   Rec = record
      Field1 : record
         Field1 : Rec;
         Field2 : real
      end;
      Field2 : char
   end;
```

(c)
```
type
    Num = 1..3;
    Rec = record
        Field1 : real
        case Field2 : Num of
            1 : (Field1 : char);
            2 : ( );
            3 : (Field4,Rec: char)
    end;
```

(d)
```
type
    Num = 1..3;
    Rec = record
        Field1 : real;
        case Field2: Num of
            1 : (Field3: char);
            2 : ( );
            2 : (Field4: boolean)
    end;
```

2. Consider the following definitions and declarations.

```
type
    String = packed array[1..20] of char;
    Date    = record
        Day : 1..31;
        Month : (jan, feb, mar, apr, may, jun,
                 jul, aug, sep, oct, nov, dec);
        Year  : 1900..2000
    end;

    Student = record
        Name : record
                FirstName : String;
                LastName  : String
            end;
        DateOfBirth : Date;
        Sex : (male, female);
        Id  : integer
    end;

var
    Person : Student;
    ClassList : array[1..30] of Student;
    Today : Date;
```

Which of the following are valid references to fields of records? If a reference is not valid state why.

(a) `read(Person.DateOfBirth.Day)` (b) `with Person, Name do`
                                       `writeln(LastName)`

(c) `Today := Person.DateOfBirth`   (d) `with ClassList[i] do`
                                       `DateOfBirth := Today`

(e) **with** ClassList[i] **do**
       writeln(Name)

(f) **with** Person **do**
       with Date **do**
          Month := feb

3. Define a variant record structure that could be used to store the information about a geometric figure. The record should store the shape (square, triangle, rectangle, or circle) and the appropriate dimensions.

Answers

1. (a) Valid   (b) Not valid   (c) Not valid.

```
type
   Num = 1..3;
   Rec = record
      Field1 : real;
      case Field2: Num of
         1 : (Field3 : char);
         2 : ( );
         3 : (Field4,Rec: char)
      end;
```

(d) Valid

2. (a) Valid   (b) Valid   (c) Valid   (d) Valid   (e) Not valid. Name is a record and cannot be used as a parameter in a writeln procedure.   (f) Not valid. Date is not a field of record Person.

3.
```
type
   ShapeName = (square,triangle,rectangle,circle);
   Figure = record
      case Shape : ShapeName of
         Square : (Side : real);
         Triangle : (Side1, Side2, Side3 : real);
         Rectangle : (Length, Width : real);
         Circle : (Radius : real)
      end;
```

One of the most common uses of computers is to prepare reports. We will now examine two such applications. The first prints a grade report for a class. The second prints the monthly year-to-date sales report for a company.

APPLICATION

Student Grade Report

We will write a Pascal program that prints a grade report based on the contents of a file that consists of student grade records. Each student record consists of the following fields:

APPLICATION

Student Grade Report (*continued*)

1. Student Last Name (Col 1–20)
2. Student First Name (Col 21–30)
3. Five programming assignment grades (Col 31–33, 35–37, 39–41, etc.)
4. A midterm examination grade (Col 50–52)
5. A final examination grade (Col 55–57)

The program will print the grade report in a clean, readable format. It will also compute the final course average for each student and print that as part of the final grade report. The final average will be calculated from the following formula:

1. The programming assignments are 50% of the final average.
2. The midterm is 20% of the final average.
3. The final is 30% of the final average.

Finally, the program will assign letter grades to each student based on the following average scores:

A   average $>= 90$
B $80 <=$ average < 90
C $70 <=$ average < 80
D $60 <=$ average < 70
F   average < 60

For example, if the input field contains the following records:

Jones	John	065	086	090	100	095	085	076
Coboller	Hack	095	095	070	100	055	044	080
Fortran	Fred	100	088	098	060	090	097	069
Pascal	Blaise	100	090	098	100	100	095	090

then the output of the program should look something like this:

Name		Programming Grades					Midterm	Final	Average	Grade
		1	2	3	4	5				
Jones	John	65	86	90	100	95	85	76	83.4	B
Coboller	Hack	95	95	70	100	55	44	80	74.3	C
Fortran	Fred	100	88	98	60	90	97	69	83.7	B
Pascal	Blaise	100	90	98	100	100	95	90	94.8	A

We can subdivide the task into smaller pieces. The program will need to print headings, read the record of a student, compute the average grade of that student, determine the student's letter grade, and output the result. This suggests the modular structure shown in Figure 10.4.

The five procedures and main program can now be coded. Note how we reformat the name so as to eliminate the spaces and insert a comma between the last and first names.

```
program GradeReport (input,output);
{**********************************
* Program to print course grades, *
* compute final course averages,   *
* assign letter grades to these    *
* averages, and print out this     *
* information.                     *
**********************************}
const
    NumOfProg = 5; {There are five programming
                             assignments}

type
    LongString  = packed array[1..20] of char;
    ShortString = packed array[1..10] of char;
    ProgList    = array[1..NumOfProg] of integer;
    StudGrades = record
       LastName   : LongString;
       FirstName  : ShortString;
       Programs   : ProgList;
       Midterm    : integer;
       Final      : integer
     end; {of record}
```

Figure 10.4
Modular structure
of program
GradeReport

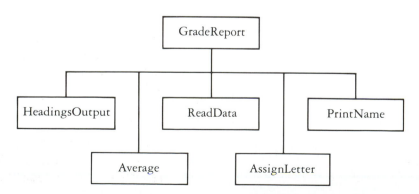

APPLICATION

Student Grade Report (*continued*)

```
var
    StuData : StudGrades;
    FinalAvg : real;
    Grade : char;
    i : integer;

procedure HeadingsOutput;

    {*******************************
    * Procedure to print headings. *
    *******************************}

    begin
        writeln ('                    CLASS GRADE REPORT');
        writeln ('                    -------------------');
        writeln;
        writeln('                              PROGRAMS        ',
                '         MIDTERM  FINAL   WEIGHTED LETTER');
        writeln(' NAME              1    2    3    4    5',
                '         EXAM    EXAM    AVERAGE  GRADE');
        writeln(' ----                       ----------------------',
                '         -------  -----  -------  -----');
        writeln;
    end; {of procedure HeadingsOutput}

procedure ReadData (var StudData: StudGrades);

    {******************************
    * Procedure to read a record. *
    ******************************}

    var
        i : integer;

    begin
        with StudData do
            begin
                read (LastName, FirstName);
                for i := 1 to NumOfProg do
                    read (Programs[i]);
                readln (Midterm, Final)
            end; {of With}
    end; {of procedure ReadData}

procedure Average (Programs : ProgList;
                              Midterm, Final : integer;
                   var FinalAvg : real);
```

APPLICATION

**Student Grade
Report**
(*continued*)

```
{*******************************
* Procedure to compute weighted *
* course average.                *
*******************************}

var
    j, Total : integer;
    ProgAvg : real;

begin
    Total := 0;
    for j := 1 to NumOfProg do
        Total := Total + Programs[j];
    ProgAvg := Total / NumOfProg;
    FinalAvg := (ProgAvg * 0.5) + (Midterm * 0.2) +
                                    (Final * 0.3)

    {the relative weights of each part of the final
     score are  50%, 20%, and 30%, as above.}

end; {of procedure Average}

procedure AssignLetter (FinalAvg : real;
                           var Grade : char);

{*****************************
* Procedure to assign letter *
* grades.                    *
*****************************}

begin
    if FinalAvg >= 90 then
        Grade := 'A'
    else
        if FinalAvg >= 80 then
            Grade := 'B'
        else
            if FinalAvg >= 70 then
                Grade := 'C'
            else
                if FinalAvg >= 60 then
                    Grade := 'D'
                else
                    Grade := 'F'
end; {of procedure AssignLetter}
```

```
procedure PrintName (LastName: Longstring;
                         FirstName : Shortstring);

  {*****************************************
   * Procedure to trim the last and first  *
   * names of excess spaces and print them *
   * separated by a comma.                 *
   *****************************************}

  var
     i,j,k : integer;
  begin
     {Print last name }

     i := 1;
     while (LastName[i] <> ' ') and (i<20) do
        begin
           write (LastName[i]);
           i := i + 1
        end;

     write (', ');

     {Print first name}

     j := 1;
     while (FirstName[j] <> ' ') and (j<20 ) do
        begin
           write (FirstName[j]);
           j :=j + 1
        end;

     {Print blanks to fill out rest of field}

     for k := i+j to 15 do
        write (' ')
  end; {of procedure PrintName}

begin {MAIN Program}

  HeadingsOutput;
  while not eof do
     begin
        ReadData (StudData);
```

APPLICATION

Student Grade Report (*continued*)

```
    with StudData do
        Average (Programs, Midterm, Final, FinalAvg);
    AssignLetter (FinalAvg, Grade);
    with StudData do
        begin
            PrintName (LastName, FirstName);
            for i := 1 to NumOfProg do
                write (Programs[i] :5);
            writeln (Midterm:10, Final:11,
                    FinalAvg:9:1,
                    ' ',Grade)
        end; {of With}
    end; {of while}
end {of MAIN program}.
```

Given the input:

```
Jones     John    065  086  090  100  095  85  076
Coboller  Hack    095  095  070  100  055  044 080
Fortran   Fred    100  088  098  060  090  097 069
Pascal    Blaise  100  090  098  100  100  095 090
```

the output will be:

```
                    CLASS GRADE REPORT
                    ------------------
```

| NAME | PROGRAMS | | | | | MIDTERM EXAM | FINAL EXAM | WEIGHTED AVERAGE | LETTER GRADE |
	1	2	3	4	5				
Jones, John	65	86	90	100	95	85	76	83.4	B
Coboller, Hack	95	95	70	100	55	44	80	74.3	C
Fortran, Fred	100	88	98	60	90	97	69	83.7	B
Pascal, Blaise	100	90	98	100	100	95	90	94.8	A

APPLICATION

Sales Report

We will now generate a sales report from records that contain the following data:

Column	Contents
1–5	Idnumber
6–20	Name
21	blank
22	Classification
	(1 = Quota, 2 = Commission)

APPLICATION

Sales Report
(*continued*)

Column	Contents
23	blank
24–31	Year-to-date Sales
32	blank
33–40	Year-to-date Returns
41	blank
42–49	Current Sales
50	blank
51–58	Current Returns

The data in the input file are, therefore, arranged as follows:

```
10001Knight, Arthur  1   52850.35   2395.35    382.15    93.48
10062Taylor, James   1    1465.50    520.00     25.00     0.00
12345Adams, Elise    2   66500.35    183.50   1572.45   981.56
```

We can represent this information in Pascal with the following record structures:

```
type
   IdInfo = record
      Number : integer;
      Name   : packed array[1..15] of char;
      Classification : (Quota, Commission)
   end;

   SalesData = record
      Sales, Returns : real
   end;

   SalesPerson = record
      Id : IdInfo;
      YearToDate : SalesData;
      Current    : SalesData
   end;
```

Note that the structure for " Salesperson" is a nested record. Given this data, the program is to calculate the new year-to-date sales and the new year-to-date returns for each salesperson. These new figures are obtained by adding the current month's data to the old year-to-date sales and returns. Additionally, we would like to com-

APPLICATION

Sales Report
(*continued*)

pute the new year-to-date net sales by subtracting the returns from the sales. Finally, we need to calculate the total new year-to-date sales, returns, and net. Thus, the printed report should have the format shown in Table 10.1.

In addition to printing each line of the report and the summary line at the end, the program must print the headings at the top of each page. We will assume that we want to print 30 lines per page. To do this, we will have to count the lines we print.

Three basic activities must be performed by the program: (1) the headings must be printed, (2) each salesperson's data must be processed, and (3) the summary line must be printed. Thus, we can start designing our algorithm by dividing the main program into three modules as diagrammed in Figure 10.5.

The PrintHeadings and PrintSummary modules do not need further subdivision. However, the ProcessSalesPerson module includes many activities and should be subdivided further. For each salesperson we must read the input data, perform the appropriate calculations, and then print the required output line. We can do this by writing two additional modules. The module ReadSalesperson reads in

Table 10.1

		Year-to-Date Sales Report **October 1981**			
Salesperson Number	**Salesperson Name**	**Classification**	**Sales**	**Returns**	**Net**
10001	Knight, Arthur	Quota	53232.50	2488.83	50743.67
10062	Taylor, James	Quota	1490.50	520.00	970.50
12345	Adams, Elise	Commission	68072.80	1165.06	66907.74
		.			
		.			
		.			
		Totals	1238675.75	457698.65	780977.05

Figure 10.5 Initial modular structure of program SalesReport

APPLICATION

Sales Report
(*continued*)

the record of a salesperson, and the module PrintReportLine performs the necessary computations and outputs a line of the report. Finally, although we do not need to rewrite it, the module PrintHeadings will be called by the ProcessSalesperson module, as well as the main program. This is because headings are printed initially in the main program and then again in the module ProcessSalesperson every time we print the maximum number of lines per page. The entire structure of our program is diagrammed in Figure 10.6.

Figure 10.6
Modular structure
of program
SalesReport

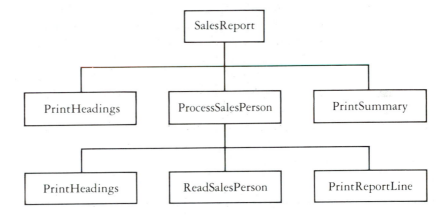

The module SalesReport, which is the main program, can now be written in pseudocode.

begin
    Read month and year
    Print headings
    Initialize line count to 0
    Initialize total sales to 0
    Initialize total returns to 0
    while data remains in input file **do**
        Process salesperson
    Print summary
end.

Writing the main program to correspond to the pseudocode we have:

```
program SalesReport (input, output);

{*****************************
* Program to print a monthly *
* year-to-date sales report. *
*****************************}
```

```
const
    Maxlines = 30;
type
    Datetype = record
        Month : packed array[1..8] of char;
        Year  : integer
    end;

    IdInfo = record
        Number : integer;
        Name   : packed array[1..15] of char;
        Classification : (Quota, Commission, Unknown)
    end;

    SalesData = record
        Sales   : real;
        Returns : real
    end;

    SalesPerson = record
        Id : IdInfo;
        YearToDate : SalesData;
        Current    : SalesData;
    end;

var
    Tot : SalesData;
    LineCount : integer;
    Date : DateType;
    i : integer;

begin {MAIN Program}

    {Read current date}

    with Date do
        begin
            for i := 1 to 8 do
                read (Month[i]);
            read (Year);
        end {of With Date};

    {Print report headings}

    PrintHeadings(Date);

    {Print report}

    LineCount := 0;
    Tot.Sales := 0.0;
```

APPLICATION

Sales Report
(*continued*)

```
   Tot.Returns := 0.0;
   while not eof do
      ProcessSalesperson(Tot);

   {Print final summary}

   PrintSummary(Tot)
end.
```

This program, of course, cannot be run without the procedures it calls. Thus, we now need the procedures that correspond to the modules at the next level: PrintHeadings, ProcessSalesperson, and PrintSummary. However, we should provide stubs for each of these modules and test the main program before proceeding to the next level. Then the next step would be to write the procedures Print Headings, ProcessSalesperson, and PrintSummary, and to test them by providing stubs for the modules of the level below. Finally, the procedures at the lowest level should be written and the entire program tested.

The complete program, with all of the procedures, is shown below. Although this is a lengthy program, it should be easy to understand because of its modular structure.

```
program SalesReport (input, output);

{*****************************
 * Program to print a monthly *
 * year-to-date sales report. *
 *****************************}

const
   Maxlines = 30;

type
   Datetype = record
      Month : packed array[1..8] of char;
      Year  : integer
   end;

   IdInfo = record
      Number : integer;
      Name   : packed array[1..15] of char;
      Classification : (Quota, Commission, Unknown)
   end;

   SalesData = record
      Sales   : real;
```

```
      Returns : real
   end;

SalesPerson = record
   Id : IdInfo;
   YearToDate : SalesData;
   Current  : SalesData;
end;

var
   Tot : SalesData;
   LineCount : integer;
   Date : DateType;
   i : integer;

procedure PrintHeadings(CurrentDate :DateType);

   {******************************
   * Procedure to print headings *
   * given the current date.     *
   ******************************}

   var
      i : integer;

   begin
      writeln;
      writeln ('                          SALES REPORT');
      write   ('                          ');
      with CurrentDate do
         begin
            i := 1;
            while Month[i] <> ' ' do
               begin
                  write (Month[i]);
                  i := i + 1
               end;
            writeln (' ',Year :1)
         end {of With CurrentDate};
      writeln;

      {Print Column Headings}

      writeln (' SALESPERSON    SALESPERSON');
      write   ('   NUMBER          NAME');
      writeln ('      CLASSIFICATION  SALES',
               '      RETURNS       NET');
      writeln
   end {of procedure PrintHeadings};
```

APPLICATION

Sales Report
(*continued*)

```
procedure ProcessSalesperson (var Summary : SalesData);

    {********************************
    * Procedure to process the data *
    * of a single salesperson.      *
    ********************************}

var
    Salesman : Salesperson;

procedure ReadSalesperson ( var Person : Salesperson);

    {*******************************
    * Procedure to input data for *
    * a salesperson.              *
    *******************************}

var
    Ch : char;
    i  : integer;

begin
    with Person do
        begin
            with Id do
                begin
                    read (Number);
                    for i := 1 to 15 do
                        read(Name[i]);
                    read (Ch); {skip blank}
                    read (Ch);
                    if Ch = '1' then
                        Classification := Quota
                    else
                        if Ch = '2' then
                            Classification := Commission
                        else
                            Classification := Unknown
                end {of With Id};

            with YearToDate do
                begin
                    read(Sales);
                    read(Returns)
                end {of With YearToDate};
            with Current do
                begin
                    read(Sales);
```

```
                              read(Returns)
                        end {of With Current}
                  end {of With Person};
            readln
      end {of procedure ReadSalesperson};

procedure PrintReportLine ( Line : SalesPerson);

    {*******************************
    * Procedure to print a detail *
    * line of the sales report.   *
    *******************************}

    var
        NewYearToDate : SalesData;

    begin
        with Line do
            begin
                with Id do
                    begin
                        write ( Number :8);
                        write ( Name : 20);
                        case Classification of
                            Quota : write ('  Quota       ');
                            Commission : write ('  Commission');
                            Unknown : write ('  Unknown    ')
                        end {of Case }
                    end {of With Id};
                with NewYearToDate do
                    begin
                        Sales := YearToDate.Sales +
                                    Current.Sales;
                        write ( Sales :10:2);
                        Returns := YearToDate.Returns +
                                    Current.Returns;
                        write ( Returns :10:2);
                        writeln ( Sales - Returns:11:2)
                    end {of With NewYearToDate}
            end {of With Line}
    end {of procedure PrintLine};

begin {of procedure ProcessSalesperson}

    ReadSalesPerson (Salesman);
    if LineCount <= Maxlines then
        begin
            with Salesman do
```

APPLICATION

Sales Report
(*continued*)

```
              begin
                  Summary.Sales := Summary.Sales +
                        YearToDate.Sales + Current.Sales;
                  Summary.Returns := Summary.Returns +
                        YeartoDate.Returns + Current.Returns
              end {of With Salesman};
            PrintReportLine ( Salesman );
            LineCount := Linecount + 1
          end {of then}
      else
        begin
            PrintHeadings(Date);
            LineCount := 0
        end {of else}
  end {of procedure ProcessSalesperson};

  procedure PrintSummary ( Totals : SalesData);

    {*************************
    * Procedure to print the *
    * summary line of the    *
    * sales report.          *
    *************************}

    begin
        writeln;
        write ('                                TOTALS  ');
        write ( Tot.Sales :10:2, Tot.Returns :10:2);
        writeln ( Tot.Sales-Tot.Returns :11:2)
    end {of procedure PrintSummary};

  begin {MAIN Program}

    {Read current date}

    with Date do
      begin
        for i := 1 to 8 do
            read (Month[i]);
          read (Year);
      end {of With Date};

    {Print report headings}

    PrintHeadings(Date);

    {Print report}

    LineCount := 0;
    Tot.Sales := 0.0;
```

APPLICATION

Sales Report
(*continued*)

```
   Tot.Returns := 0.0;
   while not eof do
      ProcessSalesperson(Tot);

   {Print final summary}

   PrintSummary(Tot)
end.
```

Given the input data:

```
OCTOBER 1982
10001Knight, Arthur    1    52850.35    2395.35    382.15    93.48
10062Taylor, James     1     1465.50     520.00     25 .00    0.00
12345Adams, Elise      2    66500.35     183.50   1572.45   981.56
```

the output of the program will be:

SALES REPORT
OCTOBER 1982

SALESPERSON NUMBER	SALESPERSON NAME	CLASSIFICATION	SALES	RETURNS	NET
10001	Knight, Arthur	Quota	53232.50	2488.83	50743.67
10062	Taylor, James	Quota	1490.50	520.00	970.50
12345	Adams, Elise	Commission	68072.80	1165.06	66907.74
		TOTALS	122795.80	4173.89	118621.91

**10.6
COMMON
ERRORS**

When using records, the most common error is specifying incorrectly the desired field. The full field selector must be used, unless the reference to the field is nested inside a **with** statement. If a record identifier is listed in the header of a **with** statement, then only the field identifier is needed to reference the fields of that record inside the **with** statement. The full field selector must be used for any other record. Given the definitions and declarations:

```
type
   Prospect = record
      Name : packed array[1..20] of char;
      Sex : (female, male);
      Income : real
   end;
   Customer = record
      CustName : packed array[1..20] of char;
      Balance : real;
      CurrentCharge : real;
```

```
        BillingDate : packed array[1..8] of char
    end;
var
    Accounts : array[1..35] of Customer;
    CurrentProspect : Prospect;
    NewCustomer : Customer;
```

the following reference to the Name field of record variable Current-Prospect is *not* valid because the record identifier is not part of the **with** header:

```
with NewCustomer do
    if Income >= 15000 then
        begin
            CustName := Name; {Error - Name not
                                      in scope of With}
            Balance := 0.0;
            CurrentBalance := 0.0;
            BillingDate := '02-JAN-83'
        end;
```

The correct reference is:

```
with NewCustomer do
    if Income >= 15000 then
        begin
            CustName := CurrentProspect.Name;
            Balance := 0.0;
            CurrentBalance := 0.0;
            BillingDate := '02-JAN-83'
        end;
```

If a variable represents an array of records, then the array subscript must be part of the field selector. If a **with** statement is used with a loop, then the **with** statement must be nested inside the loop. If this is not done, the record being manipulated will not change as the value of the subscript changes. Given the above declarations, the following loop will print the value of CustName of the first record in array Accounts thirty-five times:

```
i := 1;
with Accounts[i] do
    while i <= 35 do
        begin
            writeln(CustName);
            i := i + 1
        end
```

Variant records are particularly error prone. In spite of the fact that only certain variant fields may make sense at a particular point in a program, all fields are always accessible to it. Thus, if you are not careful, you may retrieve the wrong value for a field. You should always use the **case** control structure with the tag field to access variant fields of a record.

**10.7
CHAPTER
REVIEW**

A record is a structure consisting of a usually fixed number of components, called fields. Unlike arrays and sets, the components of a record need not be of the same type. Also, unlike arrays, the components of a record must have their own identifiers.

The general form for a record type definition is:

```
type
   RecordType = record
      Field1 : Type1;
      Field2 : Type2;
              .
              .
              .
      Fieldn : Typen
   end;
```

The identifier RecordType is associated with the record structure being defined. Each field is provided with its own identifier and data type.

There are three different ways to access the values stored in a record variable.

1. The complete record can be accessed by using a single assignment statement. This allows for the assignment of all the fields of a record to another record of the same type.

2. Individual fields of a record may be accessed by specifying the record identifier followed by the field identifier, separated by a period. Such expressions are called field designators.

3. A field can be accessed without using the full field designator if the **with** statement is used. The record identifier appears in the header of the **with** statement and all fields in the scope of the **with** are then accessed by using only the field identifier.

The form of the **with** statement is:

```
with Record Identifier do
   Statement
```

The statement that is the body of the **with** statement can be a compound statement. Within the statement, any field of the record variable can be referenced without specifying the record identifier.

More than one record identifier can be listed between the reserved words **with** and **do**. Thus, a statement of the form

```
with var1,var2,var3 do
   statement
```

is permitted. This structure is equivalent to the nested structure:

```
with var1 do
   with var2 do
      with var3 do
         statement
```

Records may be nested; that is, a component of a record may be another record. A record cannot, however, be its own component.

Variant records permit the number and type of fields to change during the execution of a program. The idea that the value of one field, the tag field, can be used to determine the structure of the rest of the record is the basis of variant records.

A variant record consists of two parts: the fixed part and the variant part. The fixed, or invariant, part consists of all the fields that are present in all variants of the records. One fixed field is designated the tag field. Its values determine the structure of the rest of the record.

The tag field is followed by a list of the variant fields. This is the variant part of the record. The declaration of each variant field consists of a constant of the same type as the tag field, followed by a colon, followed by a list of field declarations in parentheses. The list of field declarations can be empty, signifying that the variant record does not need any additional fields other than those listed in the fixed part.

10.8 EXERCISES

10.1. Fill in the blanks for each of the following:

(a) The components of a record are called _____.

(b) A record may have two parts: a _____, which contains fields that are always available, and a _____, which may change.

(c) Every field identifier must be _____ within a given record.

(d) The full name of a field within a record is represented by a _____ that consists of the _____ identifier and a _____ identifier separated by a period.

(e) A _____ statement may be used to eliminate the need to specify the record identifier each time a field of that record is referenced.

(f) The value of the _____ field determines the structure of the variant part of a particular record.

(g) A record that has a variant part is often processed by using the _____ statement so that the appropriate variant fields are referenced.

(h) When a component of a record is itself a record, the records are said to be _____.

10.2. Answer each of the following true or false. If your answer is false, state why.

(a) A record may have only a fixed part, only a variant part, or both.

(b) The components of a record are all of the same type.

(c) In the same program block, it is possible for two different record definitions to have fields with the same identifier.

(d) When two records are of the same type, it is possible to copy the entire contents of one record to the other using a single assignment statement.

(e) It is necessary to have every possible value of the tag field appear as a label on one of the variant field lists.

(f) Records may be nested within records to any desired depth.

(g) A record may be nested within itself. That is, record structures may have recursive definitions.

(h) The type of the tag field may not be real.

(i) The tag field must be present in all variant records.

10.3. Describe the function(s) performed by each of the following Pascal statements.

(a)
```
type
    Address = record
        Number : integer;
        Street : packed array[1..15] of char;
        City   : packed array[1..20] of char;
        State  : packed array[1..2] of char;
        Zipcode: integer
    end;
```

(b)
```
var
    Location : Address;
```

(c)
```
var
    Places : array[1..20] of Address;
```

(d)
```
writeln(Location.Number: 5)
```

(e)
```
for i := 1 to 20 do
    read(Location.City[i])
```

(f)
```
Location := Places[1]
```

(g)
```
with Location do
    writeln(Street)
```

```
(h)  for i := 1 to 20 do
        begin
           for j := 1 to 2 do
              read(Places[i].State[j];
           readln
        end

(i)  type
        PhoneNumber = record
           AreaCode : integer;
           Prefix   : integer;
           Number   : integer
        end;

        Info = record
           Name : packed array[1..20] of char;
           case HasPhone : boolean of
              true  : (Telephone : PhoneNumber);
              false : ( )
        end;

(j)  var
        Directory : array[1..100] of Info;
        PhoneEntry : PhoneNumber;

(k)  Directory[5].Telephone.AreaCode := 617;

(l)  with Directory[i] do
        case HasPhone of
           true  : Telephone := PhoneEntry;
           false : ;
        end
```

10.4. Given the following record definition, rewrite each of the statements that follow using **with**.

```
type
   DateType
      Day : 1..31;
      DayOfWeek : (sun, mon, tue, wed, thu, fri, sat);
      Month : (jan, feb, mar, apr, may, jun,
               jul, aug, sep, oct, nov, dec);
      Year : integer
   end;

var
   Date1, Date2 : DateType;
```

(a) `Date1.Day := 5;`

(b) `Date2.DayOfWeek := thu;`

(c) `Date1.Month := feb;`
     `Date1.Year := 1976;`

(d) `Date1.Month := nov;`
     `Date2.DayOfWeek := mon;`
     `Date1.Day := 11;`

10.5. Define a "Faculty" record with the following fields:

(a) Name (last, first)
(b) Date hired (day, month, year)
(c) Type of appointment (full- or part-time)
(d) Current rank (professor, associate, assistant, lecturer)
(e) Department of appointment
(f) If professor, associate, or assistant, then number of years of service; if lecturer, then number of courses taught

10.6. A research bureau keeps track of monthly rainfall statistics for three years as follows:

Month. Numeric value 1 - 12 (Col 1–2)
Year. (Col 4–7)
Amount of rainfall. Fractions of inches (Col 9–13)

(a) Write a Pascal program that reads the rainfall information and stores it in an array, RainStatistics, declared as follows:

```
type
   MonthType = (jan, feb, mar, apr, may, jun,
                jul, aug, sep, oct, nov, dec);
   RainData = record
      Month  : MonthType;
      Year   : integer;
      Amount : real
   end;

var
   RainStatistics : array[1..36] of RainData;
```

(b) Write a program to print the rainfall report for each year and each quarter of the year. Print the average yearly and quarterly rainfall amounts on the last line of the report.

10.7. Employee records have the following information available:

Id (Col 1–6)
Number of Dependents (Col 8–9)
Hours worked this week. Fractional hours are possible (Col 11–14)

Hourly rate in dollars and cents (Col 16–20)
Saving program code. A "1" denotes that 5% of gross salary is to be deducted. A "0" denotes no deduction. (Col 22)

Write a program that computes the gross pay and net pay for each employee. The gross pay is equal to the hours worked times the hourly rate. Hours worked beyond forty hours should be paid at time-and-a-half. The deductions for net pay computation are:

Federal tax = (Gross pay − (13 ∗ Dependents))∗0.15
FICA = Gross pay ∗ 0.06
State tax = Gross pay ∗ 0.055
Savings = 5% of Gross pay or nothing

10.8. A variable length character string may be represented as:

```
const
   Maxsize = 100;

type
   String = record
       Ch   : packed array[1..Maxsize] of char;
       Size :   0..Maxsize
   end;
```

(a) Write a procedure, ReadString, that reads a line of text from the standard input file and stores it in a variable of type String. The procedure returns the characters read, as well as the length of the line. If the line is longer than Maxsize, it truncates the line to a length of Maxsize.
(b) Write a procedure, WriteString, that prints a variable length string in a field equal to its size.
(c) Write a function, Index, that, given two strings, finds the location of the first string in the second string. If the first string is not contained in the second, the function returns a zero.
(d) Write a procedure, Delete, that, given a string, a position in the string, and a number deletes the specified number of characters from the string starting at the specified position. The size of the resulting string equals the size of the original string minus the number of deleted characters.

10.9. In mathematics, a complex number is written in the form $a + bi$, where a and b are real numbers and i is $\sqrt{-1}$. The numbers a and b are called the real and imaginary parts respectively. Given two complex numbers, $a + bi$ and $c + di$, the operations on complex numbers are defined below:

Addition: $(a + bi) + (c + di) = (a + c) + (b + d)i$
Subtraction: $(a + bi) − (c + di) = (a − c) + (b − d)i$
Multiplication: $(a + bi) ∗ (c + di) = (ac − bd) + (ad + bc)i$

Division: $\dfrac{a + bi}{c + di} = \dfrac{ac + bd}{c + d} + \dfrac{bc - ad}{c + d}\, i$

In Pascal we can implement complex numbers by using the following record structure:

```
type
   Complex = record
      RealPart : real;
      ImaginaryPart : real
   end;
```

Write procedures to implement complex number arithmetic.

10.10. A computer dating service keeps track of clients using the following Client record:

```
type
   Topics = (art, music, sports, computers);
   Client = record
      Name       : packed array[1..20] of char;
      Sex        : (female, male);
      Interests  : set of Topics;
      Age        : integer;
   end;
```

Given client information in the following form:

Name (Col 1–20)
Sex: F = female; M = male (Col 22)
Interests: an X in the column represents an interest (Col 24–27)
   art (Col 24)
   music (Col 25)
   .   .
   .   .
   .   .

write a Pascal program to read the information for a new client and to create the client record. Then the program should read the information for all remaining clients on file and print the list of compatible clients. In order to be compatible, the clients must be of opposite sex, be within six years of each other in age, and have at least two interests in common.

11. Files

11.1 FILE ORGANIZATION

As we saw in earlier chapters, a **file** is any source or destination of information. Thus, a deck of punched cards is a file and so is a reel of magnetic tape. There are two types of files: **sequential files** and **random access files.**

In a sequential file the values only can be accessed in the same sequence in which they are stored. To process such a file, we must move through successive data items in the same order as their respective locations on a storage device. In contrast the values in a random access file, sometimes also called a **direct access file,** can be accessed in any order desired by the programmer. Standard Pascal only supports sequential files; so they are the only type of file that will be described in this chapter, and our use of the term "file" will be synonymous with "sequential file."

Many people feel that the lack of random access files in Pascal is one of its major limitations. As a consequence, such files are often included as a nonstandard extension to the language.

11.2 DECLARATION AND USE OF FILES

In Pascal, a file is a structured data type consisting of a sequence of components of the same type. Although this description sounds identical to the description of an array, there are two major differences between a file and an array. First, unlike arrays, the components of a file cannot be randomly accessed. The storage space for an entire array is reserved in main storage when the array is declared; so the entire array is available to the program at any time during execution. With a file only one component, called the **file window,** is available to the program at any given point in time. All other components of the file, either before or after the window, are not accessible to the program immediately.

The second major difference between a file and an array is that the size of an array must be specified when the array is declared. A file, on the other hand, can be of arbitrary and unlimited size.

To define a file data type in Pascal, we can use a **type** definition of the following form:

type
    Type-Identifier = **file of** Base Type;

The "BaseType" specifies the data type of the individual components of the file. This BaseType can be any Pascal data type except another file. For example:

```
type
   Student =  record
      Name : packed array [1..25] of char;
      Midterm : integer;
      Final : integer;
   end;

   NumberFile = file of integer;
   CharacterFile = file of char;
   ClassList = file of Student;
   NumbLists = file of array[1..100] of real;
```

Once an identifier for a file data type has been defined, just as with other data types we may declare variables using the new data type:

```
var
   Numbers : NumberFile;
   FormLetter : CharacterFile;
   CS208 : ClassList;
   SurveyData : NumbLists;
```

The syntax diagram for a **file** definition is shown in Figure 11.1.

The declaration of a file variable will automatically create a single-element window into that file. We can think of the value in the file window as being in main storage and being directly accessible to the program for use. The other elements in the file will not be accessible until the window is moved to each of them. For the file "Numbers," declared above, we illustrate the file window in Figure 11.2.

Figure 11.1 Syntax diagram for **file** definition

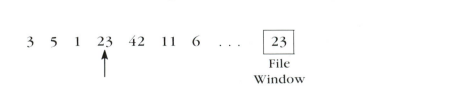

Figure 11.2 File window in Numbers

3   5   1   23   42   11   6   . . .   [23]
                                             File
                                             Window

The arrow symbol (↑) is the file pointer, and marks the position of the file window in the file. A copy of the value in the position pointed to by the file pointer is currently in main storage and is accessible to the program. The remaining values are not in main storage and so are not accessible. The file window, sometimes also called the **file buffer variable,** is referenced in Pascal by following the file name by a special symbol, usually a ↑ (up-arrow or circumflex). Sometimes the at-sign symbol (@) is also used. We will use the up-arrow notation. You should, however, find out what notation your compiler expects and use it when writing programs involving files.

The **var** declaration given earlier automatically creates the following file buffer variables:

Numbers ↑   Variable whose type is integer.
FormLetter ↑   Variable whose type is char.
CS208 ↑   Variable whose type is "Student."
SurveyData ↑   Variable whose type is an array capable of storing 100 real numbers.

The file buffer variable for the file Numbers is illustrated in Figure 11.3.

Figure 11.3 File buffer variable

3   5   1   23   42   11   6 | 23 |

Numbers ↑

We treat the file buffer variable like any other variable. That is, we can assign values to it or manipulate its value in any way that our program requires, as long as the operations we are performing are permitted for variables of that type. For example, to obtain a value from the file Numbers we write:

```
i := Numbers↑
```

where *i* is a variable of type integer. Similarly, the value of the file buffer itself will be altered by the assignment:

```
Numbers↑ := i
```

The expression:

```
writeln(Numbers↑ + 2)
```

will print the current value of the file buffer plus 2 for the file Numbers. Thus, if the value of the file buffer Numbers ↑ is as shown in Figure 11.3, a 25 will be printed.

The variable CS208 ↑ is a record. We can access its fields as with any other record:

CS208↑ .Name   Name of student whose record is in file buffer.

CS208↑ .Name[1]   First letter of name of student whose record is in file buffer.

CS208↑ .Midterm   Midterm score of student whose record is in file buffer.

CS208↑ .Final   Final examination score of student whose record is in file buffer.

Similarly, SurveyData ↑ is an array of real numbers. We can access its components the same way we would access the components of any other array:

SurveyData ↑ [1]   First component for file buffer.

SurveyData ↑ [100]   One-hundredth component of file buffer.

A file window is controlled and tested using five standard Pascal procedures and functions. These procedures and functions are reset, rewrite, get, put, and eof.

The procedure statement:

```
reset(f)
```

initializes file "f" for reading by positioning the file pointer to the first element of the file and copying the first element of the file into "f ↑ ." Every file, except for the standard input file, must be reset before being read.

The effect of a "reset(Numbers)" on file Numbers and its buffer variable is shown in Figure 11.4.

Figure 11.4 Result of reset on file buffer variable

3 5 1 23 42 11 6 | ?? |
reset(Numbers)   Numbers ↑

3 5 1 23 42 11 6 | 3 |
↑   Numbers ↑

If we followed the reset instruction with:

```
i := Numbers↑
```

the value 3 would be assigned to the variable *i*.

The procedure invocation:

get(f)

moves the file pointer ahead one element and reads the next value of the file into f ↑ . Figure 11.5 shows the result of "get(Numbers)" on the file Numbers.

Figure 11.5 Effect of get on the file window

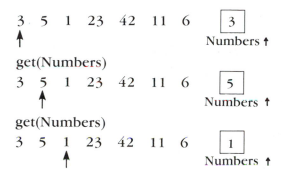

We have seen how the function eof works with the standard input file. It works the same way with an arbitrary file. The expression:

eof(f)

is false as long as the file window is positioned over a component of the file. If the window has moved beyond the last component of the file, eof(f) is true. For example, after get(Numbers) has been executed a sufficient number of times, the window will be positioned as shown in the first part of Figure 11.6. At this point the value of eof(Numbers) is false. If get(Numbers) is executed again, the window moves beyond the end of the file and eof(Numbers) becomes true.

Figure 11.6 Effect of moving file window beyond End of File

3   5   1   23   42   11   6 | 6 |
                              ↑   Numbers ↑

get(Numbers)

3   5   1   23   42   11   6 | ?? |
                                 ↑ Numbers ↑

When the window moves beyond the last element in the file f, eof(f) becomes true and f ↑ becomes undefined. An attempt to execute any additional get(f) instructions would result in run-time errors. Example 11.1 prints the contents of the file Numbers.

**EXAMPLE 11.1
Printing All
the Elements
of a File**

```
program PrintNumbers(Numbers, output);

{*********************************
 * Program to print the values of *
 * a file of integers.            *
 *********************************}

var
   Numbers : file of integer;

begin
   {Open file for reading}

   reset(Numbers);

   while not eof(Numbers) do
      begin
         {Print contents of file buffer}

         writeln(Numbers↑);

         {Move file window to next value}

         get(Numbers)
      end
end.
```

Note that we included the name of the file Numbers in the program heading. Files whose identifiers appear as parameters in the program heading are called **external files.** External files physically exist in secondary storage. Files that are not listed as parameters in the program heading are called **internal files.** Internal files exist only during the execution of the program in which they are declared. They are usually temporary files. We will see examples of internal files later in this chapter. A program may create and use both internal and external files. An external file, however, does not disappear when the program ends.

When eof(f) is true we can output a value to file f. The function eof is true only when the file is empty, or the window has been moved past the last value in the file. Thus, values can only be written to the *end* of a file. To write a value to a file, we first assign the value to the file buffer variable, and then execute a "put(f)."

The effect of assigning a value to the file buffer of the file Numbers and executing the function put(Numbers) is illustrated in Figure 11.7.

Figure 11.7 Effect of put (Numbers) on file Numbers

3   5   1   23   42   11   6   ??

↑ Numbers ↑

Numbers ↑ : = 37
3   5   1   23   42   11   6   37

↑ Numbers ↑

put(Numbers)
3   5   1   23   42   11   6   37   ??

↑ Numbers ↑

After put(Numbers) is executed, 37 is appended to the file, the value of eof(Numbers) is again true, and the value of Numbers ↑ is again undefined. We can continue to append values to the file by repeating the process as many times as we wish.

Although values can be appended to an existing file, they are most commonly written to an empty file. A program is able to put values into an empty file only after the file has been opened for output by a call to the standard procedure, rewrite.

rewrite(f)

opens the file f for output. File f is completely cleared and eof(f) is set to true. Figure 11.8 illustrates the result of executing reset(Numbers) with the file Numbers as it was midway through the previous example.

Figure 11.8 The effect of rewrite (Numbers) on the file Numbers

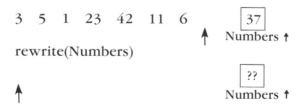

3   5   1   23   42   11   6   37

↑ Numbers ↑

rewrite(Numbers)

                                   ??

↑   Numbers ↑

As an illustration of the use of standard procedures and functions with files, consider Example 11.2, which starts with a file of students and creates two new files, the first containing only the female students and the second containing the male students.

For the next example we will assume the reverse. We have separate files for male and female students and we want to create a single

**EXAMPLE 11.2
Program to
Separate a File
into Two Files**

```pascal
program Separate (Class, FemaleStudents, MaleStudents);

{*************************************
 * Program to separate a class file *
 * into two files, one containing    *
 * the female students, the other    *
 * containing the male students.     *
 *************************************}

type
   Student = record
      Id    : integer;
      Name  : packed array [1..15] of char;
      Sex   : (Male, Female);
      Grade : integer
   end;
var
   Class, FemaleStudents, MaleStudents : file of Student;
begin
   {Open the files for input and output}

   reset (Class);
   rewrite (FemaleStudents);
   rewrite (MaleStudents);

   {Step through the Class file as long as students remain}

   while not eof(Class) do
      begin
         if Class↑.Sex = Female then
            begin
               {Student is female}

               FemaleStudents↑ := Class↑;
               put (FemaleStudents)
            end
         else
            begin
               {Student is male}

               MaleStudents↑ := Class↑;
               put (MaleStudents)
            end;

      {Obtain next student from class file}
```

**EXAMPLE 11.2
Program to
Separate a File
into Two Files**
(*continued*)

```
        get (Class)
    end
end.
```

file out of the class. Furthermore, the two individual files are sequenced by id number, and we would like the resulting file to be sequenced as well. This is a classic problem and involves **merging** two files. As an illustration of what merging two files involves, consider the following two lists of integers:

```
3  6  8  10  15  45  56  78
1  2  4  27  29  32  36  88
```

The merged list is:

```
1  2  3  4  6  8  10  15  27  29  32  26  45  56  78  88
```

The algorithm to merge the two files is:

begin
    Open class file for output
    Open female and males files for input
    while records remain in male and female files **do**
        if id from female file is less than id from male file **then**
            Copy buffer of female file into buffer of class file
            Obtain next record from female file
        else
            Copy buffer of male file into buffer of class file
            Obtain next record from male file
        Put buffer of class file into class file
    while records remain in female file
        Copy records from female file to class file
    while records remain in male file
        Copy records from male file to class file
end.

Three loops are used to merge two files into one. The first loop steps through the files to be merged as long as records remain in both files. In that loop we compare the id numbers of the corresponding records and copy the appropriate record to the merged file. The remaining loops are needed to copy the remainder of either file to the merged class file.

The corresponding program is written as in Example 11.3.

EXAMPLE 11.3
Merging Two
Files

```
program Merge (Class, FemaleStudents, MaleStudents);

{*****************************
 * Program to merge two files. *
 *****************************}

type
   Student = record
      Id    : integer;
      Name  : packed array [1..15] of char;
      Sex   : (Male, Female);
      Grade : integer
   end;
var
   Class, FemaleStudents, MaleStudents : file of Student;

begin
   {Open the files for input and output}

   reset(FemaleStudents);
   reset(MaleStudents);
   rewrite(Class);

   while (not eof(FemaleStudents)) and (not
             eof(MaleStudents)) do
      begin
         if FemaleStudents↑.Id < MaleStudents↑.Id then
            begin
               Class↑ := FemaleStudents↑;
               get(FemaleStudents)
            end
         else
            begin
               Class↑ := MaleStudents↑;
               get(MaleStudents)
            end;
         put(Class)
      end;

   {If female students remain}

   while not eof(FemaleStudents) do
      begin
         Class↑ := FemaleStudents↑;
```

**EXAMPLE 11.3
Merging Two
Files**
(*continued*)

```
            get(FemaleStudents);
            put(Class)
        end;

    {If male students remain}

    while not eof(MaleStudents) do
        begin
            Class↑ := MaleStudents↑;
            get(MaleStudents);
            put(Class)
        end;
end.
```

SELF-TEST 1

1. Write out the **type** and **var** declarations for files with the following structures:

(a) A file containing names of students. Each name is stored in 30 columns.

(b) A file containing customer information. For each customer we have the following information:

Name	20 characters
Address	20 characters
Balance	real number
Credit Limit	real number

(c) A file containing grade information about students in a class. The following information needs to be stored for each student.

Name	20 characters
5 Quiz Grades	integers
Midterm	integer
Final	integer

2. For the above definitions and declarations, show how you would reference each of the following:

(a) The name of the student in the file window for 1(a).

(b) The credit limit of the customer in the file window for 1(b).

(c) The grade on the third quiz for the student in the file window for 1(c).

3. Assume that we have two files, "In" and "Out." We are obtaining information from In and are outputting information to Out. The files currently appear as:

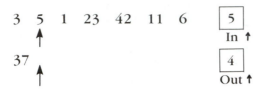

3   5   1   23   42   11   6   [5]
    ↑   In ↑

37   [4]
   ↑   Out ↑

For each of the following groups of operations, show what the affected file contains, and show the contents of the buffer variable.

(a) reset(In)   (b) put(Out);
(c) get(In); get(In)   (d) Out↑ := In↑ ; put(out)

4. Write a program that reads a file of integers and creates a new file that contains only the positive integers from the original file.

Answers

1. (a) **type**
```
        Name = packed array[1..30] of char;
        NameFile = file of Name;
    var
        Students : NameFile;
```

(b) **type**
```
    Customer = record
       Name, Address : packed array[1..20] of char;
       Balance, CreditLimit : real
    end;
    CustFile = file of Customer;
  var
    ChargeCustomers : CustFile;
```

(c) **type**
```
    Student = record
       Name : packed array[1..20] of char;
       QuizGrades : array[1..5] of integer;
       Midterm, Final : integer
    end;
    StudentFile = file of Student;
  var
    Class : StudentFile;
```

2. (a) Students↑ (b) ChargeCustomers↑. CreditLimit (c) Student File↑. QuizGrades[3]

3. (a) reset(In)

3   5   1   23   42   11   6   │ 3 │
↑   In↑

(b) put(Out);

37   4   ↑   │ ? │
                                 Out↑

(c) get(In);get(In)

3   5   1   23   42   11   6   │ 23 │
                ↑   In↑

(d) Out↑ := In↑ ; put(Out)

37   5   │ ? │
        ↑   Out↑

4.
```
program Question4 (InFile, OutFile);
var
    InFile, OutFile : file of integer;
begin
    reset(InFile);
    rewrite(OutFile);
    while not eof(InFile) do
      begin
        if InFile↑ > 0 then
          begin
            OutFile↑ := InFile↑;
            put(OutFile)
          end;
        get(InFile)
      end
end.
```

11.3 TEXT FILES

In Pascal one particular type of file is so important that it deserves special mention. The predefined file type **text** is a file of characters that is structured into lines. The standard *input* and *output* files are of type text.

A file of type text can be thought of as a file containing printable characters organized into lines. Each line in the file is separated from the next by a special character called a **line-separator.** We discussed these line separator characters in Chapter 4. Figure 11.9 shows the organization of a text file.

Figure 11.9
Structure of a file of
type Text

ccc. . .ccLScccccc. . .cLSccc. . . ccLS. . .LSEOF
line 1   line 2   line 3

Each "c" stands for a character, each "LS" stands for the special line-separator character, and the "EOF" stands for the end-of-file character. We can think of the file in Figure 11.9 as consisting of lines as follows:

ccc. . .cc	line 1
cccccc. . .c	line 2
ccc. . .cc	line 3
.	.
.	.
.	.

Input and output to text files can be done using the standard procedures get and put, which work for all files. However, because text files are so widely used, there are four special procedures to handle input and output with them. We studied these procedures earlier in the book. They are read, readln, write, and writeln. The reason we have been able to use these procedures in all of the programs we wrote prior to this chapter is because we always obtained our input values from the standard input file and output our results to the standard output file and both of these files are predefined as text files. With our present knowledge of files, we can now examine more precisely how these procedures work.

Given the declarations

```
var
   f : text;
   Symbol : char;
```

we can describe the standard Pascal text file operations as follows.

The procedure call

```
read(f,Symbol)
```

is equivalent to

```
Symbol := f↑;
get(f)
```

and

```
write(f,Symbol)
```

is equivalent to

```
f↑ := Symbol;
put(f)
```

That is, read(f,Symbol) assigns to Symbol the current value in the file window of file f and then moves the window forward one character. Similarly, the statement write(f, Symbol) assigns the value of Symbol to the file window f ↑ and then appends that value to the file. Notice that when these procedures are applied to files other than the standard input and output text files, the file identifier must be the first parameter. If the file identifier is omitted, the default name "input" is assumed for read and the default name "output" is assumed for write.

The read and write procedures can read and write more than a single value in one call of the procedure. The statement

```
read(f,Symbol1,Symbol2,...,Symboln)
```

is equivalent to

```
read(f,Symbol1);
read(f,Symbol2);
        .
        .
        .
read(f,Symboln)
```

and

```
write(f,Symbol1,Symbol2,...,Symboln)
```

is equivalent to

```
write(f,Symbol1);
write(f,Symbol2);
        .
        .
        .
write(f,Symboln)
```

For any text file f

```
eoln(f)
```

is true if the file window is on a line separator character and is false otherwise. Since different implementations of Pascal use different line separator characters, when the file window is over a line separator, Pascal assigns a blank to the file buffer variable. Thus, the line separator looks like a blank space to the program.

The execution of

```
readln(f,Symbol)
```

is equivalent to

```
Symbol := f↑;
while not eoln(f) do
   get(f);
get(f)
```

the procedure call

```
writeln(f,Symbol)
```

is equivalent to

```
f↑ := Symbol;
put(f);
f↑ := '|'; {The '|' is the line separator character}
put(f)
```

Thus readln(f,Symbol) assigns the value of the file buffer to Symbol, then moves the file window to the first character past the line separator. The execution of writeln(f,Symbol), on the other hand, appends the current value of Symbol to file f and then appends the line separator character to that file.

The procedures readln and writeln can be used to input or output more than a single value. Thus,

```
readln(f, Symbol1,Symbol2,...,Symboln)
```

is equivalent to

```
read(f,Symbol1);
read(f,Symbol2);
```

.
.
.

```
readln(f,Symboln)
```

and

```
writeln(f,Symbol1,Symbol2,...,Symboln)
```

is equivalent to

```
write(f,Symbol1);
write(f,Symbol2);
```
.
.
.
```
writeln(f,Symboln)
```

The procedures read, readln, write, and writeln, as we saw earlier, are also defined for variables of type integer and real, as well as char. While it is true that a text file is a sequence of characters, by using read and readln with integer or real parameters, we are able to automatically convert characters such as "123" to the integer 123, instead of reading them as 1, 2, 3. The automatic conversion facilities of read and readln apply to any text files, not just to the standard input file. Read and readln will assemble the required number of characters from the text file into integers or reals, whichever may be required.

Similarly, write and writeln will disassemble an integer or real value into the appropriate characters and output the characters to the text file used for output. Just as read and readln, they work with any file of type text.

We have already seen many examples involving text files. Every time we used the standard input or output files we were using text files. As an additional example of text files consider the following program, which starts with a text file and restructures it so that every line is no longer than forty characters. It reads one word at a time from an input file and adds words to the output file until a word can no longer fit on a line. That is, the program fits as many words on a line as it can, subject to a line-size limitation. This is a common problem in text processing and is sometimes called **filling** the text.

The algorithm for the text-filling program is straightforward. We alternate reading and writing words in a loop, each time testing to see if the current word fits on the current line. If it fits, we append a blank and then the word to the output file. If it does not fit, we append the line separator character to the output file.

begin
    Open the files for input and output
    Initialize current line size to 0
    Input and output first word
    Add word size to line size
    while characters remain in input file **do**
        Read word from input file
        if word fits on line **then**
            Write blank to output file
            Add 1 to line size
        else
            Write line separator to output file
            Set line size to 0
        Write word to output file
        Add word size to line size
    Write line separator to output file
end.

The program resulting from the expansion of the algorithm is illustrated in Example 11.4.

**EXAMPLE 11.4
Program to
Fill Words into
Lines of Text**

```pascal
program Fill (InFile, OutFile);

{**************************************
 * Program to fill words into lines   *
 * of text. The maximum size of       *
 * each line is given by the constant *
 * MaxLineLength.                     *
 **************************************}

const
   MaxLineLength    = 40;   {Maximum line size}
   Blank            = ' ';  {Padding character}
   MaxWordLength    = 20;   {Maximum word size}

type
   Word = packed array[1..MaxWordLength] of char;

var
   InFile   : text;              {Input file}
   OutFile  : text;              {Output file}
```

**EXAMPLE 11.4
Program to
Fill Words into
Lines of Text**
(*continued*)

```pascal
LineSize : 0..MaxLineLength; {Current line size}
WordSize : 0..MaxWordLength; {Current word size}
InWord   : Word;             {Current word}


procedure ReadWord(var f: text; var Buffer: Word;
                        var Size: integer);

    {***************************************
     * Procedure to read a word from the  *
     * input file and count the number of *
     * characters in the word.            *
     ***************************************}

    var
        ch : char;
    begin
        {Initialize size to 0 and read
         first character}

        Size := 0;
        read(f, ch);

        {Read characters until blank is encountered}

        while ch <> Blank do
            begin
                Size := Size + 1;
                Buffer[Size] := ch;
                read(f,ch)
            end
    end; {of procedure READWORD}


procedure WriteWord(var f: text; Buffer: Word; Size:
                                              integer);

    {****************************
     * Procedure to write a word *
     * to the output file.       *
     ****************************}

    begin
        write(f,Buffer: Size);
    end; {of procedure WRITEWORD}
```

EXAMPLE 11.4
Program to
Fill Words into
Lines of Text
(*continued*)

```
begin    {*** MAIN Program ***}

   {Open files for input and output}

   reset(InFile);
   rewrite(OutFile);

   {Read and write first word}

   LineSize := 0;
   ReadWord(Infile, InWord, WordSize);
   WriteWord(OutFile, InWord, WordSize);
   LineSize := LineSize + WordSize;

   {As long as characters remain in input file
    read and print words}

   while not eof(InFile) do
      begin
         ReadWord (InFile, InWord, WordSize);
         if LineSize + Wordsize < MaxLineLength then
           begin {Word fits on line}
              write(OutFile,Blank);
              LineSize := LineSize + 1
           end
         else
           begin {Word does not fit on line}
              writeln(OutFile);
              LineSize := 0;
           end;

         {Write current word to output file}

         WriteWord(OutFile, InWord, WordSize);
         LineSize := LineSize + WordSize
      end;
   writeln(OutFile)
end.
```

Given the following as contents of file "InFile":

This is sample input for the program that
fills lines.
The
lines should
be filled to a maximum length of 40 characters.

**EXAMPLE 11.4
Program to
Fill Words into
Lines of Text**
(*continued*)

the resulting contents of the file "OutFile" will be:

```
This is sample input for the program
that fills lines. The lines should be
filled to a maximum length of 40
characters.
```

Note how the above program uses procedures to input and output words. When files are passed to a procedure they *must be declared as pass-by-reference parameters.*

One final comment about the storage of file components is in order. File components are usually stored in the internal representation of the base type of the file. That is, given the declaration:

```
type
    NumberFile = file of integer;
var
    Numbers : NumberFile;
```

the components of the file Numbers will be stored in the internal representation of integers. This has two immediate consequences. First, such files cannot be prepared using a terminal keyboard and a standard text editor. Recall that when a key on a keyboard is depressed, the ASCII (or EBCDIC) representation of the character on the key is generated. Thus, depressing the key marked "1" generates the character code for the representation of 1. This is not the same as the internal binary representation of the integer 1. Thus, components of file Numbers can only be created by a program that generates such a file as output.

The second consequence of the representation of the components of a file as other than type text is that the components of a file such as Numbers cannot be readily inspected by listing the file directly or by using an editor to examine its values. Again, a program must be written to read the file and print its contents out to the standard output file.

Text files whose components are characters, on the other hand, can be prepared and examined using a text editor. When an integer is input from a text file, it is converted by the read or readln procedures from the character representation in which it is stored in the file to an internal binary integer representation. Similarly, when an integer is output to a text file using the write or writeln procedures, it is converted from an internal binary integer representation to a character representation.

Are there any advantages to files other than text files? Files of type real, integer, and boolean are often used for speed and compactness of storage. Because values of such files are stored in internal representation form, they need not be converted when input or output. Thus, input and output operations proceed more quickly. Additionally, less storage may be required for internal representation of such data types as boolean than may be required to store them as characters.

Finally, files of structured data types permit input and output of entire records instead of individual fields. Furthermore, since the components are stored in their internal representations, there are no restrictions on the data type of the components. Values for variables of user-defined types can just as readily be input and output as values for variables of standard scalar data types.

SELF-TEST 2

1. What is the difference, if any, between a text file and a file of characters?

2. Under what circumstances can a file be an argument to a procedure?

3. (a) What does the following program fragment do? Assume "Letter" is a text file.

```
Number := 0;
reset(Letter);
while not eof(Letter) do
   begin
      if eoln(Letter) then
         Number := Number + 1;
      readln(Letter)
   end;
```

(b) Would the code in 3(a) work if the file Letter were declared as:

```
Letter :  file of char;
```

Explain.

4. Write a program that reads integers from the standard input file and writes them to a file of type integer.

Answers

1. A text file is divided into lines. A file of characters is not.
2. It must be the argument of a pass-by-reference parameter.
3. (a) It counts the number of lines in the file Letter. (b) The code would not work with a file of characters because such a file is not structured into lines.
4.
```
program Question4 (input, Numbers);
type
   NumberFile = file of integer;
var
   Numbers : NumberFile;
   x       : integer;
begin
   rewrite(Numbers);
   while not eof do
      begin
         read(x);
         Numbers↑ := x;
         put(Numbers)
      end
end.
```

We will now examine two programs that utilize files.

APPLICATION

Master File Update

First, we will examine a file update problem. Business data processing often involves the manipulation of large amounts of information, which is organized into files. An important aspect of file processing is the maintenance of a file. **File maintenance** is the process of adding new records, deleting old records, modifying existing records in a file, and printing reports based on the information in a file. A file that contains permanent information is called a **master file.** A file that consists of records containing information used to update the master file is called a **transaction file.**

A typical problem is to design an algorithm to maintain the credit card master file for a small company. The master file contains information about all the holders of a credit card for the company in question. The records are sequenced by credit card number. Each day, the master file is updated to include transactions that were received that day. The transactions are written to the transaction file during the day as they are received. The transaction file is then sorted by account number, and finally, the master file is updated. The updating process takes as input the current master file and the transaction file and creates a new master file.

Each record in the master file contains the following fields:

```
Customer = record
   AccountNumber : integer;
   Name          : packed array[1..20] of char;
   Address       : packed array[1..30] of char;
   Balance       : real
end;
```

Each record in the transaction file contains the following fields:

```
Transaction = record
   AccountNumber : integer;
   case TransCode : (charge,payment,addition,deletion) of
      charge, payment : (Amount : real);
      addition : (Name : packed array[1..20] of char;
                  Address : packed array[1..30] of char);
      deletion : ( )
end;
```

Note that the transaction records are variant records. All transactions have a field for the account number of the customer and a transaction code that specifies what type of transaction we are dealing with. The remainder of the record depends on the value of the transaction code. If the code indicates a charge or a payment, then the amount of the charge or payment is also available. If the code indicates the addition of a new customer to the master file, then the name and address of the customer is available. Finally, if the code indicates the deletion of a customer from the master file, then no additional data about that customer are available.

The algorithm to update the master file is similar to the algorithm for merging two files. We step sequentially through both the old master file and the transaction file, modifying, deleting, or inserting records into the new master file as necessary.

Instead of using three loops, as we did in the file-merge algorithm, we use one loop here, which terminates only when both the old master file and the transaction file have been read to the end. In each iteration of the loop we select the id number of the record to be processed. This number becomes the current id. We then process all the records with id numbers equal to the current id. The current id is chosen by examining the id numbers of the current old master file re-

APPLICATION

**Master File
Update**
(*continued*)

cord and the current transaction file record. The smaller value becomes the current id.

The records are processed as follows. If the id number of the master file record currently being examined is equal to the id number of the current transaction record, we perform the operation specified by the transaction code. However, because there may be more than one transaction that applies to the current master file record, an inner loop is used to obtain and process all such transactions. If the id number of the current transaction record is less than the id number of the master file record, the only possible transaction is an addition and the record is processed accordingly. Finally, if the id number of the current master file record is less than the current transaction record, the master file record is transferred to the new master file.

```
begin
    Print the old master file
    Open old master file and transaction file for input
    Open new master file for output
    Input current record from old master file
    Input current record from transaction file
    while records remain to be processed in either file do
        if master record id < = transaction record id then
            Set current id to master record id
            Set temporary record to master record
            Input record from master file
        else
            Set current id to transaction record id
            Set id of temporary record to dummy value
        while transaction record id = current id do
            if temporary record id < dummy value then
                Update temporary record using
                        current transaction record
            else
                if transaction code = Addition then
                    Create temporary record from
                            transaction record
                else
                    Print error message transaction id
                            not in master file
            Input record from transaction file
        if temporary record id < high dummy value then
            Output temporary record to new master file
    Print the updated master file
end.
```

APPLICATION

**Master File
Update**
(*continued*)

The complete program follows. Study it carefully to see how it steps through both files, one record at a time. Note how a temporary record is used for the update process. On each iteration of the main loop only one new record is written to the new master file.

```pascal
program FileUpdate (OldMaster,TransFile,NewMaster,Output);

{*********************************************
* Program to update an old master file and *
* create a new updated master file.        *
* During the updating process records may  *
* be altered, deleted, or added.           *
*********************************************}

const
    DummyId = maxint; {Dummy id used in updating}
type
    Customer = record
        Id      : integer;
        Name    : packed array[1..20] of char;
        Address : packed array[1..30] of char;
        Balance : real
    end;

    {Valid transaction types}

    Transtype = (charge, payment, addition, deletion);

    Transaction = record
        Id : integer;
        case Code : Transtype of
        charge, payment : (Amount : real);
        addition : (Name : packed array[1..20] of char;
                    Address : packed array[1..30] of char);
        deletion : ( )
    end;

    Master = file of Customer;
    Trans  = file of Transaction;
var
    OldMaster   : Master;
    NewMaster   : Master;
    TransFile   : Trans;
    MasterBuf   : Customer;
```

APPLICATION

**Master File
Update**
(*continued*)

```
TempBuf     : Customer;
TransBuf    : Transaction;
CurrentId   : integer;

procedure PrintMaster (var MasterFile: Master);

    {**********************************************
     * Procedure to print contents of master file. *
     **********************************************}

    begin

        {Print Headings}

        writeln;
        writeln('  ID   ','         NAME              ',
                '             ADDRESS              ',
                '             BALANCE');
        writeln;

        {Open master file for reading}

        reset(MasterFile);

        while not eof(MasterFile)do
            with MasterFile↑ do
                begin
                    write(Id:4);
                    write(Name:22);
                    write(Address:33);
                    writeln(Balance:16:2);
                    get(MasterFile);
                end
    end {of Procedure PRINTMASTER};


procedure ReadMaster (var InFile : Master;
                      var Buffer : Customer);

    {***********************************
     * Procedure to input a record from *
     * the master file. If the file is  *
     * empty the procedure returns      *
     * the dummy id.                    *
     ***********************************}
```

```
begin
   if eof(InFile) then
      Buffer.Id := DummyId
   else
      begin
        Buffer := InFile↑;
        get (InFile)
      end;
end {of Procedure READMASTER};


procedure ReadTrans (var InFile : Trans;
                     var Buffer : Transaction);

   {**********************************
    * Procedure to input a record from *
    * the transaction file. If the      *
    * file is empty the procedure       *
    * returns the dummy id.             *
    **********************************}

   begin
      if eof(InFile) then
         Buffer.Id := DummyId
      else
         begin
           Buffer := InFile↑;
           get (InFile)
         end
   end {of Procedure READTRANS};


procedure UpdateRecord (var MBuffer : Customer;
                        TBuffer : Transaction);

   {**********************************
    * Procedure to update a record.    *
    * It checks for validity of the     *
    * transaction code. If the code is  *
    * "charge," or "payment" the        *
    * balance is updated. If the code   *
    * is "deletion" the dummy id is     *
    * returned as the id. All other     *
    * codes generate error messages.    *
    **********************************}
```

```
begin
    with MBuffer do
        if TBuffer.Code in [charge, payment, deletion,
                                 addition] then
            case TBuffer.Code of
                charge : Balance := Balance +
                                    TBuffer.Amount;
                payment : Balance := Balance -
                                     TBuffer.Amount;
                deletion  : if Balance = 0.0 then
                                Id := DummyId
                            else
                                writeln('Deletion ',
                                'error -- Customer: ',
                                Id :3,' has non-zero',
                                ' balance');
                addition : writeln('Insertion error ',
                                   '-- Customer: ',
                                    Id :3, ' already',
                                    ' in masterfile')
            end
        else
            writeln ('Update error -- Invalid transaction',
                      'code for transaction: ',Id :3)
    end {of Procedure UPDATERECORD};


procedure AddRecord (var MBuffer : Customer;
                         TBuffer : Transaction);

    {**********************************
     * Procedure to create a new master *
     * file record. The appropriate     *
     * values are transferred from the  *
     * transaction record to the master *
     * file record.                     *
     **********************************}

    begin
        with MBuffer do
            begin
                Id := TBuffer.Id;
                Name := TBuffer.Name;
                Address := TBuffer.Address;
```

```
                    Balance := 0.0
              end
      end {of Procedure ADDRECORD};

begin {** Main Program **}

    {Print old master file}

    PrintMaster(OldMaster);

    {Print headings}

    writeln;
    writeln('Update now in progress...');
    writeln;
    {Open all files for reading and writing}

    reset(OldMaster);
    reset(TransFile);
    rewrite(NewMaster);

    {Obtain first record from
     master file and transaction file}

    ReadMaster(OldMaster,MasterBuf);
    ReadTrans(TransFile,TransBuf);

    {While records remain in either file, process records}

    while (MasterBuf.Id <> DummyId) or
          (Transbuf.Id <> DummyId) do
      begin
        if MasterBuf.Id <= Transbuf.Id then

            {Id of master file record is less than
             or equal to id of transaction record}

            begin
              {Set current id to id of master
               file record, copy master file
               record to temporary working
               record for update purposes, and
               obtain next master file record}

              CurrentId := MasterBuf.Id;
              TempBuf := MasterBuf;
```

APPLICATION

**Master File
Update**
(*continued*)

```
                        ReadMaster(OldMaster,MasterBuf)
     end
  else
     {Id of master file record is greater than
      id of transaction record}

     begin

        {Set current id to transaction
         record id and id of temporary
         working record to dummy indicating
         that no transactions can be made
         against this record}

        CurrentId := TransBuf.Id;
        TempBuf.Id := DummyId
     end;

 {While id of current transaction record equals
  current id process transaction records}

 while Transbuf.Id = CurrentId do
   begin
     if TempBuf.Id <> DummyId then

        {Id of temporary working
         record is not equal to
         dummy value}

        UpdateRecord(TempBuf,TransBuf)
     else

        {Id of temporary working
         record is equal to dummy}

        if TransBuf.Code = Addition then

           {Transaction is an addition}

           AddRecord(TempBuf,TransBuf)
        else

           {Transaction is not addition.
            Customer is not in
            master file.}
```

APPLICATION

**Master File
Update**
(*continued*)

```
                          writeln(' Customer: ',
                                   TransBuf.Id,
                                   ' not in file');
                  {Obtain next transaction record}

              ReadTrans(TransFile,TransBuf)
         end; {of loop for id equal to current id}

      {If record is valid write it to new master file}

      if TempBuf.Id <> DummyId then
        begin
           NewMaster := TempBuf;
           put(NewMaster)
        end
    end; {of update loop}

  {Print new master file}

  PrintMaster(NewMaster)
end.
```

Assume that the transaction file contains the following transactions:

ID	CODE		
001	charge	2.98	
007	payment	3.00	
009	addition	Disk, floppy	69 Double Sided Rd Density AL
010	payment	15.00	
011	addition	Memory, Morris	122 Indian Lane Brooklyn NY
011	charge	12.00	
099	payment	4.95	
101	addition	Prone, Error	76 Mistake Ave Bug NH
123	deletion		
229	other		

A possible output of the program might be:

```
ID  NAME                    ADDRESS                         BALANCE

 1  River, Charles          37 Pleasant Street Needham MA    12.78
 7  Pascal, Blaise          1 rue de la Paix Paris France    78.60
```
                                    (*Output continues on next page.*)

APPLICATION   Master File Update (*continued*)

```
 19   Cobol, Hacker         13 East 47th Street N.Y. N.Y.     99.50
 99   Metropolitan, C.      755 Commonwealth Av Boston MA      1.99
100   Broom, Hilda          4 Second Ave Peru IL               5.95
101   Sequential, Access    123 Tape Drive Sarasota FL         3.98
123   Fortran, Fred         99 Math Lane Matrix CA            71.05
229   Lovelace, Ada         12 Surrey Drive Dover England      0.00
```

Update now in progress...

Customer: 10 not in file
Insertion error -- Customer: 101 already in masterfile
Deletion error -- Customer: 123 has non-zero balance
Update error   -- Invalid transaction code for transaction: 229

```
 ID   NAME                  ADDRESS                          BALANCE

  1   River, Charles        37 Pleasant Street Needham MA     15.76
  7   Pascal, Blaise        1 rue de la Paix Paris France     75.60
  9   Disk, Floppy          69 Double Sided Rd Density AL      0.00
 11   Memory, Morris        122 Indian Lane Brooklyn NY       12.00
 19   Cobol, Hacker         13 East 47th Street N.Y. N.Y.     99.50
 99   Metropolitan, C.      755 Commonwealth Av Boston MA     -2.96
100   Broom, Hilda          4 Second Ave Peru IL               5.95
101   Sequential, Access    123 Tape Drive Sarasota FL         3.98
123   Fortran, Fred         99 Math Lane Matrix CA            71.05
229   Lovelace, Ada         12 Surrey Drive Dover England      0.00
```

APPLICATION

Sorting Files

As a second application of files, we will examine an algorithm to sort files. For our master file update program to work, it is essential that both the master file and the transaction file be sequenced in the same order. Many other file-processing programs also require that a file be sequenced according to a key, such as id numbers. If a file is not in order according to some key, then it must be sorted.

Sorting a file is different from sorting an array: the elements of a file cannot be accessed at random. When sorting an array, all the elements of the array are in main storage and it is not difficult to swap any pair of elements that the sorting algorithm requires. With a sequential file, only one element is available in main storage at any point in time; thus, sorts that are used on arrays generally cannot be used to sort files.

Merging is the fundamental operation used to sort sequential files. Consider the following file, which contains integers. The integers actually may be keys to records containing additional information, but for simplicity's sake, we will restrict our attention to only the keys:

12 23 2 3 9 54 34 4 67 11 32 69

We can break the file into sequences of values that are already in order. These sequences are called **runs**:

<u>12 23</u>   <u>2 3 9 54</u>   <u>34</u>   <u>4 67</u>   <u>11 32 69</u>

The original file has five runs. The end of a run can be detected by the fact that the next value is smaller than the previous one. The end of the last run is the end of the file.

The **Merge Sort** makes use of three runs. The basic idea behind this sort is to merge runs until we are left with only one run, at which point the file is sorted. To do the sorting we will need two temporary files. We start the sort by distributing the runs of the original file into the two temporary files:

Original file	<u>12 23</u> <u>2 3 9 54</u> <u>34</u> <u>4 67</u> <u>11 32 69</u>
Temporary file 1	<u>12 23 34</u> <u>11 32 69</u>
Temporary file 2	<u>2 3 9 54</u> <u>4 67</u>

The first run is placed in Temporary file 1, the next run in Temporary file 2, the next run in Temporary file 1, and so on, until all the runs have been distributed to the two temporary files. Once the original file has been distributed to the temporary files, we can proceed to merge the runs of the temporary files back into the original file:

Temporary file 1	<u>12 23 34</u> <u>11 32 69</u>
Temporary file 2	<u>2 3 9 54</u> <u>4 67</u>
Original file	<u>2 3 9 12 23 34 54</u> <u>4 11 32 67 69</u>

The distribution-merge process is repeated until only one run remains, indicating that the original file is completely sorted:

APPLICATION

Sorting Files
(*continued*)

	Distribute
Original file	2 3 9 12 23 34 54 4 11 32 67 69
Temporary file 1	2 3 9 12 23 34 54
Temporary file 2	4 11 32 67 69
	Merge
Temporary file 1	2 3 9 12 23 34 54
Temporary file 2	4 11 32 67 69
Original file	2 3 4 9 11 12 23 32 54 67 69

The algorithm to perform the sort can be written as:

```
begin
    Print the original file
    repeat
        Open original file for input
        Open temporary files for output
        Distribute (Datafile, Temp1, Temp2)
        Distribute original file to temporary files
        Open original file for output
        Open temporary files for input
        Merge temporary files to original file, counting runs
    until sorted
    Print the sorted file
end.
```

We can now elaborate the distribution operation of the algorithm:

```
begin (Distribute)
    repeat
        repeat
            Copy a record from original file to temporary file 1
        until end of run
        if not end of original file then
            repeat
                Copy a record from original file to temporary file 2
            until end of run
    until end of original file
end (of Distribute)
```

Although it appears to be simple, the instruction to copy a record from one file to another needs elaboration. What we need to do is not only copy a record, but also determine if the record just copied represents the end of a run. The following algorithm will perform both of these functions for any two files:

begin (Copy record)
  if it is not the end of the source file **then**
    Copy record from source to destination file
    Advance file window of source file
    if it is the end of source file **then**
      Set end-of-run to true
    else
      if copied record > source file window **then**
        Set end-of-run to true
      else
        Set end-of-run to false
  else
    Set end-of-run to true
end (of Copy record)

Finally, we can design the merge algorithm as follows:

begin (Merge)
  Initialize number of runs counter to 0
  while data remain in both temporary files **do**
    repeat
      if the window of file 1 is less than the window of file 2 **then**
        Copy a record from file 1 to original file
        if end of run in file 1 **then**
          Copy a record from file 2 to original file
      else
        Copy a record from file 2 to original file
        if end of run in file 2 **then**
          Copy a record from file 1 to original file
    until end of run in either file
    Increment number of runs counter by 1
  if records remain in file 1 **then**
  Increment number of runs counter by 1
    repeat
      Copy record from file 1 to original
    until end of file 1
  if records remain in file 2 **then**
    Increment number of runs counter by 1
    repeat
      Copy record from file 2 to original
    until end of file 2
  if number of runs counter equals 1 **then**
    Set sorted to true
  else
    Set sorted to false
end (of MERGE)

APPLICATION

Sorting Files
(*continued*)

When we convert the above algorithms to code and add the code to print a file, we have the following Pascal program:

```pascal
program MergeSort(DataFile,output);

{*********************************
* Program to sort two files using *
* the merge sort.                  *
*********************************}

type
   NumberFile = file of integer;

var
   DataFile : NumberFile;
   Temp1    : NumberFile;
   Temp2    : NumberFile;
   Sorted   : boolean;


procedure CopyRecord (var Source, Destination : NumberFile;
                      var RunDone : boolean);

{*****************************************
* Procedure copies a record from the    *
* Source file to the Destination file.  *
* If the item copied is the end of a    *
* run it returns "RunDone" as true.     *
*****************************************}

   var
      CopiedRecord : integer;

   begin
      if not eof(Source) then
         begin
            CopiedRecord := Source↑;
            get(Source);
            Destination↑ := CopiedRecord;
            write(Destination↑:4);
            put(Destination);
            if eof(Source) then
               RunDone := true
            else
               if CopiedRecord > Source↑ then
```

```
                                   RunDone := true
                           else
                                   RunDone := false
                   end
                     else
                         RunDone := true
           end {of procedure COPY};


   procedure Distribute(var Source,
                            Target1, Target2 :NumberFile);

      {****************************************
       * Procedure to distribute runs from the *
       * Source file to the target files.      *
       ****************************************}

      var
         EndOfRun    : boolean;

      begin
         repeat
            writeln;
            writeln('Now distributing to temporary file 1');
            repeat
               CopyRecord(Source,Target1,EndOfRun)
            until EndOfRun;
            if not eof(Source) then
              begin
                 writeln;
                 writeln('Now distributing to temporary
                         file 2');
                 repeat
                    CopyRecord(Source,Target2,EndOfRun)
                 until EndOfRun
              end
         until eof(Source);
         writeln;
         writeln('End of distribution phase')
      end {of Procedure DISTRIBUTE};


   procedure Merge(var Source1,Source2,Target :NumberFile;
                 var Done :boolean);
```

APPLICATION

Sorting Files
(*continued*)

```
{****************************************
* Procedure to merge runs from files    *
* "Source1" and "Source2" to file       *
* "Target." The procedure also counts   *
* the runs merged. If only one run is    *
* present it returns "Done"  as true to *
* indicate that the file "Target" is     *
* sorted.                                *
****************************************}

var
    EndOfRun : boolean;
    NumberOfRuns : integer;

begin
    writeln('Merge phase beginning...');
    NumberOfRuns := 0;
    while not (eof(Source1) or eof(Source2)) do
        begin
          repeat
            if Source1↑ < Source2↑ then
                begin
                    CopyRecord(Source1,Target,EndOfRun);
                    if EndOfRun then
                        CopyRecord(Source2,Target,EndOfRun)
                end
            else
                begin
                    CopyRecord(Source2,Target,EndOfRun);
                    if EndOfRun then
                        CopyRecord(Source1,Target,EndOfRun)
                end
          until EndOfRun;
          NumberOfRuns := NumberOfRuns + 1
        end;
    if not eof(Source1) then
        begin
            NumberOfRuns := NumberOfRuns + 1;
            repeat
                Target↑ := Source1↑;
                get(Source1);
                put(Target)
            until eof(Source1)
        end;
```

```
            if not eof(Source2) then
               begin
                  NumberOfRuns := NumberOfRuns + 1;
                  repeat
                     Target↑ := Source2↑;
                     get(Source2);
                     put(Target)
                  until eof(Source2)
               end;
            if NumberOfRuns = 1 then
               Done := true
            else
               Done := false;
            writeln;
            writeln('End of merge phase');
            writeln('Number of Runs: ',NumberOfRuns:4)
         end {of procedure MERGE};


procedure PrintFile (var AFile : NumberFile);

{*****************************
* Procedure to print a file. *
*****************************}

begin
   reset(AFile);
   while not eof(AFile) do
      begin
         write(AFile↑:4);
         get(AFile)
      end;
   writeln
end {of procedure PRINTFILE};

begin {*** MAIN ***}

   {Print the original unsorted file}

   writeln ('** ORIGINAL FILE **');
   writeln;
   PrintFile (DataFile);

   {Sort original file}
```

APPLICATION

Sorting Files
(*continued*)

```
repeat
    reset(DataFile);
    rewrite(Temp1);
    rewrite(Temp2);
    Distribute(Datafile,Temp1,Temp2);
    reset(Temp1,);
    reset(Temp2,);
    rewrite(DataFile);
    Merge(Temp1,Temp2,DataFile,Sorted)
until Sorted;

{Print the sorted file}

writeln; writeln;
writeln ('** SORTED FILE **');
Printfile (DataFile)
end.
```

The following is a sample run using the same data as our previous example. Instructions to print intermediate results were added to the program so that we could trace its execution.

```
** ORIGINAL FILE **

  12   23    2    3    9   54   34    4   67   11   32   69
Now distributing to temporary file 1
  12   23
Now distributing to temporary file 2
   2    3    9   54
Now distributing to temporary file 1
  34
Now distributing to temporary file 2
   4   67
Now distributing to temporary file 1
  11   32   69
End of distribution phase
Merge phase beginning...
   2    3    9   12   23   34   54    4   11   32   67   69
End of merge phase
Number of Runs:     2
Now distributing to temporary file 1
   2    3    9   12   23   34   54
Now distributing to temporary file 2
   4   11   32   67   69
```

APPLICATION

Sorting Files
(*continued*)

```
End of distribution phase
Merge phase beginning...
   2   3   4   9  11  12  23  32  34  54  67  69
End of merge phase
Number of Runs:     1

** SORTED FILE **
   2   3   4   9  11  12  23  32  34  54  67  69
```

Note that this program makes use of files "Temp1" and Temp2," which are not listed in the program heading. These files are temporary files and exist only during the execution of the program. Such files are called **internal files**, as mentioned earlier. The program starts with one unsorted external file. When the program finishes, the external file is still there, but it is now sorted. The internal files disappear when the program terminates.

11.4 COMMON ERRORS

Probably the most common programming error involving files is reading past the end of a file. Consider the following program segment:

```
reset(AFile);
repeat
   write(AFile↑);
   get(AFile)
until eof(AFile)
```

If file "AFile" is empty, a run-time error will result. This will happen because "eof(AFile)" is true the moment the file is reset for reading. A file should always be checked for the end-of-file condition before being used. Some errors that result in reading past the end of a file are more subtle. They can occur because of the way Pascal handles type conversions with text files. Consider the following example where AFile is a text file and Number is of type integer.

```
while not eof(AFile) do
   begin
      read(AFile, Number);
      write(Number :6)
   end
```

The code certainly looks fine. However, if there are trailing blanks in AFile, the execution of the above loop will result in a run-time error. After reading the last integer, the file window AFile will be positioned on a blank. The next attempt to read the file will skip that blank and any other blanks following it. In the process, it will attempt to read past the end of the file. The above loop works only if the sole trailing blank in AFile is the last end-of-line character. The problem of trailing blanks is aggravated by the fact that many systems pad all lines to a fixed length, such as 80 characters. Sometimes such systems compensate for this, and the trailing blanks are not a problem. But often they do not. Therefore, when reading real or integer values from a text file, it is wise to include a routine to skip blanks and to invoke that routine prior to reading an integer or real value. The development of such a routine is left as an exercise.

A statement such as:

```
read(AFile, Number1, Number2, Number3)
```

is also fraught with danger because eof(Afile) cannot be checked before obtaining each of the values.

Finally, with interactive input—that is, input from a terminal during program execution—eof may not work at all.

The eoln function differs from the eof function in an important way: the eoln function works only with text files, whereas the eof function works with any file

Remember that you must reset any file (other than the standard input file) before it can be read, and that you must rewrite any file (other than the standard output file) before it can be written. Also remember that *rewrite destroys the contents of a file*. The following program segment, intended to copy one file to another, will copy only the last record.

```
reset(Source);
while not eof(Source) do
   begin
      rewrite(Object);
      Object↑ := Source↑;
      put(Object)
   end
```

On the other hand, the following segment will not work at all because eof(Source) is undefined:

```
while not eof(Source) do
   begin
      reset(Source);
      rewrite(Object);
      Object↑ := Source↑;
      put(Object)
   end
```

11.5 CHAPTER REVIEW

A file is any source or destination of information. There are two types of files: sequential files and random access files.

The values in a sequential file can only be accessed in the same sequences as they are stored. To process such a file, we must move through successive data items in the same order as their respective locations on a storage device. The values in a random access file can be accessed in any order. Standard Pascal supports only sequential files.

In Pascal, a file is a structured data type consisting of a sequence of components of the same type. Unlike arrays, we repeat that the components of a file cannot be randomly accessed. With a file, only one component, called the **file window**, is available to the program at any given point in time. All other components of the file, either before or after the window, are not accessible to the program immediately.

To define a file data type in Pascal we can use a **type** definition of the following form:

type
   Type-Identifier = **file of** BaseType;

The BaseType specifies the data type of the individual components of the file. This BaseType can be any Pascal data type except another file.

The declaration of a file variable automatically creates a single-element window into that file. We can think of the value in the file window as being in main storage and being directly accessible to the program for use. The rest of the elements in the file will not be accessible until the window is moved to each of them. The file window, sometimes also called the **file buffer variable,** is referenced by following the file identifier by a special symbol, usually a ↑ .

A file window is controlled and tested using five standard Pascal procedures and functions.

The procedure invocation

`reset(f)`

initializes file f for reading by copying the first element of the file into f ↑ . Every file, except for the standard input file, must be reset before being read.

The procedure invocation

`get(f)`

reads the next value of the file into f ↑ .

The expression

`eof(f)`

is false as long as the file window is positioned over a component of the file. If the window is positioned over the end-of-file character, eof(f) is true.

The procedure invocation

`rewrite(f)`

opens the file f for output. File f is completely cleared and eof(f) is set to true.

The procedure

`put(f)`

writes the current contents of f ↑ to the file f.

The predefined file type **text** is a file of characters that is structured into lines. The standard input and output files are of type text. The four special procedures to handle input and output with text files are read, readln, write, and writeln.

For any textfile f

`eoln(f)`

is true if the file window is positioned on a line separator character and is false otherwise. When the file window is over a line separator, Pascal assigns a blank to the file buffer variable.

11.6 EXERCISES

11.1. Fill in the blanks for each of the following:

(a) A file is any _____ or _____ of data.

(b) The five standard procedures and functions to manipulate files are _____, _____, _____, _____, and _____.

(c) If the file f is empty, reset(f) sets eof(f) to _____.

(d) After rewrite(f) is executed, eof(f) is _____.

(e) The symbol for the file buffer variable for file MasterFile is _____.

(f) A text file is a file of characters divided into _____.

(g) The function eoln(f) can be used with any file f only if the type of file f is _____.

(h) When passing a file to a procedure, it must be passed as a _____ parameter.

(i) For text file f, read(f,x) is equivalent to _____ followed by _____.

(j) The type of the standard files input and output is _____.

11.2. Answer each of the following true or false. If your answer is false, state why.

(a) Before values can be read from a file, every file must be reset.

(b) In order to write values to file f, eof(f) must be true.

(c) The procdures get and put cannot be used with text files.

(d) When the file parameter is omitted from a read procedure, it defaults to input.

(e) The end-of-line character is input as a blank.

(f) The execution of put(f) appends the current value of f ↑ to the file f; f ↑ becomes undefined.

(g) The easiest way to copy file f to file g, if the files are of the same type, is by using the assignment statement:

g := f

as with any other variables.

(h) Elements of a file, just like elements of an array, can be accessed in any order.

(i) The statement write(f, value) is equivalent to put(f); f ↑ := value.

(j) The procedure get can be used to move through a file in any direction.

11.3. Describe the function(s) performed by each of the following Pascal statements:

(a) **type**
```
     Numbers = file of integer;
```

(b) **var**
```
     NumberFile :   Numbers;
```

(c) `reset(NumberFile)`

(d) `rewrite(NumberFile)`

(e)
```
NumberFile↑ := 5;
put(NumberFile)
```

(f)
```
writeln(NumberFile↑ :5);
get(NumberFile)
```

11.4. Consider the following declaration:

var
    Numbers1, Numbers2 : **file of** integer;

(a) Write a function that will return the number of times a particular integer appears in file Numbers1.

(b) Write a procedure that will copy all integers greater than zero from file Numbers1 to file Numbers2. It should leave file Numbers1 unchanged.

(c) Write a procedure to delete all integers less than zero from file Numbers1.

11.5. Suppose that a text file contains between 1 and 80 characters. Write a program that reads that file and creates another file where all the lines are exactly 80 characters long. Shorter lines are padded with blanks, as necessary.

11.6. Write a program that takes two files of the same type and concatenates them. That is, your program should link the files to form a single file from the two files such that the elements of the first file are followed by the elements of the second file. The resulting file should replace the first file.

11.7. Write a procedure that takes a text file as input and prints it, numbering each line sequentially.

11.8. The following procedure is supposed to skip blanks in a text file until it encounters a nonblank character, or the end of the file.

procedure SkipBlanks(**var** f :text);

```
    {***************************
    * Skip blanks until eof(f) *
    * or a non-blank is found. *
    ***************************}
begin
    while not eof(f) and (f↑ = ' ') do
        get(f);
end;
```

(a) Why will it not work?

(b) Modify it so that it will work. (Hint: use an **if** statement and a boolean variable.)

11.9. Write a program that uses a file to keep track of who runs the program. The program asks for the name of the user and writes it to a file. It also, on request, provides the name of the person who last used the program.

11.10. The text of a form letter is sorted in a file named Letter. A file of names and addresses is stored in another file, MailList. The file MailList consists of records of the form:

type
    MailEntry = **record**
        Salutation : (Mr, Ms);

```
    FirstName   : packed array[1..15] of char;
    LastName    : packed array[1..15] of char;
    Street      : packed array[1..20] of char;
    City        : packed array[1..15] of char;
    State       : packed array[1..2] of char;
    ZipCode     : packed array[1..5] of char
end;
```

The form letter in file Letter contains the text of the letter with certain keywords in appropriate places. These keywords are to be replaced with information from the file MailList. The keywords and their replacement information are:

Keyword	Replacement Information
s	Salutation
fn	First name
n	Last name
a	Street address
c	City
st	State
z	ZIP code

(a) Write a Pascal program to print a personalized form letter for every entry in the file MailList using the file Letter as a template.

(b) Write a program to sort the file MailList by ZIP code.

(c) Modify your program of part (a) so that a starting and ending point in the MailList file can be specified.

11.11. The master file update program of this chapter does not allow for the correction of existing records already in the master file. Alter the master file update to add the capability to correct any field, except the id field, of any record in the master file.

11.12. One defect of the merge sort described in this chapter is that each merge operation must be preceded by a distribution operation. One way to eliminate all distributions except for the first one, is to use four files instead of three. As with the merge sort, we start out by distributing the file to be sorted, File1, into two temporary files: File2 and File3. Thereafter, merging and distributing are combined into a single merge-distribute pass. As File2 and File3 are merged, they are distributed to File1 and File4. Then, as File1 and File4 are merged, they are distributed to File2 and File3. The process continues until there is only a single run left. This sort is called a **balanced merge sort.**

Write a Pascal program to perform a balanced merge sort.

12. Dynamic Data Structures

12.1 STATIC VS. DYNAMIC STRUCTURES

In the structured data types we have studied so far (with the exception of files) the number of components and the interrelationships between these components were fixed at the time the program was written. That is, the structures remained **static** during the execution of the program. We could easily change the values of components, but we could not increase their number nor easily change the relationships between them.

For example, consider arrays. The size of an array is fixed at the time of its declaration. If, during program execution, we discover that we need a larger array, there is nothing we can do. The array must be redeclared and the program recompiled with the new size. Similarly, the structure of an array is fixed. The first component precedes the second, the second precedes the third, and so on. If we wanted to delete the second component so that the third component would now become the second, we would have to shift the *values* of all the components forward one location. We could not simply delete the second component. Arrays are **static data structures**.

Dynamic data structures, on the other hand, can expand and contract during program execution. We can, for example, easily insert new components between existing ones, or delete an existing component. That is, we can dynamically alter the interrelationships among the components of a data structure during program execution. Such structures are very useful for storage of information that is constantly changing, such as that in an airline reservation system. Such a system gives rise to data structures that may vary both in size and organization during their lifetimes.

Dynamic data structures are often constructed by **linking** the components of the structure together. To construct such structures, we need each component to have not only the ability to store the information (e.g., the passenger's name on a given flight), but also the information as to which components are linked to it (e.g., the next passenger and/or the previous passenger in alphabetical order on the same flight). The links between the components of the structure are implemented using variables called **pointers**. A passenger list may appear as in Figure 12.1, where the arrows represent pointers.

Figure 12.1 A
passenger list linked
by pointers

12.2
POINTERS

Before we study how to construct and use such linked structures as that in Figure 12.1, we will examine the definition and use of pointers. A pointer variable is a variable that points or **references** another variable. Since a variable is a location in main storage, pointers are variables that reference main storage locations. Thus, values of pointer variables are *addresses* of locations in main storage. In Pascal, when defining a pointer variable, we specify the type of value the pointer points to. The definition:

```
type
  NumberPtr = ↑integer;
```

defines the type "NumberPtr" as a pointer that references a main storage location designated to store an integer. The circumflex (ˆ) or uparrow (↑), or sometimes the at sign (@), precedes the type of the referenced variable. The syntax diagram for a pointer type definition is shown in Figure 12.2.

Once the type of a pointer variable has been defined, we can declare pointer variables in the usual way. The declaration:

```
var
  p, q : NumberPtr;
```

declares *p* and *q* as pointer variables. The declaration reserves the storage for two addresses, each with the ability to point to main storage locations containing integers. The pointers, however, are as yet undefined. They do not yet reference any specific main storage locations.

Pascal provides a standard procedure, called new, to dynamically assign a value to a pointer and simultaneously allocate the storage for the variable it references. The expressions

```
new(p);
new(q)
```

allocate the storage for two integers, and assign to the pointer variables *p* and *q* the addresses of these locations. In order to assign values to, or otherwise access, the locations that *p* and *q* point to, we use the following notation:

p↑   references the location pointed to by p
q↑   references the location pointed to by q

The assignment statement:

p↑ := 5

assigns 5 to the location referenced by the pointer *p*.

When the location pointed to by pointer *p* is no longer needed, a standard procedure, called dispose, can be used to release that location for later use. We can illustrate the dynamic allocation of storage, the assignment of a value to a location referenced by a pointer, and the release of the storage location for later use with the diagram in Figure 12.3.

Figure 12.2 Syntax diagram for pointer definition

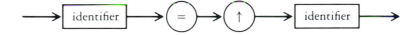

Figure 12.3 How a pointer operates

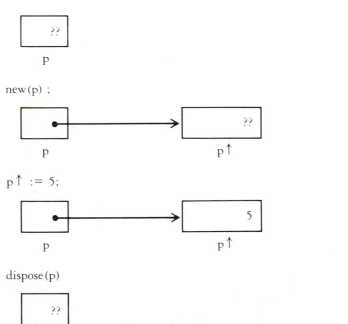

The arrow is used to represent the value of pointer p. The actual value is, of course, an address. The diagram can be summarized as follows. Initially, the pointer p is undefined. The procedure invocation new (p) allocates the storage for $p \uparrow$ and assigns to p the address of $p \uparrow$. The assignment $p \uparrow := 5$ assigns the value 5 to $p \uparrow$, the location referenced by p. Finally, dispose (p) releases the location referenced by p for possible later reallocation and makes p undefined.

We occasionally need a pointer variable that does not point to any location, but is yet defined. In Pascal this value is represented by the reserved word **nil**. The execution of the assignment

```
p := nil
```

assigns a value to p, but p does not point to any main storage location. The advantage of a **nil** pointer over a pointer that is simply undefined is that we can check it to see if it is or is not **nil**. The code below determines if the pointer p points to any main storage location. If p were undefined, the code would lead to a run-time error. The value of **nil** can be assigned to any pointer, irrespective of the data type that is referenced by the pointer.

```
if p = nil then
    writeln('The pointer is NIL')
else
    writeln('The pointer points to a location')
```

We can examine the value of a pointer only by determining if it is **nil**, or by comparing it to the value of another pointer of the same type. The following code checks to see if p and q have the same value; that is, whether p and q point to the same location.

```
if p = q then
    if p <> nil then
        writeln('The pointers point to the same location')
    else
        writeln('Both pointers are NIL')
else
    writeln('The pointers have different values')
```

In addition to assigning a value to a pointer by using the standard procedure new or by assigning the value **nil**, the value of one pointer can be assigned to another pointer of the same type. The following code first assigns a new value to the pointer p, then assigns the same value to the pointer q. As a result, p and q point to the same location.

```
new(p);
q := p
```

The values of pointer variables are addresses and are therefore represented in the internal representation the system uses for such values. These values cannot be printed, nor can we use them in arithmetic expressions to perform calculations.

The variables referenced by pointers, on the other hand, can be used like any other variables of the same type. For example, we can read or print values referenced by pointers as follows:

```
read(p↑);
writeln(p↑)
```

Pointer variables may be defined to point to structured variables such as records, as well as to scalar variables such as integers. The pointer "BookPointer," below, references a variable of type "Book," which is a record.

```
type
  BookPointer = ↑Book;

  Book = record
      Author : packed array[1..15] of char;
      Title  : packed array[1..30] of char;
      Publisher : packed array[1..20] of char;
      Year : integer
  end;

var
  ThisBook : BookPointer;
```

The execution of

```
new(ThisBook)
```

allocates the storage for the record and assigns to ThisBook the address of the record.

1. Name two differences between static and dynamic structures.
2. Given the pointer definitions and variable declarations:

```
type
  IntPtr = ↑integer;
  CharPtr = ↑char;

var
  Ptr1, Ptr2 : IntPtr;
  Ptr3, Ptr4 : CharPtr;
```

show the output produced by each of the following:

```
(a) new(Ptr1);
    new(Ptr2);
    Ptr1↑ := 10;
    Ptr2↑ := Ptr1↑ + 5;
    writeln(Ptr1↑ :3, Ptr2↑ :3)


(b) new(Ptr1);
    Ptr1↑ := 10;
    Ptr2 := Ptr1;
    new(Ptr1);
    Ptr1↑ := Ptr2↑ div 2;
    writeln(Ptr1↑ :3, Ptr2↑ :3)

(c) new(Ptr3);
    new(Ptr4);
    Ptr3↑ := 'A';
    Ptr4↑ := succ(Ptr3↑);
    writeln(Ptr3↑ :3, Ptr4↑ :3)


(d) new(Ptr3);
    Ptr3↑ := 'B';
    Ptr4 := Ptr3;
    Ptr3↑ := pred(Ptr4↑);
    writeln(Ptr3↑ :3, Ptr4↑ :3)
```

3. Given the data-type definitions and variable declarations of question 2, determine which of the following statements are valid and which are not valid. For the ones that are not valid, state why. Assume that all pointer variables have been assigned non-**nil** values.

(a) `Ptr1↑ := 10;`
`Ptr2↑ := sqr(Ptr1);`

(b) `read (Ptr3↑);`

(c) `if Ptr3 = Ptr4 then`
`writeln(Ptr3↑)`

(d) `Ptr2 := Ptr2 + 1`

(e) `Ptr1 := nil;`
`Ptr1↑ := 5;`

(f) `dispose(Ptr3↑);`

Answers

1. (a) The number of components in static structures cannot be changed during program execution. The number of components in dynamic structures can change while the program is executing. (b) The interrelationships between the components of static variables cannot be altered. The structure of dynamic variables can be changed during program execution.

2. (a) 10 15   (b) 5 10   (c) AB   (d) AB

3. (a) Not valid. The values of pointer variables are addresses; they cannot be used in arithmetic expressions. (b) Valid (c) Valid, provided Ptr3 ↑ is defined. (d) Not valid. The values of pointer variables are addresses, they cannot be used in arithmetic expressions. (e) Not valid. (f) Not valid. The argument of dispose should be a pointer, not the value it references.

12.3 LINKED DATA STRUCTURES

Most pointers are used to reference records rather than simple scalar types. Furthermore, most pointers are used to construct linked structures. In order to build linked structures, we need records with at least one field that is a pointer to another record of the same type. Consider the following definitions and declarations:

```
type
  String = packed array[1..15] of char;

  PassPointer = ↑Passenger;

  Passenger = record
      Name : String;
      Seat : 1..200;
      NextPassenger : PassPointer
  end;

var
  PassList : PassPointer;
```

We first defined a pointer, PassPointer, which points to a variable of type "Passenger." Next we defined a record, Passenger, with three fields—with the third field containing a pointer to another record of type Passenger. Taken together, the definitions appear circular: we use Passenger to define PassPointer and we use PassPointer to define Passenger. This is the one place where Pascal violates the requirement that a structure must be defined in terms of previously defined structures. There is, in fact, no way to get around the circularity. Pascal simply requires that the pointer type be defined prior to the record type to which it points.

Records such as the above can be linked together into a structure called a **linked list**. Figure 12.4 illustrates a linked list formed with such records.

The variable PassList points to the first record of the list. Each record consists of three fields. The Name field is used to store a passenger's name. The Seat field is used to store the seat number. The NextPassenger field stores a pointer to the next record on the list. The NextPassenger field of the last record has the value **nil**. The **nil** value is used as a sentinel to indicate the end of the list. It is represented in this book by the symbol:

The procedure of Example 12.1 reads names from the standard input file and builds the list shown in Figure 12.4. We assume that seat assignments are yet to be made, thus the Seat field of each record remains undefined.

Figure 12.4 A
linked list

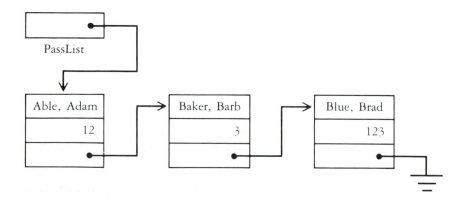

**EXAMPLE 12.1
Creating a
Linked List**

```pascal
procedure CreateList(var PassList : PassPointer);

{**************************************
* Procedure to read passenger names  *
* and create a linked list. The      *
* names are linked in the order they *
* are input.                         *
**************************************}

var
   CurrentPassenger, LastPassenger: PassPointer;
   i : integer;

begin
   {Create first record of the list}
   new(PassList);

   {Read name of first passenger}
   if not eof then
       for i := 1 to 15 do
           read(PassList↑.Name[i]);

   {Assume this is end of list. Set sentinel value}
   PassList↑.NextPassenger := nil;
   LastPassenger := PassList;

   {Read names of remaining passengers and add them to list}

   while not eof do
       begin
           {Create new record}
           new(CurrentPassenger);

           {Link new record to end of list}
           LastPassenger↑.NextPassenger := CurrentPassenger;

           {Reset pointer to end of list}
           LastPassenger := CurrentPassenger;

           {Read a name}
           for i := 1 to 15 do
               read(CurrentPassenger↑.Name[i]);
           readln
       end;
   {Set sentinel for end of list}
   LastPassenger↑.NextPassenger := nil
end;
```

First, we input and store the name of the first passenger. Then we proceed to input and link the remaining names to the list. In each case we proceed as follows. We dynamically create a new record using the statement new (CurrentPassenger). The statement LastPassenger ↑ .NextPassenger := CurrentPassenger causes the NextPassenger field of the current last record to point to the newly created record. The newly created record is thereby linked to the end of the list. The value of CurrentPassenger is then assigned to LastPassenger so that LastPassenger continues to point to the end of the list. Figure 12.5 illustrates the process. Assume that the first passenger is already on the list.

Figure 12.5 Adding a new passenger to the end of the list

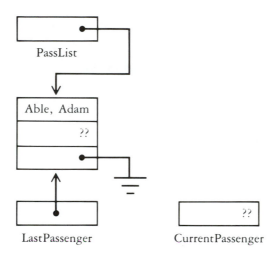

new (CurrentPassenger)

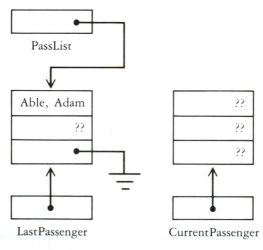

Figure 12.5
(*continued*)

LastPassenger ↑.NextPassenger := CurrentPassenger

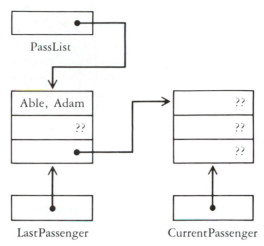

LastPassenger := CurrentPassenger

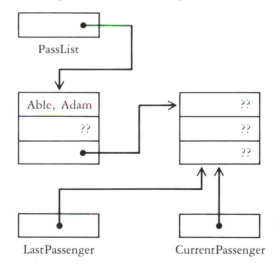

Once the record is created and properly linked to the list, the name of the new passenger can be read into the appropriate field of the record referenced by CurrentPassenger. Note that when pointers point to a record, the fields of the record are accessed in the usual manner; that is,

`CurrentPassenger↑.Name`

refers to the Name field of the record CurrentPassenger ↑.

Figure 12.6 A linked list with header

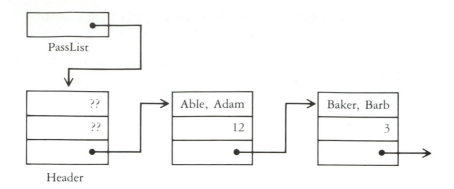

We had to handle the first record in the list differently from all the other records. This is because it is pointed to by PassList instead of the NextPassenger field of a previous record. We can simplify the algorithm to create the list (and other algorithms to manipulate the list) by including a dummy record at the front of the list, called a **list header** or simply a **header**. Figure 12.6 shows a list with a header record.

The Name and Seat fields of the header record are not important. The NextPassenger field points to the first actual record on the list. A list with only a header record, and with the NextPassenger field equal to **nil** is considered empty. If the passenger list uses a header record, then we can simplify our procedure to build the linked list as shown in Example 12.2.

EXAMPLE 12.2 Creating a Linked List with Header

```
procedure CreateList ( var PassList : PassPointer);

{****************************************
* Procedure to read passenger names    *
* and create a linked list with a      *
* header record. The names are         *
* linked in the order they are input.  *
****************************************}

var
   CurrentPassenger, LastPassenger: PassPointer;
   i : integer;

begin
   {Create the header record}
   new(PassList);
```

**EXAMPLE 12.2
Creating a
Linked List
with Header**
(*continued*)

```
{Last record pointer points to header}
LastPassenger := PassList;

{Read names of passengers and add them to list}

while not eof do
    begin
      {Create new record}
      new(CurrentPassenger);

      {Link new record to end of list}
      LastPassenger↑.NextPassenger := CurrentPassenger;

      {Reset pointer to end of list}
      LastPassenger := CurrentPassenger;

      {Read a name}
      for i := 1 to 15 do
          read(CurrentPassenger↑.Name[i]);
      readln
    end;

  {Set sentinel for last record}
  LastPassenger↑.NextPassenger := nil
end;
```

Suppose we wish to locate the record of a passenger on the list to modify it (e.g., make a seat assignment), delete it, or simply determine if the passenger is on the list. To modify a record we will need a pointer to the record. To delete it we will need a pointer to the previous record because we must reconnect the pointer of the previous record to the record *following* the deleted one. Otherwise we will lose the end of the list! Thus, our procedure to locate a particular record will return two pointers: one to the record we are looking for, the other to the preceding record. In Example 12.3 we assume the list has a header record.

When the search procedure terminates, it returns the values of two pointers: Current and Previous. If the value of Current is **nil**, then the record we were searching for is not in the list. Otherwise, Current points to the record we were looking for and Previous points to the preceding record. The search algorithm is a linear search and is similar to a linear-search algorithm for an array.

EXAMPLE 12.3
Procedure to
Locate a
Record in a
Linked List

```
procedure Search (PassList :PassPointer;
                  SearchName :String;
                  var Current, Previous : PassPointer);

{***************************************
* Procedure to locate a record on      *
* passenger list with name equal to    *
* "SearchName". Procedure is passed     *
* a pointer to the header record of     *
* the list and the name to look for.   *
* It returns a pointer to the record   *
* sought and a pointer to the          *
* previous record. If the record       *
* sought is not on the list, it        *
* returns "Current" as NIL.            *
***************************************}

var
  Found : boolean;
begin
  {Initialize Previous to point to header
   and Current to point to first record on the list}

  Previous := PassList;
  Current := PassList↑.NextPassenger;

  Found := false;
  while (Current <> nil) and (not Found) do
      if Current↑. Name = SearchName then
          Found = true
      else
          begin
              {Advance the pointers}
              Previous := Current;
              Current := Current↑.NextPassenger
          end
end;
```

Once we have located a record we can delete it using the procedure illustrated in Example 12.4. Figure 12.7 illustrates how the "DeleteAfter" procedure works.

EXAMPLE 12.4 Procedure to Delete a Record from a List

```pascal
procedure DeleteAfter(Previous : PassPointer);

{*****************************************
* Procedure to delete the record after *
* the record pointed to by "Previous." *
*****************************************}

var
   Current : PassPointer;

begin

   {Set "Current" to point to record to be deleted}
   Current := Previous↑.NextPassenger;

   {Link the "NextPassenger" pointer of the previous
    record to the record following the one to be deleted
    and dispose of the record to be deleted}

   if Current <> nil then
     begin
       Previous↑.NextPassenger := Current↑.NextPassenger;
       dispose(Current)
     end
end;
```

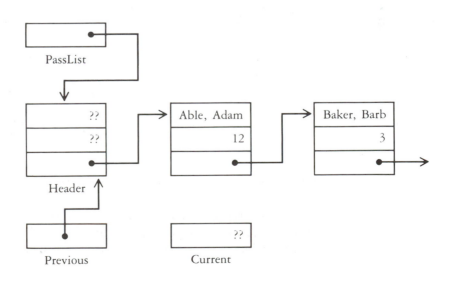

Figure 12.7 Deleting a record from a linked list

Figure 12.7
(*continued*)

Current := Previous↑.NextPassenger

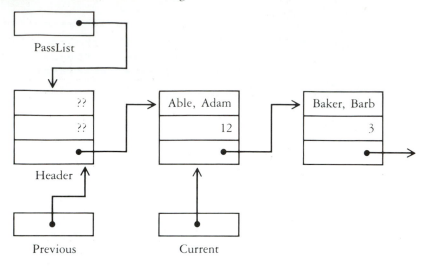

Previous↑.NextPassenger := Current↑.NextPassenger

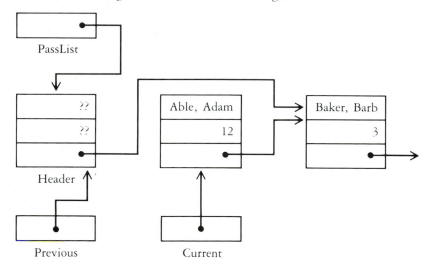

Figure 12.7
(*continued*)

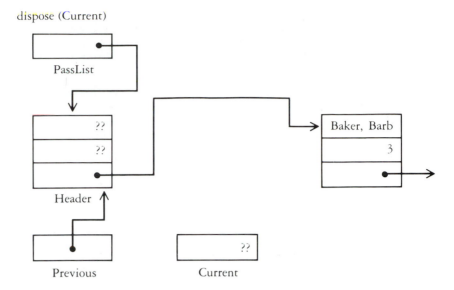

dispose (Current)

As another example of procedures that can be used with linked lists, consider a procedure to insert a record at any point in the list, given in Example 12.5. Just as with the procedure to delete a record, we insert a record after the record pointed to by the pointer passed to the procedure.

Drawing the appropriate figures to illustrate the insertion process is left as an exercise.

EXAMPLE 12.5
Procedure to Insert a Record into a Linked List

```
procedure InsertAfter(Previous : PassPointer;
                      NewName:String);

{****************************************
 * Procedure to insert a record after   *
 * the record pointed to by "Previous". *
 ****************************************}

var
   Current : PassPointer;

begin
   if Previous = nil then
      writeln ('Error -- NIL pointer')
   else
```

```
        begin
           {Create new record and store new name
            in name field}

           new(Current);
           Current↑.Name := NewName;

           {Link record into list}

           Current↑.NextPassenger := Previous↑.NextPassenger;
           Previous↑.NextPassenger := Current
        end
  end;
```

SELF-TEST 2

1. Write a procedure that prints the names of all passengers on a passenger list. (a) Assume the list does not have a header record. (b) Assume the list has a header record.

2. What does the following procedure do?

```
procedure Mystery (p : PassPointer);

var
  q : PassPointer;

begin
  q := p↑.NextPassenger;
  if q <> nil then
     begin
        p↑ := q↑;
        p↑.NextPassenger := q↑.NextPassenger;
        dispose(q)
     end
end;
```

3. Why is the **if** statement necessary in procedure "Mystery" in question 2?

Answers

```
1. procedure PrintListNoHeader(PassList : PassPointer);
   var
      Current : PassPointer;
```

```
    begin
      {Initialize "Current" pointer to first passenger}
      Current := PassList;

    while Current <> nil do
        begin
            writeln(Current↑.Name);


            {Advance pointer to next passenger}
            Current := Current↑.NextPassenger
        end
end;
procedure PrintListWithHeader(PassList : PassPointer);

var
  Current : PassPointer;

begin

  {Initialize "Current" pointer to first passenger}
  Current := PassList↑.NextPassenger;

  while Current <> nil do
      begin
          writeln(Current↑.Name);


          {Advance pointer to next passenger}
          Current := Current↑.NextPassenger

      end
end;
```

2. The procedure deletes the record that p is pointing to by first copying the contents of the next record into p ↑ and deleting the next record.

3. The **if** statement is necessary because the procedure will not work if p points to the last record on the list.

12.4 NONLINEAR STRUCTURES: TREES

In the previous section we saw how linked structures can be constructed using pointers. The structure we examined used one pointer to point to the next record in the structure. As a consequence, the components of the structure were arranged linearly, one after the other. It is possible to construct structures that use more than one pointer to link components together. One such structure, which uses two pointers, finds many applications in computer science and is called a **binary tree**. A binary tree is illustrated in Figure 12.8.

A binary tree is a collection of records, usually called **nodes**. Each node usually has three fields. One field is used to store information; the remaining fields are pointers. If we were to store the information of our passenger list in a binary tree, we could define each tree node as follows:

```
type
  String = packed array[1..15] of char;
  TreePointer = ↑Node;

  Node = record
      Name : String;
      Seat : 1..200;
      LeftPointer : TreePointer;
      RightPointer : TreePointer
  end;

var
  Tree : TreePointer;
```

Here, each node is a record consisting of four fields. The fields "Name" and "Seat" are used to store information. The fields "Left-Pointer" and "RightPointer" point to other nodes on the tree. The resulting binary tree is illustrated in Figure 12.9.

For the binary tree in Figure 12.9, passenger information is stored in such a way that the left pointer of any node points to pas-

Figure 12.8 A binary tree

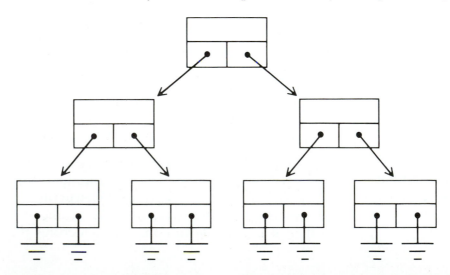

Figure 12.9 A passenger list as a binary tree

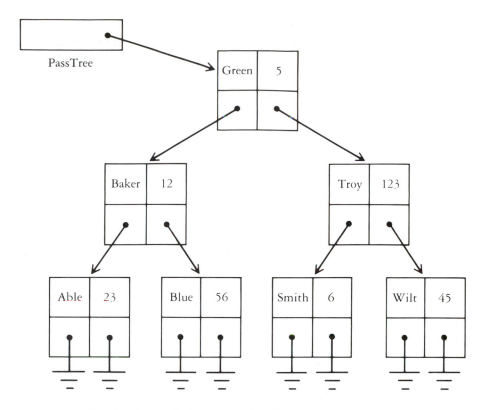

sengers earlier in the alphabet, and the right pointer points to passengers further down the alphabet. This arrangement of passengers into a tree structure makes searching for passengers very efficient. This type of a tree is often called a **binary search tree**.

We can easily design an algorithm to search the tree for a passenger with a given name. We start at the first node of the tree, usually called the **root node**. If this is the name we are looking for, then we are done. If the name stored at the node is less than the name we are looking for, then we follow the right pointer. If it is greater than the name we are looking for, then we follow the left pointer. This process is repeated until we encounter a **nil** pointer or locate the name we are searching for. The algorithm below returns a pointer to the passenger we were searching for if the passenger is found. It returns a **nil** pointer if the passenger is not in the tree.

begin
    Initialize current pointer to root node
    while (current pointer is not **nil**) **and** (name is not found) **do**
      if name sought is name at current node **then**
        Set found flag to true

```
        else
            if name sought is less than name at current node then
                Set current pointer to left pointer of
                    current node

            else
                Set current pointer to right pointer of
                    current node
        if found flag is true then
            Return pointer to current node
        else
            Return nil pointer
    end.
```

Converting this algorithm to a Pascal function is straightforward, and has been done in Example 12.6.

The function in Example 12.6 also can be written recursively. Binary trees can, in fact, be defined recursively. We can think of a tree as being empty (that is, consisting of a **nil** pointer), or as consisting of a single node (the root node), or as consisting of the root node with its pointers each pointing to binary trees (the left subtree and the right subtree).

**EXAMPLE 12.6
Function to
Search a
Binary Tree**

```
function SearchBinaryTree (Tree :TreePointer;
                           SearchName :String): TreePointer;

{*************************************
 * Function to search a binary tree. *
 *************************************}

var
   Current : TreePointer;
   Found : boolean;

begin
   Found := false;
   Current := Tree;

   while (Current <> nil) and (not Found) do
       if SearchName = Current↑.Name then
           Found := true
       else
           if SearchName < Current↑.Name then
               Current := Current↑.LeftPointer
           else
               Current := Current↑.RightPointer;
```

**EXAMPLE 12.6
Function to
Search a
Binary Tree**
(*continued*)

```
if Found then
    SearchBinaryTree := Current
else
    SearchBinaryTree := nil
end;
```

The function of Example 12.7 is a recursive version of the tree search algorithm. It makes use of the recursive nature of the binary tree structure. The algorithm inspects the root node of the tree. If the root node is **nil**, then the name is not on the tree and the **nil** pointer is returned. If the name sought is less than the name at the root node, we search the subtree whose root node is pointed to by the left pointer. If the name sought is greater than the name at the root node, we search the subtree whose root node is pointed to by the right pointer. If neither of these conditions holds, the name we are looking for must be at the root node.

**EXAMPLE 12.7
Recursive Tree
Search Func-
tion**

```
function Search (Tree :TreePointer;
                 SearchName :String): TreePointer;

{************************************
* Function to search a binary tree  *
* using a recursive algorithm.      *
************************************}

begin
  if Tree = nil then
     Search := nil
  else
    if SearchName < Tree↑.Name then
      {Search left subtree}
      Search := Search(Tree↑.LeftPointer,SearchName)
    else
      if SearchName > Tree↑.Name then
          {Search right subtree}
          Search := Search(Tree↑.RightPointer,SearchName)
      else
          {Name being sought equals name at this node}
          Search := Tree
end;
```

In order for the tree search algorithm to work, the names must be stored properly. The procedure in Example 12.8 will read names from the standard input file and enter them into a binary search tree.

**EXAMPLE 12.8
Procedure to
Build a Binary
Search Tree**

```
procedure BuildBinarySearchTree (var Tree : TreePointer);

{*********************************
 * Procedure to read names from  *
 * a file and construct a binary *
 * search tree.                  *
 *********************************}

var
   First, Second :TreePointer;
   i : integer;
   NewName : String;

begin
   {If file is not empty, read the first name
    and insert it into a single node binary tree}
   Tree := nil;
   if not eof then
      begin
         new(Tree);
         for i := 1 to 15 do
            read(Tree↑.Name[i]);
         readln;
         Tree↑.LeftPointer := nil;
         Tree↑.RightPointer := nil;
         First := Tree;
         Second := Tree
      end;

   {Read and enter into tree the remaining names}
   while not eof do
      begin
         First := Tree;
         for i := 1 to 15 do
            read(NewName[i]);
         readln;

         {Traverse tree to find location where to insert}
         while (NewName <> Second↑.Name) and
               (First <> nil) do
            begin
               Second := First;
```

EXAMPLE 12.8
Procedure to
Build a Binary
Search Tree
(*continued*)

```
                              if NewName < Second↑.Name then
                                  First := Second↑.LeftPointer
                              else
                                      First := Second↑.RightPointer
               end;

               {Check if name already in tree}
               if NewName = Second↑.Name then
                   writeln ('Passenger: ',NewName,' has',
                                ' reservation already')
               else
               begin
                   {Insert name}
                   new(First);
                   First↑.Name := NewName;
                   First↑.LeftPointer := nil;
                   First↑.RightPointer := nil;

                   {Attach new node to tree}
                   if NewName < Second↑.Name then
                       Second↑.LeftPointer := First
                   else
                       Second↑.RighytPointer := First
               end
          end {of WHILE NOT eof}
end;
```

The above procedure could also be written recursively. This is left as an exercise.

As a final example of an algorithm using trees, we will design a recursive algorithm to print the binary search tree in alphabetical order. To print the tree in alphabetical order we must traverse it (that is, visit every node) in the proper sequence. The correct sequence can be described as follows:

1. First, visit the left subtree of the tree.
2. Next, visit the root of the tree.
3. Finally, visit the right subtree of the tree.

The Pascal procedure to implement the algorithm is surprisingly easy, as we see in Example 12.9.

As our first example of an application of dynamic data structures, we will look at a simple character manipulation application involving mathematics.

**EXAMPLE 12.9
Procedure to
Print Search
Tree in Sorted
Order**

```
procedure LeftNodeRight ( Tree : TreePointer);

{*************************************
* Procedure prints the contents of  *
* a tree by first printing the left *
* subtree, then the root node, and  *
* finally the right subtree.         *
*************************************}

begin
  if Tree <> nil then
    begin
        {Traverse left subtree}
        LeftNodeRight(Tree↑.LeftPointer);

        {Visit the root}
        writeln(Tree↑.Name);

        {Traverse right subtree}
        LeftNodeRight(Tree↑.RightPointer)
    end
end;
```

APPLICATION

**Polynomial
Addition**

A polynomial of arbitrary degree can be represented as a linked list of coefficient-exponent pairs, in descending order of exponents. For example, the polynomial:

$$p(x) = 8x^5 - 5x^2 + 6x + 3$$

may be represented as in Figure 12.10.

Figure 12.10
Linked list
representation of a
polynomial

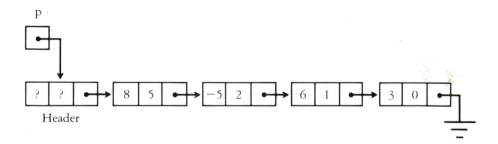

APPLICATION

**Polynomial
Addition**
(*continued*)

We can declare the data structure to store a term of such a polynomial as follows:

```
type
  TermPointer = ↑Term;
  Term = record
      Coefficient : real;
      Exponent : integer;
      NextTerm : TermPointer
  end;
```

If we assume that a polynomial such as the above would be input as:

4 85 −52 61 30

we can readily write a procedure to read a polynomial. First it will
read an integer indicating the number of terms in the polynomial;
then it will read the string of coefficient-exponent pairs from which
it will build a linked representation of the polynomial. The program
to read and print polynomials is very similar to what we did with the
passenger list earlier in this chapter.

```
program PolynomialArithmetic (input, output);

{*****************************
* Program to read and print  *
* polynomials implemented as *
* linked lists.              *
*****************************}

type
  TermPointer = ↑Term;

  Term = record
      Coefficient : real;
      Exponent : integer;
      NextTerm : TermPointer
  end;

  Polynomial = TermPointer;
var
  p,q : Polynomial;
```

APPLICATION

Polynomial Addition (*conintued*)

```pascal
procedure ReadPolynomial ( var p : Polynomial);

{*********************************
 * Procedure to read a polynomial *
 *********************************}

var
    NumberOfTerms : 0..maxint;
    Count : integer;
    CurrentTerm, NewTerm : TermPointer;
begin

    {Read the number of terms}
    read(NumberOfTerms);

    {Create header}
    new(p);
    p↑.NextTerm := nil;

    {Read and attach the values for each term}
    CurrentTerm := p;
    Count := 1;
    while Count <= NumberOfTerms do
        begin
            new(NewTerm);
            with NewTerm↑ do
                read(Coefficient, Exponent);

            {Attach term to polynomial}

            CurrentTerm↑.NextTerm := NewTerm;
            CurrentTerm := NewTerm;
            Count := Count + 1
        end;
    readln;
    CurrentTerm↑.NextTerm := nil
end;

procedure PrintPolynomial (p : Polynomial);

{*********************************
 * Procedure to print a polynomial *
 *********************************}
```

APPLICATION

Polynomial Addition
(*continued*)

```
var
    Sign : char;
    CurrentTerm : TermPointer;

begin
    {Set pointer to first term of polynomial}

    CurrentTerm := p↑.NextTerm;

    while CurrentTerm <> nil do
        with CurrentTerm↑ do
            begin
                if Exponent <> 0 then
                    begin
                        if Coefficient > 0 then
                            Sign := '+'
                        else
                            Sign := ' ';
                        write(' ',Sign,Coefficient :4:2);
                        if Exponent <> 1 then
                            write(Sign,'x**',Exponent :1)
                        else
                            write(Sign,'x')
                    end
                else
                    if Coefficient < 0 then
                        write('   ',Coefficient :4:2)
                    else
                        write(' +',Coefficient);
                CurrentTerm := CurrentTerm↑.NextTerm
            end;
end;

begin {** Main program **}

    ReadPolynomial(p);
    ReadPolynomial(q);
    write('p(x) =');
    PrintPolynomial(p);
    writeln;
    write('q(x) =');
    PrintPolynomial(q)

end.
```

APPLICATION

**Polynomial
Addition**
(*continued*)

Given the input data:

```
3 3  2 9 1    1 0
5 1 8 5 6  −7 5  6 1 1 0
```

The program will produce the following output:

```
p(x)  =  +3.00+x**2  +9.00+x    +1.00
q(x)  =  +1.00+x**8  +5.00+x**6    −7.00  x**5  +6.00+x    +1.00
```

Now we would like to write a procedure that will perform polynomial addition. Given the polynomials $p(x)$ and $q(x)$, above, we would like to compute polynomial $r(x)$ such that:

$$r(x) = p(x) + q(x)$$

specifically:

$$r(x) = 1x^8 + 5x^6 - 7x^5 + 3x^2 + 15x + 2$$

To perform the addition, we need three auxiliary pointers: two to move down the linked lists representing each of the polynomials to be added, and one to keep track of the end of the linked list representing the sum. Two pointers, p and q, are used to move along the terms of $p(x)$ and $q(x)$. If the exponents are equal, the coefficients are added and a new term is created for $r(x)$, the sum. If the exponent of the current term of $p(x)$ is less than the exponent of the current term of $q(x)$, then a duplicate of the current term of $q(x)$ is created and attached to the result, $r(x)$. Pointer q is advanced to the next term of $q(x)$. Similar action is taken on the exponent of $p(x)$ if the exponent of the current term of $p(x)$ is greater than the exponent of the current $q(x)$ term. A pointer, r, is used to keep track of the last term of $r(x)$. The complete program to input two polynomials, add the polynomials, and print them is shown below.

```
program PolynomialArithmetic (input, output);

{*****************************
* Program to read and print  *
* polynomials implemented as *
* linked lists.              *
*****************************}

type
  TermPointer = ↑Term;
```

APPLICATION

Polynomial Addition
(*continued*)

```pascal
Term = record
     Coefficient : real;
     Exponent : integer;
     NextTerm : TermPointer
end;

Polynomial = TermPointer;

var
  p,q,r : Polynomial;


procedure ReadPolynomial ( var p : Polynomial);

    {**********************************
    * Procedure to read a polynomial *
    **********************************}

    var
        NumberOfTerms : 0..maxint;
        Count : integer;
        CurrentTerm, NewTerm : TermPointer;

    begin

        {input the number of terms}
        read(NumberOfTerms);

        {Create header}
        new(p);
        p↑.NextTerm := nil;

        CurrentTerm := p;
        Count := 1;
        while Count <= NumberOfTerms do
            begin
                new(NewTerm);
                with NewTerm↑ do
                    read(Coefficient, Exponent);

                {Attach term to polynomial}
                CurrentTerm↑.NextTerm := NewTerm;
                CurrentTerm := NewTerm;
                Count := Count + 1
```

APPLICATION

**Polynomial
Addition**
(*continued*)

```
          end;
     readln;
     CurrentTerm↑.NextTerm := nil
end; {of Procedure PrintPolynomial}


procedure PrintPolynomial (p : Polynomial);

   {*********************************
   * Procedure to print a polynomial *
   *********************************}

   var
      Sign : char;
      CurrentTerm : TermPointer;

   begin
      CurrentTerm := p↑.NextTerm;
      while CurrentTerm <> nil do
         with CurrentTerm↑ do
            begin
               if Exponent <> 0 then
                  begin
                     if Coefficient > 0 then
                        Sign := '+'
                     else
                        Sign := ' ';
                     write(' ',Sign,Coefficient :4:2);
                     if Exponent <> 1 then
                        write(Sign,'x**',Exponent :1)
                     else
                        write(Sign,'x')
                  end
               else
                  if Coefficient < 0 then
                     write('  ',Coefficient :4:2)
                  else
                     write(' +',Coefficient);
               CurrentTerm := CurrentTerm↑.NextTerm
            end;
   end; {of Procedure PRINTPOLYNOMIAL}


procedure AddPolynomial(p,q : Polynomial;
                        var Sum : Polynomial);
```

APPLICATION

**Polynomial
Addition**
(*continued*)

```
{*********************************
* Procedure to add polynomials "p" *
* and "q" and return sum in "Sum"   *
**********************************}

var
    r : TermPointer;


procedure AttachTerm(Coef: real; Exp: integer;
                           var r : TermPointer);

    {*******************************
    * Procedure to attach new      *
    * term to end of a polynomial. *
    * Returns pointer to new term   *
    *******************************}

var
    NewTerm : TermPointer;

begin
    new(NewTerm);
    NewTerm↑.Coefficient := Coef;
    NewTerm↑.Exponent := Exp;
    r↑.NextTerm := NewTerm;
    r := NewTerm;
end; {of Procedure ATTACHTERM}


begin {AddPolynomials}
    {Create header node}
    new(Sum);
    r := Sum;
    r↑.NextTerm := nil;
    p := p↑.NextTerm;
    q := q↑.NextTerm;
    while (p<>nil) and (q<>nil) do
        begin
            if p↑.Exponent < q↑.Exponent then
                begin
                    AttachTerm(q↑.Coefficient,
                             q↑.Exponent,r);
                    q := q↑.NextTerm
                end
```

APPLICATION

**Polynomial
Addition**
(*continued*)

```
                else
                    if p↑.Exponent > q↑.Exponent then
                        begin
                            AttachTerm(p↑.Coefficient,
                                       p↑.Exponent,r);
                            p := p↑.NextTerm
                        end
                    else
                        begin
                            if p↑.Coefficient+q↑.Coefficient
                              <>0 then
                                AttachTerm(p↑.Coefficient+q↑.Coefficient,
                                           p↑.Exponent,r);
                            p := p↑.NextTerm;
                            q := q↑.NextTerm
                        end
            end;

        {Attach rest of q}

        while q <> nil do
            begin
                AttachTerm(q↑.Coefficient,q↑.Exponent,r);
                q := q↑.NextTerm
            end;

        {Attach rest of p}

        while p <> nil do
            begin
                AttachTerm(p↑.Coefficient,p↑.Exponent,r);
                p := p↑.NextTerm
            end
    end; {of procedure ADDPOLYNOMIAL}

begin {** Main program **}
    ReadPolynomial(p);
    ReadPolynomial(q);
    write('p(x) =');
    PrintPolynomial(p);
    writeln;
    write('q(x) =');
    PrintPolynomial(q);
    writeln;
```

APPLICATION

**Polynomial
Addition**
(*continued*)

```
AddPolynomial(p,q,r);
write('The sum is');
PrintPolynomial(r);
writeln
end.
```

Given the input data of our previous program, the output will be:

```
p(x) = +3.00+x**2 +9.00+x   +1.00
q(x) = +1.00+x**8 +5.00+x**6  −7.00 x**5 +6.00+x   +1.00
The sum is +1.00+x**8 +5.00+x**6   −7.00 x**5 +3.00+x**2 +15.00+x   +2.00
```

APPLICATION

**Computer
Guessing
Game**

As another example of the use of dynamic data structures, consider the guessing game sometimes called "Animal." This is a popular computer game in which the computer attempts to guess the name of an animal by asking questions with "yes" or "no" answers. If the computer fails to guess the animal, it requests information about it, thus "learning" about a new animal.

The structure used to represent the computer's knowledge of animals is a tree. The tree in Figure 12.11 represents the computer's initial knowledge about animals. To play the game, the computer first asks the question at the root of the tree. Based on the answer, it guesses either "Bird" or "Fish." If the guess is incorrect, it asks for the name of the correct animal and for a question that distinguishes

Figure 12.11 An
animal tree (binary)

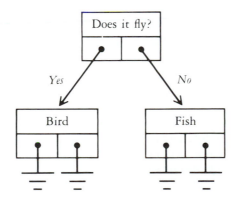

the correct animal from the guess. It then adds the information to the tree. For example, given the above tree, the following dialogue might result. The human answers to the computer's questions have been underlined to distinguish them from what the computer types.

Are you thinking of an animal? <u>yes</u>
Does it fly? <u>no</u>
Is it a fish? <u>no</u>
I give up.
The animal you are thinking of is a(n): <u>dog</u>
Please type a question that would distinguish a dog from a fish
<u>Does it bark?</u>
For a dog the answer to your question is yes or no? <u>yes</u>
Are you thinking of an animal? <u>yes</u>

.
.
.

The game continues, with the computer now armed with information about a dog as well as a bird and a fish. Adding the information about the dog to the tree changes the initial tree to that pictured in Figure 12.12. Note that the names of the animals are stored at the lowest level of the tree, usually called the **leaves** of the tree.

The data structures we will need to program Animals can be defined as:

```
const
  Maxsize = 20;

type
  String = record
      St : packed array[1..Maxsize] of char;
      Length : 0..Maxsize
  end;

  NodePointer = ↑Node;
  Node = record
      Entry : String;
      Yes : NodePointer;
      No : NodePointer
  end;
```

APPLICATION

**Computer
Guessing
Game
(*continued*)**

Figure 12.12 Revised animal tree (binary)

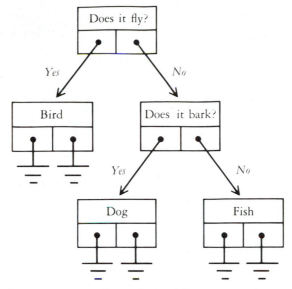

The entry at each node is either a question or the name of an animal.
Each node also has two pointers. The main algorithm to play the
game can be written as follows:

begin
   Print headings
   Initialize the game
   repeat
      Ask 'Are you thinking of an animal?'
      Get Answer
      if Answer is yes **then**
        Initialize prior question pointer to root
        Initialize current question pointer to root
        Ask question referenced by current question pointer
        if answer to question is yes **then**
          Advance current question pointer to yes
      else
        Advance current question pointer to no
      while current question pointer is not **nil do**
        Set old question pointer to prior question pointer
        Set prior question pointer to current question pointer
        Ask question referenced by current question pointer
        if answer to question is yes **then**
          Advance current question pointer to yes

            else
                    Advance current question pointer to no
            if answer is yes **then**
                    Ask 'Want to play again?'
                    Get Answer
                    if Answer is not yes **then**
                            Set play flag to false
                else
                    Get name of new animal
                    Get question about new animal
                    Update tree
            else
                Set play flag to false
            until play flag is false
        Thank player for game
end.

The algorithm uses three pointers to traverse the tree. The leading pointer points to the most current node. The other two pointers point to the last two nodes that were visited.

The complete program with all the required procedures is:

```
program Animal (input,output);

{*********************************************
* Program to play the animal guessing game. *
*********************************************}

const
  Maxsize = 20;

type
  String = record
      St : packed array[1..Maxsize] of char;
      Length : 0..Maxsize
  end;

  NodePointer = ↑Node;
  Node = record
      Entry : String;
      Yes : NodePointer;
      No : NodePointer
  end;

var
  Tree : NodePointer;
```

APPLICATION

**Computer
Guessing
Game**
(*continued*)

```
Parent, PriorQuestion, CurrentQuestion: NodePointer;
Quest, NewAnimal : String;
Play, Resp,YesAnswer: boolean;
Answer : char;


procedure Initialize(var t : NodePointer);

   {****************************************
   * Procedure to initialize tree to start *
   * the game.                             *
   ****************************************}

begin
   new(t);
   with t↑ do
       begin
           {Initialize root node}

           Entry.St := 'Does it fly?         ';
           Entry.Length := 12;
           {Create and initialize 'yes' node}
           new(Yes);
           Yes↑.Entry.St := 'bird              ';
           Yes↑.Entry.Length := 4;
           Yes↑.Yes := nil;
           Yes↑.No := nil;
           {Create and initialize 'no' node}
           new(No);
           No↑.Entry.St := 'fish              ';
           No↑.Entry.Length := 4;
           No↑.Yes := nil;
           No↑.No := nil;
       end
end; {of Procedure INITIALIZE}


procedure ReadString (var s : String);

{*************************************
* Procedure to read a string. It     *
* returns the string and its length. *
*************************************}

var
  i : integer;
```

APPLICATION
_____

**Computer
Guessing
Game**
(*continued*)

```
begin
  {Clear string to blanks}

  for i := 1 to Maxsize do
      s.St[i] := ' ';

  {Input string}

  i := 1;
  while (i <= Maxsize) and (not eoln) do
      begin
          read(s.St[i]);
          i := i + 1
      end;
  readln;
  s.Length := i - 1
end; {of Procedure READSTRING}



procedure Ask (var p: NodePointer; var Answ: boolean);

{*********************************************
* Procedure to ask a question  and advance   *
* the appropriate pointer depending on the    *
* answer. If answer is 'yes,' the pointer is  *
* advanced to Yes otherwise the pointer is    *
* advanced to no.                             *
*********************************************}

begin
  {Display question}
  if p↑.Yes <> nil then
      write(p↑.Entry.St :p↑.Entry.Length,' ')
  else
      write('Is it ',p↑.Entry.St :p↑.Entry.Length,'? ');
  {Obtain response and advance pointer}
  readln(Answer);
  writeln;
  if (Answer ='y') or (Answer = 'Y') then
      begin
          Answ := true;
          p := p↑.Yes
      end
  else
```

APPLICATION

**Computer
Guessing
Game**
(*continued*)

```
        begin
             Answ := false;
             p := p↑.No
        end
  end; {of Procedure ASK}


  procedure GetNewAnimal(var Info : String);

  {********************************
   * Procedure to obtain new animal *
   ********************************}

  var
     i : integer;

  begin
     write ('The animal you are thinking of is a(n): ');
     ReadString(Info);
     writeln
  end; {of Procedure GETNEWANIMAL}


  procedure GetQuestion( Animal: String; Guess : NodePointer;
                         var Question: String;
                         var Yes: boolean);

  {*******************************************
   * Procedure to obtain the question about *
   * the new animal.                        *
   *******************************************}

  begin
     {Obtain question to distinguish new animal
      from previous one}
     write('Please type a question that would distinguish');
     writeln('a ',Animal.St :Animal.Length,' from a ',
             Guess↑.Entry.St :Guess↑.Entry.Length);
     ReadString(Question);
     writeln;
     {Obtain answer to question}
     write ('For a ',Animal.St :Animal.Length,
            ' the answer to your question is yes or no? ');
     readln(Answer);
```

```
    writeln;
    if (Answer = 'y') or (Answer = 'Y') then
        Yes := true
    else
        Yes := false
end;


procedure Attach(QuestPtr,NamePtr: NodePointer;
                    Animal, Question: String; Yes: boolean);

{********************************
* Procedure to attach nodes for *
* new animal to tree.           *
********************************}

var
   NewQuest,NewAnimal : NodePointer;

begin
   {Create new nodes and insert entries}
   new(NewQuest);
   new(NewAnimal);
   NewAnimal↑.Entry := Animal;
   NewAnimal↑.Yes := nil;
   NewAnimal↑.No := nil;
   NewQuest↑.Entry := Question;
   {Attach nodes to tree}
   if Yes then
       begin
           NewQuest↑.No := NamePtr;
           NewQuest↑.Yes := NewAnimal
       end
   else
       begin
           NewQuest↑.Yes := NamePtr;
           NewQuest↑.No := NewAnimal
       end;
   if QuestPtr↑.No = NamePtr then
       QuestPtr↑.No := NewQuest
   else
       QuestPtr↑.Yes := NewQuest
end;
```

APPLICATION

**Computer
Guessing
Game**
(*continued*)

```
begin {*** MAIN Program ***}

    {Print headings}
    writeln ('Welcome to the game of Animal.');
    writeln;
    writeln ('I will try to guess the animal');
    writeln ('you are thinking of. I will ask you
                questions');
    writeln ('about the animal. Please answer these');
    writeln ('with a "yes" or "no" answer.');
    writeln;
    {Initialize tree for game}
    Initialize(Tree);
    {Play game}
    repeat
        write ('Are you thinking of an animal? ');
        readln (Answer);
        writeln;
        if (Answer = 'y') or (Answer = 'Y') then
            begin
                Play := true;
                PriorQuestion := Tree;
                CurrentQuestion := Tree;
                Ask(CurrentQuestion,YesAnswer);
                while CurrentQuestion <> nil do
                    begin
                        Parent := PriorQuestion;
                        PriorQuestion := CurrentQuestion;
                        Ask(CurrentQuestion,YesAnswer)
                    end;
                if YesAnswer then
                    begin
                        write('Want to play again? ');
                            readln(Answer);
                        writeln;
                        if (Answer <> 'y') and
                            (Answer <> 'Y') then
                                Play := false
                    end
                else
                    begin
                        writeln ('I give up.');
                        GetNewAnimal(NewAnimal);
```

APPLICATION

**Computer
Guessing
Game**
(*continued*)

```
                    GetQuestion(NewAnimal,PriorQuestion,
                                Quest,Resp);
                    Attach(Parent,PriorQuestion,
                                NewAnimal,Quest,Resp);
                        end
                end
            else
                Play := false
        until not Play;
        writeln;
        writeln('Thank you for game!')
    end.
```

A sample game session is shown below. Again, the information typed by the player is underlined to distinguish it from what is typed by the computer.

```
Welcome to the game of Animal.

I will try to guess the animal
you are thinking of. I will ask you questions
about the animal. Please answer these
with a "yes" or "no" answer.

Are you thinking of an animal? yes
Does it fly? no
Is it fish? no
I give up.
The animal you are thinking of is a(n): dog
Please type a question that would distinguish a dog from
a fish
Does it swim?
For a dog the answer to your question is yes or no? no
Are you thinking of an animal? yes
Does it fly? no
Does it swim? no
Is it dog? no
I give up.
The animal you are thinking of is a(n): cat
Please type a question that would distinguish a cat from
a dog
Does it purr?
For a cat the answer to your question is yes or no? yes
Are you thinking of an animal? yes
Does it fly? no
```

APPLICATION

Computer Guessing Game (*continued*)

```
Does it swim? no
Does it purr? yes
Is it cat? yes
Want to play again? no
Thank you for game!
```

12.5 COMMON ERRORS

Programs involving pointers are especially difficult to debug because pointer values cannot be examined directly.

Undefined variables are just as troublesome with pointers as with other types of variables. With pointers, however, there are more ways to go wrong. Not only can a pointer be undefined, but so can the variable to which the pointer points. Consider the following definitions and declarations:

```
type
  ItemPointer = ↑Item;

  Item = record
      Data : packed array[1..10] of char;
      Next : ItemPointer
  end;

var
  FirstItem : ItemPointer;
```

At the beginning of the program, the pointer "FirstItem" is undefined. Any attempt to reference it, such as:

```
if FirstItem = nil then
    writeln('Empty list')
```

will lead to a run-time error. Assigning a value to FirstItem using the new procedure still leaves the variable to which FirstItem points undefined. Any reference to FirstItem ↑ such as:

```
writeln (FirstItem↑.Name);
FirstItem := FirstItem↑.Next
```

will lead to run-time errors. If the value **nil** is assigned to FirstItem any attempt to reference FirstItem ↑ , as above, will also lead to run-time errors.

It is easy to run off the end of a list or to forget that a list may be empty. When searching a linked list or, for that matter, an array, it is tempting to forget that boolean expressions are evaluated fully even when it is not logically necessary to do so. Thus, we are often tempted to write a search loop as follows:

```
CurrentItem := FirstItem;
while (CurrentItem <> nil)
        and (DataSearched <> CurrentItem↑.Data) do
    CurrentItem := CurrentItem↑.Next;
```

Such a loop will result in a run-time error if "DataSearched" is not in the list.

When pointers need to be reconnected, such as in insertion and deletion of items in a list, reconnecting them in the incorrect sequence may lead to the loss of all or part of the list. The following version of a function to insert a record into a list and return a pointer to the newly inserted record loses that part of the list following the inserted record.

```
function InsertAfter(Prior: ItemPointer): ItemPointer;

{*** Function loses part of a list ***}

var
  CurrentItem : ItemPointer;

begin
  new(CurrentItem);
  Prior↑.Next := CurrentItem;
  Current↑.Next := Prior↑.Next
end;
```

The last two assignment statements were done in reverse order. The new record was first attached to the list at the correct location. In the process, however, the pointer to the rest of the list was lost.

Finally, for debugging purposes, it is useful to write and use procedures that print the contents of entire structures. When working with a list or a tree, incorporate into your program a procedure to print the list or the tree to see that it is working properly, even if your program does not require such a procedure. If data values are incorrectly entered into the structures, your program cannot produce correct results.

**12.6
CHAPTER
REVIEW**

Dynamic data structures are data structures that can expand and contract during program execution. Such structures can also dynamically alter the interrelationships among their components. They are very useful for storage of information that is constantly changing.

Each component of a dynamic data structure not only stores the information that is needed for the particular application, but also links to other components. The links between the components of the structure are implemented using variables called **pointers**.

A pointer is a variable that references main storage locations. Therefore, the value of a pointer variable is an address of a location in main storage. When defining a pointer variable in Pascal we specify the type of value the pointer points to. The definition:

```
type
  NumberPtr = ↑integer;
```

defines a pointer variable that points to an integer.

Pascal provides a standard procedure called "new" to dynamically assign a value to a pointer and simultaneously allocate the storage for the variable it references. The expression:

```
new(p);
```

allocates the storage for an integer and assigns the address of this location to the pointer, p. We use the following notation to access the variable referenced by the pointer, p:

```
p↑
```

When a location pointed to by pointer p is no longer needed, the standard procedure "dispose" can be used to release that location for later use.

We occasionally need a pointer variable that does not point to any location, but is yet defined. In Pascal this value is represented by the reserved word **nil**.

Pointers are used to build linked data structures. The components of such structures contain at least one pointer field. Two common linked data structures are **linked lists** and **binary trees**.

**12.7
EXERCISES**

12.1. Fill in the blanks in each of the following:

(a) The value of a pointer is a(n) _____.

(b) Pointers are often used to build _____ data structures.

(c) The _____ and the _____ between the components of dynamic data structures may change while the program is executing.

(d) In order to construct a linked structure at least one field of the records that constitute the components of the structure must be _____.

(e) An example of a nonlinear linked structure is a _____.

(f) Recursive algorithms are common with _____ structures.

(g) To allocate storage to a dynamic variable, the procedure _____ is used.

(h) To release the storage allocated to a dynamic variable for future reallocation the procedure _____ is used.

12.2. Answer each of the following true or false. If your answer is false, state why.

(a) When defining a pointer type, the type of the referenced variable need not be specified.

(b) Integers can be assigned to pointer variables.

(c) **nil** can be assigned to any pointer irrespective of the type of the variable being referenced.

(d) Pointer values may not be printed.

(e) To build a linked list we need a pointer variable as one of the fields for each element of the list.

(f) A tree structure requires two pointers at each node.

(g) The variable referenced by a **nil** pointer is undefined.

(h) The procedure "delete" sets a pointer to **nil**.

(i) The procedure "new" is used to assign values to pointers.

12.3. Why does the delete procedure for linked lists require a pointer to the preceding record?

12.4. Write a program to insert names into a passenger list in alphabetical order.

12.5. Write a function to count the number of records in a linked list.

12.6. Write a procedure that, given a pointer to a record in a list, inserts a record into the list in front of the record referenced by the pointer. (*Hint*: you may need to copy records.)

12.7. In a doubly linked list, each record contains not only a pointer to the record that follows it but also a pointer to the preceding record. To make the passenger list into a doubly linked list we could define Passenger as follows:

```
type
  PassengerPointer = ↑Passenger
  Passenger = record
      Name : String;
      Seat : 1..200;
      PrecedingPassenger : PassengerPointer;
      NextPassenger : PassengerPointer
  end;
```

Write versions of insert and delete for doubly linked lists.

12.8. A *queue* is a list where all insertions are done at the rear, and all deletions are done from the front. Write the following procedures and functions to manipulate a queue where the queue is implemented as a linked list with header.

(a) A function, called Empty, which checks to see if a queue is empty.

(b) A procedure Enqueue, which adds an element to the queue.

(c) A procedure Dequeue, which removes an element from the queue.

12.9. Modify the game-playing program of this chapter so that it "remembers" what it learns from session to session. You will need to modify the initialization procedure so that it reads the information from a file and builds the initial tree from that information. You will also need to add a procedure to write the tree to a file each time the game terminates, or upon a request by the player. Each time the game is played the tree is reinitialized to its state at the end of the previous game.

12.10. The binary search tree can be used to sort data. Data is read and entered into the tree; then the tree is printed in the order described in the text: first the left subtree is printed, then the root node, and finally the right subtree. The resulting sort algorithm is called a **tree sort**. Using the procedures provided in the text write a tree sort algorithm.

12.11. Write a program that generates a cross-reference list, for text material written in English. Your program should do the following:

(a) Input lines of text and output each line prefixed by a line number.

(b) The output of the printed text is to be followed by a cross-referenced concordance that lists all the words in the text and gives for each word a list of all the line numbers on which it appears.

Since you do not know how many different words are in the text, nor on how many different lines a word may appear, you should use dynamic structures. One approach is to use a linked list of words and a linked list (actually a queue—see problem 12.8) of line numbers for each word. The data structures could be defined as follows:

```
type
    LinePointer = ↑LineRecord;

    LineRecord = record
        Line : integer;
        NextLine : LinePointer
    end;

    String = packed array[1..15] of char;

    WordPointer = ↑WordRecord;
```

```
WordRecord = record
    Word : String;
    FirstLine : LinePointer;
    LastLine : LinePointer;
    NextWord : WordPointer
end;
```

Note that each entry in the list of words not only provides for a field to store the word, but also three pointers. One pointer will point to the first line on which the word occurs, while another pointer will point to the current last line on which the word occurs. Because line numbers will be obtained sequentially, it is easy to add line numbers to the list. They are simply added to the end of the list, using the pointer to the last line. There is also a pointer pointing to the next word on the list. The cross-reference list should be alphabetical.

12.12. Write a program to simulate some simple functions of an airline reservation system. The program should respond to the following commands:

's' Schedule a new flight;
     input data: flight number, number of seats available.
'r' Reserve seats for a passenger;
     input data: flight number, passenger's name,
     number of seats requested.
'p' Print the list of passengers:
     input data: flight number.
'a' Seat availability report; input data: none.
'c' Cancel passenger's reservation; input data: flight number, passenger's name.
'd' Departure; input data: flight number.

Use a linked list to represent the flight data. Each entry on the list should contain the flight number, the count of the seats currently available, a pointer to the next flight on the list, and a pointer to a binary search tree representing the list of passengers for this particular flight. Each node on the passenger tree has to contain the passenger's name, the count of the seats allocated to this passenger, and pointers to the left child and the right child in the tree.

Appendices

Reserved Words

and	array	begin
case	const	div
do	downto	else
end	file	for
function	goto	if
in	label	mod
nil	not	of
or	packed	procedure
program	record	repeat
set	then	to
type	until	var
while	with	

Predefined Identifiers

Constants

false   true   maxint

Types

boolean	char	integer
real	text	

Files

input   output

Functions

Name	Parameter	Result	Description
abs(x)	integer or real	same as parameter	Absolute value of "x"
arctan(x)	real	real	Inverse tangent of "x"
chr(x)	integer	char	Character whose ordinal value is "x"
cos(x)	real	real	Cosine of "x"

Name	Parameter	Result	Description
eof(f)	file	boolean	End-of-file for file "f" Standard input file assumed if no other file given
eoln(f)	file	boolean	End-of-line for file "f" Standard input file assumed if no other file given
exp(x)	real	real	**e** raised to the power of "x"
ln(x)	real	real	Natural logarithm
odd(x)	integer	boolean	True if "x" is odd
ord(x)	scalar other than real	integer	Ordinal value of "x"
pred(x)	scalar other than real	same as parameter	Predecessor of "x"
round(x)	real	integer	"x" rounded
sin(x)	real	real	Sine of "x"
sqr(x)	integer or real	same as parameter	Square of "x"
sqrt(x)	real	real	Square root of "x"
succ(x)	scalar other than real	same as parameter	Successor of "x"
trunc(x)	real	integer	"x" truncated

Procedures

Name	Description
dispose(p)	Returns the variable referenced by pointer "p" to free storage. The pointer "p" becomes undefined.
get(f)	Advances window of file "f" to the next component.
new(p)	Allocates storage to the variable referenced by the pointer "p."
pack(a,i,b)	Copies the elements of array "a" beginning at position "i" into packed array "b."

Name	Description
put(f)	Appends the value in the file window of file "f" to the file.
read(x)	Reads data from a text file.
readln(x)	Reads data from a text file and advances file window to the beginning of the next line.
reset(f)	Opens a file for reading and positions window at first component.
rewrite(f)	Clears a file and opens it for writing.
unpack(b,a,i)	Copies packed array "b" into array "a" starting at location "i."
write(x)	Writes data to a text file.
writeln(x)	Writes data to a text file and appends an end-of-line character.

B. CHARACTER CODES

ASCII (American Standard Code for Information Interchange)

Left Digit(s)	Right Digit									
	0	**1**	**2**	**3**	**4**	**5**	**6**	**7**	**8**	**9**
3				!	"	#	$	%	&	'
4	(	)	*	+	'	−	.	/	0	1
5	2	3	4	5	6	7	8	9	:	;
6	<	=	>	?	@	A	B	C	D	E
7	F	G	H	I	J	K	L	M	N	O
8	P	Q	R	S	T	U	V	W	X	Y
9	Z	[	\	]	^	_	`		a	b	c
10	d	e	f	g	h	i	j	k	l	m
11	n	o	p	q	r	s	t	u	v	w
12	x	y	z	{	|	}	~			

Codes 00–31 and 127 are nonprintable control characters. A blank space is 32.

EBCDIC (Extended Binary Coded Decimal Interchange Code)

Left Digit(s)	Right Digit									
	0	1	2	3	4	5	6	7	8	9
6										
7					¢	.	<	(	+	|
8	&									
9	!	$	*	)	;	¬	-	/		
10							—	,	%	__
11	>	?								
12		`	:	#	@	'	=	"		a
13	b	c	d	e	f	g	h	i		
14						j	k	l	m	n
15	o	p	q	r						
16		~	s	t	u	v	w	x	y	z
17										
18				[						]
19			{	A	B	C	D	E	F	G
20	H	I							}	J
21	K	L	M	N	O	P	Q	R		
22							S	T	U	V
23	W	X	Y	Z	/					
24	0	1	2	3	4	5	6	7	8	9

Codes 00–63 and 250–255 are nonprintable control characters. A blank space is 64.

C. PASCAL SYNTAX DIAGRAMS

program

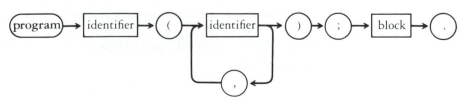

identifier

block

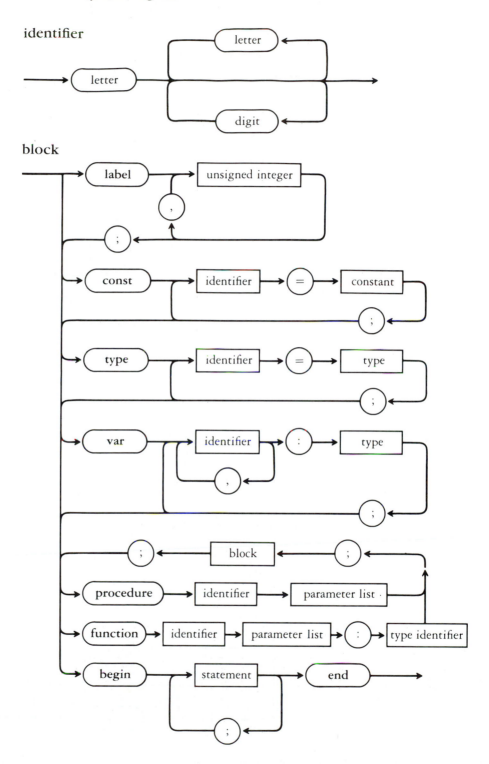

unsigned integer

unsigned number

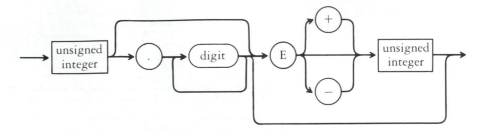

constant

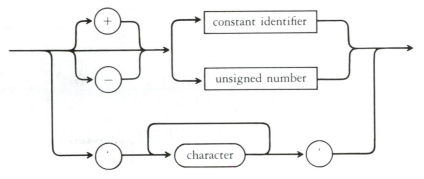

unsigned constant

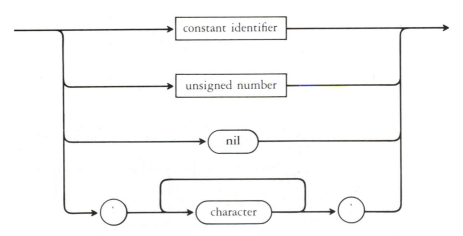

simple type

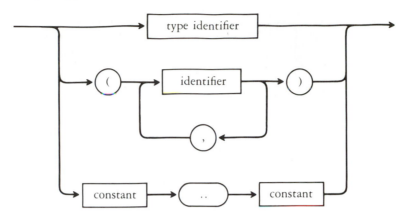

type

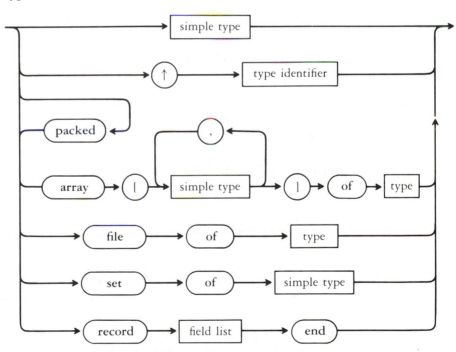

variable

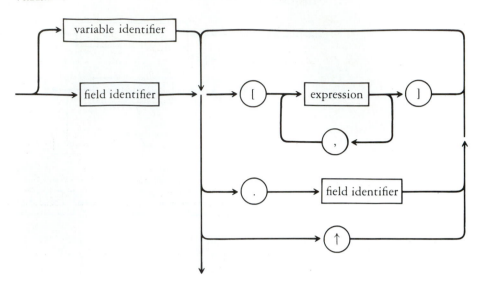

parameter list

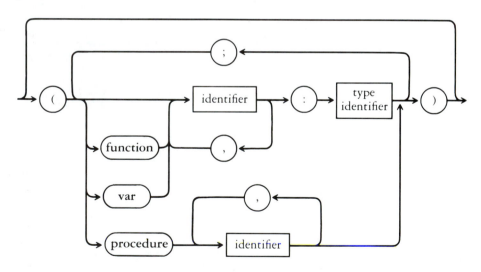

term

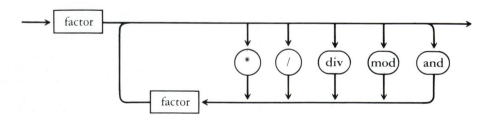

simple expression

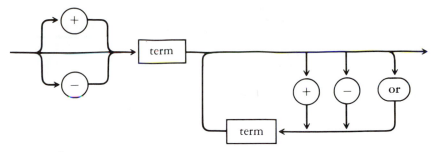

expression

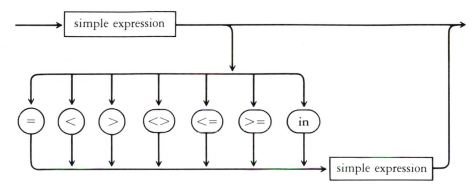

field list

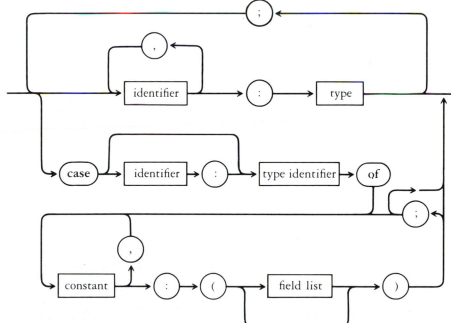

factor

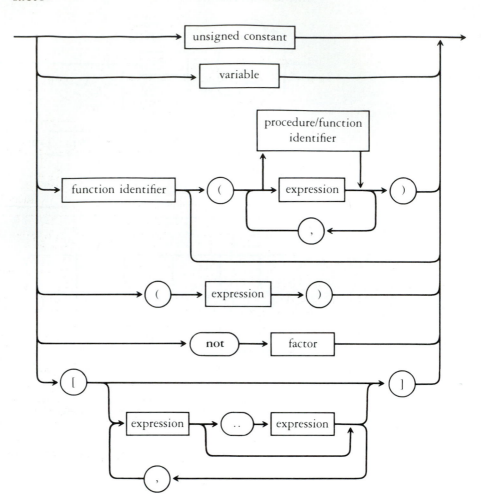

statement

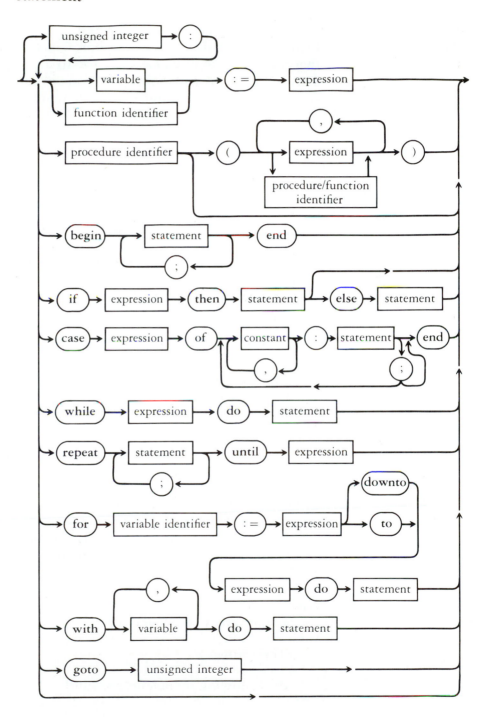

**D.
SELECTED
PASCAL
IMPLEMEN-
TATIONS**

The version of the Pascal language described in this text conforms to
the ISO (International Standards Organization) Pascal. Most Pascal
compilers, especially those written for the commercial environment, have nonstandard extensions. These extensions are features
that make the language easier to use in a production environment.
This appendix presents some common deviations from the proposed
standard for a small number of implementations. Specifically it discusses implementation differences in the following areas:

1. The use of packed arrays of characters as parameters to the procedures read and readln.

2. The existence of predefined-character string data types and procedures and functions to manipulate character strings.

3. The existence of an "escape" clause for the **case** statement.

4. The capability of binding external files to internal file variables.

5. The use of external, precompiled library routines.

6. The limitations on set data types.

7. The procedures used to manage dynamic storage allocation.

8. The special provisions for interactive I/0.

The above features are not meant to be exhaustive. They represent the typical areas where implementations tend to differ from the
standard and from each other. The Pascal compilers discussed in this
appendix also represent only a small sample of the available Pascals.

AAEC Pascal 8000

Pascal 8000 Version 2.0 is a version of Pascal that can be obtained
from the Australian Atomic Energy Commission and that commonly
is used on IBM System 360/370 computers.

   1. It allows for use of character strings as parameters to read
and readln procedures. Thus, given the following data definitions
and declarations,

type
   String = **array** [1..20] **of** char;
var
   Name : String;

the following statements are valid:

read(Name);
readln(Name);

In both cases, the number of characters equal to the length of the string will be read.

2. This version has no provisions for a predefined-character string data type and hence no functions and procedures to manipulate character strings.

3. This version has a predefined case label **otherwise**, which can be used with **case** statements as follows:

case i **of**
    1, 2 : z : = sin(x);
    3 : z : = cos(x);
    otherwise z : = 0
end

4. Binding of external files to file variables is possible only through the program heading. On most systems additional JCL (Job Control Language) must be provided with the program to associate external file names with file variables.

5. The reserved words **extern** or **Pascal** are used to identify separately compiled procedures and functions. Either of these reserved words must appear in place of the function or the procedure body. For example:

procedure Example (**var** x,y : real);**Pascal**;

or

procedure Example (**var** x,y : real);**extern**;

are valid references to precompiled-Pascal procedures.

6. The base type of any set must have its associated ordinal values in the range 0..63. The one exception to this rule is **set of** char.

7. In addition to "new" and "dispose," the procedures "mark" and "release" are used to manage dynamic storage allocation. Mark stores the value of a pointer that is later used by release. When release is executed, storage allocated since the last mark invocation is released.

8. There are no special provisions for interactive I/O.

DEC VAX—11 Pascal

This Pascal compiler is available from Digital Equipment Corporation for VAX computers running VMS.

    1. Packed arrays of characters may be passed as parameters to read and readln. The number of characters corresponding to the size of the array will be input.

    2. Character strings can be defined as **varying of** char. For example, the declaration

var Name : **varying** [20] of char

reserves storage for a string with maximum size of 20. Procedures and functions are available to manipulate character strings defined in this way.

    The functions are:

Bin(x,Size)—Converts the value of x to its equivalent binary representation and returns the resulting value as a character string, "Size" characters long.

Hex(x,Size)—Does the same thing as Bin, but returns the hexadecimal representation instead.

Oct(x,Size)—Also does the same thing as Bin, but instead returns the octal representation of x.

Length(s)—Returns the length of string s.

Index(s1,s2)—Locates and returns the position of the first occurrence of s2 in s1. If s2 is not in s1, it returns a 0.

Pad(s,FillChar,Size)—Pads the string s using the character FillChar until s is of length Size.

Substr(s,Start,Size)—Extracts and returns a substring of length Size from string s starting at location Start.

    The procedures are:

readv(s,parameter-list)—Reads from string s values for each parameter on the list.

writev(s,parameter-list)—Writes to string s the values of the variables on the parameter list).

    3. The predefined case label **otherwise** is provided with the **case** statement. It is used the same way as in AAEC Pascal 8000 Version 2.0.

4. The procedures "open" and "close" are used to associate external files with file variables as follows:

> Open(f,FileName)—Binds the external file FileName to the file variable *f*. It should be executed just prior to "reset(f)" or "rewrite(f)."
>
> Close(f,FileName)—Releases the external file FileName and breaks its association with the file variable *f*.

5. Previously compiled procedures and functions may be declared by using the predefined attribute **extern** as follows:

procedure Example (**var** a : integer);**extern**;

6. The maximum number of elements in a set is 256.

7. Dynamic storage allocation is managed by using the standard procedures "new" and "dispose."

8. The next character of interactive input is not read until needed. It is input when a read occurs or when eoln or eof is tested.

IBM Personal Computer Pascal

The IBM Personal Computer Pascal is available for the IBM PC Microcomputer using the DOS operating system.

1. Strings may be passed as parameters to the procedures read and readln.

2. There are two predefined character string types. The predefined type "String(n)" is equivalent to **packed array** [1..n] **of** char, and the predefined type "LString" is equivalent to **packed array** [0..n] **of** char. The first element (element 0) contains the length of the string. The predefined constant **null** is the empty string LString(0). Procedures and functions to manipulate variables of type String and LString are provided. To manipulate variables of type LString, we have the procedures:

> Concat(s1,s2)—Appends string s2 to the string s1. The length of s1 is increased by the length of s2.
>
> Delete(s,Start,Size)—Deletes Size number of characters from string *s* starting at location Start.
>
> Insert(s1,s2,i)—Inserts the string s2 into the string s1 starting at location *i*. The length of s1 is increased by the length of s2.
>
> Copylst(s1,s2)—Copies string s1 to string s2.

The following procedures and functions are used to manipulate variables of type String and LString.

> Positn(s1,s2,i)—Function to locate the first occurrence of string s1 in string s2 starting at location *i*. It returns 0 if s1 is not found.
>
> Scaneq(i,ch,s,Start)—Function to scan string *s* starting at location Start and to return the number of characters skipped. It stops scanning when a character equal to ch is encountered or location *i* is reached.
>
> Scanne(i,ch,s,Start)—Function like Scaneq, but it stops scanning when a character not equal to ch is encountered.
>
> Copystr(s1,s2)—Procedure to copy string s1 to string s2. The remaining characters of s2 are set to blanks.

3. The **case** statement may use an **otherwise** clause whose statements are executed when the value of the selector expression is not one of the case labels. The syntax of the clause is the same as for AAEC Pascal 8000.

4. Binding of external files to internal file variables is achieved by using the procedures "Assign" and "Readfn." For example, the procedure invocation

Assign(f, ´b:info.dat')

binds the file info.dat on drive *b* to the file variable *f*. The procedure Assign must be invoked prior to the invocation of the procedure reset.

The invocation

Readfn(f,f1,f2,..,fn)

reads from file *f* the external file names for file variables f1 through fn. It binds these file names to the corresponding file variables in the same manner as Assign.

5. External, precompiled library routines may be designated as **extern**.

6. The ordinal value of the base type of a set must be in the range 0..255.

7. The standard procedures "new" and "dispose" are used to manage dynamic storage allocation.

8.   The predeclared type INTERACTIVE, which is similar to the type text, is provided. This simplifies the handling of single-character I/0 for interactive terminal devices.

OMSI Pascal

OMSI Pascal Version 1.2 can be obtained from Oregon Software Inc. and commonly is used on DEC PDP-11 computers running RSTS/E and other operating systems.

1.   As with Pascal 8000, read, and readln will take packed arrays of characters as parameters. Reading begins at the current position in the text file being read and reads the number of characters equal to the size of the array or until eoln is true, in which case the rest of the array is filled with blanks.

2.   OMSI does not have a predefined character string data type, hence it makes no provisions for predefined functions and procedures to manipulate character strings.

3.   OMSI allows for an optional **else** clause to appear in a **case** statement. For example

```
case ch of
    'A' : ACount : = ACount + 1;
    'E' : ECount : = ECount + 1;
    'I' : ICount : = ICount + 1;
    'O' : OCount : = OCount + 1;
    'U' : UCount : = UCount + 1;
    else Other : = Other + 1;
end
```

is a valid statement. Control passes to the **else** clause if the value of ch is any character different from A, E, I, O, or U. If no **else** clause is present, control passes to the statement following the **case** statement.

4.   The program heading is optional and is ignored. Three optional parameters may appear with either the reset or rewrite functions to bind an external file name with an internal file variable. The general forms of the reset and rewrite procedure calls are:

reset(f,FileName,DefaultName,Size)
rewrite(f,FileName,DefaultName,Size)
where the parameters have the following data types:

f—any file variable.

FileName—any literal character string or a packed array of characters.

DefaultName—same data type as FileName.

Size—integer variable.

The statement

reset(f,'ids','.txt',Size)

binds the external file ids.txt to the file variable *f*. For reset, the external file ids.txt is opened for reading. The variable Size is equal to the number of records in file *f*. If −1 is returned as a value for Size, an error occurred. For rewrite, the new external file ids.txt is created. The parameter Size specifies the initial storage to be allocated to the new file.

5. The reserved word **external** is used to provide access to separately compiled procedures and functions and to program libraries. The keyword **external** appears in place of the procedure or function body to indicate it has been compiled separately. For example, the procedure definition:

procedure Sample (**var** x : integer); **external**;

indicates that Sample has been compiled separately.

6. Sets are limited to a maximum of 64 elements.

7. The procedures "new" and "dispose" are used to manage the allocation of storage to dynamic variables.

8. When an interactive file is reset, the file window is set to blank and eoln is set to false, but no actual I/0 transmission occurs. Thus an empty line will seem to consist of one blank.

UCSD Pascal

UCSD Pascal is distributed by Softech Microsystems and runs on many microcomputers. It runs under its own operating system, utilities, editor, linker, and assembler.

1. UCSD Pascal allows character strings to be used as parameters with read and readln.

2. It provides the predeclared type "String" for working with packed arrays of characters. A variable of type String is equivalent to a **packed array** [1..upper-bound] **of** char. The predefined proce-

dures "insert" and "delete" and the predefined functions "length," "pos," "copy," and "concat" are available to work with variables of type String. Examples of string variables are:

var
    s1 : String; {Default size is 80}
    s2 : String[100]; {Size is 100}
    s2 : String[255]; {Maximum size is 255}

The procedures are:

Insert (s1,s2,n)—Inserts string s1 into string s2 at position *n* of string s2.
Delete(s,n,size)—Deletes from string *s*, size number of characters beginning at location *n*.

The functions are:

Length(s)—Returns the length of string *s*.
Pos(s1,s2)—Returns the starting position of string s1 in string s2. If no match is found, Pos returns 0.
Copy(s,n,size)—Returns a string of the size specified taken from string *s* starting at position *n*.
Concat(s1,s2,...)—Returns a string that is the concatenation of the strings s1,s2. . . .

3. It does not provide for an "escape" clause for the **case** statement. However, processing simply drops through to the statement following the **case** statement if the selector expression is evaluated to a value that does not correspond to a case label.

4. External files, other than the standard predefined files, require a special form of reset and rewrite to bind the external file to the internal file variable: Thus,

reset(f,'filename')
rewrite(f,'filename')

will bind the file variable *f* to the external file whose name is filename.

5. UCSD Pascal allows for a collection of separately compiled procedures and functions to be incorporated into a program.

6. Variables of type set may have at most 4080 elements.

7. It does not provide the procedure "dispose" to free storage allocated to dynamic variables. Instead the more primitive "mark" and "release" procedures are provided.

8. The predeclared type INTERACTIVE, which is similar to the type text, is provided. This simplifies the handling of single-character I/0 for interactive terminal devices. The standard files input and output are of type interactive.

Answers to Selected Exercises

Chapter 1 (p. 29)

1.1. (a) central processing unit (c) hardware (e) central processing unit (g) printers, terminals

1.2. (a) true (c) false. It translates assembly language programs to machine language. (e) false. It accepts data from main storage. (g) true

1.3. The major hardware elements of a computer system are: the central processing unit, main storage, and input-output units. The central processing unit interprets and executes program instructions. Main storage holds data and instructions. Input units accept data in machine-readable form and store them in main storage. Output units make data available for human use.

1.5. (a) 21 (c) 32

1.6. (a) 0010000000001111
       0011000000010000
       0101000000010000
       0000000000

(c) 0010000000000100
    0011000000000101
    0110000000000110
    0101000000000111
    0000000000

1.9. Software is a set of programs associated with the operation of a computer system.

1.11. (a) Source code is a program written in either an assembly or high-level language. It is the input to an assembler or a compiler. (b) Object code is a set of statements derived from source code by a translator program, usually machine executable.

1.13. Assembly and machine languages are still useful because they provide access to the full capabilities of a computer. Generally more efficient programs can be written in machine or assembly languages than in high-level languages because the programs need not be translated, or the translation process is a one-for-one substitution. Hence, the actual instructions of the machine can be used directly.

Chapter 2 (p. 77)

2.1. (a) declaration (c) comment (e) program heading (g) constants, variables (i) maxint (k) **div, mod**

2.2. (a) false. It helps the programmer to read a program. (c) false. They may be redefined, although this is not recommended. (e) true (g) true (i) false. An expression with one or more integer operands may also produce a real result.

2.3. (a) Program heading. It provides a name for the program and specifies that the program will use the standard output file. (c) Variable declaration. It declares the variables Length, Width, and Area to be variables of type real. (e) Reserved word **end**. It marks the end of the program. (g) It assigns the product of Length and Width to the variable area. (i) It outputs the values of the variables Length, Width, and Area. (k) This is a comment describing the function of a part of a program. (m) It declares Employee to be of type integer. (o) It assigns to Depreciation the value of the expression (Cost − Salvage)/Life. (q) It outputs the values 1, 27, − 142, and − 142 in fields 3, 3, 4, and 5 columns wide, respectively. (s) It outputs the value − 0.98 in a field 9 columns wide with 3 places to the right of the decimal. (u) It prints a single quote. (w) It inputs the values of Length and Width.

2.4. (a) incorrect. The operator ∗∗ is not a Pascal operator. (c) correct (e) incorrect. Parentheses not balanced.

2.5. (a) 2 (c) skips to a new line (e) '

2.6. (a) **PROGRAM TaxesDue (input, output);**

(c) **VAR**
```
    TotalPay, HourlySalary : real;
    ID, HoursWorked : integer;
```

2.7. (a) `writeln(' * WEEKLY PRODUCTIVITY SUMMARY * ')`

(c) `writeln(' --EMPLOYEE NUMBER-- --UNITS PRODUCED-- ')`

(e) `writeln (' *** TOTAL UNITS ***', u1+u2+u3+u4+u5 : 6)`

2.9. (a) **PROGRAM PartA (output);**

```
    BEGIN
        writeln(1:2, 2:2, 3:2, 4:2, 5:2, 6:2, 7;2, 8:2,
                9:2, 10:3)
    END.
```

(c) **PROGRAM PartC (output);**

```
        BEGIN
           writeln('            *');
           writeln('           ***');
           writeln('          *****');
           writeln('         *******');
           writeln('        *********');
           writeln('           ***');
           writeln('           ***');
           writeln('         *******')
        END.
```

(e) **PROGRAM** PartE (output);

```
        BEGIN
           writeln('            *');
           writeln('           ***');
           writeln('          *****');
           writeln('         *******');
           writeln('        *********');
           writeln('         *******');
           writeln('          *****');
           writeln('           ***');
           writeln('            *');
        END.
```

2.11. **PROGRAM** Question11 (input, output);

```
    VAR
        Gallons1, Gallons2, Gallons3, Gallons4, Gallons5 : real;
        Miles1, Miles2, Miles3, Miles4, Miles5 : real;
        GallonsTotal, MilesTotal : real;

    BEGIN
        readln(Gallons1, Miles1);
        readln(Gallons2, Miles2);
        readln(Gallons3, Miles3);
        readln(Gallons4, Miles4);
        readln(Gallons5, Miles5);

        writeln ('Miles per Gallon for period 1: ', Miles1/Gallons1 :8:2);
        writeln ('Miles per Gallon for period 2: ', Miles2/Gallons2 :8:2);
        writeln ('Miles per Gallon for period 3: ', Miles3/Gallons3 :8:2);
        writeln ('Miles per Gallon for period 4: ', Miles4/Gallons4 :8:2);
        writeln ('Miles per Gallon for period 5: ', Miles5/Gallons5 :8:2);
```

```
        GallonsTotal := Gallons1 + Gallons2 + Gallons3 + Gallons4 +
                        Gallons5;
      MilesTotal := Miles1 + Miles2 + Miles3 + Miles4 + Miles5;

      writeln ('Miles per Gallon for all periods: ',
               MilesTotal/GallonsTotal :8:2);
  END.
```

2.13. **PROGRAM** Question13 (output);

```
       VAR
           Power : integer;

       BEGIN
           Power := 2;
           writeln(Power);
           Power := Power*2;
           writeln(Power);
           Power := Power*2;
           writeln(Power);
           Power := Power*2;
           writeln(Power);
           Power := Power*2;
           writeln(Power);
           Power := Power*2;
           writeln(Power);
           Power := Power*2;
           writeln(Power);
           Power := Power*2;
           writeln(Power);
           Power := Power*2;
           writeln(Power);
           Power := Power*2;
           writeln(Power);
           Power := Power*2;
           writeln(Power);
           Power := Power*2;
           writeln(Power);
           Power := Power*2;
           writeln(Power);
           Power := Power*2;
           writeln(Power);
           Power := Power*2;
           writeln(Power);
           Power := Power*2;
           writeln(Power);
       END.
```

This problem is very repetitious and cries for the ability to repeat the execution of some statements. We will see how this can be done in the following chapters.

Chapter 3 (p. 123)

3.1 (a) problem definition, algorithm design (c) input, output (e) coding (g) flowcharts (i) usage, maintenance

3.2. (a) true (c) false. Comments should be inserted while the program is being written. (e) false. The compiler detects only compile-time errors. (g) false. A program should be tested with invalid as well as valid data.

3.3. (a) (1) *Problem Outline*: We wish to compute the average of three real numbers.

(2) *Input*: The input to the program will consist of a line of data with three real numbers.

(3) *Output*: The output of the program is to consist of the average of the three real numbers printed in the following format:

AVERAGE: ddddd.dd

where the *d*'s represent decimal digits.

(4) *Exceptional Conditions*: No exceptional conditions will be handled.

3.3 (c) (1) *Problem Outline*: We wish to compute the hypotenuse of a right triangle given the lengths of the perpendicular sides.

(2) *Input*: The input to the program will consist of a line of data with two real numbers representing the lengths of the perpendicular sides of a right triangle.

(3) *Output*: The output of the program is to consist of the lengths of the original sides and the length of the hypotenuse printed in the following format:

Side A	Side B	Hypotenuse
ddddd.dd	ddddd.dd	ddddd.dd

where the *d*'s represent decimal digits.

(4) *Exceptional Conditions*: If either of the sides is less than or equal to zero, the following message should be printed:

ERROR: Zero or negative length.

3.3 (e) (1) *Problem Outline*: We wish to write a program that prints a mailing label given the name and address.

(2) *Input*: The input to the program will consist of three lines of data. The first line will contain the name; the second line the street address; and the third the city, state, and ZIP code.

(3) *Output*: The output of the program is to consist of three lines of text printed in the following format:

FirstName LastName
No Street
city ST ZIP

where ST represents the two letter designation for the state and ZIP represents the ZIP code.

(4) *Exceptional Conditions*: No provisions for exceptional conditions.

3.4. None of the algorithms below handle the exceptional conditions. You should return to some of these problems after completing Chapter 4 and incorporate the handling of the exceptional conditions.

(a) BEGIN
        Input the three numbers.
        Compute their average.
        Print the average.
     END.

(c) BEGIN
        Input the lengths of the two sides.
        Compute the hypotenuse.
        Print the headings.
        Print the lengths of the sides and the hypotenuse.
     END.

(e) BEGIN
        Input name.
        Print name.
        Input street address.
        Print street address.
        Input city, state, and ZIP code.
        Print city, state, and ZIP code.
     END.

3.5. (a) **PROGRAM PartA** (input, output);
          VAR
              Number1, Number2, Number3, Average : real;

          BEGIN
              read (Number1, Number2, Number3);
              Average := (Number1 + Number2 + Number3)/3;
              writeln (' AVERAGE : ', Average :9:2)
          END.

      (c) **PROGRAM PartC** (input, output);

          VAR
              Side1, Side2, Hypotenuse : real;

          BEGIN
              read (Side1, Side2);
              Hypotenuse := sqrt(sqr(Side1)+sqr(Side2));
              writeln('Side A   Side B   Hypotenuse');

```
        writeln (Side1 :9:2, Side2 :9:2, Hypotenuse :9:2)
END.
```

3.6. (a) **1.500000E+00   3.333333E-01 6.666666E-01**
        1.000000E+01 7.000000E+00

3.7. A run-time error, indicating division by zero, would result.

3.9. (a) The program without syntax errors is

```
PROGRAM Question9 (input,output);

VAR
  Number, Digit1, Digit2, Digit3 : integer;
 BEGIN
  read (Number);
  Digit1 := Number DIV 100;
  Number := Number MOD 100;
  Digit2 := Number DIV 10;
  Digit3 := Number MOD 0;
  writeln (Digit1, Digit2, Digit3)
END.
```

(b) The line Digit3 : = Number MOD 0 will cause a run-time error. It should be corrected to read Digit3 : = Number MOD 10.

(c) The program decomposes a three-digit integer into its individual digits.

```
PROGRAM Question9 (input,output);

{**************************************
* Program to decompose a three-digit *
* integer into its digits            *
**************************************}

VAR
  Number, Digit1, Digit2, Digit3 : integer;

BEGIN
  read (Number);

  {Obtain left-most digit}
  Digit1 := Number DIV 100;

  {Eliminate left-most digit}
  Number := Number MOD 100;
```

```
{Obtain middle digit}
Digit2 := Number DIV 10;

{Obtain right-most digit}
Digit3 := Number MOD 10;

writeln (Digit1, Digit2, Digit3)
END.
```

Chapter 4 (p. 168)

4.1. (a) **if ... then ... else** (c) false (e) true (g) lower (i) last unused (k) a run-time error

4.2. (a) false (c) true (e) false. Because there are parentheses, the expression in the parentheses must be evaluated first; thus, the − will be performed second. (g) false. Only the **else** may be omitted. (i) true (k) true (l) false. Subtraction will be performed before > = .

4.3. (a) It checks to see if *a* equals one and prints the appropriate message. (c) If HoursWorked is greater than 40.00, it assigns to Overtime the value HoursWorked − 40.00; otherwise Overtime is assigned the value 0. (e) If DayOfyear equals 200, it writes the message "This must be July," sets Month to 7, and writes the message "We should go swimming." (g) First it checks if Sex equals 1 or 2. If this is true, then if Sex equals 1, it writes the message "female"; otherwise it writes the message "male." IF Sex is neither 1 nor 2, it writes the message "code is incorrect." (i) If *a* equals 5 and *b* equals 6, it writes the message "7"; otherwise it writes the message "8." (k) If *a*, *b*, and *c* equal 1, it writes the message "someone likes 1s." (m) If Sex equals 1, it writes "female," and if Sex equals 2, it writes "male." (o) It divides Grade by 10. If the answer is 9 or 10, it writes "excellent"; if 8, "good"; if 7, "satisfactory"; if 6, "pass"; if 4 or 5, "failed—should work harder"; and if 0, 1, 2, or 3, "hopeless."

4.4. (a) false (c) false (e) false false (g) true false (i) true (k) true

4.5. (a)
```
IF TestGrade >= 60 THEN
     writeln('passed')
   ELSE
     writeln('failed')
```

(c)
```
IF Rain THEN
   writeln('It is raining')
 ELSE
   writeln('It is not raining')
```

(e)
```
IF (0<= Hours) AND (Hours <= 30) THEN
   writeln('excessive absence')
 ELSE
   IF Hours <= 50 THEN
      writeln ('normal')
```

```
        ELSE
          IF Hours <= 70 THEN
            writeln('excessive overtime')
          ELSE
            IF Hours <=100 THEN
              writeln('crazy')
```

(g) CASE p MOD 2 OF
```
      0 : writeln('even');
      1 : writeln('odd')
    END
```

4.7. PROGRAM Question7 (input, output);

```
    VAR
        a, b, c, d : integer;

    BEGIN
        read(a,b,c,d);
        IF a > b THEN
          IF a > c THEN
            IF a > d THEN
              writeln ('largest is a')
            ELSE
              writeln ('largest is d')
          ELSE
            IF c > d THEN
              writeln ('largest is c')
            ELSE
              writeln ('largest is d')
        ELSE
          IF b > c THEN
            IF b > d THEN
              writeln ('largest is b')
            ELSE
              writeln ('largest is d')
          ELSE
            IF c > d THEN
              writeln ('largest is c')
            ELSE
              writeln ('largest is d')
    END.
```

As you can see by comparing the solution for three numbers with solution for four numbers, this approach, if used with ten numbers, would be very difficult and long.

4.9. ```
PROGRAM Question9 (input, output);

   VAR
      Die1, Die2, Sum : integer;

   BEGIN
      read(Die1, Die2);
      Sum := Die1 + Die2;
      CASE Sum OF
         2, 3, 12   : writeln (' You lose');
         7, 11   : writeln (' You win');
         4,5,6,8,9,10   : writeln (' Your point is ', Sum :1,
                                    ' - roll again')
      END
   END.
```

**Chapter 5** (p. 231)

5.1. (a) loop (c) counter controlled (e) termination, repetition (g) sentinel (i) the number of times the loop is to be repeated (k) **downto** (m) quotes (o) in a **type** definition, in a **var**iable declaration.

5.2. (a) false. A **repeat . . . until** loop terminates when the condition is true. (c) false. The body is executed once. (e) false. The letter *e* will cause a run-time error when read as an integer. (g) false. It can be any scalar type other than real. (i) true (k) true (m) true

5.3. (a) A loop that will repeat statements in the body until some condition becomes true. (c) A loop that will repeat the statement in the body a fixed number of times. (e) It adds 1 to Count. (g) It computes Salary as Hours Worked times Rate plus Overtime. (i) It writes the value of Number ten times. (k) It counts all the blanks in the input file. (m) It defines an enumerated data type for the days of the week. (o) It declares Year to be of type integer. (q) It defines the type Letter to be the subrange of characters from *A* to *Z*.

5.4. (a) ```
Total := 0;
Count := 0
```

(c) ```
Total := Total + Number
```

(e) ```
BEGIN
   Count := Count + 1;
   Sum := Sum + Number
END
```

(g) `read (Number);`

```
   WHILE Number <> -1 DO
      BEGIN
         Sum := Sum + Number;
         read(Number)
      END
```

(i)
```
VAR
   Letter, Digit, SpecialSymbol : char;
```

(k)
```
TYPE
   WorkingDay = (monday, tuesday, wednesday,
                 thursday, friday)
```

5.5.
```
PROGRAM Question5 (output);

   VAR
      i, SumSquares : integer;

   BEGIN
      SumSquares := 0;
      FOR i := 1 TO 50 DO
         SumSquares := SumSquares + sqr(i);
      writeln(SumSquares)
   END.
```

5.7.
```
PROGRAM Question7 (output);

   VAR
      i, j : integer;
      Factorial : real;

   BEGIN
      i := 1;
      WHILE true DO
         BEGIN
            Factorial := 1.0;
            FOR j := i DOWNTO 1 DO
               Factorial := Factorial * j;
            writeln('Factorial of ',i:1,' = ',Factorial);
            i := i + 1
         END
   END.
```

```
5.9.  PROGRAM Question9 (output);

          VAR
              First, Second, Count, Sum : integer;
              Ratio : real;

          BEGIN
              First := 1;
              Second := 1;
              Ratio := First/Second;
              writeln (Ratio :10:5);
              FOR Count := 3 TO 30 DO
                  BEGIN
                      Sum := First + Second;
                      First := Second;
                      Second := Sum;
                      Ratio : First/ Second;
                      writeln(Ratio :10:5)
                  END
          END.
```

```
5.11.  PROGRAM Question11 (output);

    VAR
        Celsius, i : integer;
        Fahrenheit : real;

    BEGIN
        writeln('CELSIUS                          FAHRENHEIT');
        writeln('----------------------------------------------------');
        writeln;
        Celsius := 0;
        WHILE Celsius <= 100 DO
            BEGIN
                write (Celsius : 1,' - ', Celsius+9 :1);
                FOR i := 0 TO 9 DO
                    BEGIN
                        Fahrenheit := (9/5)*(Celsius+i) + 32;
                        write(Fahrenheit :15:3)
                    END;
                writeln
            END
    END.
```

```
5.13. PROGRAM Question13 (output);

     VAR
        Months : integer;
        Interest, Principal, Prin, Increment : real;

     BEGIN
        writeln('          AMOUNT REMAINING ON DEPOSIT');
        writeln('          --------------------------');
        writeln;
        write('MONTH          1.0%    1.1%    1.2%    1.3%    1.4%    1.5%');
        writeln('  1.6%    1.7%    1.8%    1.8%');
        write('-----          ----    ----    ----    ----    ----    ----');
        writeln('  ----    ----    ----    ----');
        writeln;
        Principal := 1000.0;
        FOR Months := 1 TO 30 DO
           BEGIN
              write(Months :6);
              Interest := 0.01;
              Increment := 0.0;
              Prin := Principal;
              FOR i := 1 TO 10 DO
                 BEGIN
                    Prin := Prin*(1+Interest+Increment);
                    write(Prin :15:2);
                    Increment := Increment + 0.001
                 END;
              Principal := Principal*(1.01)
           END
     END.

                    5.15. (a) PROGRAM Question15A (output);

                              VAR
                                 Row, Stars : integer;

                              BEGIN
                                 FOR Row := 1 TO 5 DO
                                    BEGIN
                                       FOR Stars := 1 TO Row DO
                                          write('*');
                                       writeln
                                    END
                              END.
```

```
PROGRAM Question15C (output);

VAR
    Row, Blanks, Stars : integer;

BEGIN
    FOR Row := 1 TO 5 DO
        BEGIN
            FOR Blanks := 1 TO 5-Row DO
                write(' ');
            FOR Stars := 1 TO Row DO
                write('*');
            writeln
        END
END.
```

Chapter 6 (p. 290)

6.1. (a) structured (c) array variable (e) integer, real (g) assignment (i) relational, output, constant (k) 480 (m) integer (o) 630

6.2. (a) true (c) true (e) true (g) true (i) true (k) false. They have different index types. To have variables of the same type you must declare them to be the same named type. (m) false. The array must be printed one component at a time. (o) true (q) true (s) true

6.3. (a) It declares an array to hold 20 integers. (c) It stores the value 0 in every component of the array Midterm. (e) It copies the array Midterm into the array Final. (g) It divides every component of array Final by 100. (i) It sums all 50 components of array Final. (k) It reads the 20 characters for the string Name. (m) It assigns a value to the string Address. (o) It assigns the value empty to every component of array Board.

6.5.

```
PROGRAM Question5 (input, output);

VAR
    Counters : ARRAY[0..5] OF integer;
    Salary : real;
    Index : integer;

BEGIN
    {Initialize the counters}

    FOR Index := 0 TO 5 DO
        Counters[Index] := 0;
```

```
WHILE NOT eof DO
   BEGIN
      readln(Salary);
      Index := trunc(Salary/100);
      IF Index > 5 THEN
          Index := 5;
      Counters[Index] := Counters[Index]+1
   END;
   writeln ('Number in range $50  - $99.99 : ',Counters[0] :4);
   writeln ('Number in range $100 - $199.99 : ',Counters[1] :4);
   writeln ('Number in range $200 - $299.99 : ',Counters[2] :4);
   writeln ('Number in range $300 - $399.99 : ',Counters[3] :4);
   writeln ('Number in range $400 - $499.99 : ',Counters[4] :4);
   writeln ('Number $500  and over : ',Counters[5] :4)
END.
```

6.7.
```
PROGRAM Question7 (input, output);
VAR
    List : ARRAY[1..100] OF integer;
    Count, Index, Largest, Second : integer;
BEGIN
    read(Count);
    FOR Index := 1 TO Count DO
       read(List[Index]);
    {Find largest}

    Largest := List[1];
    FOR Index := 2 TO Count DO
       IF Largest < List[Index] THEN
          Largest := List[Index];
    {Find second largest}
    IF List[1] <> Largest THEN
       Second := List[1]
    ELSE
       Second := List[2];
    FOR Index := 2 TO Count DO
       IF (List[Index] <> Largest) THEN
          IF (Second < List[Index]) THEN
             Second := List[Index];

    {Print the largest and second largest}

    writeln('Largest: ',Largest :5);
    writeln('Second largest: ',Second :5)
END.
```

```
6.9. PROGRAM Question9 (input, output);

    VAR
        x : ARRAY[1..100] OF integer;
        Index, Largest, LocLargest, Count : integer;
    BEGIN
        {Part a) input the integers}

        Index := 1;
        WHILE (NOT eof) AND (Index <= 100) DO
            BEGIN
                read(x[Index]);
                Index := Index + 1
            END;
        IF Index > 100 THEN
            Count := Index - 1
        ELSE
            Count := Index -2;

        {Part b) find the value of the largest integer}

        Largest := x[1];
        FOR Index := 2 TO Count DO
            IF Largest < x[Index] THEN
                Largest := x[Index];
        writeln ('Largest : ', Largest : 5);

        {Part c) Find and print the location of the largest value.
         Assume the largest value is unique.}

        LocLargest := 1;
        FOR Index := 2 TO Count DO
            IF x[LocLargest] < x[Index] THEN
                LocLargest := Index;
        writeln ('Location of largest : ',LocLargest :5);

        {Part d) Find and print the location of the largest value.
         Assume the largest value may not be unique.}

        {Locate largest as above.}

        writeln ('The largest value is at the following locations...');
        FOR Index := 1 TO Count DO
            IF x[Index] = x[LocLargest] THEN
                write (Index :5);
        writeln
    END.
```

6.11. **PROGRAM** Question11 (input, output);

```
CONST
    Maxsize = 100;

TYPE
    List = ARRAY[1..Maxsize] OF integer;

VAR
    Original, Sorted : List;
    Index, LocSmallest, Start, Count : integer;

BEGIN
    read(Count);
    FOR Index := 1 TO Count DO
       read(Original[Index]);

    {Sort}

    FOR Start := 1 TO Count DO
       BEGIN
          LocSmallest := Start;
          FOR Index := Start+1 TO Count DO
             IF Original[LocSmallest] > Original[Index] THEN
                   LocSmallest := Index;

          {Copy into second array}

          Sorted[Start] := Original[LocSmallest];
          Original[LocSmallest] := maxint;
       END;

    writeln('Sorted array...');
    writeln;
    FOR Index := 1 TO Count DO
       write(Sorted[Index]);
    writeln
END.
```

6.12. (a) **PROGRAM** Question12a (input, output);

```
    VAR
       List : ARRAY[1..100] OF integer;
       i, j, n, Temp : integer;
```

```
BEGIN
    read(n);
    FOR i := 1 TO n DO
        read(List[i]);

    {Sort}

    FOR i := 1 TO n-1 DO
        FOR j := 1 TO n-1 DO   {Perform pass}
            IF List[j] < List[j+1] THEN
                BEGIN
                        Temp := List[j];
                        List[j] := List[j+1];
                        List[j+1] := Temp
                END;
    writeln('Sorted array...');
    FOR i := 1 TO Count DO
        write(List[i]);
    writeln
END.
```

6.13.
```
PROGRAM Question13 (input, output);

CONST
    Blank = ' ';
    Period = '.';

VAR
    Line : ARRAY[1..100] OF char;
    i, Count : integer;

BEGIN
    Count := 0;
    REPEAT
        Count := Count + 1;
        read(Line[Count])
    UNTIL Line[Count] = Period;

    Start := Count;
    WHILE Start > 1 DO
        BEGIN
            WHILE Line[Start] = Blank DO
                BEGIN
                        write(Line[Start]);
```

```
                              Start := Start - 1
                    END;
                Finish := Start;
                WHILE Line[Finish] <> Blank DO
                    Finish := Finish - 1;
                FOR i := Finish+1 TO Start DO
                    write(Line[i]);
                Start := Finish
            END
    END.
```

Chapter 7 (p. 368)

7.1. (a) **function** (c) number and type (e) after (g) actual (i) function invocation (k) as many as desired (m) pass-by-value and pass-by-reference (o) pass-by-reference (q) is (s) block (u) global (w) side effect (y) recursive

7.2. (a) false. It is the formal parameter list. (c) true (e) false. They must also agree in type. (g) false. A local variable does not exist between function invocations. (i) false. Call-by-reference parameters must be used. (k) true (m) false. It can be redeclared in another block. (m) true (p) false. No special declaration is required.

7.3. (a) function heading (c) procedure heading (e) procedure heading for a **forward** declaration

7.4. (a) 3
          5
(c) 1   2   3
    1   2   10

7.5. Formal parameters are place holders. They are variables local to a function or procedure. Actual parameters are the actual values passed to a procedure or function.

7.7.
```
FUNCTION Count(S : String; Size : integer; Ch : char): integer;

VAR
   i : integer;
   Counter : integer;
BEGIN
   Counter := 0;
   FOR i := 1 TO Size DO
      IF s[i] = Ch THEN
         Counter := Counter + 1;
   Count := Counter
END;
```

7.9.

```
PROCEDURE Hang(Errors :integer);
PROCEDURE Draw1;

BEGIN
    writeln;
    writeln;
    writeln;
    writeln;
    writeln;
    writeln;
    writeln('x');
    writeln('x');
    writeln('x');
    writeln('x');
    writeln('x');
END;
PROCEDURE Draw2;

BEGIN
    writeln;
    writeln('x');
    writeln('x');
    writeln('x');
    writeln('x');
    writeln('x');
    writeln('x');
    writeln('x');
    writeln('x');
    writeln('x');
    writeln('x');
END;

PROCEDURE Draw3;

BEGIN
    writeln('xxxxxxxxx');
    writeln('x');
    writeln('x');
    writeln('x');
    writeln('x');
    writeln('x');
    writeln('x');
    writeln('x');
    writeln('x');
    writeln('x');
    writeln('x');
END;
```

```
PROCEDURE Draw4;

BEGIN
    writeln('xxxxxxxxx');
    writeln('x            |');
    writeln('x            0');
    writeln('x');
    writeln('x');
    writeln('x');
    writeln('x');
    writeln('x');
    writeln('x');
    writeln('x');
    writeln('x');
END;

PROCEDURE Draw5;

BEGIN
    writeln('xxxxxxxxx');
    writeln('x            |');
    writeln('x            0');
    writeln('x          -===-');
    writeln('x          | X |');
    writeln('x          | X |');
    writeln('x            X');
    writeln('x');
    writeln('x');
    writeln('x');
    writeln('x');
END;

PROCEDURE Draw6;

BEGIN
    writeln('xxxxxxxxx');
    writeln('x            |');
    writeln('x            0');
    writeln('x          -===-');
    writeln('x          | X |');
    writeln('x          | X |');
    writeln('x            X');
    writeln('x          / \');
    writeln('x         /   \');
    writeln('x        -     -');
    writeln('x');
END;
```

```
BEGIN
    CASE Errors OF
        1 : Draw1;
        2 : Draw2;
        3 : Draw3;
        4 : Draw4;
        5 : Draw5;
        6 : Draw6
    END
END;
```

7.10. (a)
```
PROCEDURE Encode (VAR English : String ; Dispacement : integer;
                  VAR Code : String; Size : integer);
VAR
    i : integer;
BEGIN
    FOR i := 1 TO Size DO
        Code[i] := chr(ord(English[i])+Displacement)
END;
```

(c) To break the code, simply try all the displacements from 0 to 25.

7.11. (a)
```
PROCEDURE Encode (VAR English, Code, Key : String; Size : integer);

VAR
    i, Index : integer;
BEGIN
    FOR i := 1 TO Size DO
        BEGIN
            Index := ord(English[i])-ord('A')+1;
            IF (Index < 1) OR (Index > 26) THEN
                Code[i] := English[i]
            ELSE
                Code[i] := Key[Index]
        END
END;
```

(c)
```
PROCEDURE EncodeAndGroup (VAR English, Code, Key : String; Size :
    integer);

VAR
    i, Counter, Index : integer;
BEGIN
    Counter := 1;
```

```
FOR i := 1 TO Size DO
    BEGIN
        IF English[i] <> ' ' THEN
            BEGIN
                Index := ord(English[i])-ord('A')+1;
                IF (Index < 1) OR (Index > 26 THEN
                    IF (Counter MOD 5) <> 0 THEN
                        Code[Counter] := English[i]
                    ELSE
                        BEGIN
                            Code[Counter] := ' ';
                            Counter := Counter + 1;
                            Code[Counter] := English[i]
                        END
                ELSE
                    IF (Counter MOD 5) <> 0 THEN
                        Code[Counter] := Key[Index]
                    ELSE
                        BEGIN
                            Code[Counter] := ' ';
                            Counter := Counter + 1;
                            Code[Counter] := Key[Index]
                        END;
                Counter := Counter + 1
            END
END;
```

7.15. Hint: When handling subtraction, generate two random numbers, add them, and display the sum and sign of the numbers. This will avoid negative answers. Do something similar to avoid fractional answers for division.

Chapter 8 (p. 420)

8.1. (a) modular (c) module (e) stub (g) exercise all paths

8.2. (a) true (c) true (e) false. A module should perform a single function. (g) false. A stub should be used in top-down testing.

8.3. The use of global variables does not allow a programmer to isolate modules from each other. Side effects are likely, and debugging is more difficult.

8.5. (a) Lower-level modules suggested by the algorithm are "PrintHeadings" to print the headings, "Initialize" to initialize the game, "GetMove" to obtain each player's move, "PrintBoard" to display the board, and "Winner" to determine if the game is won.

```
(b) PROGRAM TicTacToe (input, output);

    TYPE
        Entry = (Empty, X, O);
        BoardType = ARRAY[1..9] OF Entry;

    VAR
        Board : BoardType;
        Player, MoveCounter : integer;
        WinFlag : boolean;

    PROCEDURE PrintHeadings;

        BEGIN
            writeln ('TIC TAC TOE');
            writeln
        END;
    PROCEDURE Initialize (VAR B : BoardType; VAR Win : boolean;
                              VAR MoveCounter : integer);

        VAR
            i : integer;
        BEGIN
            FOR i := 1 TO 9 DO
                B[i] := Empty;
            Win := false;
            MoveCounter := 1
        END;

    PROCEDURE PrintBoard (B : BoardType);

        BEGIN {stub}
            writeln (ord(B[1]:2, ord(B[2]:2, ord(B[3]:2);
            writeln (ord(B[4]:2, ord(B[5]:2, ord(B[6]:2);
            writeln (ord(E[7]:2, ord(B[8]:2, ord(B[9]:2);
        END;

    PROCEDURE GetMove ( Player : integer; VAR Move : integer);

        BEGIN {stub}
            writeln ('Player ',Player :1,' Please enter move');
            read (Move)
        END;

    FUNCTION Winner(B: BoardType) : boolean;

        VAR {stub}
            Answer : char;
        BEGIN
            writeln('Is there a winner?');
```

```
            read(Answer);
            IF Answer = 'y' THEN
                Winner := true
            ELSE
                Winner := false
        END;
BEGIN { Tic-tac-toe }

    PrintHeadings;
    Initialize(Board,WinFlag,MoveCounter);
    Player := 1;

    REPEAT
                    IF Player = 1 THEN
            BEGIN
                GetMove(1,Move);
                Board[Move] := X
                PrintBoard(Board);
                IF Winner(Board) THEN
                    BEGIN
                        writeln('Player 1 wins');
                        WinFlag := true
                    END
                ELSE
                    Player := 2
            END
        ELSE
            BEGIN
                GetMove(2,Move);
                Board[Move] := O;
                PrintBoard(Board);
                IF Winner(Board) THEN
                    BEGIN
                        writeln('Player 2 wins');
                        WinFlag := true
                    END
                ELSE
                    Player := 1
            END;
        MoveCounter := MoveCounter + 1
    UNTIL (MoveCounter > 9) OR (WinFlag)
    IF NOT WinFlag THEN
                    writeln('It is a draw')
END.
```

(c) To test the top level module play the game for a win by either player and a draw.

Chapter 9 (p. 449)

9.1. (a) elements (c) universal (e) 4 (g) + (i) * (l) **in**

9.2. (a) false. In Pascal square brackets are used, [and]. (c) false. Only subranges of scalar data types can be used. (e) true (g) false. It is the set of all values in *a*, but not in *b*. (i) true (k) false. It is true if every element of *a* is an element of *b*. (m) true (o) true

9.3. (a) It defines the type LetterSet to be a set of characters. (c) It declares the variable Letters to be of type set of characters. (e) It declares the variable Month to be an array with base type Week, which is a set type. (g) It initializes Letters to the alphabet. (i) It initializes the components of array Month, the set of the days of the week. (k) It initializes the set Numbers to the first 50 positive integers, then removes from the set the even integers. (m) It checks to see if set Week contains Saturday or Sunday and prints an appropriate message. (o) It prints a message if Letter is a vowel. (q) It validates that Ch is a vowel, then processes each vowel accordingly.

9.4. (a) `Ch IN ['A'..'Z']`

(c) `Ch IN ['A'..'Z','0'..'9']`

(e) `(Number1 IN [0..9]) AND (Number2 IN [0..9])`

9.5. (a) [1,3,5] (c) true (e) true

9.7.
```
PROGRAM Question7 (input, output);

   CONST
      Period = '.';
   VAR
      Sent1, Sent2 : SET OF char;
      Letter : char;
   BEGIN
      {Read first sentence and form a set of letters}

      read(Letter);
      Sent1 := [];
      WHILE Letter <> Period DO
         BEGIN
            IF Letter IN ['A'..'Z','a'..'z'] THEN
               Sent1 := Sent1 + [Letter];
            read(Letter);
         END;

      {Read second sentence and form a set of letters}

      read(Letter);
      Sent2 := [];
```

```
            WHILE Letter <> Period DO
                BEGIN
                    IF Letter IN ['A'..'Z','a'..'z'] THEN
                        Sent2 := Sent2 + [Letter];
                    read(Letter);
                END;
            {Compute set difference}


            Sent1 := Sent1-Sent2;


            {Print the set}

            Letter := 'A';
            WHILE Sent1 <> [] DO
                BEGIN
                    IF Letter IN Sent1 THEN
                        BEGIN
                            write(Letter);
                            Sent1 := Sent1-[Letter]
                        END;
                    IF Letter <> 'Z' THEN
                        Letter := succ(Letter)
                    ELSE
                        Letter := 'a'
                END
        END;
```

```
9.11 PROCEDURE SetIntersection (S1,S2 : ArraySet; VAR S3 : ArraySet);

    {*******************************************
    * Procedure to compute the intersection of *
    * sets S1 and S2 and store the             *
    * result in S3.                            *
    *******************************************}

    VAR
        I : BaseType;

    BEGIN
        FOR I := 1 TO Maxsize DO
            S3[I] := S1[I] AND S2[I]
    END {of PROCEDURE SetIntersection};
```

Chapter 10 (p. 503)

10.1. (a) fields (c) unique (e) **with** (g) **case**

10.2. (a) true (c) true (e) true (g) false. Record structures may not be defined recursively. (i) false. The tag field may be omitted.

10.3. (a) It defines a record type with the appropriate fields to store an address. (c) It declares an array whose components are records of type Address. (e) It inputs the 20 characters constituting the City field of the record Location. (g) It prints the value of the field Street of the record Location. (i) First, it defines the record type PhoneNumber with the fields Area Code, Prefix, and Number. Then, it defines the record type Info with the fields Name, HasPhone, and Telephone. The field Name is a fixed field, the field HasPhone is a tag field, and the field Telephone is a variant field. The data type of the field Telephone is the record type PhoneNumber. (k) It assigns the value 617 to the field AreaCode of the record Telephone, which is itself a field of the record Directory[5].

10.4. (a)
```
WITH Date1 DO
     Day := 5;
```

(c)
```
WITH Date1 DO
   BEGIN
      Month := feb;
      Year := 1976
   END
```

10.5.
```
TYPE
   Rank = (professor, associate, assistant, lecturer);
   NameType = RECORD
      First = PACKED ARRAY[1..15] OF char;
      Last = PACKED ARRAY[1..20] OF char
   END;
   Date = RECORD
      Day : 1..31;
      Month : 1..12;
      Year : 1900..1990
   END;
   Faculty = RECORD
      Name : NameType;
      DateHired : Date;
      TypeOfAppointment : (Fulltime, Parttime);
      Department : PACKED ARRAY[1..15] OF char;
      CASE CurrentRank : Rank OF
         Professor,
         Associate,
         Assistant : ( YearsOfService : integer);
         Lecturer : (NumberOfCoursesTaught : integer)
   END
```

10.7. PROGRAM Report (input, output);

```
TYPE
    EmployeeRec = RECORD
        Id : integer;
        NumbDependents : integer;
        HoursWorked : real;
        Rate : real;
        Savings : boolean
    END;

VAR
    Employee : EmployeeRec;
    GrossPay, NetPay : real;
    FederalTax, StateTax, FICA, Save : real;


PROCEDURE ReadInfo(VAR Empl : EmployeeRec);

    VAR
        SavProg : integer;
    BEGIN
        WITH Empl DO
            BEGIN
                read(Id, NumbDependents, HoursWorked, Rate);
                read (SavProg);
                IF SavProg = 1 THEN
                    Savings := true
                ELSE
                    Savings := false
            END;
        readln
    END;


BEGIN

    {Print headings}

    writeln(' ID     NUMBER OF      HOUR     HOURLY GROSS',
            ' FED TAX  FICA   SAVINGS    NET');
    writeln('        DEPENDENTS    WORKED   RATE    PAY ',
            '                        PAY');
    writeln;

    {Process each employee}
```

```
            WHILE NOT eof DO
               BEGIN
                  ReadInfo(Employee);
                  WITH Employee DO
                     BEGIN
                        OverTime := 0.0;
                     IF HoursWorked > 40.0 THEN
                        BEGIN
                           OverTime := HoursWorked - 40.0;
                           HoursWorked := HoursWorked - OverTime
                        END;
                     GrossPay := Rate*HoursWorked +Rate*1.5*OverTime;
                     FederalTax := (GrossPay-(13*NumbDependents))*0.15;
                     FICA := GrossPay * 0.06;
                     StateTax := GrossPay * 0.55;
                     IF Savings = true THEN
                        Save := 0.05 * GrossPay
                     ELSE
                        Save := 0;
                     NetPay := GrossPay - FederalTax - FICA
                                 - StateTax - Save;

                     {Print record}

                     write(Id :6, NumbDependents :4, HoursWorked :6:2);
                     write(GrossPay :8:2, FederalTax :8:2, FICA :8:2);
                     writeln(StateTax :8:2, Save :8:2, NetPay :8:2)
               END
         END
   END.
```

10.8. (a)
```
           PROCEDURE ReadString(VAR S : String);

           {*****************************
           * Procedure to input a line. *
           *****************************}

           VAR
              i : integer;
           BEGIN
              i := 0;
              WHILE (i < Maxsize) AND (NOT eoln) DO
                 BEGIN
                    i := i + 1;
                    read(S.Ch[i])
                 END;
              S.Length := i
           END;
```

(c) `FUNCTION Index(VAR S,T :String; Start:integer):integer;`

```
{********************************
* Function to locate string S    *
* in target string T. The        *
* function returns the position  *
* of the first character of the  *
* first occurrence of S in T.    *
* If S is not in T it            *
* returns 0. The search begins   *
* at location Start of T.        *
********************************}

VAR
    i,j            : integer;
    Uneq           : boolean;
BEGIN
   {Validate Start}

   IF Start<1 THEN
      Start:=1;

   {Check if remainder of T is long enough to
    contain S}

   IF (Start+T.Length>S.Length+1) OR (T.Length=0) THEN
      Locate:=0
   ELSE
      BEGIN
         i:=Start-1;
         REPEAT
            i:=i+1;
            j:=0;
            REPEAT
               j:=j+1;
               Uneq:=T.Ch[j]<>S.Ch[i+j-1];
            UNTIL Uneq OR (j=T.Length);
         UNTIL (NOT Uneq) OR (i=S.Length-T.Length+1);
         IF Uneq THEN
            Index:=0
         ELSE
            Index:=j

      END
END;
```

```
10.9.  TYPE
         Complex = RECORD
             RealPart : real;
             ImaginaryPart : real
         END;

       PROCEDURE ComplexAddition(a,b : Complex; VAR Sum : Complex);

       {*******************************
       * Procedure to perform         *
       * addition of complex numbers. *
       *******************************}

       BEGIN
           Sum.RealPart := a.RealPart + b.RealPart;
           Sum.ImaginaryPart := a.ImaginaryPart + b.ImaginaryPart
       END;

       PROCEDURE ComplexSubtraction(a,b : Complex; VAR Difference : Complex);

       {**********************************
       * Procedure to perform            *
       * subtraction of complex numbers. *
       **********************************}

       BEGIN
           Difference.RealPart := a.RealPart - b.RealPart;
           Difference.ImaginaryPart := a.ImaginaryPart - b.ImaginaryPart
       END;

       PROCEDURE ComplexMultiplication(a,b : Complex; VAR Product : Complex);

       {*******************************
       * Procedure to perform         *
       * addition of complex numbers. *
       *******************************}

       BEGIN
           Product.RealPart := a.RealPart * b.RealPart;
           Product.ImaginaryPart := a.ImaginaryPart * b.ImaginaryPart
       END;

       PROCEDURE ComplexDivision(a,b : Complex; VAR Quotient : Complex);

       {*******************************
       * Procedure to perform         *
       * division of complex numbers. *
       *******************************}
```

```
BEGIN
   Quotient.RealPart := ((a.RealPart * b.RealPart) +
                            (a.ImaginaryPart * b.ImaginaryPart)) /
                            (b.RealPart + b.ImaginaryPart);
   Quotient.ImaginaryPart := ((a.ImaginaryPart * b.RealPart) -
                                (a.RealPart * b.ImaginaryPart) /
                                (b.RealPart + b.ImaginaryPart);
END;
```

Chapter 11 (p. 553)

11.1. (a) source, destination (c) true (e) MasterFile ↑ (g) text (i) get (f); x := f ↑

11.2. (a) false. You need not reset the standard file "input." (c) false. They may be used with any files. (e) true (g) false. Files must be copied one component at a time. (i) false. It is equivalent to f ↑ : = value; put(f)

11.3. (a) It defines Numbers to be a file whose components are integers. (c) It opens the file NumberFile for reading by setting the window on the first component of the file. (e) It writes a 5 to the file NumberFile.

11.4. (a)
```
TYPE
     NumberFile = FILE OF integer;

FUNCTION Count (VAR f : NumberFile ; n : integer): integer;

VAR
   Counter : integer;

BEGIN
   reset(f);
   Counter := 0;
   WHILE NOT eof(f) DO
      BEGIN
         IF f↑ = n THEN
            Counter := Counter + 1;
         get(f)
      END
   Count := Counter
END;
```

(c)
```
PROCEDURE DeleteNegative (VAR f : NumberFile);

   VAR
      Temp : NumberFile;

   BEGIN
      reset(f);
      rewrite(Temp);
```

```
        WHILE NOT eof(f) DO
            BEGIN
                IF f↑ >= 0 THEN
                    BEGIN
                        Temp↑ := f↑;
                        put(temp)
                    END;
                get(f)
            END;
        reset(Temp);
        rewrite(f);
        WHILE NOT eof(Temp) DO
            BEGIN
                f↑ := Temp↑;
                put(f);
                get(Temp)
            END
    END;

    DeleteNegative(Numbers1)
```

11.5.
```
PROGRAM Make80(File1, File2);

VAR
    File1, File2 : Text;
    Size : integer;
    Ch : char;

BEGIN
    reset(File1);
    rewrite(File2);
    WHILE NOT eof(File1) DO
        BEGIN
            Size := 0;
            WHILE NOT eoln(File1) DO
                BEGIN
                    read(File1, Ch);
                    Size := Size + 1;
                    write(File2, Ch)
                END;
            WHILE Size <= 80 DO
                BEGIN
                    write(File2,' ');
                    Size := Size + 1
                END;
```

```
                     writeln(File2)
               END;
         WHILE Size <= 80 DO
             BEGIN
                 write(File2,' ');
                 Size := Size + 1
             END;
         writeln(File2)
   END.
```

11.7.
```
PROCEDURE NumberFile ( File1 : text);

VAR
    Count : integer;
    Ch : char;
BEGIN
    reset(File1);
    Count := 0;
    WHILE NOT eof(File1) DO
        BEGIN
            Count := Count + 1;
            write (Count :4,' ');
            WHILE NOT eoln(File1) DO
               BEGIN
                   read(File1, Ch);
                   write(Ch)
               END;
            writeln
        END
END;
```

11.9.
```
PROGRAM Snoop (input, output, Log);

TYPE
    NameType = PACKED ARRAY[1..20] OF char;
    LogFile = FILE OF NameType;

VAR
    Name : NameType;
    Log : LogFile;

BEGIN
    reset(Log);
```

```
        WHILE NOT eof(Log) DO
           get(Log);

        writeln (' Enter your name');
        i := 1;
        WHILE (i <= 20) AND (NOT eoln) DO
           BEGIN
              read(Name[i])
              i := 1 + 1
           END;
        Length := i - 1;
        FOR i := Length + 1 TO 20 DO
           Name[i] := ' ';

        Log↑ := Name;
        put(Log)
     END;
```

Chapter 12 (p. 603)

12.1. (a) address (c) number, relationship (e) tree (g) new

12.2. (a) false. The type of the referenced variable must be specified. (c) true (e) true (g) true (i) false. It assigns values to pointers by creating the variable referenced by the pointer.

12.3. The delete procedure for linked lists requires a pointer to the preceding record because we need access to that record in order to modify its pointer. Since the list is linked in only one direction, the only way we can access this record is by providing a pointer to it. We cannot backup.

12.5. `FUNCTION NumberOfNodes(List : NodePointer);`

```
{***************************************
* Function counts number of nodes on  *
* a linked list. The list has a       *
* header record.                      *
***************************************}

VAR
   p : NodePointer;
   Count := integer;

BEGIN
   Count := 0;
   p := List↑.Next;
```

```
                        WHILE p <> NIL DO
                           BEGIN
                              Count := Count + 1;
                              p := p↑.Next
                           END;
                        NumberOfNodes := Count;
                     END;
```

12.7. TYPE
```
      String = PACKED ARRAY[1..20] OF char;
      PassengerPointer = ↑Passenger;
      Passenger = RECORD
         Name : String;
         Seat : 1..200;
         PrecedingPassenger : PassengerPointer;
         NextPassenger : PassengerPointer
      END;
```

```
PROCEDURE InsertAfter (p : PassengerPointer, NewName : String
                          ReservedSeat : integer);
```

VAR
```
   q : PassengerPointer;
```

BEGIN
```
   new(q);
   q↑.Name := NewName;
   q↑.Seat := ReservedSeat;
   q↑.PrecedingPassenger := p;
   q↑.NextPassenger := p↑.NextPassenger;
   p↑.NextPassenger := q;
   IF q↑.NextPassenger <> NIL THEN
      q↑.NextPassenger↑.PrecedingPassenger := q
END;
```

```
PROCEDURE Delete (p :PassengerPointer);
```

VAR
```
   q : PassengerPointer;
```

BEGIN
```
   q := p;
   IF p↑.NextPassenger <> NIL THEN
      p↑.NextPassenger↑.PrecedingPassenger := p↑.PrecedingPassenger;
```

```
      IF p↑.PrecedingPassenger <> NIL THEN
         p↑.PrecedingPassenger↑.NextPassenger := p↑.NextPassenger;
      dispose(q);
   END;
```

12.8. (a) ```FUNCTION Empty (q : Queue): boolean;```

```
{*********************************************
 * Function to check for an empty queue.     *
 * Queue is implemented with a header node.  *
 *********************************************}

BEGIN
   Empty := q.Front = q.Rear
END;
```

(c) ```PROCEDURE Dequeue (q : Queue; VAR OldData : InfoType);```

```
{*********************************************
 * Procedure to remove data from queue       *
 * and return it as "OldData."               *
 * Queue is implemented with a header node.  *
 *********************************************}

VAR
   a : NodePointer;
BEGIN
   IF NOT Empty(q) THEN
      BEGIN
         OldData := q.Front↑.Next↑.Data;
         a := q.Front↑.Next;
         q.Front := a↑.Next
         dispose(a)
      END
END;
```

Index